'A life told with panache and elegance by Eleanor Fitzsimons. A must-read not just for those interested in the early years of feminism, or in children's literature, but for anyone who cares about the complexities of the human soul.'
Anthony McGowan, award-winning author of Henry Tumour

'A fascinating insight into late 19th century/ early 20th century bohemian literary life, and a rare glimpse into the world of an unconventional, enigmatic and staunchly socialist children's author. I loved it.'
Cathy Cassidy, children's author of The Chocolate Box Girls

'I knew nothing about the extraordinary, surprising life of this great figure in children's literature. Eleanor Fitzsimons's account is so gripping that I read this biography in two days.'
Gretchen Rubin author of the #1 New York Times bestseller of The Happiness Project

'An exceptional biography about an absolutely fascinating individual.'
Adam Roberts (via Twitter)

'Absolutely superb!'
Hilary McKay, author of The Skylarks War (shortlisted for the Costa Children's Book Awards), via Twitter

'One of the greatest children's writers, and an acknowledged much loved influence on Joan Aiken – E. Nesbit is celebrated in this wonderful new biography by Eleanor Fitzsimons.'
Lizza Aiken, daughter of Joan Aiken

'A fascinating, thoughtfully organized, thoroughly researched, often surprising biography of the enigmatic author of The Railway Children.'
Kirkus Reviews

'Fitzsimons delivers a sprightly and highly readable life of a writer who deserves even wider recognition.'
Publisher's Weekly

'As an author, [Nesbit] was one of a kind, and Fitzsimmons makes a compelling case for her stature as an important writer. This biography is long overdue.'
Booklist, starred review

THE LIFE AND LOVES OF E. NESBIT

Eleanor Fitzsimons

DUCKWORTH

This edition first published in the United Kingdom
by Duckworth in 2019

Duckworth Books
1 Golden Court, Richmond
TW9 1EU United Kingdom
www.duckworthbooks.co.uk

For bulk and special sales please contact
info@preludebooks.co.uk

A catalogue record for this book is available from the British Library

Typeset by Danny Lyle
DanJLyle@gmail.com

Printed and bound in Great Britain by Clays

9780715651469

1   3   5   7   9   10   8   6   4   2

For Derek, Alex and Ewan

CONTENTS

INTRODUCTION

When I was a little girl who borrowed weekly adventures from my local library, my favourite stories were by E. Nesbit. Best of all were her tales of magic and of these the book I loved most was *The Story of the Amulet*. I accompanied her fictional children to ancient Egypt, Babylon and the lost city of Atlantis. I met Emperor Julius Caesar as he stood on the shores of Gaul looking across towards England. I was filled with hope on reading her account of a utopian London where everyone is happy and wise. In "Praise and Punishment", chapter nine of *Wings and the Child*, her manual for a successful childhood, Nesbit herself explained:

> There is only one way of understanding children; they cannot be understood by imagination, by observation, nor even by love. They can only be understood by memory. Only by remembering how you felt and thought when you yourself were a child can you arrive at any understanding of the thoughts and feelings of children.[1]

Confirming that the children in *The Story of the Amulet* were 'second cousins once removed' of her beloved Bastables from earlier books, she confided:

> The reason why those children are like real children is that I was a child once myself, and by some fortunate magic I remembered exactly how I used to feel and think about things.[2]

The key to her brilliance was that she was one of us and her magical adventures felt as if they could easily happen to you or to me. Her entry in the *Dictionary of National Biography* explains this:

Her characters were neither heroes nor moral dummies, but real young human beings behaving naturally. This gift of character drawing, aided by the ease and humour of her style, place her in the highest rank among writers of books for children.[3]

A profile published in September 1905 in *The Strand Magazine*, where Nesbit's most popular stories were serialised, praised her 'astonishing versatility' and her 'almost uncanny insight into the psychology of childhood'.[4] A review in *John O'London's Weekly* noted: 'Take a book by E. Nesbit into any family of boys and girls and they fall upon it like wolves.'[5] Of her own style, she wrote: 'I make it a point of honour never to write down to a child.'[6] In an interview with the *Dundee Evening Telegraph*, she insisted: 'It's quite natural that children should believe in fairies.'[7]

In *Treasure Seekers and Borrowers*, Marcus Crouch suggested of E. Nesbit: 'No writer for children today is free of debt to this remarkable woman.' He believed that she 'managed to create the prototypes of many of the basic patterns in modern children's fiction'.[8] Nesbit came of age in the Victorian era but she did not leave us more of the stiff, moralising tales that characterised the nineteenth century. Instead, as Crouch explained, she 'threw away their strong, sober, essentially literary style and replaced it with the miraculously colloquial, flexible and revealing prose which was her unique contribution to the children's novel'. She wove her whimsy and magic into the everyday lives of children and they would not easily let this go.

It helped that Nesbit's own life was just as extraordinary as anything found in the pages of her books. A nervous child with a vivid imagination capable of conjuring up phantoms at every turn, she experienced tragic loss and displacement as a child. In adulthood, she became, as Humphrey Carpenter puts it, 'an energetic hack, keen to try anything to support her wayward husband and her odd household'.[9] Her abiding passion was for poetry with a socialist theme, but she rarely had the time to indulge it, something for which generations of children have reason to be grateful.

E. Nesbit lived through a time of extraordinary political upheaval and she was instrumental in introducing socialist thinking into British intellectual life. A founder member of the Fabian Society, she counted George Bernard Shaw and H.G. Wells among her closest friends. She was tireless in campaigning for the alleviation of poverty in London and she expended considerable time and energy in helping poor children living on her doorstep in Deptford. Yet she enjoyed the finer things in life and made no apology for doing so. She had a keen eye for nature and detested the creeping urbanisation she saw all around her. Some of her finest writing celebrates the beauty of the British countryside.

A strikingly attractive woman with a keen sense of fun, E. Nesbit attracted a circle of young admirers who left fascinating glimpses of her in their letters and memoirs. Some of her closest friendships were with her young fans. She included them in her stories, and the letters she sent them are exceptionally revealing. She put the best of herself into her books for children. E. Nesbit is one of our most important writers. She has entertained and inspired generations of us. Yet just two full biographies have been devoted to her and both have been out of print for years. I believe she deserves a third, and here it is.

Chapter 1

The Mummies of Bordeaux

On a day in September 1867, little Daisy Nesbit, who had just turned nine and was wearing her 'best blue silk frock', waited impatiently at the entrance to the bell tower of the church of Saint Michel in the French city of Bordeaux.[1] She was clutching the hand of her older sister – whether this was Minnie, aged fifteen, or Saretta, her half-sister, who was twenty-three, she does not make clear in the account she left – and 'positively skipping with delicious anticipation' as an aged French guide fumbled with the keys to the crypt. At last, he unlocked the ancient door and led the young tourists through an archway and down a low-lit, flagstone passage.

Daisy was an exceptionally imaginative and high-spirited child. She was also intensely homesick and had grown 'tired of churches and picture-galleries, of fairs and markets, of the strange babble of foreign tongues and the thin English of the guide-book'.[2] When she learned that Bordeaux contained a cryptful of mummies, she imagined the 'plate-glass cases, camphor, boarded galleries, and kindly curators' familiar from visits to the British Museum. She begged to be taken to see them: 'As one Englishman travelling across a desert seeks to find another of whom he has heard in that far land, so I sought to meet these mummies who had cousins at home, in the British Museum, in dear, dear England,' she explained.[3]

Any one of the many thousands of visitors who had traversed that dank passageway before her could have warned her that what lay beyond bore no resemblance to the 'cousins' who lay in twin rows of angled cases in the centre of the bright and airy room where Egyptian antiquities were displayed at the British Museum. In 1791, when alterations were being made to the church of Saint Michel, one of the oldest surviving medieval churches in Europe, it became necessary to exhume the bodies interred in the adjoining cemetery. Rather than unearthing the skeletal remains they expected, startled workmen were confronted with seventy human forms, weirdly intact and dressed in the rags and tatters of their burial clothing, their shrivelled, grey-brown skin still cleaving to their bones. New Zealand newspaper the *Otago Daily Times* suggested 'the earth around the church seems to have something peculiarly antiseptic in its nature'.[4]

Rather than reburying these desiccated corpses, the church authorities arranged them upright against the crypt walls of the bell tower, which stood some distance from the church. Soon these eerie new inhabitants were attracting visitors in their droves, among them celebrated French writers Gustave Flaubert and Victor Hugo. Flaubert appeared unmoved. 'I can testify,' he wrote, 'that all have skin as drum-tight, leathery, brown and reverberant as ass hides.'[5] In contrast, the unsettling experience made Hugo gloomy and filled him with a foreboding of disaster.[6]

The reporter from the *Otago Daily Times* described a rough-looking guide, likely the same man who led Daisy and her sisters, who clutched a flickering candle on a stick and thumped each body in turn with a stout club in order to demonstrate its soundness. In voluble French, he drew attention to the 'excellent calves' of one desiccated man and the perfectly preserved lace chemise worn by a young woman who had died four centuries earlier.[7] Here too was 'The Family Poisoned by Mushrooms', and over there 'The General Killed in a Duel'. He became particularly animated when he reached one 'poor miserable' who had been buried alive: 'See how his head is turned to one side and the body half turned round in the frantic effort to get out of the coffin, with his mouth open and gasping,' he exclaimed. Little wonder the *Otago Daily Times* declared the whole thing 'a disgusting and demoralising show'.[8]

In 1837, three decades before Daisy arrived, a trio of eminent doctors took skin and muscle samples in order to determine what kept these corpses intact. Their detailed notes describe a descent of thirty or forty steps into a 'circular space, the walls of which are tapestried by dead bodies all standing erect'.[9] They left a particularly vivid description of one 'miserable creature':

> The mouth open and horribly contracted, the inferior members strongly drawn to the body – the arms, one twisted by convulsions is thrown over the head, the other folded beneath the trunk and fixed to the thigh by the nails, which are deeply implanted in the flesh; the forced inflexion of the whole body, gives the expression of ineffable pain, all announcing a violent death. Unfortunate wretch! had he died in this state, or rather, had

he been buried alive, and assumed this position in the horrible agonies of awakening?[10]

Little Daisy walked down that same passage with its tang of damp earth and negotiated that same flight of narrow stone steps, each one slippery with mould. Her French was poor, so she missed the guide's warning of 'natural mummies'. Instead, she anticipated 'a long clean gallery, filled with the white light of a London noon, shed through high skylights on Egyptian treasures'.[11] Yet the darkness made her wary and she tightened her grip on her sister's hand.

With a triumphant cry of 'Les voilà!', their guide threw open a 'heavy door barred with iron' and Daisy was confronted with a sight that horrified her for the rest of her life:

A small vault, as my memory serves me, about fifteen feet square, with an arched roof, from the centre of which hung a lamp that burned with a faint blue light, and made the guide's candle look red and lurid. The floor was flagged like the passages, and was as damp and chill. Round three sides of the room ran a railing, and behind it – standing against the wall, with a ghastly look of life in death – were about two hundred skeletons. Not white clean skeletons, hung on wires, like the one you see at the doctor's, but skeletons with the flesh hardened on their bones, with their long dry hair hanging on each side of their brown faces, where the skin in drying had drawn itself back from their gleaming teeth and empty eye-sockets. Skeletons draped in mouldering shreds of shrouds and grave-clothes, their lean fingers still clothed with dry skin, seemed to reach out towards me. There they stood, men, women, and children, knee-deep in loose bones collected from the other vaults of the church, and heaped round them. On the wall near the door I saw the dried body of a little child hung up by its hair.[12]

Paralysed with horror, she scarcely remembered retracing her steps. She dared not turn her head 'lest one of those charnel-house faces' would peep out 'from some niche in the damp wall'.[13]

That evening, as she sat alone in her hotel bedroom while her mother and sisters dined below, she grew convinced that the mummies had followed her and were lurking in a curtained alcove set into the wall. The young French waiter who delivered her supper was confronted with a distraught child in desperate need of comfort. He spoke no English and she hardly any French, but he drew back the curtain to dispel her fears, helped her fetch more candles, and took her onto his knee, singing softly and feeding her bread and milk while she clung to his neck until the others returned.

In *My School Days*, a series of articles published in the *Girl's Own Paper* between October 1896 and September 1897, Daisy, who was thirty-eight by then and writing under her given name of Edith, or E. Nesbit, insisted:

> The mummies of Bordeaux were the crowning horror of my childish life; it is to them, I think, more than to any other thing, that I owe nights and nights of anguish and horror, long years of bitterest fear and dread. All the other fears could have been effaced but the shock of that sight branded it on my brain, and I never forgot it. For many years I could not bring myself to go about any house in the dark, and long after I was a grown woman I was tortured, in the dark watches, by imagination and memory, who rose strong and united, overpowering my will and my reason as utterly as in my baby days.[14]

She admitted: 'It was not till I had two little children of my own that I was able to conquer this mortal terror of darkness, and teach imagination her place, under the foot of reason and the will.' Years later, she kept a human skull and a small collection of bones in her house in order to familiarise her children with artifacts that had terrified her in childhood. 'My children, I resolved, should never know such fear,' she explained. 'And to guard them from it I must banish it from my own soul. It was not easy but it was done.'[15]

This early scare instilled a lifelong fear of the risen dead, which Edith explored in her fiction. In a story she wrote in childhood, she has a young girl named Mina descend a secret flight of steps and walk towards a dim light before reaching 'a round room with doors all around'. Behind one is 'a corridor lined with dead bodies'.[16] In 'Man-size in Marble', a horror story she wrote for *Home Chimes* magazine in December 1887, the effigies of two long-dead knights come alive and stride down the nave of a church. In 'From the Dead', which is included in her collection *Grim Tales* (1893), a widower wakes to find his shroud-clad wife standing at the foot of his bed. In 'Hurst of Hurstcote', published in *Temple Bar* magazine in June 1893, the body of a deceased bride does not decay. In 'The Power of

Darkness', which she wrote for *The Strand Magazine* in April 1905, a man descends into the catacombs of the Musée Grévin in Paris and discovers that the wax effigies on display have come to life.

Generations of children had their first encounter with terror in the pages of Edith's best-loved books. Her braver characters scoff at such fanciful notions in a way she could not. In *The Wouldbegoods* (1901), her young narrator Oswald Bastable informs readers: 'My uncle he always upheld that that dead man was no deader than you and me, but was in a sort of fit, a transit, I think they call it, and looked for him to waken into life again some day.'[17] The Bastable children imagine that a body kept behind glass at the top of a tower will come alive and lock them in. In *The Wouldbegoods,* young Dora Bastable fears she may encounter 'a skeleton that can walk about and catch at your legs when you're going up-stairs to bed'.[18] In *The Enchanted Castle* (1907) her child protagonists lure the terrifying Ugly-Wuglies, oddly animated collections of old clothing and bric-a-brac, 'hollow, unbelievable things' that had no insides to their heads, into a dark passageway reminiscent of the one populated by the mummies of Bordeaux.[19]

Edith had an exceptionally fertile imagination, and her anxieties were intensified by the upheaval she experienced in early life. She populated her stories with people and events from her past, and wrote alternative outcomes to exorcise her fears and phobias. In *My School Days,* she described how she prayed 'fervently, tearfully, that when I should be grown up I might never forget what I thought and felt and suffered then'.[20] She was three years old when tragedy blighted her life. On Sunday morning, 30 March 1862, her father, John Collis Nesbit, aged just forty-three, died at Elm Bank House in Barnes, the home of his 'intimate friend' and publisher, George Parker Tuxford.[21]

An obituary in the *Illustrated London News* confirmed that John Nesbit had died from 'consumption' after a 'long wearing illness'. He was eulogised as 'one of the most celebrated analytical chemists' in England, a 'pioneering educationalist, and principal of a highly regarded agricultural college in Kennington'.[22] His remains were interred in the public vaults of the Anglican catacombs at West Norwood Cemetery in London, a place not dissimilar to the crypt in Bordeaux since its entrance lies at the base of ancient steps and the ground is desperately uneven.

Edith's fiction is replete with missing parents. The Bastable children often recall the trauma of losing their mother. The children in the

Psammead Series are separated from their father without warning. In *The Railway Children* (1906) young Bobbie clings to her father as tightly as she can and cries 'Oh! My Daddy, my Daddy!' The magnitude of Edith's own loss is suggested by the inclusion of a near identical scene on the final page of *The House of Arden* (1908): 'and in one flash she was across the room and in her father's arms, sobbing and laughing and saying again and again – "Oh, my daddy! Oh, my daddy, my daddy!"' She was in the habit of recycling plots and scenes.

Edith had few memories of her father, but she did recall being terrified when he turned his fur-lined travelling coat inside-out in order to dress up as a bear when playing with her older brothers, Alfred and Harry. 'The first thing I remember that frightened me was running into my father's dressing-room and finding him playing at wild beasts with my brothers,' she revealed, 'his roars were completely convincing.'[23] In *The Wouldbegoods* timid Daisy is confronted by the sight of the Bastable boys, Dicky and Noël, dressed in tiger-skin rugs. She 'stopped short and, uttering a shriek like a railway whistle, she fell flat on the ground'.[24] Edith must have felt guilty for remembering her father, a kind-hearted man by all accounts, as a frightening figure. She has her narrator, Oswald Bastable, ridicule Daisy's response by scoffing that it was just a game. She also makes her surrogate Alice Bastable dress up as a bear to frighten timid Denny.

Edith Nesbit, the fifth child of Sarah and John Nesbit, was born on 15 August 1858. Sarah also had a daughter, 'Saretta', from her first marriage to a grocer named Charles Green. Widowed in her twenties, she raised Saretta alone for three years before she married John Nesbit in 1851. Saretta and she moved into the Nesbit College of Agriculture and Chemistry at 38 and 39 Kennington Lane, a middle-class residential street just around the corner from the Oval Cricket Ground. Both houses were demolished during Edith's lifetime to make way for more modest terraced dwellings, and the district was absorbed into Greater London. Back in 1851, John, Sarah and Saretta shared their lively home with assorted members of the Nesbit family, boarders at the college who ranged in age from thirteen to twenty-three, and three domestic servants.

Edith's grandfather, Anthony Nesbit, who had established the college in 1841, was still living there when she was born. The son of a Northumberland farmer, he had taught himself mathematics while working as a farm labourer from four in the morning until four in the afternoon. An account of his early life, written by his grandson Paris

Nesbit, described how he 'maintained himself' from the age of eight, when he left his family home.[25] His extraordinary aptitude for maths and science gave him access to the teaching profession, and he earned recognition as a committed educationalist and an excellent if somewhat severe teacher. He also wrote extensively on the natural sciences and became a noted adversary of Charles Darwin.[26]

A profile of Edith published in *The Strand Magazine* in September 1905, included the information that 'her English blood is modified by a trace of Irish, to which those who are strong on racial influences may attribute something of the humour which can be found in her work'.[27] This would appear to be a reference to her 'Irish grandmother', Mary Collis, who married Anthony Nesbit on 9 February 1817. A notice of their marriage appeared in the *New Monthly* magazine:

> At Leeds, Mr Anthony Nesbit, master of the Commercial and Mathematical School, Bradford, to Mary, daughter of the late Rev. David Collis, of Fairfield, near Manchester.[28]

Anthony Nesbit established a series of general schools during his lifetime. He educated his children at home and required them to assist him in the running of his schools from an early age. It was Edith's father, John Nesbit, Anthony's eldest son, who took over the running of the college in Kennington on his retirement and renamed it the 'College of Agriculture and Chemistry, and of Practical and General Science' to reflect his own area of expertise. A talented chemist with a practical bent, he was admitted as a Fellow to both the Geological Society of London and the Chemical Society of London in 1845, when he was twenty-seven years old. He pioneered the teaching of natural science, lecturing extensively in 'a most familiar and easy manner'. He also built up an extensive practice as a consulting analytical chemist and was an early advocate for the use of superphosphate fertilisers in agriculture. Somehow, he found time to write several highly regarded books on agricultural science, his central theme being the fertilising properties of Peruvian guano, a far cry from his youngest daughter's future output.[29]

Father and son were passionate and progressive educationalists who set out their enlightened ethos in *An Essay on Education* (1841):

> THE FIRST AND GRAND CONSIDERATION in bringing up and educating Youth, is to endeavour to preserve and promote their Health

and the Buoyancy of their Spirits, by making them comfortable, cheerful and happy; for without Health and Spirits, little progress will ever be made in the Acquisition of Knowledge.[30]

'The Happiness of Parents and also that of their children are inseparably bound up together,' they insisted.[31]

Anthony Nesbit died at home on 15 March 1859, five months short of Edith's first birthday. He was lauded as a man 'known for half a century in all our principal colleges and schools in connection with his many valuable mathematical works'.[32] One can scarcely imagine what he would have made of his youngest granddaughter's febrile imagination and her struggles with long division. 'Beware of reading tales and novels,' he warned in *An Introduction to English Parsing*, 'for they generally exhibit pictures that never had any existence, except in the airy imaginations of the brain.'[33]

On 8 June 1857, fourteen months before Edith was born, John and Sarah lost their firstborn son, John Collis Nesbit, when he was just four years old. The cause of his death was recorded as 'bilious remittent fever combined with hydrocephalus', a redundant and largely descriptive medical term that covered a wide range of childhood conditions and infections.[34] When Edith was born, on August 15, 1858, Saretta was fourteen; Mary, known affectionately as Minnie, was six; Alfred was three; and Henry, always called Harry, was just two. When the three youngest children were christened on June 25, 1859, family legend had it that precocious little Edith, affectionately known as Daisy, removed her tiny kid shoes in order to float them in the font as boats.[35]

The Nesbit home stood on three acres of land, a portion of which was given over 'for experimental purposes and the recreation of the students'.[36] In *Wings and the Child* (1913), an instruction manual for parents keen to give their children a good start in life, Edith described this wonderland for urban children:

It was in Kennington, that house – and it had a big garden and a meadow and a cottage and a laundry, stables and cow-house and pig-styes [sic], elm-trees and vines, tiger lilies and flags in the garden, and chrysanthemums that smelt like earth and hyacinths that smelt like heaven.[37]

She described her childhood playroom:

Our nursery was at the top of the house, a big room with a pillar in the middle to support the roof. 'The post,' we called it: it was excellent for playing mulberry bush, or for being martyrs at. The skipping rope did to bind the martyrs to the stake.[38]

In her late thirties she recast her siblings and herself as the Bastable children. In *The Story of the Treasure Seekers* (1899), she has Oswald and Dicky bury wimpish Albert-next-door in the garden while twins Alice and Noël, surrogates for Edith herself, watch on approvingly. She drew on an incident from her own childhood when her mischievous brothers buried her so firmly in their garden that she had to be rescued by adults. In 'The Twopenny Spell', from *Oswald Bastable and Others* (1905), young Lucy is affronted at being buried up to her waist by her brother Harry. She gets her revenge by casting a spell that swaps their personalities, with disastrous consequences. After Saretta covered her face with a hideous mask to play an old gypsy women bent on abducting Edith, who played a 'highborn orphan,' her dreams were haunted for decades. This sight informed her eerie Ugly-Wuglies from *The Enchanted Castle*.

The boarders at the agricultural college often stepped in to sooth little Edith's fears. She was terrified of a two-headed calf, a 'terrible object' her father had purchased during a three-week tour of the north of England taken with a dozen pupils from the college. Her brothers used to chase her with this hideous article but she lost her fear after a kindly student tucked her under one arm and the 'two-headed horror' under the other to chase Alfred and Harry around the college.[39] More terrifying was the empty skin of an emu, which had been nailed to a wall 'with its wiry black feathers that fluttered dismally in the draught'. Edith regarded this as 'no mere bird's skin' but a malevolent creature that wished her ill. Every time she walked past it, she would cover her eyes. 'It was always lurking for me in the dark, ready to rush out at me,' she remembered. 'It was waiting for me at the top of the flight, while the old woman with the mask stretched skinny hands out to grasp my little legs as I went up the nursery stairs.'[40] A kindly student cured her fear by convincing her to stroke it.

Edith's early childhood was overshadowed by her father's protracted illness. In April 1861, almost a year before he died, he travelled with her mother to the Castle Hotel in Hastings, leaving the children behind with their nurse. This term-time trip was most likely prompted by a Victorian faith in the restorative properties of sea air for consumptive patients. An exceptionally loving letter Sarah wrote to her 'Pretty little Daisy' almost certainly dates to this holiday. 'I shall be so glad to have you down in my bed and hug and kiss you,' she wrote, assuring her, 'I shall be home soon now.' She promised to bring 'darling little Daisy' a 'baby doll'. Edith treasured this letter throughout her life, and it closes with the words: 'Papa and Mama send you lots of love and kisses.'[41] Perhaps this doll is the one she described in *Wings and the Child*:

> I had a 'rag doll', but she was stuffed with hair, and was washed once a fortnight, after which nurse put in her features again with a quill pen, and consoled me for any change in her expression by explaining that she was 'growing up'.[42]

After John died, Sarah, who was twice widowed by her mid-forties, attempted to step into her husband's shoes. The *Illustrated London News* reported: 'Mrs. Nesbit, and the large staff of assistants, will continue the business to which for a long time past her late husband has been totally unable to attend.'[43] Since John's reputation as an analytical chemist had attracted students from across the British Isles, Sarah faced an overwhelming task, but she did her best and entrusted the care of her younger children to a 'Nurse' named Mary Ann Moore, who was aided by an under-nurse.[44] In *My School Days*, Edith portrays Moore as a warm and sympathetic young woman who soothed her fears. Decades later, she could recall perfectly her enduring fear of the dark:

> For to a child who is frightened, the darkness and the silence of its lonely room are only a shade less terrible than the wild horrors of dreamland. One used to lie awake in the silence, listening, listening to the pad-pad of one's heart, straining one's ears to make sure that it was not the pad-pad of something else, something unspeakable creeping towards one out of the horrible dense dark. One used to lie quite, quite still, I remember, listening, listening.[45]

While she was tucking little Edith into bed one night, Moore noticed that her pillow was wet with 'the dews of agony and terror'. Although she had completed her duties and her time was her own, this kindly young woman sat in the day nursery with the door ajar so her young charge would see a reassuring sliver of light as she drifted off to sleep.[46] The little girls in *The Story of the Treasure Seekers* also sleep with the door ajar, and

Denny in *The Wouldbegoods* cannot sleep without 'the gas being left a little bit on'.[47]

Yet timid little Daisy, who was so nervous of the dark, had an adventurous streak too and loved to explore the vast city that lay beyond her idyllic urban farm. Her dichotomous nature may explain why she wrote herself as the Bastable twins: intrepid, courageous Alice and fragile, sensitive Noël, who wrote poetry, as she did. Accompanied by Alfred and Harry, she would visit her beloved British Museum, or head to Madame Tussaud's to marvel at relics from the French Revolution, 'the waxen heads of kings and democrats, the very guillotine itself'.[48]

Her favourite destination was the Crystal Palace, which had been moved to Penge Common by then, five miles south of Kennington Lane. There, she would marvel at elegant water temples surrounded by pools filled with water lilies. She loved the Egyptian Court with its sphinxes and elaborately decorated pillars, and the Spanish Court with its mosaic of gold, blue and red, its tinkling fountain, and beautiful marble arches. In the Grecian Court, she came face to face with a reproduction of the Venus de Milo. It was on Penge Common that she encountered Benjamin Waterhouse Hawkins' magnificent dinosaur park complete with thirty-three life-sized beasts. She described them in *Wings and the Child*:

They set up, amid the rocks and reeds and trees of the island in that lake, life-sized images of the wonders of a dead world. On a great stone crouched a Pterodactyl, his vast wings spread for flight. A mammoth sloth embraced a tree, and I give you my word that when you came on him from behind, you, in your six years, could hardly believe that he was not real, that he would not presently leave the tree and turn his attention to your bloused and belted self.

Edith needed to touch them in order to be sure they were not real:

Convinced, at last, by the cold feel of his flank to your fat little hand, that he was but stone, you kept, none the less, a memory of him that would last your life, and make his name, when you met it in a book, as thrilling as the name of a friend in the list of birthday honours.[49]

Paleontologist Sir Richard Owen had hosted a dinner party inside the hollow iguanodon on New Year's Eve 1853. Edith remembered one of her brothers giving her a 'leg-up' so she could 'explore the roomy interior of the Dinosaur with feelings hardly to be surpassed by those of bandits in a cave'.[50] She put these stone beasts into *The Enchanted Castle*: 'Their stone flanks, their wide ungainly wings, their lozenge crocodile-like backs show grey through the trees a long way off.' When the children wonder what to do with their dressing-up clothes, Mabel suggests the iguanodon: 'We'll hide them inside the great stone dinosaur,' she says. 'He's hollow.' Kathleen insists: 'He comes alive in his stone.' 'Not in the sunshine he doesn't,' Mabel replies.[51] After dark, Edith's stone creatures come alive:

> There was a crunching of the little stones in the gravel of the drive. Something enormously long and darkly grey came crawling towards him, slowly, heavily. The moon came out just in time to show its shape. It was one of those great lizards that you see at the Crystal Palace, made in stone, of the same awful size which they were millions of years ago when they were masters of the world, before Man was.[52]

Edith had a portal to the past on her very English doorstep, a point of access to the wonders of the ancient world. Little wonder her fictional children in *The Phoenix and the Carpet* (1904) ride an enchanted carpet that 'swirled their senses away and restored them on the outskirts of a gleaming white Indian town'. In *The Story of the Amulet* (1906), a charmed artifact allows them to swap Regent's Park for the banks of the River Nile. Those joyous days came to an end before Edith reached her tenth birthday. By then she was far from home and longing for the familiar landmarks of early childhood.

CHAPTER 2

'FAREWELL THE TRANQUIL MIND! FAREWELL CONTENT!'

Early in 1866, when Edith was seven years old, the happy, stable life Sarah Nesbit had created was thrown into utter disarray. Fifteen-year-old Mary developed symptoms of tuberculosis, the disease that had taken her father. Determined not to lose another child, Sarah sold the college in Kennington, placed their possessions in storage and moved to Brighton where Mary might benefit from healthy sea air. Their lodgings on Western Road were a significant come-down from the three-acre paradise at Kennington Lane. In *Wings and the Child*, Edith recalled the 'hard and hot' pavement of Western Road with its 'long rows of dazzling houses' and their 'small gritty garden where nothing grew but geraniums and calceolarias'.[1]

Edith mourned the loss of the nursery where she and her brothers had played with 'a large rocking horse, a large doll's house (with a wooden box as annexe), a Noah's Ark, dinner and tea things, a great chest of oak bricks, and a pestle and mortar'.[2] The bricks, which she recalled with 'fond affection', had disappeared in the move. She assumed they must have been too heavy, or could not be accommodated in their cramped new home. Sarah bought 'a small box of deal bricks made in Germany', but these proved hopelessly inadequate and Edith's disappointment lasted a lifetime. In *Wings and the Child*, which she wrote in her early fifties, she described her lost bricks in precise detail:

> Our bricks were well and truly cut: they were of seasoned oak, smooth and pleasant to touch – none of the rough-sawn edges which vex the hand and render the building unstable; they were heavy – a very important quality in bricks. They 'stayed put'.[3]

Edith, who had a lifelong passion for building, lamented the fact that 'there was no building at Brighton except on the beach'. In a passage that illustrates perfectly what an imaginative child she was, she described the disappointing sand:

> Sand is as good as anything in the world to build with – but there is no sand on the beach at Brighton, only sandiness. There are stones – pebbles you call them, but they are too round to be piled up into buildings. The only thing you can play with them is dolls' dinner parties. There are plenty of oyster shells and flat bits of slate and tile for dishes and plates – and it is quite easy to find stones the proper shape and colour for boiled fowls and hams and roast legs of mutton, German sausages, ribs of beef, mince pies, pork pies, roast hare or calf's head. But building is impossible.[4]

Perhaps it was while she was digging on the stony beaches of Brighton and wishing for better sand that she dreamed up her Psammead, star of *Five Children and It*, one of her best-loved books. It was 'brown and furry and fat', and it crawled out of the sand where her fictional children had been digging:

> Its eyes were on long horns like a snail's eyes, and it could move them in and out like telescopes; it had ears like a bat's ears, and its tubby body was shaped like a spider's and covered with thick soft fur; its legs and arms were furry too, and it had hands and feet like a monkey's.[5]

In Brighton, Edith was enrolled as a weekday boarder at Mrs Arthur's school. During outings, she would walk right past her rented home:

> I remember the hot white streets, and the flies, and Brill's baths, and the Western Road, and the bitter pang of passing, at the end of a long procession, our own house, where always some one might be at the window, and never any one was. I used to go home on Saturdays, and then all bitterness was so swallowed up in the bliss of the homereturning, that I actually forgot the miseries of my school-life; but I was very unhappy there.[6]

The main source of her unhappiness was the relentless bullying she endured at the hands of a little girl dressed in 'Stuart Plaid', who destroyed her few remaining toys out of sheer malice: 'She tortured me unremittingly,' Edith recalled. Her account of her childish attempt to replenish the paint set this callous girl destroyed makes it clear that she never told her mother:

> When I had been at school a week or two my paint-box suffered at her hands, but I bore it meekly and in silence, only seeking to replace my Vandyke brown by mud from the garden. Chinese white I sought to manu-facture by a mixture of chalk picked up on the sea-shore, and milk from my mug at tea-time. It was never a successful industry.[7]

Illness brought deliverance. 'I suppose no prisoner ever hailed the falling of his fetters with the joy I felt when at last, after three or four days of headache and tears, I was wrapped in a blanket and taken home with the measles,' she recalled.[8] She recovered in time for their midsum-mer holiday.

Alfred and Harry had been released from school by then, and Sarah rented 'a lovely cottage among the beech-woods of Buckinghamshire', a glorious haven swathed in 'royal red roses, and jasmine, and tall white lilies'. All around stood 'lovely trees, acacias and elms, and a big cop-per beech... and in the hedge by the gate, sweet-briar and deep-cupped white convolvulus'.[9] For breakfast they feasted on 'honey in the comb', 'new-laid eggs', and 'cool raspberries... trimmed with fresh green leaves'. Edith watched her mother 'in a cool cotton gown pouring out tea, and purring with pleasure at having all her kittens together again'.[10] Alfred gave her 'a white rabbit with pink eyes – in a hutch he had made himself'. Harry offered to share two dormice he kept in an old tea-caddy in 'a nook among the roots of the copper beech'.

'That was summer indeed,' she wrote in *My School Days*, but sum-mer never lasts. Come September, she was sent to a 'select boarding establishment for young ladies and gentlemen' in faraway Stamford in Lincolnshire. 'I venture to think,' she recalled, 'that I should have preferred a penal settlement.' Turned feral by the freedom of heady summer days, she struggled to conform to the strict regime. Her first difficulty, she explained, was her unruly hair:

> My hair was never tidy... this got me into continual disgrace. I am sure I tried hard enough to keep it tidy – I brushed it for fruitless hours till my little head was so sore that it hurt me to put my hat on. But it never would look smooth and shiny... It was always a rough, impossible brown mop.

She also struggled to keep her hands clean:

My hands were more compromising to me than anyone would have believed who had ever seen their size, for, in the winter especially, they were never clean. I can see now the little willow-patterned basin of hard cold water, and smell the unpleasant little square of mottled soap with which I was expected to wash them. I don't know how the others managed, but for me the result was always the same – failure; and when I presented myself at breakfast, trying to hide my red and grubby little paws in my pinafore, Miss— used to say: 'Show your hands, Daisy – yes as I thought. Not fit to sit down with young ladies and gentlemen. Breakfast in the schoolroom for Miss Daisy.'

Most distressing was her inability to grasp the intricacies of long division:

[Day] after day the long division sums, hopelessly wrong, disfigured my slate, and were washed off with my tears. Day after day I was sent to bed, my dinner was knocked off, or my breakfast, or my tea.

A second term brought no relief:

Night after night I cried myself to sleep in my bed – whose coarse home-spun sheets were hotter than blankets – because I could not get the answers right. Even Miss Fairfield [the kind headmistress], I fancied, began to look coldly on me, and the other children naturally did not care to associate with one so deficient in arithmetic.[11]

It was during these desperate days that Sarah arrived with dreadful news. Mary's doctors, believing she would not survive another damp Brighton winter, had advised Sarah to take her to the south of France once she was well enough to travel. Sarah planned to take Saretta too, leaving Edith in England with her brothers. Since Edith was inconsolable, Sarah agreed to take her along. 'When I was small and teachable,' she recalled, 'my mother was compelled to much travel and change of scene by the illness of my elder sister; and as she liked to have me more or less within reach, I changed schools as a place-hunter changes his politics.'[12] From then on, her school attendance was sporadic and largely unsuccessful. Years later, she told a friend:

Once at school where I had been quite contented I was one term wretched – for reasons – and wrote home saying so and imploring to be taken away... They did not <u>come</u> – they wrote saying I would feel all right and happy again soon and I didn't. I was miserable the whole term and refused to return at the end.[13]

It is no coincidence that her fictional children, who are of school-going age, rarely attend school. The Bastables are removed when their father's business fails. Of her Railway Children, she wrote, they 'got used to not going to school'.[14]

Yet she was precociously intelligent and a voracious reader. A profile in *The Strand Magazine* confirmed:

She read Scott and Longfellow at the age of five. She began to write verse as soon as she could write at all, and her first published poem appeared when she was only sixteen.[15]

The night crossing from Newhaven to Dieppe proved a terrible ordeal for an overwrought little girl. Laid low by debilitating seasickness, Edith arrived in Rouen in a state of utter exhaustion. While travelling to their lodgings from the train station, she glimpsed the words *Débit de Tabac** and they became lodged in her febrile imagination. Drifting between wakefulness and sleep, she formed a weird association between this innocuous phrase and her own last name:

I lay awake in the dark, the light from the oil lamp in the street came through the Persiennes [louvered shutters] and fell in bright bars on the wall. As I grew drowsier I seemed to read there in letters of fire '*Débit de Tabac*'. Then I fell asleep, and dreamed that my father's ghost came to me, and implored me to have the horrible French inscription erased from his tomb – 'for I was an Englishman,' he said.[16]

Wide-awake and filled with terror, she crept across the corridor to Sarah's room. This, she realised, was her first memory of having an abiding 'terror of the dead, or of the supernatural'.

Travelling on to Paris, they spent three days at the International Exposition of 1867; Edith found it 'large, empty and very tiring'. She was

---

* Tobacconist.

pleased to leave the city once the weather turned cold. In Poitiers, in an old Byzantine church, she picked up a bone she believed to be human. In *My School Days*, she recalled how she swaddled it in cotton wool and kept it hidden in a drawer. She 'wove many romances round the little brown relic', until her brother Alfred, roaring with laughter, told her it was 'half a fowl's back'.[17] She was content in Bordeaux until her encounter with the mummies. 'After that,' she wrote: '"Farewell the tranquil mind, farewell content."'[18]

After ten days in Bordeaux they continued south, staying in a series of affordable lodging houses but never settling anywhere for long. In *Wings and the Child*, Edith wrote:

> It is a mistake to suppose that children are naturally fond of change. They love what they know. In strange places they suffer violently from home-sickness, even when their loved nurse or mother is with them. They want to get back to the house they know, the toys they know, the books they know.[19]

In November they found a comfortable *pension* in the city of Pau, fifty miles short of the Spanish border and popular on account of its mild winter climate. In a letter to her Uncle Edward in Australia, Mary admitted "the air agreed with none of us"; they decided to move on.[20]

Concerned about the break in Edith's education and her inability to speak French, Sarah arranged for the little girl to spend three months with the Lourdes family in Pau. As she listened to the wheels of her mother's carriage rolling away from the door, the enormity of Edith's situation dawned on her: 'Then I was left, a little English child without a word of French in the bosom of a French family, and as this came upon me I burst into a flood of tears,' she recalled.[21] Yet she enjoyed the routine of ordinary family life and she formed a close friendship with Marguerite Lourdes, a sweet-natured little girl of similar age. As Marguerite spoke no English Edith made rapid process in French. She spent Christmas there and wept bitter tears when a maidservant arrived to reunite her with her mother and sisters.

In Edith's absence Mary's health had worsened, so Sarah took her to Biarritz. On Boxing Day they played croquet in the sunshine, then gathered late roses from the churchyard hedge and maidenhair fern from a sea cave on the shoreline. 'The fresh sea breezes quite set us up again,' Mary told Uncle Edward.[22] In 'glorious weather' they crossed the Spanish border to visit Irun and San Sebastián. Mary and Saretta enjoyed the trip but Sarah was unhappy with the standard of Spanish inns. After Christmas they swapped Biarritz for the spa town of Bagnères-de-Bigorre in the high foothills of the Pyrenees, where they planned to stay for several months. In her letter to Uncle Edward, Mary described 'innumerable streams of clear, sparkling water, running in and round and even under the houses'. Once Edith joined them, she found the town delightful:

Streams cross the roads, streams run between the houses, under the houses, not quiet, placid little streams, such as meander through our English meadows, but violent, angry, rushing, boiling little mountain torrents that thunder along their rocky beds. Sometimes one of these streams is spanned by a dark arch, and a house built over it. What good fortune that one of these houses should have been the one selected by my mother – on quite other grounds, of course – and, oh! the double good fortune I, even I, was to sleep in the little bedroom actually built on the arch itself that spanned the mountain stream! It was delightful, it was romantic, it was fascinating. I could fancy myself a princess in a tower by the rushing Rhine as I heard the four-foot torrent go thundering along with a noise that would not have disgraced a full-grown river. It had every charm the imagination could desire, but it kept me awake till the small hours of the morning. It was humiliating to have to confess that even romance and a rushing torrent did not compensate for the loss of humdrum, commonplace sleep, but I accepted that humiliation and slept no more in the little room overhanging the torrent.[23]

She missed Marguerite desperately and took little interest in the letter writing that kept her mother and sisters occupied. 'It is not so easy to amuse yourself in-doors on a wet day as older people seem to think,' Oswald Bastable complains in *The Wouldbegoods*, 'especially when you are far removed from your own home, and haven't got all your own books and things.'[24] In childhood she read Hans Christian Andersen and at one time had an edition of *The Arabian Nights* with woodcut pictures, but they may not have survived the move to France.[25] Kind-hearted Saretta, who was 'a refuge on wet days when a fairy-story seemed to be the best thing to be had', took her to visit a shepherdess, but she was desperately disappointed when the magical maiden she hope for turned out to be a wizened old crone.[26]

Their stay in Bagnères de Bigorre was cut short by news from Harry's boarding school in England that he had contracted whooping cough and was desperately ill. Sarah considered sending for him but decided to travel to England instead. Day and night, they traversed central France by carriage. Travelling from Aurillac to Murat, they grew nervous when their surly driver, 'a blue-bloused ruffian of plausible manners', picked up an equally disreputable looking companion. He assured them that this man was his stepson. Further along the road he picked up his 'father and brother-in-law', then a 'cousin' and his 'uncle', all with 'villainous-looking faces'. Edith recalled:

> The uncle, who looked like a porpoise and smelt horribly of brandy, was put inside the carriage with us, because there was now no room left in any other part of the conveyance. The family party laughed and jolted in a patois wholly unintelligible to us. I was convinced that they were arranging for the disposal of our property and our bodies after the murder. My mother and sisters were talking in low voices in English.[27]

It was almost midnight by the time they reached their halfway house in one of the loneliest spots in the mountains of Auvergne. Sarah complained to their landlady, but she turned out to be the driver's mother. When she demanded double the agreed fare, quick-thinking Sarah hid their valuables and convinced her they had only the fare agreed and a ten-franc piece to pay for their supper. Without further incident, they were deposited in Murat, where they spent the night at a filthy inn. They sat up until dawn rather than lie on the soiled sheets provided and caught the first train out next morning.

Once Harry was well again, Sarah returned to France to find a house for the summer. Edith was dispatched to a small English boarding school presided over by Mrs MacBean, 'one of the best and kindest women that ever lived'. She kept in touch with her for years. Letters to Sarah were addressed care of St Martin's le Grand, the headquarters of the Royal Mail in London, but Edith, who had no idea where her mother was, became convinced this must be in Paris. She was not yet ten years old when Sarah sent for her, and she travelled alone by train and boat to Saint-Malo in Brittany.

Together for the first time in months, the family spent that summer in La Haye, close to Dinan in Brittany, in a rustic farmhouse with whitewashed walls and a steep slate roof. Edith's description makes it sound heavenly:

There never was such another garden, there never will be! Peaches, apricots, nectarines, and grapes of all kinds, lined the inside walls; the avenue
that ran down the middle of it was of fig trees and standard peach-trees.
There were raspberries, cherries and strawberries, and flowers mingling
with fruits and vegetables in a confusion the most charming in the world.
Along the end of the garden was a great arcade of black, clipped yews, so
thick and strong that a child could crawl on the outside of it without falling through. Above the dairy and coach-house was an immense hay-loft,
a straw-loft over the stable and cow-house. What play-rooms for wet days!
Beyond the chicken-house was the orchard, full of twisted grey apple trees,
beneath whose boughs in due season the barley grew. Beyond, a network
of lanes, fringed with maiden-hair, led away into fairyland.[28]

Here, in 'the dearest home of my childhood', Edith and her brothers
were given the freedom they craved: 'My mother,' she wrote, 'with a
wisdom for which I shall thank her all my days, allowed us to run wild.'
All Sarah asked was that they present themselves for meals with 'some
approach to punctuality, and with hands and faces moderately clean'.[29]
They climbed trees, explored lanes and meadows, built forts of hay and
straw, and recruited the resident goats, cow and black English pig for
their boisterous games. They had ponies to ride, Judy and frisky little
Punch, who threw Edith three times in one morning. Decades later, she
could describe their play in minute detail:

> In the courtyard of our house in France there was an out-house with a
> sloping roof and a flat parapet about four feet high. We used to build little
> clay huts along this, and roof them with slates, leaving a hole for a chim-
> ney. The huts had holes for windows and doors, and we used to collect bits
> of candle and put them in our huts after dark and enjoy the lovely spec-
> tacle of our illuminated buildings till someone remembered us and caught
> us, and sent us to bed. That was the curse of our hut-building – the very
> splendour of the result attracted the attention one most wished to avoid.[30]

Her lifelong belief in ghosts dated to the day they came upon a dilapidated and boarded up château. Peering through gaps in the planks, they
could see a bare room with a heap of straw in its centre. Without warning,
this straw swirled up and formed a rope that reached the ceiling. The terrified children ran down the driveway. An old woman who emerged from

a cottage near the gate called out, '*Je vois, mes enfants, que vous avez vu la dame qui file.*'[31] They searched for this château but never found it again.

Many of the adventures in *The Story of the Treasure Seekers* and *The Wouldbegoods* have their origins in that perfect summer in La Haye. The Bastable children populate their circus with farm animals; the English pig became the truculent black pig that reluctantly plays an elephant. Just like Edith and her brothers, they play shipwrecked mariners on the roof of the hen house. Alice Bastable describes how they follow a stream to its source, just as Edith, Alfred and Harry had:

> I cannot tell you about all the windings of the stream; it went through fields and woods and meadows, and at last the banks got steeper and higher, and the trees overhead darkly arched their mysterious branches, and we felt like the princes in a fairy tale who go out to seek their fortunes.[32]

Those weeks at La Haye were a key period of stability and happiness in Edith's turbulent childhood. 'The happy memories of that golden time crowd thickly upon me,' she wrote.[33] She rose early each morning to enjoy the day to the full, and many of her fictional characters do likewise. For the rest of her life she could conjure up at will the scents of dead leaves and wood smoke that marked the end of their stay.

Autumn arrived and the boys returned to England. Edith was sent to Mademoiselle Fauchet's school in Dinan, but a misunderstanding saw her arrive five days early. She was 'bored to extinction', so she ran away. Rather than return her, Sarah enrolled her in the Ursuline Convent in Dinan, where she enjoyed fleeting happiness among kindly nuns whose patience she tried to the limit. Mère Marie Madeline instructed her to tell her mother that she was a '*bon petit diable*'. She translated this as 'a proper little devil, a holy terror', and signed her letter 'your young Diable, Edie Nesbit, Little Daisy', adding a perfect little drawing of a daisy at the bottom of the page.[34]

In *Daphne in Fitzroy Street* (1909), a largely forgotten novel for adults, Daphne is introduced as a mischievous, tree-climbing, poetry-writing girl who feels confined in her convent school. Edith described how 'long, narrow horse-shoe tables, spread with coarse unbleached linen, were outlined by a vivid, varying fringe of girls, mostly eating thin soup and wide slabs of *pain de ménage*. The English girls ate eggs and drank chocolate.' Forbidden from talking, they would gossip 'without moving one's lips, in a voice too low to be heard above the clatter of plate and spoon and the setting down of the yellow mug after drinking'.[35]

Edith missed Sarah desperately. When Alfred, who was in school nearby, told her that their mother was away from home, information the nuns had kept from her, she pleaded: 'Mama do come home.'[36] Her letters home were playful and deeply affectionate. In 1869, she instructed Sarah to 'buy a locket for Minnie on her birthday and give it her from me'. She enclosed a lock of hair with instructions that it be placed inside along with a photograph.[37] Perhaps she hoped her thick, dark hair would act as a talisman. In *Wet Magic* (1913), a mermaid presents four young siblings with locks of her hair, which she instructs them to wear around their necks at all times in order to survive in the kingdom of the Merpeople.

On 3 November 1869, Mère Marie Madeline wrote to Saretta, who had better French than Sarah, to inform her of the nuns' disappointment at finding two empty wine bottles in eleven-year-old Edith's room: 'I regret that Daisy should have taken wine,' she explained. 'I believe this has been the cause of her tempers. It was her brother who brought it to her and the little girl wished to drink some of it.' This kindly nun expressed concern for Edith, who had 'been crying a lot'.[38] 'The nuns are all very kind to me,' she told Sarah, 'though I have been very naughty, but I am very sorry and intend to be good now.' She asked if she might become a Catholic and if she might 'learn singing', since she wanted to 'so very much indeed'. Her concern for a family pet provides an insight into her warmth and humour: 'How is that queen of dogs that splendid lady that estimable that lovely loving lovable Trot,' she asked. 'I hope Her Majesty is in bonne santé, that she has sufficinetay of daintys to please her royal palate, and a sprightly family of hippopotami to be a comfort in her old age.'[39]

In November 1869, Edith, Alfred and Harry were sent to schools in Germany, she to a school run by Moravian Sisters near Düsseldorf and they to a boarding school nearby. She was so unhappy that she attempted to run away three times, but her poor German prevented her from reaching her brothers' school and hunger forced her back on each occasion. She was saved by geopolitics. When the Franco-Prussian war was declared in 1870, the English siblings sang *La Marseillaise* in the street. Edith harboured anti-German sentiments throughout her life.[40] Although she was given permission to join her mother in France, hostilities obliged her to travel via Southampton where her boat was held up in fog for three days. Not yet twelve years old, she was travelling alone once again, only this time she was the only female on board.

She spent the months that followed in a series of boarding schools and the unfamiliar homes of relatives and friends. On census night, 2 April 1871, she was recorded as a pupil at Brunswick House School in Hammersmith; Alfred was there too. She recalled one 'strange house' in Sutherland Gardens in East Sheen, 'a house with large rooms and heavy hangings – with massive wardrobes and deep ottoman boxes'. During her first night, she lay 'trembling in the chill linen of a strange bed', gripped by a terror that 'in the black silence something might be stealthily creeping – something which would presently lean over you, in the dark – whose touch you would feel, not knowing whether it were the old woman in the mask or some new terror'.[41] She persuaded her hosts to leave the gaslight burning, but they dimmed it while she slept and she woke 'in a faint light' convinced she could see 'a corpse laid out under white draperies, and at its foot a skeleton with luminous skull and outstretched bony arm'.[42]

She also stayed for a time at 15 Claremont Square in Islington, home to Sarah Bolton, née Nesbit, a distant relative of her late father. Peering out between the 'brown wire blinds' that obscured each window, she grew increasingly despondent as she watched tradesmen's carts rattle past. These may have inspired 'the carts of butchers and bakers and candle-stick makers' in *The Railway Children*. In *Five Children and It*, she wrote: 'London is like a prison for children, especially if their relations are not rich.' In *My School Days*, she described the 'sordid ugliness of Islington' which outraged the feelings of a child who had always found her greatest pleasures and life's greatest beauties in the 'green country'.[43]

She described the Boltons as 'the kindest hearted people in the world', who would have done anything to please her had they understood what she desired, but she was desperately bored there. Sarah Bolton, who had 'a heart full of kindness', spoke of nothing but the court circular* while her daughters, Rose, Fanny and Helen, all older than Edith, were merely kind 'in their way'. As the house had few books, she reread the 'few old bound volumes of *Good Words*† again and again'. Books were enormously important to her. 'I can remember my fourth birthday,' she wrote in *Wings*

---

*   The official record of royal engagements.
†   An improving periodical.

and the Child, 'but I cannot remember a time when I could not read.' She advocated for children to be given access to books as early as possible:

> For a child from ten onwards it is no bad thing to give the run of a good general library. When he has exhausted the storybooks he will read the ballads, the histories and the travels, and may even nibble at science, poetry, or philosophy.[44]

She had eclectic taste and liked to be challenged. 'I myself, at the age of thirteen,' she remembered, 'browsed contentedly in such a library – where Percy's anecdotes in thirty-nine volumes or so divided my attention with Hume, Locke and Berkeley. I even read Burton's *Anatomy of Melancholy*, and was none the worse for it.'[45]

Edith took a keen interest in Dr Robert Bolton's infrequent observations on his patients and their ailments. One evening, filled with mischief, she crept into his surgery, uncorked the medicine bottles he had left ready for dispatch, mixed their contents in a large jug, then refilled each bottle with her concoction and replaced each cork. Later that night, she woke in an absolute panic, convinced that some unsuspecting patient would die as a result of her naughtiness and that she would be hanged for murder.

By morning, she had resolved to let matters take their course. Should Dr Bolton be put on trial for murder, she decided, she would step forward and admit her guilt. Warming to her theme, she pictured herself confessing 'among the sympathetic tears of usher and jury, the Judge himself not remaining dry-eyed'.[46] No longer bored, she wept over this notional murder and exalted in her future heroics. She revived this episode in *The Story of the Treasure Seekers*: the Bastable children mix a batch of medicine and test it on Noël before selling it to the general public. Albert-Next-Door's uncle is not amused:

> 'Look here,' he said, 'you're old enough not to play the fool like this. Health is the best thing you've got; you ought to know better than to risk it. You might have killed your little brother with your precious medicines. You've had a lucky escape, certainly.'[47]

A week elapsed with no word of an unexplained death, and Edith's anxiety gave way to 'acute boredom'. She wrote 'a frantic letter' to Sarah, who was staying in Penshurst, near Sevenoaks in Kent, begging to be removed from the Bolton household. Since she had no stamps, she asked Sarah Bolton to post it for her. An inveterate letter-opener herself, Edith would discover later in life that the punishment for opening a letter destined for someone else was often unhappiness with its contents. When Sarah Bolton read this exceptionally unflattering critique of her hospitality, she added a note urging Sarah Nesbit to remove her daughter without delay.

Edith left in disgrace, but she could not conceal her delight at exchanging dreary Islington for 'the splendour of a blaze of buttercups' in Penshurst churchyard. She sat contentedly beneath the outstretched branches of a silver-white may tree, listening to the skylarks that sang overhead. Sarah offered only 'gentle reproaches', but one of her sisters, it's not clear which, was 'exceedingly angry'. 'Try and be a good girl, and not make dear Mamma unhappy,' she urged. Edith was willing to comply as long as she was allowed to remain 'among the golden buttercups and silver may-bushes'.[48]

Aged thirteen, she was on the verge of putting away childish things. The upheaval that characterised her early life continued when her play-box went missing during the crossing from France. She was desperately upset at the loss of a favourite toy, which she described in *Wings and the Child*:

> I had a black-and-white china rabbit who was hard enough, in all con-science, but then he never pretended to be anything but a china rabbit, and I bought him with my own penny at Sandhurst Fair. He slept with me for seven or eight years, and when he was lost, with my play-box and the rest of its loved contents, on the journey from France to England, all the dignity of my thirteen years could not uphold me in that tragedy.[49]

This 'crockery rabbit, white with black spots, crouched on a green crockery grass-plot' makes an appearance in *Daphne in Fitzroy Street*.[50]

Although Mary Nesbit's short life had been blighted by tuberculosis, that beautiful, sweet-natured young woman had not withdrawn from society entirely: 'How many balls has Minnie been to?' Edith had enquired of her mother in a letter she sent from the Ursuline Convent in 1869. Mary spent much of her adolescence convalescing in France, yet she attracted the attention of at least one young man back in England. In her late teens, she became engaged to Pre-Raphaelite poet Philip Bourke Marston.

CHAPTER 3

'DIM LIGHT OF FUNERAL LAMPS'

Mary Nesbit's involvement with Philip Bourke Marston brought Edith into
contact with the Pre-Raphaelite circle that dominated literary London, a
circumstance that had a profound impact on the trajectory of her life.
Philip, who was born in London on 13 August 1850, was the third child
and only son of Eleanor Jane Marston, née Potts, and John Westland
Marston, an exceptionally well-connected dramatist, critic and host of
one of London's most influential literary salons. Marston Senior's close
friend Charles Dickens wrote a prologue to his play *The Patrician's Daughter*,
and Henry Irving, manager and lead actor at the Lyceum Theatre, held a
benefit performance of Byron's *Werner* for him on 1 June 1887, played the
lead, and presented him with a cheque for £928. Philip was named after
Philip James Bailey, author of *Festus*, who was also his godfather. His godmother was bestselling novelist Dinah Maria Craik, whose most popular
short poem, 'Philip, my King', was addressed to him.

Regular visitors to the Marston home in Chalk Farm, regarded as 'one of
the chief literary resorts in London', included William Makepeace Thackeray,
Ford Madox Brown, brothers William and Dante Gabriel Rossetti, William
Morris, and Algernon Charles Swinburne.[1] Several of these luminaries recognised in Philip a precocious talent for poetry. It was said that he was 'almost
adopted by Swinburne from the age of fourteen'.[2] Dante Gabriel Rossetti,
founder of the Pre-Raphaelite Brotherhood, spoke of him 'ever in the highest
terms, and regarded him as undoubtedly the most gifted of all the younger
men'.[3] Responding to a sonnet Philip wrote in praise of his verse, Rossetti
composed 'To Philip Bourke Marston, inciting me to poetic work'.

Yet Philip's childhood was far from charmed. In infancy, his eyesight was
damaged when an excessive dose of belladonna was administered to prevent
him contracting scarlet fever from his older sister Nellie. When he was three
years old, a blow to his head during boisterous play caused inflammation in

both eyes and an almost total loss of vision. An operation provided temporary respite, but his sight deteriorated over time. To his great credit, he bore his disability with good humour. He insisted that he could distinguish between 'night and day, and even sunshine and cloud-gloom', and could 'discern the difference between men and women by their relative sizes and the shape of their garments'.[4] He never let his blindness hold him back and even developed a passion for sea swimming.

Little was made of Philip's disability, although popular novelist Lady Duffus Hardy did admit to being 'perplexed by the way in which he was wont to run up against chairs and tables as if he had miscalculated their distances'.[5] Her family was connected to the Marston family through a mutual friendship with painter Ford Madox Brown, a close confidante of both John Westland Marston and her husband, Sir Thomas Duffus Hardy, Deputy Keeper of the Public Record Office. Philip cultivated a lifelong friendship with Iza, the Duffus Hardys' only child, a delicate, bookish girl who became a successful novelist like her mother. It was Lady Duffus Hardy who introduced Philip to Iza's friend Mary Nesbit while she was staying in their home, a 'pretty house, standing in the midst of a large and well-wooded garden in St John's Wood'.[6]

In March 1887 drama critic Thomas Purnell, who regarded himself as 'Philip's first intimate', noted that his friend was 'passionately devoted' to the 'sister of Mr A. A. Nesbit, the eminent analytical chemist'.* He declared her 'one of the most beautiful girls I ever saw'.[7] Purnell was not alone in remarking on Mary's beauty. In the *Pall Mall Gazette* she was described as 'a very beautiful girl with whom he [Philip] was madly in love'.[8] Richard Garnett, in the *Dictionary of National Biography*, referred to her as 'a young lady of great personal and other attractions'.[9] Edith too described Mary in her sonnet 'To My Sister's Portrait', which she wrote around the time of Mary's engagement:

A SONNET
To my Sister's Portrait

It is so lovely! Yet that portrait shews
But one half of her beauty, auburn hair
Falls o'er her shoulders and her throat, small fair
Soft hands, and a delicate Grecian nose!
Those eyes, those wells of truth and love and light

---

* Alfred had followed in his late father's footsteps. Brilliantly inventive as a chemist, he would prove to be a poor businessman.

> Speak volumes to a colder heart than mine
> They are as tranquil those blue eyes of thine
> As summer sea beneath a moonlit night.
> Thy cherry lips make happy slaves of those
> Who hear thee speak through them their *Christian* name.
> Some love thee sadly without hope of love
> Some give thee love while hoping for the same.
> Some love thee with a love that cannot die
> And, Maris Stella, such a one am I.[10]

Philip too was physically striking. In her introduction to his *Collected Poems*, Louise Chandler Moulton, his friend and fellow poet, described him as 'a slight, rather tall man... very young-looking even for his age', with 'a wonderfully fine brow':

> His brown eyes were still beautiful in shape and colour. His dark-brown hair and beard had glints of chestnut; and all his colouring was rich and warm. His was a singularly refined face, with a beautiful expression when in repose – keenly sensitive but with full, pleasure-loving lips, that made one understand how hard his limitations must be for him to whom beauty and pleasure were so dear.[11]

His nature was as sweet as his face. According to William Sharp, who claimed him as 'my chief friend', he was a sweet, gentle young man, 'passionately fond of flowers' and 'intensely happy' in Mary's company.[12] Mary took Edith to visit Philip's friends. She remembered playing hide-and-seek with Dante Gabriel Rossetti and visiting Christina Rossetti at the home she shared with her mother, Frances.* It was meeting Christina that inspired her to become a poet.

In 1871 *Song-Tide and Other Poems*, Philip Bourke Marston's debut collection, was published to wide acclaim. He presented the first copy to Mary, who had inspired many of its sonnets and love-poems. Yet his joy was tainted with despair. A short time earlier, he had lost his beloved mother who had been devoted to him and who had written out his poems as he composed them. He told Louise Chandler Moulton that 'the whole world

---

* Philip Marston was uncharitable about Frances: 'She never seemed to me to be a lovable old lady,' he wrote, 'but I suppose she was, since she won the hearts of her children' (Charles Churchill Osborne, Philip Bourke Marston, *Times Book Club*, 1926, p. 27).

had gone to pieces'. She recognised the importance of his relationship with Mary during this difficult time:

It almost seemed like a miracle of mercy when he met Mary Nesbit and her sweet young voice lured him back to a fresh interest in this world. He loved her, as poets love, – suddenly, romantically and with an adoring and idealising devotion that at once expressed itself in the fifty-seven sonnets which form the first division of his earliest book.[13]

Although it was written for his mother, the dedication in *Song-Tide and Other Poems* proved tragically prophetic:

TO THE MEMORY OF
ONE WHOSE LOVE WAS THE CHIEF JOY OF MY LIFE
AND WHOSE LOSS
IS ITS INCONSOLABLE AFFLICTION

For many years Mary had faced her illness with great stoicism, but her symptoms were worsening. As William Sharp recalled:

Miss Nesbit was far from robust, but only a few friends knew that she had developed symptoms of consumption. She bore her unseen crown of sorrow bravely, and only when it became certain that her life was no longer secure for any length of time did she endeavour to warn her lover of the inevitable. But love had blinded his inner vision, and he either did not realise or else refused to allow himself to believe what was with infinite gentleness hinted to him.[14]

On 30 November 1871, while she was staying with friends at La Haute Motte, Châteauneuf-d'Ille-et-Vilaine, in Normandy, Mary lost her battle with the disease that had blighted her life. She was just twenty years old. Philip and Sarah were with her and it was reported that Philip had found her lifeless body, although his father was adamant that this was not the case. Afterwards he kept vigil by her lifeless body for hours. Christina Rossetti wrote to her brother, Dante Gabriel Rossetti: 'Poor Philip Marston, what a terrible sorrow for him in his blindness.'[15] He in turn told poet and physician Thomas Gordon Hake that 'poor Philip Marston' was 'just back from Brittany where he went not to see – poor fellow – but to be with a beautiful girl his betrothed who has just died of consumption'.[16] Swinburne wrote to his mother: 'I have told you of Philip Bourke Marston, the blind youth who was engaged to be married at 21 to a very beautiful girl who died before the wedding day.'[17]

Mary's body was shipped to England in a stout French coffin made of pale wood bound with iron hasps and fleurs-de-lys. On 1 December 1871 her remains were placed on the top shelf of vault 81 in the public vaults of the Anglican catacombs at West Norwood Cemetery, close to the resting place of her father, John Collis Nesbit.[18] Edith seemed haunted by this loss. In 'A Strange Experience', an unsettling Gothic tale she wrote for *Longman's Magazine* in March 1884, Isabel, a beautiful but utterly demented young woman with 'waves and ripples of... auburn hair', a 'red perfect mouth' and 'wildrose-coloured cheeks', insists on staying with the body of her murdered twin sister, 'Edith'. To soothe Isabel's mania, Edith's body is buried and replaced with a wax effigy.[19]

Philip was described as being 'absolutely prostrate' with grief after Mary's death, and Thomas Purnell believed that his friend's 'soul, as well as his body, was left in the dimness of anguish'.[20] His second collection, *All in All* (1875), is filled with sonnets that lament his lost love. He inscribed a copy 'presented to Anthony Nesbit from his friend Philip Bourke Marston'.* Sadly, this was merely the latest in a string of misfortunes that blighted his life, tragedies that, as his biographer Sir Leslie Stephen explained, 'might well excuse the morbid element in his views of life and nature'.[21] 'If one were not too insignificant for the metaphor,' Philip complained to William Sharp, 'I could with bitter truth assert that the stars in their courses have ever fought against me.'[22]

In 1874 Philip's close friend Oliver Madox Brown died of blood poisoning. He was just nineteen. In 1878 he lost his sister Cicely, who had been a source of great comfort after Mary's death. His other sister Nellie, who was married to poet Arthur O'Shaughnessy, died in January 1879. O'Shaughnessy himself died two years later on the eve of contracting a second marriage. Dante Gabriel Rossetti, Philip's greatest poetic inspiration, died of Bright's disease in April 1882. A short time later, poet James Thompson, having wandered the streets of London, lost to drink and despair, sought refuge in Philip's lodgings before being taken to University College Hospital, where he died. Philip too found solace in alcohol.

---

* Edith's brother Alfred sometimes went by his middle name, Anthony.

Although he grew increasingly moribund, Edith stayed loyal to him until he too died, aged just thirty-seven, on 13 February 1887.

After Mary's death, Sarah decided to settle in England with her surviving children, who were as mischievous as ever. Years later, Edith confessed that during a trip to see the illuminations organised in February 1872 to celebrate the recovery of the Prince of Wales from typhoid fever, they had tossed firecrackers into the mouths of the trombone and cornopean* 'to the amazement and terror of the band'.[23] Sarah settled on the picturesque village of Halstead in her native Kent. Perhaps she was attracted by its name, which is derived from the Anglian 'Hald', meaning refuge or shelter, and the Old English 'Stede', meaning place, hence 'safe place, or place of refuge'.

When falling sugar prices stimulated the jam industry, Halstead became a haven of fruit farms. Local woodland was grubbed up to make way for strawberries, while damson trees, known locally as 'skegs', lined the hedgerows. Smallholder's huts were erected hurriedly, then replaced with stone cottages. Boisterous groups of itinerant pickers were often spotted emerging from one or other of the village pubs, The Rose and Crown and The Cock. Sarah leased Halstead Hall, a substantial detached house, from Caroline Man whose late husband, Harry Stoe Man, had purchased it using a legacy of six hundred pounds her mother had left her.[†] The Man family was notorious in the village. Harry had made himself extremely unpopular in the late 1820s when he annexed the pond adjacent to Halstead Hall, the main source of water for the village. He was eventually prosecuted for nuisance and imprisoned for failing to pay a fine of £100 imposed by the court. Although use of the pond reverted to the villagers, Man stoked up further enmity by opposing an application by the parish vestry to exempt Halstead's poorest cottagers from the payment of rates.[24]

It was said that Halstead Hall was haunted. Long before the Nesbits arrived, the local rector had carried out a ceremony of exorcism on the stairway. This event may have informed Edith's horror story 'The Portent of the Shadow', in which she wrote: 'On the staircase, the feeling used to be so awful that I have had to bite my lips till they bled to keep myself from running upstairs at full speed.'[25] Yet she described her 'Kentish home' as 'dearer to me than all'. In *My School Days* she wrote:

---

*   A large-valved horn or trumpet.
†   Mrs Man lived at Halstead Lodge in nearby Carshalton with her daughter Eleanor.

After many wanderings my mother took a house at Halstead, 'The Hall' it was called but the house itself did not lend itself to the pretensions of its name. A long, low, red-brick house, that might have been common-place but for the roses and ivy which clung to the front of it, and the rich, heavy jasmine which covered the side. There was a smooth lawn with chestnut-trees round it and a big garden, where flowers and fruit and vegetables grew together, as they should, without jealousy or class-distinction. There never were such peonies as grew among our currant-bushes, nor such apricots as hung among the leaves on the sunny south wall. From a laburnum-tree in a corner of the lawn we children slung an improvised hammock, and there I used to read and dream, and watch the swaying green gold of leaf and blossom.[26]

The Man family had long vacated Halstead Hall, but Septimus Man, Caroline's youngest son, lived in a cottage in the village. A tragic figure, he was believed to have suffered heatstroke while practising as a barrister in India. On returning to England, he developed 'brainfever' and fell into a coma so deep that he was declared dead. He was laid out 'with a penny on each eye and a plate of salt on his chest', but he woke in the dead of night and attempted to strangle his brother.[27] Afterwards he grew increasingly eccentric. In his confused state, he would squat in Halstead Hall whenever it was empty of tenants, and it was his shadowy presence that fuelled rumours suggesting the house was haunted. Edith remembered him well:

The only really exciting thing was the presence, within a stone's throw of our house, of our landlady's son, who lived all alone in a little cottage standing in the fields. He was reported mad by the world, eccentric by his friends; but, as we found him, perfectly harmless. His one delusion, as far as I know, was that he was the rightful owner, nay, more, the rightful tenant of our house, and about once in six months he used to terrify the whole household by appearing with a carpet bag at the front door and announcing that he had come to take possession. This used to alarm all of us very much, because if a gentleman is eccentric enough to wish to 'take possession' of another person's house there is no knowing what he may be eccentric enough to do next. But he was always persuaded to go away peaceably, and I don't think we need have been so frightened. Once while he was in the drawing-room being persuaded by my mother, I peeped into the carpet bag he had left in the hall: It contained three empty bottles that had held mixed pickles, a loaf of bread and a barrister's wig and gown. Poor gentleman, I am afraid he was very eccentric indeed.[28]

Although Alfred and Harry were sent to school, Edith, to her great relief, was excused. She missed her brothers desperately and longed for school holidays when their adventures could resume. Then they would sail across the once-contested pond on a raft the boys had built, or roam through the 'gold-dim woodlands', which were 'starred with primroses', and 'light copses where the blue-bells and wind-flowers grow'. In *My School Days*, she described these glorious days in vivid prose:

Oh, those dewy mornings – the resurrection of light and life in the woods and fields! Would that it were possible for all children to live in the country where they may drink in, consciously or unconsciously, the dear delights of green meadow and dappled woodland! The delight in green things growing, in the tender beauty of the evening light on grey pastures, the glorious splendour of the noonday sun on meadows golden with buttercups, the browns and purples of winter woodlands.[29]

When Alfred shot a fox, mistaking it for a rabbit, he hid the corpse in his bedroom. He scoffed at Edith's suggestion that they give it a funeral and persuaded her to help him stuff it instead. They bought a shilling book on taxidermy and the chemicals they needed, skinned the poor creature and buried its innards, before nailing its pelt to the inside of a cupboard door, but their efforts were a failure and they soon abandoned the project. Next day they rose early, before the maids had stirred, and reunited the pelt with its contents. In *My School Days*, Edith recalled that 'the dew was grey on the grass, and the scent of the wet earth was sweet and fresh'.[30] In *The Wouldbegoods*, when the Bastable children shoot a fox in error they give it the elaborate funeral Edith had desired. 'The fox was cold,' she wrote, 'but its fur was so pretty, and its tail and its little feet.'[31] She even composed a eulogy for it.

Edith loved the bright little bedroom she had been allocated, with its window facing westward over a garden filled with roses, shrubs and fruit trees. She arranged bright potted plants along her window ledge, so they might be 'encouraged by the western sun'. To her delight, they blossomed profusely. In her short story 'The Brute', a large-eyed, dark-haired girl, with a passion for poetry, leans out of a 'jasmine-muffled lattice window' overlooking 'the dewy stillness of the garden'. The 'cloudy shadows that had clung in the earliest dawn about the lilac bushes and rhododendrons had faded like grey ghosts, and slowly on lawn and bed and path new black shadows were deepening and intensifying'. The girl gazes out over the 'green garden, the awakened birds, the roses that still looked asleep, the scented jasmine stars! She saw and loved it all'. She is 'full of the anxious, trembling longing that is youth's unnecessary joy'.[32]

A hatch built into Edith's bedroom ceiling provided an entrance to a secret place, 'by turn a treasure and a charm'. By treading carefully on the crossbeams in the attic, she could traverse the narrow passage that ran underneath the eaves until she reached a narrow wooden door that opened out onto a flat space at the centre of the roof with tiled ridges sloping up on each side. Alfred and Harry had access to a trapdoor in the linen closet next to their bedroom. They revelled in those 'happy, vanished days, when to be on the roof and to eat tinned pineapple in secret constituted happiness!'[33] Edith included this refuge in *The Wouldbegoods* and its sequel, *The New Treasure Seekers* (1904). Oswald Bastable, equipped with 'a book and a few apples', enters 'a square trapdoor in the ceiling of the linen room' to reach 'the wonderful, mysterious place between the ceiling and the roof of the house':

> The roof is beams and tiles. Slits of light show through the tiles here and there. The ceiling, on its other and top side, is made of rough plaster and beams. If you walk on the beams it is all right – if you walk on the plaster you go through with your feet… it was splendid… He walked along a dark, narrow passage. Every now and then cross-beams barred his way, and he had to creep under them. At last a small door loomed before him with cracks of light under and over. He drew back the rusty bolts and opened it. It opened straight on to the leads, a flat place between two steep red roofs, with a parapet two feet high back and front, so that no one could see you. It was a place no one could have invented better than, if they had tried, for hiding in.[34]

Of her own secret roof space, Edith wrote: 'This until the higher powers discovered it was a safer haven (for privacy) than even the shrubbery'. The shrubbery in question was a tangle of lilacs and laburnums that grew thickly around the pond at Halstead Hall. When she needed a refuge 'secure from the insistent and irritating demands so often made on one's time by one's elders', she would crawl deep inside, equipped with a volume of Mrs Ewing's tales.[35]

Although Edith missed Alfred and Harry, she did make friends locally. She grew particularly close to Violet Oakley,* daughter of the Very Reverend John Oakley and his wife Clara, who were regular visitors to Halstead. Violet was almost seven years her junior, but they remained friends into adulthood. It is thought she was referring to the Oakley family when she told a friend:

> When I was sixteen I stood at a window with a girl-friend of mine and her brother [Frank] whom I did not particularly care for; and she said, looking out at the stars, 'Let us three promise always to think of each other when we see The Great Bear' and I have done so ever since![36]

Edith was also friendly with the Sikes family, who lived at the rectory on Church Lane, a short distance from Halstead Hall. The Sikes children, Arthur, Francis and Edward, were too young for her to play with, so she invented stories for them instead. Frances Sikes, their mother, lent her books. Before long, she had finished the complete novels of Walter Scott. With Alfred and Harry, she played tennis on an improvised court marked out on the rectory lawn. Sometimes they would run down Cadlocks Hill to the railway track that ran along a deep cutting at its base before it disappeared into distant tunnels in either direction. The fictional railway line running along the field at the end of the garden in *The Railway Children*, her most celebrated novel for children, appears to draw on memories of Halstead and how she would walk the railway line with her brothers.[37] The 'great bridge with tall arches running across one end of the valley' may be the imposing brick viaduct that spanned the next valley along, to the east of Chelsfield.[38]

According to an article in *The Poets and the Poetry of the Century*, Edith started writing poetry when she was just eleven years old, three years before she arrived in Halstead.[39] An old mahogany bookcase with a deep top drawer that let down to form a writing table stood underneath the

---

* Violet was born Lucy Violet Oakley. As an adult, she lived with her aunt Janey de Brissac Phelps, who ran an orphanage in Camberwell. Violet acted as secretary to the orphanage. Neither woman ever married. Frank Page Oakley, who was four years younger than Edith, trained as an architect and set up his own practice in Manchester in 1887.

window of her bright new bedroom. There, she would scribble away in secret, locking her work away if her brothers were around, since she knew they would pour scorn on it. The few poems she shared with them were humorous ditties designed to make them laugh. Years later, she would write similar verses for her own children. She had unassailable confidence in her literary talent and believed she would become 'a great poet, like Shakespeare, or Christina Rossetti'. In 'When I was a Girl', an article she wrote for *John O'London's Weekly*, she described the adolescent style of her early poems:

> I don't know whether it was the influence of the poetry I read or merely a tendency natural to my age, but from fourteen to seventeen all my poems were about love and the grave. I had no sweetheart in real life, but in my poems I buried dozens of them and wept on their graves quite broken-heartedly.[40]

Edith signed her early poems 'D. Nesbit'. Sarah sent several of them to Alexander Hay Japp, literary adviser to publishers Alexander Strahan and a member of the editing team on *Good Words* and the *Sunday Magazine* and he agreed to publish them. Edith described her joy at seeing her work in print:

> The first poem I ever had published was a non-committal set of verses about dawn, with a moral tag. It was printed in the Sunday Magazine. When I got the proof I ran round the garden shouting 'Hooray!' at the top of my voice, to the scandal of the village and the vexation of my family.[41]

During the autumn of 1875 Sarah Nesbit gave up the lease on Halstead Hall. The impetus may have been Saretta's marriage, on 1 September 1875, to John Deakin, a general merchant from Liverpool and a former pupil of the Nesbit agricultural college.

It is also possible that a shortage of funds obliged her to leave her lovely home. It was suggested that her sons, Alfred in particular, had drained her of her remaining resources.[42] Aged twenty-one, he was earning a reputation as an excellent agricultural chemist by then. Harry, who was nineteen, planned to leave for Australia.

Before they moved to cheaper lodgings at 6 Mount Pleasant, Barnsbury Square in Islington, Edith and Sarah stayed for a time with Saretta in

Manchester. While they were there, Edith, who was seventeen, befriended Ada Breakell. She would become a significant figure in her life. The warm letters they exchanged are filled with gossip and fascinating insights into Edith's often-capricious state of mind.

Many of Edith's stories feature people who are obliged to leave their homes but come into riches in the nick of time. In 'Thor and the Hammer', from *These Little Ones* (1909), a little girl finds a will containing terms that allow her to stay in her lovely home. In 'The White Cat', from *The Magic World* (1912), she wrote: 'the wicked lawyer's taken nearly all mother's money and we've got to leave our lovely big white house, and go and live in a horrid little house with another house glued on its side'. An ornamental cat is found to contain the key to a safe filled with money and jewels.[43] In *My School Days*, Edith wrote:

> My book of memories lies open always at the page where are the pictures of Kentish cherry orchards, field and farm and gold-dim woodlands starred with primroses, light copses where the blue-bells and wind-flowers grow.[44]

She was on the verge of leaving her childhood home, but she would never forget the happy days she spent there and soon she would introduce her future husband to her old haunts.

CHAPTER 4

'A PARTICULARLY AND PECULIARLY MASCULINE PERSON'

Little trace can be found of Sarah and Edith at 6 Mount Pleasant, Barnsbury Square in Islington. What we do know is that, shortly after she arrived in London, Edith, who was in her teens, agreed to marry a young bank clerk named Stuart Smith. It is always a challenge to identify someone with the most common surname in Britain. The census of 1881, however, includes an accounts clerk named Stuart Smith who lodged, with his older brother Frederick, an insurance clerk, at 70 Thornhill Road, also on Barnsbury Square in Islington. Their landlord was William Lambeth, a bookbinder from Oxford.

Since this Stuart Smith was baptised on 16 March 1860, it would appear that he was younger than Edith, information that fits the account given to her biographer Doris Langley Moore by Ada Breakell, her 'dearest and oldest friend'. Ada remembered that he was eighteen months younger than Edith and 'a very young man' when they became engaged.[1]

Ada also left an account of a visit she paid, with Edith, to the 'money changer's office, (or bank)' where Smith worked:*

> H[ubert]. Bland was also working there, and one day, on our going in to change a note, Stuart introduced Mr. Bland to us; and that was the first time E. Nesbit saw H.B. as far as I know... personally, I never thought seriously of her engagement to Stuart and the next time I went to London to stay with them (in 1878) she was engaged to Mr. Bland.[2]

Edith's letters to Ada suggest that she was besotted with this charismatic young man. 'How different I was this time last year!', she

---

* In Edgar Jepson's *Memories of an Edwardian and Neo-Georgian* (1937), he writes that Edith told him she met Hubert at a picnic and they shared a plate of strawberries and cream. Yet Ada was adamant that her account was accurate.

exclaimed in one. 'Now I see the world through "larger, other eyes".'[3] Bland, who was two-and-a-half years older than her, was born on 3 January 1855, to a well-established Woolwich family that had thrived as a result of hard work. His paternal grandfather, Cornelius Bland, was a plumber and glazier. His father, Henry Bland, had trained as a commercial clerk and became a successful businessman whose many interests included a directorship of the River Steam Packet Company and a position as clerk to the Woolwich Burial Board. A proud man, he described himself as a 'Gentleman' on Hubert's birth certificate. Hubert's mother, Mary Anne, was a member of the Lacey family, an equally prominent Woolwich family. His maternal grandfather, John Lacey, kept the Red Lion Inn at Mulgrave Place. His wife, Elizabeth, took over when he died and it trades to this day.

Life was filled with promise for young Hubert, an intelligent boy with a compelling personality. Keen to expose him to the best education available, his parents enrolled him at Whiteley School on Woolwich Common and, later, Godwin's School at Blackheath. He also attended several local crammers with a view to passing the entrance exams for the Royal Military Academy in Woolwich, where he would train as a commissioned officer of the Royal Artillery or Royal Engineers. These ambitions were dashed on 5 September 1866, when Henry Bland died, aged fifty-eight, after 'a very brief but trying illness of spasmodic asthma'. The *Kentish Independent* reported:

> No man was better known, or more highly respected than Mr. Bland. The son of a leading Woolwich tradesman, he formerly took a very active part in all movements which were connected with the improvement of the town, and the development of its trade. He was for many years one of the Commissioners of the old Court of Requests; had served the office of Churchwarden, Local Commissioner, and indeed almost every other office of honour and credit, in connection with the parish. Latterly he withdrew himself from nearly all active local movements. At the time of his death, he held the offices of Chairman of the Woolwich Steam Package Company, and Clerk and Collector to the Woolwich Equitable Gas Company.[4]

Due to the sudden and catastrophic nature of his illness, Henry had made little provision for his widow and his eleven-year-old son. Mary Anne was obliged to swap her well-appointed home at 29 Frances Street for a more modest house, 46 Samuel Street, also in Woolwich. When her daughter Helen married local man Louis Tasche later that year, Hubert, who was eleven years younger than his sister, became her last dependent child. His considerably older brothers, Henry and Percy, had left home years earlier, and another brother, William, the first child born to the Blands, had died in childhood.[5] The census of 1871 recorded that Mary Anne Bland, an 'annuitant' aged fifty-seven, lived at 46 Samuel Street with her sixteen-year-old son Hubert, a scholar, and a general servant named Margaret, who was also sixteen.

This adjustment in Hubert's circumstances ended all prospect of military training. His education curtailed, he tried for the civil service but became a clerk instead. Yet he retained a lifelong interest in the military and he joined the Artists Rifles, a volunteer light infantry unit. Physically imposing and standing well over six feet tall, he was an athletic man who showed great prowess at swimming, boxing, running and jumping. 'Hubert Bland was a very big man,' his friend Cecil Chesterton wrote in an introduction to *Essays by Hubert Bland* (1914). 'That was the first impression that anyone who met him received.'[6] In a letter to Archibald Henderson, George Bernard Shaw, who also knew him well, described him as:

A man of fierce Norman exterior and huge physical strength ... a strong Conservative and Imperialist by temperament ... [He] was never seen without an irreproachable frock coat, tall hat, and a single eyeglass which infuriated everybody. He was pugnacious, powerful, a skilled pugilist, and had a voice like the scream of an eagle. Nobody dared be uncivil to him.[7]

Henderson noted that Hubert possessed 'strong individuality and hard common sense'.[8] Certainly he had a rebellious streak; he smoked heavily and was, by his own admission, 'adventurous' with drugs; 'I have taken opium in all its forms,' he claimed. 'I have eaten haschish [sic], and soothed my sorrows with Indian hemp.'[9] The monocle that Shaw took such exception to was a necessity rather than an affectation. He suffered from chronic short-sightedness that was markedly worse in his left eye and had adopted this eccentric but practical aid when he was seventeen. He attached it to a watered silk ribbon that was thoroughly in keeping with his flamboyant dress code: silk hat and frock coat by day and tailcoat, worn with gleaming stiff collar and cuffs, gloves, and a silver-topped cane, in the evening.

Hubert was popular with his peers and attractive to the point of irresistibility to women. As Cecil Chesterton observed:

In regard to the sexes he knew that men were men and that women were women. His virility would have forbidden him to desire any alteration in this condition of things even if he had thought such an alteration practicable.[10]

He regarded himself as 'a particularly and peculiarly masculine person' and had essentialist notions of men and women being fundamentally different but complementary. An ardent womaniser, he claimed to have had his 'first love-affair at the age of eight'. By twelve, he was 'formally engaged to the most charming of her sex'.[11]

Before meeting Edith, Hubert had entered an understanding with Yorkshire-born Maggie Doran, who lived with her family at 86 Powis Street, less than fifteen minutes' walk from the home he shared with his mother.[12] Maggie's father, Thomas, a Londoner by birth and a dyer by trade, was proprietor of a family business and had trained her as a dyer's assistant. She may also have acted as a paid companion to Hubert's mother. Maggie believed that Hubert intended to marry her. By the time he was courting Edith she was pregnant with his child.

Family sources confirm that Maggie gave birth to a son shortly after Hubert met Edith, but no record of him can be found in birth records or census returns and he may have been put up for adoption.[13] Edith, who knew nothing of this, took to spending her days in the beautiful old library at Guildhall in London, reading, writing or losing herself in her thoughts while she waited for Hubert to take his lunchtime break. Lengthy letters to Ada contain expressions of existential angst and concern for her future. 'I'm worried with trying to <u>understand</u> things,' she admitted:

> What good is my life to me? What good can I do with it? <u>Can</u> I do <u>anything</u>? Is life a dream and death a reality? – Or is <u>death</u> the substance? – I think on – and on – I <u>nearly</u> get an answer and then – just as I think I am attaining to what I so desire, it slips – and I lose my chance and then – I have only to 'dry my eyes and laugh at my fall' and humbly begin my train of thought all over again – I shall never be answered – I think still and from my thoughts <u>gain</u> nothing – <u>attain</u> nothing, <u>see</u> nothing of all that my soul longs to grasp.

She realised how ridiculously self-absorbed she sounded and closed by writing:

I better stop, I think. I shall only sink into a veritable miry slough, represented by my own ridiculous system of bad metaphysics – and, as I don't want to drag you down with me I won't go on – on paper – In my thoughts I sink or swim – done – [14]

As 1878 reached its end, Edith presented Hubert with a little leather-bound notebook. She painted a pretty sheaf of daisies on the front and wrote: 'To Hubert Bland from Daisy Nesbit, for Xmas 1878'. Inside, she had copied out *Sonnets from the Portuguese*, the intimate sequence of poems Elizabeth Barrett Browning had written for her husband, Robert. They both admired the Brownings and enjoyed reading their sonnets aloud to one another. In October 1881 they joined the newly established London Browning Society, although Robert Browning, who was very much alive at the time, observed wryly that 'it was 300 years too early for a Browning Society'.[15]

Early in their relationship, Edith took Hubert to her beloved Halstead. There, they wandered through the woods and had lunch in a 'funny, old-fashioned Inn'. She appears to recapture that idyllic day in her short story 'A Holiday'. A fictional couple who are strangers to each other spend several sublime hours strolling through lush green parkland in Halstead 'where tall red sorrel and white daisies grew high among the grass that was up for hay'. They 'talked of all things under the sun'. While they are there, '[the] gold sun shone, the blue sky arched over a world of green and glory'. 'It seemed,' Edith wrote, 'that the green country was enchanted land, and they under a spell that could never break.'

Yet this is not a relationship between equals. The man is 'eager to impress her with that splendid self of his'. The woman is 'anxious to show herself not wholly unworthy'. She impresses on him that 'she, too, had read her Keats and her Shelley and her Browning – and could cap and even overshadow his random quotations'.[16] She takes him to a copse of beech trees that she used to visit with her brothers when she was a child. She believes they share a special bond:

To the end of her days no one will know her soul as he knew it that day, and no one ever knew better than she that aspect of his soul which he chose that day to represent as its permanent form.[17]

Yet there is a sting in this tale. The lovers agree to preserve in their memories this one perfect day. They part, vowing never to meet again. The woman is certain she will never meet a man to equal this stranger and rejects 'an excellent solicitor who may have made her happy'. She never marries but grows 'faded and harassed' as her life unfurls in an unsatisfactory manner. The man writes a poem inspired by the woman's eyes. He sells it to the *Athenaeum* for two guineas and considers his day trip to have been extremely worthwhile.[18]

Edith may have explored doubts in her fiction, but her description of the day she spent in Halstead with Hubert, which she included in an exuberant and curiously childish letter to Ada, contained no hint of foreboding; 'The country was <u>fresh, young and jolly. So were we</u>,' she exclaimed.[19] As the summer of 1879 drew to a close, she was pregnant with Hubert's child. The poems she wrote at this time indicate a deepening relationship, but she appears terrified of losing his regard. In *Après*, an unpublished poem she wrote in her personal journal in July 1879, she lamented:

So now our bright, brief love is done
How sweet its dreams, my dear –
The joy you coveted is won,
The end you chose is here.
The end of all you cared to give –
A love too weak to live![20]

She is more explicit in *Aimer*, which she wrote on 7 June 1879 and subtitled '*C'est être voue a la douleur, sans retour*' [to be devoted to pain without return]:

This is the end that has always grown
From a woman's love, and a man's desire![21]

She signed herself 'Daisy Bland, Aug. 27, 1879' in the cheap, black linen-covered notebook that contained her poems. Later, she added 'deeply regretted', which she underlined. That month, she left the Islington home she shared with her mother and, with Hubert's help, secured lodgings with the Knowles family at 8 Oxford Terrace, just off Blackheath Hill in Greenwich, within walking distance of Woolwich. She shared this busy home with watchmaker Alfred Knowles, his wife, Sarah, and their four young children. They knew her as 'Edith Bland'.

Edith took to telling people that she had married Hubert in 1879, most likely in an attempt to legitimise their firstborn child. She included this information in a letter to anthropologist Francis Galton.[22] Certainly Ada believed Edith was married by the time she visited her in London during the winter of 1879. Edith, who would have entered the middle trimester of pregnancy by then, took her friend skating.

Yet as her pregnancy advanced she remained single and Hubert continued to live with his mother. Perhaps he didn't believe in the institution of marriage. In *The Prophet's Mantle*, a novel he wrote with Edith as 'Fabian Bland' in 1885, a socialist man explains to his pregnant lover that he cannot betray his principles and marry her since he doesn't believe in the convention of marriage:

> The true marriage, he had maintained, was fidelity, and mutual love was more binding than could be a ceremony in which one of the performers did not believe. He loved her, he had said, far too dearly to wish to deceive her in the smallest degree about his sentiments, and so he felt bound to tell her that to him a legal marriage would be for ever impossible. In spite of that, would she not be noble enough to trust her life entirely to him, and be his wife?[23]

When the woman rejects this arrangement, she is obliged to rely on the kindness of strangers.

Hubert often expressed hostile views on marriage and was quoted as follows in the *Lichfield Mercury*:

> Marriage, as we know it, is the inevitable slayer of romance. Before the intimacy of marriage, says Mr. Hubert Bland, romance disappears like a mist wreath in the blazing sun.[24]

In his essay 'Some Ways of Love' he declared: 'The worst of friendship is that it may end in matrimony; the best of matrimony is that it may end in friendship.'[25] In 'Hobson's Choice' he asked readers to consider 'the feeble passive way in which men fall into the one and drift into the other'. 'How many men who marry under thirty have the slightest intention of speaking the fatal word until it is spoken in spite of themselves?' he enquired:

> How many begin their courting with any end in view at all but that of a more or less harmless flirtation – the delightful past-time or an idle hour?

And then, before they know where they are, a hint from a candid friend that people are talking, that the girl is being compromised, or the tacit claims of honour decide the point.[26]

Men, he insisted, 'may face the altar' only because they lack the courage to 'take so irretrievable a step as to face the grave'.[27]

It may have been Edith who was sceptical. Twenty-one-year-old Katherine, protagonist of her novel *The Incredible Honeymoon* (1916), insists: 'When I marry… it won't be just because I want to get myself out of a scrape.'[28] Katherine declares:

I've always thought that even if I cared very much for some one I should be almost afraid to marry him unless I knew him very, very well. Girls do make such frightful mistakes. You ought to see a man every day for a year, and then perhaps, you'd know if you could really bear to live with him all your life.[29]

Yet Katherine is desperate to quit her stifling home and she tells a man she barely knows: 'I wish I could come with you without being married.' He urges her to: 'Come then, come on any terms. I'll take you as a sister if I'm not to take you as a wife.' Elsewhere, she worries: 'What if he were to regret the adventure? What if he were to like her less and less… while she grew to like him more and more?'[30]

In 'To a Lady' Hubert declared, rather ominously: 'I think women find it easier to "settle down" in marriage with a partner they don't love than men do.'[31] The vast majority of women, he insisted, 'do not marry for love'. Marriage, he reasoned, was a profession for women and 'one needs not to love a profession or anyone in it to adopt it'. Conversely, men must marry for love since they have nothing to gain from marriage 'but the satisfaction of that instinct, that impulse'. He drew a clear distinction between love and 'raw passion', and insisted that the latter 'can always be satisfied without anything so drastic and so irrevocable, and so generally bothersome as marriage'.[32]

Hubert insisted that women could only find sexual satisfaction in marriage. For women and men, he believed:

There have been, are, and always will be two standards of sex morality which the Law has been, is, and always will be impotent to reduce by one, for these two standards are established by Nature's decree.[33]

In 'The Love Interest' he declared: 'Love is the ever-present possibility, one is never safe from it.'[34] Since he made little effort to resist temptation it seems reasonable to suppose that Edith had him in mind when she wrote of one character in *The Incredible Honeymoon*: 'The temperamental needle of Edward Basingstoke followed the magnet of romance.'[35] Yet Hubert believed a marriage could be made to work. In 'Hobson's Choice' he declared: 'It doesn't follow because you didn't freely choose your wife that therefore your marriage must turn out a failure, and your children rise up and call you cursed.'[36] This seems at odds with his statement in 'About Divorce' where he warned:

To-day we all know that to marry in haste is to do something more than to prepare for oneself a leisured repentance; it is in all probability to bring into the world offspring whose lives will be one long expiation of their parents' ghastly error.[37]

Ghastly or not, Hubert and Edith had made their error. As her pregnancy advanced, she may have pushed him to legitimise their situation since the consequences of a baby born outside the confines of marriage would be far worse for her than for him. In 'Observations on the Art of Life' Hubert described how, 'at the age of twenty-five or thereabouts', men 'love women best, admire them most, find most pleasure in their society, clutch with most avidity at the faintest signs of their favour, write most letters to them, make most assignations with them, feel most keenly, most convincedly, that in them is the top of life'.[38] He was twenty-five years old when he married Edith, who had just turned twenty-one.

Although civil wedding ceremonies were unusual at that time, Hubert Bland and Edith Nesbit were married at a London registry office on 22 April 1880. She was seven months pregnant at the time and still living at Oxford Terrace with the Knowles family. Hubert gave his address as 17 Devonshire Square, a building known as Commercial Chambers that was subdivided into '18 or 20 offices'.[39] This address was associated with Clarke, Bland & Co., a brush manufacturing partnership he had entered with John Reade Clarke a short time beforehand. He had left the bank and invested what capital he had in this enterprise. Edith may have been nervous on her wedding day, since her father's name is recorded as Henry rather than John. Their witnesses appear to have been strangers to them and no members of either family were present. Ada Breakell, who insisted that Sarah Nesbit 'did <u>not</u> like Hubert Bland', also believed that Hubert did not tell his own mother that he was married 'for quite a long time'.[40]

Edith rarely mentioned her wedding day, and it must be hoped that it did not resemble the dispiriting ritual that Katherine and Edward endure in *The Incredible Honeymoon*:

> The dingy house with the grimy doorstep, and the area where dust and torn paper lay, the bare room, the few words that were a mockery of what a marriage service should be, the policeman who met them as they went in, the charwoman who followed them as they went out, the man at the end of the long, leather-covered table… who wished them joy with, as it were, his tongue in his cheek. And there was the signing of names and dabbing of them with a little oblong of pink blotting-paper crisscrossed with the ghosts of the names of other brides and bridegrooms… and then they were walking down the sordid street, she rather pale and looking straight before her, and in her white-gloved hand the prize of the expedition, the marriage certificate.[41]

It is to be hoped too that Hubert did not share Edward's regret. He 'wished the day's work undone' and lamented: 'Freedom was over, independence was over, and all his life lay at the mercy of a girl.'[42]

In her semi-autobiographical novel *The Red House* (1902), Edith has her protagonist Chloe, a newly married woman, suggest that men 'feel injured at the mere idea a girl they like might marry someone else'. Len, her husband, replies: 'It's only that women believe in marriage and men don't.'[43] Chloe too disparages traditional weddings, as Len explains:

> 'What an ideal beginning to a honey-moon!' said my wife. 'Fancy walking straight home to your own house. No broughams and slippers and things, no long railway journey and horrid hotels and lodgings, with the rice dropping out of you in showers every time you move an inch, and everybody grinning sympathetically after you.'[44]

Whether she desired it or not, an expensive ceremony would have been beyond Edith's means and, in any case, it was considered improper for a heavily pregnant woman to participate in an elaborate celebration.

Paul Cyril Bland was born on 22 June 1880, two months to the day after his parents' wedding day. When Hubert's brush manufacturing business failed a short time later, they were plunged into desperate financial uncertainty. Hubert always insisted that his business partner had absconded abroad with the funds, yet records indicate that Clarke, Bland & Co. had been 'dissolved by mutual consent' on 9 July 1880, less than three weeks after Paul was born.[45] Whatever the truth, Edith was required to muster what resources, determination and ingenuity she had to support her family. For years she earned a small, sporadic income from her poetry and her drawing. At that time there seemed little prospect of her writing some of the most popular and influential children's books ever published.

CHAPTER 5

'MORE LIKE A LOVER
THAN A HUSBAND'

George Bernard Shaw was an occasional visitor to the Bland marital home at 28 Elswick Road, off Loampit Vale in Lewisham, South-East London. He included a description of this modest terraced house in his *An Unfinished Novel* (1958). Noting the 'cheap oilcloth on the hall floor & untrustworthy chairs', he went on to describe how:

> The furniture was not all of one set. The carpet was very old, the sofa was concealed by a cretonne cover that hid it to the very casters, and the rest of the moveables were clearly spare pieces from the stock of father or mother.[1]

In 'The Force of Habit', a Gothic tale she wrote for *Ainslee's Magazine*, Edith has a young married woman move into 'a little new red-brick Queen Anne villa' that was 'damp as any cloud'.[2] She described the difficulties of living in a 'microscopic' little 'bandbox' house, with a minuscule backyard in *The Red House*.

The census for 1881, taken on 3 April, recorded Edith Bland, 'Authoress', aged twenty-two and married, as head of the household at 28 Elswick Road. Also present was baby Paul Bland, aged ten months, and his grandmother Sarah Nesbit, who may have been visiting. There were two live-in domestic servants: Elizabeth Knight, aged thirty-four, and Elizabeth Rule, aged fourteen. Hubert was at his mother's home in Woolwich that night. His occupation was recorded as 'brush manufacturer' and, although he would celebrate his first wedding anniversary less than three weeks later, he was registered as 'unmarried'. This deception may have been prompted by the presence that evening of Maggie Doran, who is registered as a visitor. There was no record of their child.

Hubert may have been quarantined in his mother's house at that time. A virulent outbreak of smallpox gripped London in 1881, and he fell victim to this life-threatening illness.* He bore the scars for the rest of his life. Family accounts suggest that it was baby Paul who had come into contact with an infectious patient when a maid took him to visit her family. He developed no symptoms but somehow infected his father. In fact Hubert contracted the disease twice, and he kept his distance from his wife and infant son while he fought it.

It was while he was ill that Hubert's partner in the brush business defrauded him. On 8 March 1881 Hubert wrote an intriguing letter to the editor of the *Sporting Times* expressing fury at a man who had fled England some months earlier. 'Dear Sir,' he enquired:

Can you, or any of your readers inform me whether the 'Timothy Knapp' whose letter [posted in San Diego in America] you published in your yesterday's issue is a certain clerk who left England rather hurriedly last autumn in order to avoid a horse-whipping? Do you happen to know if he is likely to come back, as he is anxiously 'wanted'? Information on this subject will greatly oblige yours very truly,

Hubert Bland,
Bowater Crescent, Woolwich, S.E.[3]

A Minnie Williams responded several weeks later:

Dear Sir, – Mr. Bland is quite right in his surmises as to 'Timothy Knapp'. This person was a clerk in the city up to the time when he found it convenient to leave England 'hurriedly'. After threatening women and slandering men he ran away to escape the unpleasant alternative.[4]

A second letter, from an Emmeline de Vere, was published that June:

Sir, – I believe Timothy Knapp is the man wanted by Mr. H. Bland. His real name is J.H. Since he hurried away last autumn he has been adding to his list of dirty tricks and writing false and slandering letters. I think it's not likely he'll come back now when the account is so much heavier against

---

* The smallpox epidemic placed great strain on available hospital beds in London. To ease the situation the Metropolitan Asylums Board chartered two old wooden warships from the Admiralty to be converted into hospital ships; the *Atlas*, a 91-gun man-of-war built in 1860, and the *Endymion*, a 50-gun frigate built in 1865. George Bernard Shaw contracted the disease during the same outbreak.

him than when he was so prudent before to get the herring pond between those he has injured and himself.[5]

This absconder was most likely Irish-born John Reade Clarke, the man registered as Hubert's partner. In 1908, an obituary in the *Emmetsburg (Iowa) Democrat* confirmed that Clarke and his wife had arrived in Iowa in 1881 'at the wish of his uncle and aunt, Mr. and Mrs. T.R. Crawford'. This Clarke, it was reported, had 'prospered and is quite contented with this country'.[6]

Ada Breakell confirmed that the brush business had ended disastrously. According to another friend named Alice Hoatson:

> Every penny he [Hubert] had which he had put into a brush factory had been embezzled by his partner. Not a penny was left, that was how it came about they were in such ghastly poverty – all the money gone and much of the stock. Hubert retained a few brushes and gave them to friends as gifts.[7]

In *The Story of the Treasure Seekers* Mr Bastable is defrauded in a similar fashion: 'Father was very ill,' Oswald Bastable explains, 'and while he was ill his business-partner went to Spain – and there was never much money afterwards.'[8] In *The New Treasure Seekers* (1904), father learns that his 'wicked partner who ran away with his money was in France'.[9] When the Bastable children see an advertisement in the *Lewishment Recorder* promising '£100 secures partnership in lucrative business for sale of useful patent', a 'Generous Benefactor' cautions: 'I don't advise you to enter into that partnership. It's a swindle.'[10] In 'Miss Eden's Baby', a story from *The Literary Sense* (1903), Miss Eden's father dies of a heart attack brought on by the shock of his partner running off with all his money.

In *The Story of the Treasure Seekers* Oswald Bastable describes the debt collectors who called to their door. They 'got very angry and said they were calling for the last time before putting it in other hands'.[11] Edith suffered similar humiliations when Hubert was ill, and it fell to her to generate income for rent and tradesmen's bills. She told Ada Breakell that she was '*fiendishly* busy sometimes'.[12] As if life wasn't difficult enough, by the spring of 1881 she was pregnant for a second time. Like professional writer Laura in her chilling tale 'Man-size in Marble', Edith became the breadwinner in the family. It is revealing that Laura's patronising husband, Jack, who calls her 'Pussy' as Hubert did Edith, trivialises her work and refuses to take her seriously. His attitude leads to a tragedy.[13]

When Hubert advised Edith that no editor could resist a manuscript presented by a beautiful woman, she walked the length of Fleet Street, hawking her sketches and poems. It was reported in *Current Literature* that this was how she secured a commission for one of her best-regarded poems in 1883:

> [Her] first hit was made with her poem 'Absolution', in the pages of Longman's magazine; a perfect stranger, she called one day at the office and read the poem to the editor; it was accepted then and there, and for its appearance in the magazine she received $75.[14]

In *Daphne in Fitzroy Street*, the eponymous Daphne declares: 'Someone had said last night that the only way to sell your stuff for magazines was to call on editors yourself.'[15] She dons 'her quietest hat and gown' and heads 'down into the City to call on editors', but she 'returned heavy footed' when her 'brown paper parcel of sketches, whose string had been untied so often and so wearily, had grown strangely heavy to carry'.[16] She explains how demoralising this is:

> 'I've been trying to sell my drawings,' said Daphne, suddenly. 'Oh, editors are hateful – even when you see them – and when you don't, and you generally don't – they're fiends, I believe.'[17]

In *The Red House*, Chloe too believes 'to be on the spot is the thing', since 'work is given to the people who look after it'.[18] She 'went to town twice a week to wring remunerative orders for illustrations from the flinty hearts of editors'. In *The Railway Children*, Mother, whom Edith modelled on herself, earns a precarious living this way:

> Mother, all the time, was very busy with her writing. She used to send off a good many long blue envelopes with stories in them – and large envelopes of different sizes and colours used to come to her. Sometimes she would sigh when she opened them and say: 'Another story come home to roost. O dear, O dear!' and then the children would be very sorry. But sometimes she would wave the envelope in the air and say: 'Hooray, hooray. Here's a sensible Editor.' Whenever an Editor was sensible, there were buns for tea.[19]

Much of Edith's modest income at this time came from decorating blank greeting cards with pretty illustrations, many of them drawn from nature. It helped enormously that she could compose verse for the inside too. Ada Breakell recalled the manager of one 'Jewish firm of colour printers located in the City' refusing to accept a pack of decorated cards because she completed them two days later than agreed. He relented when she burst into tears. This firm was almost certainly Raphael Tuck and Sons, a leading manufacturer of greeting cards in London at that time. Perhaps Edith had entered the nationwide design competition they launched in October 1880, which helped establish the custom of sending Christmas cards.[20] In time, she developed an excellent relationship with Gustave Tuck, chairman and managing director. He remembered her as a 'high-spirited, charming, whimsical' woman, with a penchant for inventing verse on the spot and a playful habit of reading the palms of Tuck employees.[21]

Edith gave birth to a baby girl on 2 December 1881. They named her Mary but always called her by her middle name, Iris.

A short time later, Edith, who was in the habit of opening other people's letters,* opened one Maggie Doran had written to Hubert. She learned that their relationship was ongoing and that Maggie had absolutely no idea Hubert was married with two children.[22] Although she had every right to be furious, she realised that this woman had been duped just as much as she had. Living up to what Ada Breakell described as her 'very loving and forgiving disposition', she set about befriending her unwitting rival.[23]

Never one to waste a good plot, Edith drew on this incident when she wrote her cautionary tale 'After Many Days' for *Longman's Magazine* in November 1893. A woman named Margaret is abandoned by her fiancé. He quits his job in the bank and sets off to seek his fortune, but his ventures fail and he descends into desperate poverty.[24] In 'From the Dead', from *Grim Tales*, a woman opens a letter addressed to her brother and justifies her prying by explaining that she knows both sender and recipient. Matters end badly. In 'Dick, Tom and Harry' Harriet reads a letter intended for her fiancé and discovers that she is at the centre of a love triangle.

Although Ada Breakell was certain that Edith 'could not help seeing what sort of a man H.B. was', she could not recall her friend ever saying

---

* Her son John confirmed this in an interview with Doris Langley Moore. George Bernard Shaw incorporated this trait into his pen portrait of Edith in *An Unfinished Novel*.

a word against him, nor complaining about the infidelities he took so little trouble to conceal.[25] Hubert seemed unrepentant and could be playful when justifying his flirtations. In *The Happy Moralist* he declared: 'the Don Juans of the world generally are good-tempered, genial, generous fellows'. The woman he is addressing responds: 'It is comforting to feel that one's husband never so much as smiles at another woman, of course; but it is rather cold comfort if he never smiles at you either.'[26] She lists the advantages of not having a 'Don Juan' for a husband:

> It's nice to know that no part of his income goes on jewels to other women, but one would like a few shillings of it to go in flowers for oneself. A man should spend his evenings at home, of course; but then it does rather depend upon how he spends them there doesn't it? If he sits reading the evening papers or dozing in an arm-chair, he might almost as well be anywhere else mightn't he?[27]

This woman points to Drelincourt, 'the most charming and attentive of husbands'. He writes to his wife every day and she is 'one of the merriest women in London'. She exclaims: 'He makes love – I don't believe he can help it – to every woman he knows and yet see how delightful he is.' She declares admiringly: 'he is more like a lover than a husband'.[28]

For quite some time Hubert was in no position to buy jewels for other women. Happily the couple's finances improved dramatically in 1883, when he was appointed as secretary to the newly established London Hydraulic Power Company. A business acquaintance described him at this time:

> He dressed in the usual conventional get up of the London business man, frock coat, top hat, etc. He told me that he was considered much too eccentric in being a socialist* and he could not afford further eccentricities such as Bernard Shaw's mustard coloured loose fitting tweed suits and 'Trilby' hat![29]

A letter Hubert wrote in his capacity as secretary was published in the *Engineer* on 4 August 1885, under the heading 'Novel Method of Erecting Bridgework'. Yet he lacked any technical qualifications and an engineer

---

* Hubert and Edith had developed an interest in socialism by this time and Shaw, a fellow socialist, dressed eccentrically in a Jaeger suit.

was hired in his place. Perhaps that explains Edith's reference, in *The Red House*, to 'the late deplorable action of the London Water Companies'.[30] Once again it fell to her to earn the greater part of the household income.

Many of the insights we have into Edith's state of mind at this time come from a series of letters she exchanged with her close friend Ada Breakell, who had sailed for Australia in January 1884 to join her fiancé, Edith's brother Harry. Certain she would never see her friend again, Edith confessed that she was 'grieving after' her and exclaimed: 'No one has loved you so long as I – (outside your own people I mean) and I don't think anyone could love you *more*.' She felt no inclination to mix with others; 'I hate strangers,' she declared. In an exceptionally intimate passage, she admitted:

> I think so often of those few minutes in the bedroom at Dulwich. It was then I first felt and <u>realized</u> what it <u>meant</u> for you to be going away. If I live to be a hundred I shall never forget that evening. <u>My</u> Ada – my dear – my friend'.

Edith appears to have been crying as she wrote these words, since she goes on: 'I don't want to mar the superlative neatness of this large blue sheet by blots or anything of that nature'. She asked Ada to imagine how she would feel if it were she who had been 'left behind, longing and yearning and feeling <u>your</u> heart ache very very bitterly for <u>my</u> sake – as I now for <u>yours</u> my dear and for the loss of you'. She closed by assuring her: 'I long for you and love you so my darling.' She signed this heart-wrenching letter 'Dai'.

Her letters are filled with news of her life with Hubert and 'the bunnies', her affectionate name for their two tiny children. So changed was her life that she declared: 'I seem to have lived three or four lives right through since those old times.'[31] On Easter Sunday 1884 she described a scene of perfect domesticity: 'the kettle is singing on the fire and the kitten purring before it', she wrote. 'I have just got Iris to sleep, and laid her down and Paul is standing watching my scribbling pen.' She mused: 'Iris ought certainly to have been the boy – and Paul the girl,' adding. 'They are very good children, I think, as children go – and if only we don't add to their number I am satisfied. But that is a big "if".'[32]

On 11 April 1884 she admitted to Ada: 'I am not doing any painting just now, I am sorry to say – so I try to write as many stories as I can – but it is uphill work – writing when you don't feel a bit inclined.'[33] Poetry was her true passion: 'I'm sure to quote poetry sooner or later if I'm not restrained,' she exclaimed, then complained:

> What seems to be the worst of my present life is that I have no time to do any good work – in the way of writing verse I mean. I want to write another longish poem or two and there don't seem to be any blank sheets of time lying loose round to scribble it down on.[34]

Released from the London Hydraulic Power Company, Hubert too turned to writing and discovered he had a talent for it. His greatest pleasure, by his own account, was to read his work aloud to an attentive crowd, made up primarily of young women dressed in 'greenish and yellowish velvet and silk drapery, all curled up in sinuous poses, and looking… like a lot of dear little caterpillars.'[35] He collaborated with Edith under the pseudonym 'Fabian Bland' and they received £10, the equivalent of two months' wages, for a story published in the *Longman's Magazine* Christmas number for 1884; 'Hubert wrote the first part and we finished it together,' Edith told Ada.[36] They also received £3 a week for 'The Social Cobweb', a series of twelve loosely themed stories that ran in the *Weekly Dispatch* until March 1884. 'Did I tell you I am writing nothing now by myself except poems,' she told Ada. 'In all stories Hubert and I "go shares". I am sure it is much better when we write together than when we write separately.' In *The Red House*, Chloe and Len write collaboratively; Len starts each story for Chloe to finish. She resents having to write through financial necessity too:

> I longed to write the stories because I wanted the money they would bring to me. The longing was keen enough to be painful, not strong enough to get itself satisfied. It was not a desire for the thing in itself – not a desire to achieve, to attain – but depended for its vitality on a secondary motive.[37]

In *The Story of the Treasure Seekers*, Noël, who is a surrogate for Edith, tells the editor of the *Daily Recorder* that he does not write for money but because he wants to. 'Art for art's sake eh?' the editor responds.

Edith's greatest challenge was coming up with plots. 'If ever you think of any plots – mind you let me know,' she wrote to Ada. 'They are our great difficulty. The writing is a much more simple matter than the construction.' She asks if Harry might suggest 'even central ideas for stories', since 'they are so hard to hit upon'. She was astonished that she had received no news of her brother: 'But you did not tell me <u>any-thing</u> about Harry,' she complained. 'How is he? How does he look? Is he well? Is he much altered?' The truth was that Ada's relationship with Harry had faltered by then and she was making plans to return to England alone.* She had been supplanted somewhat by a new friend Edith had met when she visited Warwick House in Salisbury Square, the offices of *Sylvia's Home Journal*, early in 1882, clutching a story she had written with Hubert.[38]

In the account of their first meeting that she gave to Doris Langley Moore, Alice Hoatson, manuscript reader for *Sylvia's Home Journal*, recalled that Edith was 'pale as a ghost and shivering with cold' when she arrived.[39] As the magazine was due to go to press that day, the office was bustling with activity. Edith was ushered in to see editor-in-chief Charlotte Elizabeth Graham, who was in her late twenties and had made her name as a prolific writer and editor of publications targeted at women. As 'Madge' she dispensed advice on etiquette, which was also the theme of several books she had written, among them *How To Be Pretty Though Plain* (1899). She must have been heavily pregnant at that time, since her daughter Pearl was born in April 1882.

Graham was sympathetic, but she insisted that she could not publish Edith's story unless Alice Hoatson approved it. Decades later Alice told Doris Langley Moore that she felt desperately sorry for this young woman, who had gone to such lengths to have her story accepted. She promised to read it as soon as she could and invited her to sit by the fire and drink a cup of cocoa. They chatted companionably for an hour or so. Alice's account is somewhat unreliable. She recalled that she read Edith's story that day and sent her a personal note to let her know she was recommend-ing it for publication. She was therefore amazed to find her back at the offices of *Sylvia's Home Journal* early the following morning, in a state of extreme agitation. Hubert, it transpired, had submitted the same story to the *Weekly Dispatch* and it was to be published the following Saturday. In response, Alice insisted that she agreed Edith could swap her story for one she had written alone. Yet no story by E. Nesbit appeared in *Sylvia's Home Journal* during this period. Perhaps she used a pseudonym.

---

* On 6 September 1893 Harry Nesbit married Jessie Emily Rosser Rogers in Queensland and they had a son whom they named Collis Anthony Artis Nesbit. Harry died on 14 February 1925, aged 68. He is buried in Brisbane, Australia.

CHAPTER 6

'A COMMITTED IF ECCENTRIC SOCIALIST'

Mid-way through 1884 Edith discovered she was pregnant once more; Fabian Bland was born on 8 January 1885. The name his parents chose, one they had used when collaborating on stories, honoured a new political movement that was occupying increasing amounts of their time. Life with three tiny children, few resources and a desperately uncertain future threw up challenges that Edith had to grapple with every day. She mustered every creative impulse to fund the necessities of family life. Yet she made time to indulge her intellect too. 'We are going out a good bit just now,' she told Ada, 'to all sorts of places and meeting all sorts and conditions of men.' It was not always fun. 'Sometimes I enjoy myself,' she confessed, 'and sometimes I don't – which is the way of the world I suppose.' They joined the Browning Society, the Shelley Society, and the Lewisham Literary Society, which, she complained, 'has three secretaries who between them can never get a notice out in time'.[1]

In 'The Faith I Hold', a paper Hubert read before the Fabian Society in December 1907, he described himself at this time as:

> A young man with his heart in the right place and in search of ideas, hungry for ideas, ready to listen to anybody who had ideas to offer; particularly political ideas, ideas that might lead to action, that might set one doing something.

He admitted that his 'old friends the Tories were bankrupt of ideas', and he felt 'embittered and too prejudiced to listen to anything a Liberal had to say'. When he learned that 'William Morris was calling himself a socialist', he decided 'If William Morris was a socialist, whatever else socialism might be it would not be ugly'. It was then that Hubert Bland 'turned to the socialists, who just then were beginning to make a clamour'.[2] He might not have been so effusive had he overheard Morris tell trade unionist and Labour politician John Lincoln Mahon: 'The debate at the Fabian last night was a very absurd affair only enlivened by a flare up between me & that offensive snob Bland.'[3]

Edith too admired Morris, a leading light in the vibrant Pre-Raphaelite movement. She was drawn to what Hubert described as the 'simple, beautiful ideals of mediaeval England' that Morris incorporated into his painting and poetry. These, she believed, provided an antidote to the 'insistent sordidness and blatant ugliness' that had crept into society. They included a pen portrait of Morris in *Something Wrong*, the serial they wrote for the *Weekly Dispatch*. In *The Story of the Amulet* (1906), Edith's fictional children travel forward in time to a verdant, utopian London where school is delightful, mothers and fathers share the burden of child-care, and everyone dresses in comfortable clothing. This episode owes a debt to Morris's *News from Nowhere* (1900) in which he envisaged a utopian society founded on common ownership and democratic control of the means of production.

Disillusioned with the creeping commercialism that had gripped society, Morris joined the radical Social Democratic Federation (SDF), which had been founded as the Democratic Federation by Henry Mayers Hyndman in 1881. Hyndman, a devotee of Karl Marx, realised that Morris could be relied upon to deliver a fiery sermon and welcomed him with enthusiasm. He left a wonderful description of him:

> His imposing forehead and clear grey eyes, with the powerful nose and slightly florid cheeks, impressed upon you the truth and importance of what he was saying, every hair on his head and in his rough shaggy beard appearing to enter into the subject as a living part of himself.[4]

Morris addressed SDF meetings throughout the UK, and insisted that beauty had a place in any workable model for a socialist future. However, by December 1884 he had decided that the SDF was not sufficiently revolution-ary, and he left to help establish the Socialist League. He was co-author of its manifesto. By then, Hubert had become captivated by what he described as Hyndman's 'air of cocksuredness, his breezy bonhomie, the exhilarating atmosphere of optimism which seemed to exhale from his very presence'. In 'The Faith I Hold' he acknowledged that Hyndman was 'the predominant factor in my own conversion to the Socialist Faith'.[5]

Hyndman had impressed Edith too. After hearing him lecture on socialism, she declared him 'very good indeed'.[6] Hubert outlined their motivation in embracing this new doctrine:

> We felt that we had had the misfortune to be born in a stupid, vulgar, grimy age, an age, too, that was getting stupider, grimier, more vulgar, every day, and so we turned away from it to a little world within a world, a world of poetry, of pictures, of music, of old romance, of strangely designed wall-papers, and of sad-coloured velveteen.[7]

Although he acknowledged that Hyndman's 'prediction of the social revolution for the year 1889', was absurd, Hubert admitted that he 'more than half hoped that it might be true'. 'Personally,' he declared, 'I gave the capitalist regime at least another ten years of life.'[8] They included Hyndman in *Something Wrong* as a thinly disguised 'Gottheim', the genial yet strident leader of the United Pioneers of Labour.

In *The Record of an Adventurous Life* (1911) Hyndman wrote:

> About this time too, men and women of great ability joined our body. It is indeed sad to look back and see the number of really capable people who joined us in this year, and then to note that, instead of remaining with us and constituting a great party, so many of them drifted away and formed cliques. In addition to [William] Morris there were with us at this time, [Edward] Carpenter, Bernard Shaw, Bland and Mrs Bland, [Henry 'Harry'] Quelch, [Andreas] Scheu, [Sydney] Olivier, Graham Wallas and others.[9]

Hyndman was appointed editor of *Justice*, a weekly socialist newspaper subtitled 'Organ of the Social Democracy', which appeared on 19 January 1884 and was sold on the streets of London by members of the SDF for one penny. 'We started well,' he recalled:

> Morris, Shaw, Hubert Bland and Mrs Bland, Joynes, Salt, Champion, Helen Taylor and others made up a good staff; the paper itself was well printed, and the whole effect of it was good. But the trouble was with the circulation.[10]

As was the case for Morris, the SDF failed to provide the radicalism Edith and Hubert sought and they turned elsewhere. There was much political turmoil at the time. Edward R. Pease, a disillusioned young stockbroker, the sixth of fifteen children born to a devout Quaker couple, noted that London was 'full of half-digested ideas'. He attributed this, in part at least, to the recent death of Charles Darwin while his unsettling theories were still being hotly debated.[11] He summarised the ethos of the assortment of self-interested aristocrats and industrialists who governed Britain at that time and were utterly disengaged from the overwhelming social problems that blighted the lives of citizens:

> Pauperism was still to be stamped out by ruthless deterrence: education had been only recently and reluctantly taken in hand: factory inspection alone was an accepted State function.[12]

Edith was similarly disillusioned. In 'Porro Unum Est Necessarium'* she wrote: 'The Devil's gospel of laissez-faire still inspires the calloused heart of man. Every man for himself, and Mammon for the foremost.' She was dismayed by the lack of empathy that pervaded society and declared:

> But so dulled and stupefied is our sense of beauty, our sense of brother-hood, that our brother's wounds do not hurt us. We have not imagination enough to know how it feels to be wounded. Just as we have not imagination enough to see the green fields that lie crushed where Manchester sprawls in the smoke – the fair hills and streams on which has grown the loathsome fungus of Stockport.[13]

During the summer of 1883 Pease attended a meeting of the SDF and encountered 'the oddest little gathering'. It consisted of 'twenty characteristically democratic men with dirty hands and small heads, some of them obviously with very limited wits, and most with some sort of foreign accent'. He joined them when he realised that their manifesto, 'Socialism Made Plain', sought nothing less than the overthrow of capitalism.

Pease was drawn to the teachings of Thomas Davidson, a mesmeric 'wandering scholar', the illegitimate son of a Scottish shepherd who had devoted his life to the betterment of society. In 1883 Davidson travelled

---

* 'But one thing is needed', Christ to Martha, Luke 10:42.

to England from his adopted American home in order to whip up support for a 'secular brotherhood' dedicated to the promotion of ethical perfection. He described this as 'a Vita Nuova, a Fellowship of the New Life'. Fired with enthusiasm, Pease discussed these radical ideas with Frank Podmore, a post office clerk and fellow member of the Society for Psychical Research, which had been established to examine the bona fides of the many mediums, clairvoyants, hypnotists and spiritualists operating in London. Pease was secretary of the haunted-house committee of this organisation and Podmore and he discussed their shared interest in socialist politics when they spent a night in a house in Notting Hill that was reputed to be haunted.

On 23 October 1883 Pease invited Podmore, social reformer Henry Havelock Ellis, and Percival Chubb, a young civil servant with an interest in establishing a utopian community, to a meeting in his rooms at 17 Osnaburgh Street, near Regent's Park. Havelock Ellis described Davidson as 'the most remarkable man, the most intensely alive man, I had ever met'.[14] Also present on that occasion were 'a couple of junior clerks in the civil service, a medical student, an architect, some aspiring journalists, and half a dozen ladies of advanced opinions'.[15] That evening the Fellowship of the New Life was established.

Ernest Belfort Bax, who had left the SDF to establish the Socialist League with William Morris, left a tongue-in-cheek account of the foundation of the Fellowship of the New Life:

> Early in the year 1883 a group of nice young persons of both sexes met together in a London drawing room and resolved to form a Society for mutual aid in soaring, whither none of them exactly could say – but soar they meant to, above the lusts of the flesh into certain unspecified regions of plain living and high thinking.[16]

Since Chubb considered Hubert to be 'morally promising', he invited him to a second meeting, which was convened a fortnight later. Chubb was rather taken aback when his guest enquired if he should attend wearing evening dress. Hubert too fell under Davidson's spell, and described him as 'a spiritual tonic'. In *The Faith I Hold* he explained: 'one came away from an evening's talk with him with a sharpened appetite for ideas. I think it was he who rid me of the last clinging mud of the pessimist bog.'[17]

Hubert was in the chair on 7 December 1883 when the Fellowship ratified a draft constitution designed to foster 'the cultivation of a perfect character in each and all'. A rather vague guiding principle promised 'the subordination of material things to spiritual things'. This was to be achieved by means of four equally vague actions:

1. The supplanting of the spirit of self-seeking by that unselfish regard for the general good.
2. Simplicity of living.
3. The highest and completest education of the young.
4. Introduction as far as possible of manual labour in conjunction with intellectual pursuits.

Before long ideological cracks began to appear and Hubert was branded the catalyst. As Belfort Bax put it:

The leader of the malcontents was Hubert Bland, who, having grave doubts as to the practical utility of plain living and high thinking, proposed that the Society should adopt new lines, and make a serious attempt to tackle social problems upon the socialist basis, then first becoming generally known in this country.[18]

An anonymous note pencilled into the margin of the Fellowship Minute Book described Hubert as 'the materialistic cuckoo who was to affect the dispersal of the Davidsonian brood of spiritual singing birds'. Differences came to a head at a meeting Hubert chaired on 4 January 1884, which Edith attended. 'Cuckoo hatched' noted the anonymous penciller.[19]

One faction, led by Chubb, who would soon join Davidson in America, believed that the spiritual must take primacy over the political. They advocated the establishment of a utopian community in the Lake District, although this plan was scaled back to an experimental commune operating out of a house in London. Hubert led the rival faction, supported by Pease and Podmore. This formed the nucleus of what became the Fabian Society, which was named, at Podmore's suggestion, after the Roman general Fabius Cunctator, whose victorious tactics against Hannibal were lauded as forthright, pragmatic and perfectly timed. This group insisted that economics and the equitable distribution of wealth must take primacy. As Belfort Bax put it, the Fabian Society 'relegated "plain living and high thinking" to the position of a purely private matter'.[20]

In *The Wouldbegoods* Dora Bastable declares: 'when people want to do good things they always make a society'. The aim of the Bastable children's society is 'nobleness and goodness, and great and unselfish deeds'. They are endearingly idealistic: 'We wish to spread our wings and rise above the kind of interesting things that you ought not to do, but to do kindnesses to all, however low and mean,' they announce. They write the rules of the 'NEW SOCIETY FOR BEING GOOD IN' in their minute book:

1. Every member is to be as good as possible.
2. There is to be no more jaw than necessary about being good. (Oswald and Dicky put that rule in.)
3. No day must pass without our doing some kind action to a suffering fellow-creature.
4. We are to meet every day, or as often as we like.
5. We are to do good to people we don't like as often as we can.
6. No one is to leave the Society without the consent of all the rest of us.
7. The Society is to be kept a profound secret from all the world except us.
8. The name of our Society is... the Society of the Wouldbegoods.

Although considerably more worldly than the Fellowship of the New Life, the Fabian Society's ambitions were just as lofty. Their stated aim was the reconstruction of society 'in such manner as to secure the general welfare and happiness'.[21]

Edith was an enthusiastic Fabian from the start: 'the talks after the Fabian meetings are very jolly,' she told Ada Breakell. 'I do think the Fabians are quite the nicest set of people I ever knew.'[22] They met on alternate Fridays to discuss 'the Condition of England and what might be done about it'.[23] Pease admitted, with admirable frankness:

At this stage our chief characteristic was a lack of self-confidence unusual amongst revolutionaries. We had with considerable courage set out to reconstruct society, and we frankly confessed that we did not know how to go about it.[24]

Yet when George Bernard Shaw joined them in 1885, he observed:

If you consider that we are all persons of strong individuality and very diverse temperaments, and take along with that the fact that no one of us is strong enough to impose his will on the rest, or weak enough to allow himself to be overridden, you will... allow me to claim our escape from the quarrels which have rent asunder both the Federation and the League as a proof that our methods do stand the test of experience in the matter of keeping our forces together.[25]

All was not as harmonious as it appeared. Pease, who regarded Hubert as 'always something of a critic... a Tory by instinct wherever he was not a socialist', thought that, 'whilst thoroughly united with the others for all purposes of the Society, he [Hubert] lived the rest of his life apart'.[26]

In *Fabianism and Culture* Ian Britain wrote of 'an air of comfort, refinement and charm about Fabian Society gatherings which a body like the Socialist League could never match'.[27] Pease believed that a perception of privilege attracted opprobrium:

We used to be plentifully sneered at as fops and arm-chair socialists for our attention to these details; but I think it was by no means the least of our merits that we always, as far as our means permitted, tried to make our printed documents as handsome as possible, and did our best to destroy the association between revolutionary literature and slovenly printing on paper that is nasty without being cheap. One effect of this was that we were supposed to be much richer than we really were, because we generally got better value and a finer show for our money than the other socialist societies.[28]

In March 1886 an entertaining though far from even-handed article was published in the *Morning Star*. Its author, Arnold White, journalist and unsuccessful Liberal candidate, characterised the Fabians as 'eloquent in theory but unpractical in method'.[29] He described a Fabian Society meeting he had attended at the invitation of Edward Pease. It was held, he insisted, in a 'well-appointed and fashionably-situated mansion', which was representative of the 'residential pretentiousness affected by other prominent members of the socialistic movement in London in its air of well-to-do ease and comfort'. Warming to his theme, he described how 'more than one Fabian arrived and went in his own carriage', and how guests were greeted by a 'blue-coated, gold-buttoned manservant'. On entering, he observed that:

[A] 'dim religious light' from the duplex burner of a pink shaded lamp bathed the session chamber of the Fabians in a ruddy and mysterious soft-ness. Standing on the threshold of the room one felt instinctively that he was entering into a society of dreamers – into the charmed realms of those whose theories are the theories of the etherealist.[30]

White portrayed Hubert in unflattering terms: 'Difference of opinion, said the hon. treasurer in his shrill, excitable way, is our raison d'être.'

The Fabian Society was riven by ideological differences, which Edith outlined succinctly in a letter to Ada:

There are two distinct elements in the F.S. The practical and the vision-ary – the first being much the strongest – but a perpetual warfare goes on between the parties wh. gives to the Fabian an excitement wh. it might otherwise lack. We belong – needs say – to the practical party, and so do most of our most intimate friends – Stapleton, Keddell, Watts, Estcourt.[31]

Matters came to a head on 17 September 1886, when Hubert sec-onded a motion proposed by prominent Fabian Annie Besant at a meeting convened in Anderton's Hotel on Fleet Street:

That it is advisable the socialists should organise themselves as a political party for the purposes of transferring into the hands of the whole working community full control over the soil and the means of production and distribution of wealth.[32]

The ensuing debate was so robust that it was noted in the minutes:

Subsequently to the meeting, the secretary received notice from the man-ager of Anderton's Hotel that the Society could not be accommodated there for any further meetings.[33]

Besant's skills as an orator were extraordinary. As one commenta-tor observed, 'she speaks as correctly as she writes and her voice is as melodious as a silver bell'.[34] White, in his article for the *Morning Star*, admired how she had 'soared into one of the most eloquent passages of the evening', and described how 'other lady members' were 'crouching at her feet'. He added that 'she might have been a queen holding court in the midst of her maids of honour'.

Short and delicate of feature, she was eleven years older than Edith and had also lost her father in early childhood. Unable to support her, her mother had placed her in the care of Ellen Marryat, an evangelical spinster who raised her to be grave and overly religious. At the age of twenty she married evangelical Anglican clergyman Frank Besant, who was attracted by her religious fervour. They had two children by the time Annie began to question her faith. She obtained a legal separation in 1873 and moved back in with her mother, bringing her daughter with her. She was not granted custody of her son.

Increasingly radicalised, Besant joined the National Secular Society, established by charismatic, militant atheist Charles Bradlaugh, who Edith 'loathed' since she considered him 'innately bestial'.[35] Besant resolved to give herself wholly 'to propagandist work, as a Freethinker and a Social Reformer'. She would, she declared, 'use my tongue as well as my pen in the struggle'.[36] She co-edited the *National Reformer* and worked with Bradlaugh on republishing Charles Knowlton's *The Fruits of Philosophy, or The Private Companion of Young Married People*. They were tried for obscenity as a result and, although they were acquitted, Annie lost custody of her daughter.

As a campaigner Besant radiated pure energy. It was said of her, 'she has held so many opinions in her time that everybody is bound to find himself in agreement with some of them'. That same commentator claimed that she 'combined the crusader's zeal with the journalist's alert outlook for new "stunts"'.[37] In 1883 she founded *Our Corner*, a six-penny monthly journal featuring a column titled 'Fabian Society and Socialist Notes'. She commissioned articles from prominent Fabians, including Edith and Hubert whose writing she admired. Commenting on 'Something Wrong', which they wrote for the *Weekly Dispatch* under their 'nom de guerre Fabian Bland', she noted that it opened 'vigorously', adding, 'I hear it will deal with the socialist agitation, and that some of the best-known leaders therein will be sketched as the story proceeds.' She singled Edith out: 'By the way E. Nesbit's short poems in the same paper are quite above ordinary newspaper verse, and sometimes deserve higher praise.'[38]

Besant claimed that she had joined the Fabian Society because she found it 'less hotly antagonistic to the Radicals than the other two socialist societies'. She listed the members she admired most:

Sidney Webb, G. Bernard Shaw, Hubert and Mrs Bland, Graham Wallas – these were some of those who gave time, thought, incessant work to the popularising of socialist thought, the spreading of sound economics, the effort to turn the workers' energy toward social rather than mere political thought.[39]

Before long Besant was appointed to the executive and worked closely with Hubert on several campaigns. When both stood as Progressive candidates in the School Board elections of November 1888, she was successful but he was not. When trade unionist Clementina Black had delivered a speech on Female labour at a Fabian Society meeting in June of that year she had outlined the appalling pay and conditions endured by women working at the Bryant and May match factory. Besant was horrified. Her article 'White Slavery in London' helped prompt a strike and Hubert, along with several fellow Fabians, joined the campaign. George Bernard Shaw noted in his diary: 'Met Mrs Besant and Bland at Cannon Street Station to bring down the strike money to the Bryant and May girls.'[40] Edith sympathised too. In *The House of Arden* Richard refuses to return to modern day London because 'they make people work fourteen hours a day for nine shillings a week, so that they never have enough to eat or wear, and no time to sleep or be happy in'.[41] Annie Besant was a wonderful asset to the Fabian Society, but her attention was diverted when she met the theosophist Madame Blavatsky in 1890. Pease crossed her name off the Fabian list with a red pen and wrote 'gone to Theosophy' beside it.

Edith's letters to Ada are delightfully revealing when it comes to her opinions on her fellow Fabians. She liked Pease 'very much' because he was 'always smiling' and had 'the cheerful serenity and self-containedness common to the sect [Quakers]'. Although she thought J. Glode Stapleton 'the nicest' of the Fabians, she found his excessive spiritualism tiresome and declared:

He has given up Christianity on insufficient grounds, I think and being unable to face the outer darkness and desolation of materialism has taken refuge in Spiritualism – and this is always cropping up in his talk in a most aggravating way.[42]

She added, somewhat mischievously, that he was 'a man of wide read-ing and an extremely subtle mind – and can always see the negative of every positive'.

Edith could not resist commenting on the appearance of some of the men. Although she conceded that Sidney Webb, a leading light in the movement, was 'no fool... in fact an absolute master of political economy', she remarked rather spitefully that 'a face like a fat billy goat and a wild profusion of red spots do not combine to give him an attractive appearance'. She decided that Harold Cox, future Liberal MP for Preston, had 'a crooked face', while Walter Coffin had a 'dark face' that she found 'inscrutable'. She thought Sydney Olivier, who was later appointed Governor of Jamaica and Secretary of State for India in the first government of Ramsay MacDonald, a 'very nice looking young man with a romantic name'.[*] At one Fabian gathering, held at her home, she noticed that the sleeve of his smoking jacket was hanging loose and she repaired it for him without fuss. Turning her attention to Thomas Bolas and W.K. Burton, two 'working men' who had writ-ten *The Practical Socialist*, she described them as 'a rather funny sort of Siamese twins'.

When it came to the women, Edith could be waspish. She regarded Charlotte Wilson as a rival and described her, rather disingenuously, as a 'Girton girl' who was 'the life and soul of the executive council'. In fact Wilson, a surgeon's daughter, had studied at Newnham College. 'Cambridge was the porch through which I entered the world,' she told Shaw.[43] Yet she appeared disillusioned and dissatisfied with the orthodox economic theory she had studied there. In a letter to Ada, Edith insisted she was 'trying very hard not to dislike' Wilson, but complained:

> She is sometimes horribly rude, and will never speak to a woman if she can get a man to talk to. I don't mean she is a flirt – she isn't, but I suppose women are not clever enough for her to talk to.[44]

She was out of step with others as Wilson was enormously popular among Fabian Society members. In 'Select Socialists', Margaret Mary Dilke, prominent suffrage campaigner and widow of radical Liberal Ashton Dilke MP, wrote:

---

[*] The actor Laurence Olivier was his nephew.

Charlotte Wilson is a splendid worker, the ready champion of every neglected cause, and one of the few people who really practise what they preach in every-day life. She and her husband live in a workman's cottage out at Hampstead, keeping no servant, and indulging in no luxuries; all the remainder of their income is devoted to the cause.[45]

Edith was scathing about Wilson's decision to leave her 'very charming house at Hampstead', which had been paid for out of 'what she tersely terms the "wages of iniquity"'. She thought Arthur Wilson, her stockbroker husband, 'very nice and a perfect gentleman'. She described their new home, Wyldes Farmhouse in Hampstead Heath, as 'a quite little cottage where she means to keep herself by keeping fowls!' Later she admitted it was 'a charming and quite idyllic little farm', though she sneered at the 'idealised farm kitchen, where of course no cooking is done'.[46] Wilson is caricatured as 'Mrs Coburn' in *Something Wrong*.

Ironically Edith had much in common with Charlotte Wilson. Margaret Dilke noted a 'curious family resemblance between the Fabian ladies' and explained 'they mostly affect aesthetic garments; they cut their hair short, and at their meetings they all take their hats off'. Of Charlotte Wilson, she wrote:

Mrs Wilson walked into the hall dressed in a long, straight ulster coat; she sat down in front of me, flung her large floppy hat on the seat, ran her fingers through her short black hair, and settled down to the debate with rapt attention. In spite of the manliness of her movement, there was something distinctly attractive in the pale delicate face and large brown eyes with their absorbed intense expression.[47]

In 1884 Wilson established the 'Karl Marx Club', a radical political study group that met fortnightly to study Marxist and anarchist theory and was later renamed the Hampstead Historic Club. Edith attended several of what Sidney Webb called 'Mrs. Wilson's economic tea parties'. Edward Pease, who described them as 'the most delightful of their social gatherings', insisted these gatherings 'had much to do with settling the Fabian attitude towards Marxian economics and historical theory'.[48]

It was clear that Charlotte Wilson's nihilist views were more radical than those of her fellow Fabians. Shaw believed that, after she joined, 'a sort of influenza of Anarchism soon spread through the society'. In 1885, aided by Edward Pease and Annie Besant, she organised the 'Society of Friends of Russia'. She also wrote an account of anarchism in *What Socialism Is*, which became Fabian Tract No. 4 and was published in June 1886. The following year she resigned from the executive and joined forces with Russian anarchist Pyotr Alexeyevich Kropotkin, who had informed a character in *The Prophet's Mantle*. Together they established the Freedom Press and financed, edited and published *Freedom*, an anarchist newspaper to which Edith contributed.

Like Charlotte Wilson, Edith too caused a stir at Fabian meetings. She cut her hair short, in a style she described as '*deliciously* comfortable', and she adopted simple aesthetic clothing made from natural fibres; these new costumes were 'deliciously pleasant to wear'.[49] She also took up smoking, a habit long considered the preserve of men, rolling her own cigarettes and inserting them into an elegant amber holder. On occasion she even smoked theatrical black cheroots.[50] In *Something Wrong* (1893), a collection of eight gothic stories that were likened in style to those of Edgar Allen Poe, her character Nora takes up smoking as a protest against gender prejudice. In 'The Pavilion', published in *The Strand Magazine* in November 1915, she scorned 'ladies who had not yet learnt that a cigarette is not exclusively a male accessory like a beard or a bass voice'. Here too she praised 'the freedom of modern dress and coiffure, and the increasing confidence in herself which the modern girl experiences'.[51] In *The Story of the Treasure Seekers* Alice Bastable, her fictional alter ego, insists that the hairdresser cut her hair short and 'always will play boys' parts'.

Edward Pease described Edith as 'the most attractive and vivacious woman of our circle'.[52] When Havelock Ellis sat behind her at a meeting he described:

> A woman, young and beautiful it seemed to me, and certainly full of radiant vitality; she turned around and looked into one's face with a frank and direct gaze of warm sympathy which in a stranger I found singularly attractive so that I asked afterwards who she was. I never spoke to her and never saw her again.[53]

With Hubert beside her in his velvet evening coats, yellow neckties and ever-present monocle, they must have made an arresting pair. A report on the Fabian delegation to the International Socialist and Trade Union Congress at the Queens Hall in 1896 noted 'Mr. Hubert Bland, looking like a stray bank director, imparted a soothing air of respectability to his vicinity.'[54]

Of course, Edith performed far more than a decorative role at Fabian meetings. She was elected to the pamphlet committee in March 1884; 'Now can you fancy me on a committee?' she asked Ada, 'I really surprise myself sometimes.'[55] That year she helped produce the first Fabian pamphlet, *Why Are the Many Poor?*, written by W.L. Phillips, a house painter who helped runaway slaves in America, then scrutinised line by line by members of the committee before it was signed off. Edith seemed unimpressed: 'Personally I don't think much of it,' she told Ada, 'but you can't expect working men's style to be <u>much</u> and his <u>facts</u> are all right.' She softened the blow by writing of Phillips, 'I like him so much.'[56]

In February 1886 Edith was elected onto the Fabian Society Conference Committee. The minutes of a meeting held on 6 May 1887 recorded: 'Mrs Bland recommended the holding of classes in political economy as a development of the society's work.' A fortnight later she was elected to a 'committee to make suggestions for amending the printed statement of the Basis, Aims, etc. of the society'.[57] She also contributed to the Fabian Society journal *To-Day*, which she helped Hubert edit for a time.

Yet she could be disruptive too. Several members recalled how she would demand glasses of water or faint during meetings, particularly if she had been crossed in an argument. It was Shaw as usual who provided the most entertaining account. After attending a meeting on 1 January 1886, at which Edward Carpenter read a paper on private property, he wrote:

Awfully dull meeting. Wilson yawning like anything – no wonder! Infernal draft from the window, Coffin fidgeting – putting coals on the fire, distributing ipecacuanha lozenges, & so on. Miss Coffin sitting on the landing, evidently bored… Something making a frightful noise like the winding of a rusty clock. Mrs Bland suspected of doing it with the handle of her fan. Wish she wouldn't. Two or three meetings like this could finish up any society.[58]

He refused to sit beside her unless she promised not to interrupt him by asking for a glass of water or 'staging a faint'.[59] Uncommonly tall and fiery-haired, Shaw was in his late twenties by then and was described by one friend as looking like a 'fairly respectable plasterer, his cuffs trimmed with scissors, his boots shabby and cracked, and his tall hat worn back to front because the brim was broken'.[60] Yet he had a compelling personality and Edith was one of dozens of women who fell madly in love with him.

Chapter 7

The Summer of Shaw

In a diary entry dated 21 February 1920, poet and writer Wilfrid Scawen Blunt wrote of George Bernard Shaw: 'He is an ugly fellow, too, his face pasty white, with a red nose and a rusty red beard, and little slatey-blue eyes.'[1] Above these eyes, Frank Harris noted, were 'straight eyebrows tending a little upwards at the outside and thus adding a touch of the familiar Mephistophelian sarcasm to the alert keen expression'.[2] Fellow Fabian Sydney Olivier wrote about Shaw's 'dead white complexion and orange patches of whisker about his cheek and his chin', and recalled Henry Hyde Champion likening him to 'an unskillfully poached egg'.[3] Poor Shaw had only grown his 'straggly beard' to conceal scars left by smallpox, which he, like Hubert, had contracted in 1881.

Hubert, who was a careful and flashy dresser, remarked on Shaw's shabbiness:

'When I first knew Bernard Shaw,' said Hubert Bland, the journalist, author and Fabian, 'his costume was unmistakably, arrantly Bohemian… Shaw wore a pair of tawny trousers, distinguished for their baggy appearance, a long cutaway coat which had once been black, but was then a dingy green, cuffs which he was now and then compelled, cruel though it was, to trim to the quick, and a tall silk hat, which had been battered down so often that it had a thousand creases in it from top to crown. Ah, that was a wonderful hat!' Mr. Bland laughed heartily over the recollection, 'Shaw had to turn it around when he put it on, because it was broken in the middle, and if he wore it in the usual way it would fall limply together when removed from his head.'[4]

Poverty dictated Shaw's careless appearance. When he received a life assurance payment on the death of his father, he bought a suit from the newly opened Dr Jaeger's Sanitary Woollen System shop on Fore Street in London. He insisted that this get-up, made from undyed wool stockinette, allowed his body to breathe, but Frank Harris remarked that he looked like 'a forked radish in a worsted bifurcated stocking'.[5] Shaw had plenty to say about Hubert's appearance too. He dubbed him 'the eyeglassed and indomitable Bland', and counted him among a group of Fabian men of 'exceptional character and attainments'.[6] His comments on Hubert were reported in an article for the *Evening Dispatch*:

He was always a very striking figure. He was an enormously powerful man physically; he had such immense shoulders that none of us would sit next to him in a room, because his shoulders occupied the space of three chairs. He had to leave room between the Hubert and the Bland and a chair space on either side of him to allow his shoulders to work.[7]

Most people understood that Shaw's attractions lay beneath the superficial. As Harris noted, he was 'above all a charming talker with enough brogue to make women appraise him with an eye to capture'.[8] Blunt declared:

Shaw's appearance, however, matters little when he begins to talk, if he can ever be said to begin, for he talks always in his fine Irish brogue. His talk is like his plays, a string of paradoxes, and he is ready to be switched on to any subject one pleases and to talk brilliantly on all.[9]

It was a fellow Fabian who provided the best encapsulation: 'Mr Shaw's position, as I understand it, is one of pure, unadulterated individualism.'[10] He could be infuriatingly enigmatic. Asked what he thought of 'G.B.S.,' he replied that G.B.S. was 'one of the most successful of my fictions' and 'about as real as a pantomime ostrich'.[11] In fact he was excruciatingly shy and described himself as 'nervous and self-conscious to a heartbreaking degree'. Since he spilled over with opinions on every topic, he cultivated a deceptive 'air of impudence'.[12]

George Bernard Shaw, nicknamed 'Sonny' in boyhood, was born on 26 July 1856 at 3 Upper Synge Street in the lower-middle-class Portobello district of Dublin city. He was the youngest child and only son of George Carr Shaw, an ineffectual, alcoholic civil servant turned corn merchant, and his wife, Lucinda Elizabeth 'Bessie' Shaw, an accomplished amateur singer. His two older sisters were Lucinda, always called Lucy, and Elinor Agnes, whom they called 'Yuppy'. He told the actress Ellen Terry that his was 'a devil of a childhood... rich only in dreams, frightful and loveless in realities'.[13]

Shaw's mother, whom he regarded as 'a Bohemian anarchist with ladylike habits', introduced music into his life, but remained distant otherwise.[14] In adulthood he dreamt she was also his wife, a fantasy that would have intrigued Freud. Interestingly, it was said that Freud remarked: 'Shaw does not understand sex. He has not the remotest conception of love. There is no real love affair in his plays.'[15] The young Shaw was strongly influenced by Bessie Shaw's singing teacher, George John Vandeleur Lee, a man he considered 'mesmeric' and 'daringly original'. It was Lee who prompted Shaw's lifelong habits of eating brown bread and sleeping with the windows open. Although Lee lived with the family for a time, Shaw insisted that his relationship with Bessie was purely professional. He told Frank Harris:

I was brought up in a *ménage à trois* (we kept joint household with a musician who was a bit of a genius as a teacher of singing and conductor, with my mother as his prima donna and lieutenant).[16]

When Lee moved to London in May 1873, Bessie followed with Yuppy and Lucy in tow. Lucy became a successful music hall singer, but poor Yuppy died of pulmonary tuberculosis in a sanatorium on the Isle of Wight in March 1876. Shaw remained in Dublin with his father, a man he regarded as 'humane and likable' although he was utterly undone by drink.[17] He accepted a junior clerkship with a firm of estate managers. For £18 a year he sat in 'a stuffy little den counting another man's money'. He did well there and was promoted, but he regarded the whole enterprise as a 'damnable waste of human life'. In March 1876 he too left for London.

In London Shaw tried unsuccessfully for the civil service. He drifted for three years before accepting a job as Wayleave Manager with the Edison Telephone Company where he was responsible for securing permission for the running of telephone lines through private property. He resigned in June 1880. That December he moved with his mother to an unfurnished apartment at 37 Fitzroy Street, close to the newly electrified reading room at the British Museum. By then he had written *Immaturity*, a semi-autobiographical novel that was rejected time and time again. By the time it was published by Constable in 1931 its author was fêted as a celebrated playwright and intellectual.

Shaw spent his evenings at lectures and society meetings where he mixed with the most radical thinkers in London. Soon he was contributing from the floor during every debate. He styled himself an 'independent radical' in search of a political home. He was on the verge of joining the SDF when he met Hubert in the offices of the *Christian Socialist* in May 1884. Sensing a potential convert, Hubert invited Shaw to attend the next meeting of the Fabian Society and sent him a copy of Fabian Tract Number One – *Why Are the Many Poor?*

It seemed clear to Shaw that the Fabians represented 'a body of educated middle-class intelligentsia, my own class in fact'.[18] He attended a meeting on 16 May 1884 and wrote in the minutes 'this meeting was made memorable by the first appearance of Bernard Shaw'.[19] In September he was accepted as a member and he was elected to the Executive the following May. That same month, in a stirring address, he outlined seventeen propositions that were adopted as the first Fabian Society manifesto. Edward Pease described them as 'unqualified Shaw'.[20]

According to Ada Chesterton, Cecil's wife, Bernard Shaw and Hubert Bland were the 'star turns' of the Fabian Society:

Some of the committee members suggested a diet of nuts and undiluted vitamins but their drabness faded at the sight of G.B.S.'s flaming red head and general flamboyance. Hubert Bland, refulgent in eyeglass, smartly cut clothes, stiff shirt and collar and exotic tie, looked like a dashing company promoter at a Convocation of Rural Deans, or a sinister international spy at a meeting of the Junior Navy league.[21]

Another Fabian, Jerome K. Jerome, attributed the theatrical atmosphere of their meetings to the presence of Shaw. In autumn 1886 Shaw delivered a lecture on 'Socialism and the Family'. Afterwards he pencilled in the minute book: 'This was one of Shaw's most outrageous performances'. He could be deadly serious too. Edith regarded him as 'the most interesting' of the Fabians. She painted a perfect little pen portrait for Ada Breakell:

G.B.S. has a fund of dry Irish humour that is simply irresistible. He is a very clever writer and speaker – is the grossest flatterer (of men, women and children impartially) I ever met, is horribly untrustworthy as he repeats everything he hears, and does not always stick to the truth, and is <u>very plain</u> like a long corpse with a dead white face – sandy sleek hair, and a loathsome small straggly beard, and yet is one of the most fascinating men I ever met.[22]

In *Daphne in Fitzroy Street* Edith cast Shaw as Daphne's love interest, Mr Henry, and has her declare: 'I wish he would fall in love with me. I'd soon put him in his place. It would be a real pleasure to do it. But he's not likely to. I believe he hates me, really.'[23] Edith would have benefited from the advice offered by fellow Fabian Beatrice Webb, who declared: 'You cannot fall in love with a sprite and Shaw is a sprite in such matters, not a real person.'[24] Peevish at times and inclined to hypochondria, Shaw seemed an unlikely object of romantic desire. He could be infuriatingly self-absorbed and exceptionally set in his ways. Once, when Lady Randolph Churchill invited him to lunch, he telegraphed 'Certainly not! What have I done to provoke such an attack on my well-known habits?' To her credit, she replied 'Know nothing of your habits. Hope they are not as bad as your manners.'[25] Lunch rarely figured in Shaw's daily routine, which he outlined in a letter to E.D. Girdlestone:

I do not smoke, though I am not intolerant of that deplorable habit in others [he later admitted that he hated to see women smoke]. I do not eat meat nor drink alcohol. Tea I also bar, and coffee. My three meals are Breakfast – cocoa and porridge; Dinner – the usual fare with a penn'orth of stewed Indian corn, haricot beans or whatnot in the place of the cow; and "Tea" – cocoa and brown bread, or eggs. [Sunday dinner was] brown bread and cheese, with a glass of milk and an apple.[26]

Yet, for all his eccentricity, Shaw had survived several romantic entanglements by the time Edith was extolling his virtues. He portrayed himself as hapless prey and told Frank Harris: 'I did not need to pursue women; I was pursued by them.'[27] This appeared to irk him. 'Whenever I have been left alone in a room with a susceptible female,' he told Hesketh Pearson, 'she has invariably thrown her arms round me and declared that she adored me.'[28] In Shaw's novel *Love Among the Artists* (1881) young women are drawn inexplicably to taciturn musical composer Owen Jack. 'He was not conventionally handsome,' admits one admirer, 'but there was something about him that I cannot very well describe. It was a sort of latent power.'[29]

Beatrice Webb wrote in her diary: 'Adored by many women, he [Shaw] is a born philanderer.'[30] Hubert, who was a serial and unapologetic womaniser, declared that Shaw seemed 'obsessed by Woman… terrified by Woman, dominated by Woman'.[31] While convalescing from scarlet fever at the home of a maternal uncle in 1882, he had become embroiled in a desultory romance with trainee nurse Alice Lockett. To keep up their connection after he left, she took music lessons from his mother. This relationship appears to have been comparatively chaste; Shaw's biographer Stanley Weintraub described it as more epistolary than physical.[32] It was over by 1885 but they corresponded for years and he lent her money when her husband was called up during the First World War.[33] She inspired the spirited Gertrude Lindsay in his novel *An Unsocial Socialist* (1887).

Shaw's relationship with Jenny Patterson, a friend and pupil of his mother's, was far more significant. She informed hot-tempered Blanche Sartorius in *Widowers' Houses* (1892) and stormy Julia Craven in *The Philanderer* (1893). In a diary entry dated 26 July 1885, his twenty-ninth birthday, he noted that he lost his virginity to Patterson, an event he described as 'a new experience'.[34] Insisting this was his 'first connection of the kind', he wrote: 'I was an absolute novice. I did not take the initiative in the matter.'[35] Yet he was being coy since he had recorded on 18 July that he had purchased 'some fl', an abbreviation of French letters.[36]

Shaw's attitude to sex was distinctly odd. When Cecil Chesterton asked him if he was 'puritan in practice', he was reported to have replied that 'the sexual act was to him monstrous and indecent and that he could not understand how any self-respecting couple could face each other in the daylight after spending the night together'.[37] Hesketh Pearson insisted that Shaw believed the most satisfactory way of procreating 'would be for a crowd of healthy men and women to meet in the dark, to couple, and then to separate without having seen one another's faces'.[38] Shaw himself wrote: 'I was not impotent; I was not sterile; I was not homosexual; and I was extremely susceptible, though not promiscuously.'[39]

His friendships with women, although often platonic, were more intimate than was generally the case at that time. In 1886 he withdrew from a burgeoning relationship with fellow Fabian Annie Besant because he was fearful that it 'threatened to become a vulgar intrigue'.[40] Yet it was he who had suggested they cohabit since she was not free to marry. She responded by presenting him with a list of terms that he deemed 'worse than all the vows of all the churches on earth'.[41] She had been helpful to him professionally, serialising his novels and employing him as art critic for *Our Corner*. She was impressed by his commitment to socialism: 'I found that he was very poor,' she wrote, 'because he was a writer with principles and preferred starving his body to starving his conscience; that he gave time and earnest work to the spreading of socialism.' Besant inspired the heroic Raina Petkoff in his play *Arms and the Man* (1894).

In a similar fashion, Shaw withdrew from a potential relationship with William Morris's daughter May, who was an exceptionally accomplished artist in her own right. They had become staunch friends after they met at a lecture he delivered. Although she sent him a beautiful valentine card in February 1886, nothing developed between them. In 1890 she married Henry Halliday Sparling, secretary of the Socialist League. Shaw stayed with the couple in 1892 when the drains needed mending at 29 Fitzroy Square. He described his time there as 'probably the happiest passage in our three lives'. For some reason he became convinced that he had experienced a 'mystic betrothal' with May.[42] Yet he stopped short of a full-blown love affair and told Hesketh Pearson:

> To be welcomed in his [Sparling's] house and then steal his wife was revolting to my sense of honour and socially inexcusable; for though I was as extreme a freethinker on sexual and religious questions as any sane human being could be… I knew that a scandal would damage both of us and damage The Cause as well.[43]

The marriage did not survive and Sparling, who had little interest in the nuances of a 'mystic betrothal', left for Paris. He confided in journalist Holbrook Jackson, who explained:

> After completely captivating his wife Shaw suddenly disappeared, leaving behind him a desolate female who might have been an iceberg so far as her future relations with her husband went.[44]

Shaw's relationships were not always so fraught or damaging. He became what he described as a 'Sunday husband' to Eleanor Marx while she was ensnared in a desperately one-sided free union with Edward Aveling, an untrustworthy philanderer. Edith too befriended Marx and invited this troubled young woman to her home. Ashamed that she was not free to marry Aveling, who had not divorced his first wife, she explained: 'I could not bear that one I feel such deep sympathy for as yourself should think ill of, or misunderstand us.'[45] She clearly had no idea how unconventional Edith's marriage was. As Shaw noted, Hubert, in direct contradiction to his own philandering, 'held the most severe and rigid sentiments in all sex questions', and took 'a violently condemnatory tone in denouncing everybody who made any attempt at sexual freedom'. Shaw did point out that his position was 'fundamentally a little weak'.[46]

Although he regarded Hubert as 'an affectionate, imaginative sort of person', Shaw acknowledged that he was 'not a restful husband'.[47] Little wonder Hubert informed Hector Hushabye, the roguish womaniser from *Heartbreak House* (1919). Hushabye is a 'very handsome man of fifty, with mousquetaire moustaches, wearing a rather dandified curly brimmed hat, and carrying an elaborate walking-stick'. This passage of dialogue could have been lifted from one of Hubert's essays, although there are elements of Shaw here too:

She has the diabolical family fascination. I began making love to her automatically. What am I to do? I can't fall in love; and I can't hurt a woman's feelings by telling her so when she falls in love with me. And as women are always falling in love with my moustache I get landed in all sorts of tedious and terrifying flirtations in which I'm not a bit in earnest.[48]

On 6 March 1885 Shaw called on Eleanor Marx and found Edith there with Philip Bourke Marston. Three days later Edith and Shaw met once again at Marx's house. Afterwards they walked together to Charing Cross station where he waited with her until she boarded her train.[49] Soon Shaw was a regular visitor to the Bland home. On occasion, Hubert and he would don boxing gloves to engage in a bout of sparring; Shaw noted one such occasion in his diary on May 18, 1885. According to Frank Harris:

Edith Nesbitt [sic], poetess and fairy-tale writer, rather mischievously set him sparring once or twice with her husband, Hubert Bland, a really formidable heavy-weight, who was fortunately merciful.[50]

Hubert was a skilled boxer, but Shaw was the taller of the two and had a longer reach. He had also competed in the Queensberry Amateur Boxing Championships of 1883.

When Shaw paid a visit to the Bland home in August 1885, Edith, Hubert and he got caught up in 'an energetic discussion on the subject of whipping children'.[51] He bumped into Edith at the British Museum a few days later and they continued this discussion. From March 1886 onwards, Edith's name begins to appear with greater frequency in Shaw's diary. They would bump into each other in the reading room of the British Museum and head for lunch or hot chocolate. On Saturday 26 June, Shaw noted:

Mrs Bland at museum. I did some German and read a little P E [Political Economy] for my lecture; but on the whole the day was devoted to Mrs Bland. We dined together, had tea together and I went out to Lee with her, and played and sang there until Bland came in from his volunteer work. A memorable evening![52]

Underneath he totted up the expenses he had incurred. He had been obliged to borrow money from Edith to pay for first-class train tickets, an extravagance that was almost certainly motivated by their desire for privacy. When he repaid her loan by postal order the following Monday, she sent a playful letter of thanks and told him she was looking forward to meeting him at Annie Besant's house the following day, since she wanted his opinion on something she had written; 'make fun of it as much as you like, to *me*', she teased.[53] In *Daphne in Fitzroy Street*, Mr Henry dismisses Daphne's drawings as 'rubbish' and advises her to burn them. 'What's the good of getting a little money if you can't look yourself in the face afterward?' he chastises.[54] They left Annie Besant's house together and had supper at the Wheatsheaf, one of Shaw's favourite vegetarian restaurants.

On 8 July Edith and Shaw attended a meeting of the Vigilance Committee of the Tower Hamlets Radical Club. Afterwards they took a cab to Ludgate Hill and a train to Blackheath, then walked almost as far as Edith's home in Lee. It took Shaw more than two hours to trudge back to his lodgings on Osnaburgh Street, which he reached sometime after half past three in the morning. He took Edith back there two weeks later. However, he was taken aback when she turned up early the following morning while he was having breakfast with his mother. They arranged to meet in Regent's Park at ten o'clock and walked for an hour. At least one account has it that Edith was walking arm in arm with Shaw in Regent's Park, chatting in a ladylike fashion, when she suddenly exclaimed, 'Shaw, I do believe it's going to rain like Hell.' This outburst was thought to have influenced a scene in *Pygmalion*. When Freddy asks Eliza if she is going to walk across the park, she replies, 'Walk? Not bloody likely!'[55]

Decades later, when he recalled this period of his life, Shaw described Edith as 'very attractive' and insisted he had been 'very fond of her and paid her all the attention I could'.[56] Yet by September 1886 he was reverting to his evasive habits. A peevish diary entry for 15 September records that Edith 'would not be denied coming back here to tea'. Three days later he 'began composing a song to Mrs Bland's words'.[57] His desire to bring matters to a close may be evident in his refusal to continue paying for first-class rail travel. They travelled second-class to Finsbury on the evening of 25 October before switching to third-class, 'for the sake of company' he noted in his diary, and disembarking at Enfield, where they endured a miserable walk in the rain. At least Shaw relented and bought Edith a hot whisky before accompanying her first-class to Pentonville, where she was staying at the time. On Halloween night they met at Portland Road Station at ten o'clock, in the rain, in order to walk 'along Camden Road, Caledonian Road and Barnsbury Square' where they planned to 'look at the house she lived in as a girl'. He left her in Claremont Square and walked home alone.[58]

As 1886 came to a close, Shaw, who liked to sum up each year at the back of his diary, noted:

E.B. (Mrs Bland known as Edith Nesbit by her poetry.) One of the women with whom the Fabian Society brought me into contact. On the 26th June 1886 I discovered that she had become passionately attached to me. As she was a married woman with children and her husband my friend and colleague, she had to live down her fancy. We remained very good friends.[59]

He was fully aware of the dangers involved. 'It is only natural that a man should establish friendly relationships with the wives of his friends,' he told Hesketh Pearson, 'but if he is wise he puts all idea of sex out of the question.'[60] Pearson believed that Shaw 'steered' Edith 'through her infatuation as best he could, finally keeping her just off the rocks'. In *Don Giovanni Explains*, an autobiographical short story Shaw wrote in the summer of 1887, he declared:

People who are much admired often get wheedled or persecuted into love affairs with persons whom they would have let alone if they themselves had been let alone.[61]

Little wonder fellow Fabian Grace Black, sister of trade unionist Clementina Black and another would-be-lover, begged him to 'care more for people for that is where you seem to fail'.[62] He remained resolute. 'Women are nothing to me,' he told actress Janet Achurch. 'This heart is a rock: they will make grindstones for diamonds out of it after I am dead.'[63] In *Daphne in Fitzroy Street*, Daphne criticises Shaw's *Man and Superman*, prompting Mr Henry to ask: 'You think it's always the men who do the running.' 'Isn't it?' she replies. 'Yes,' he agrees. 'In books.'[64]

It seems their relationship remained unconsummated. Shaw confirmed as much in a letter to American actress Molly Tompkins, dated 22 February 1925:

> I remember a well known poetess (now no more) saying to me when I refused to let her commit adultery with me, 'You had no right to write the preface if you were not going to write the book.'[65]

Edith channelled her disappointment into her poetry. In 'The Depths of the Sea', a poem inspired by the Edward Burne Jones painting of the same name, she likened herself to a mermaid who yearns for a mortal man before dragging him to his death.

> So I – seeing you above me – turn and tire,
> Sick with an empty ache of long desire
> To drag you down, to hold you, make you mine!

Denied her prize, she laments:

> So I – I long for what, far off, you shine,
> Not what you must be ere you could be mine,
> That which would crown despair if it were won.

Shaw set this poem to music and it was published in *To-day* in September 1886.

In a second poem titled 'Bewitched', Edith referred to Shaw's 'white malign face' but she changed this to 'dark malign face' in order to conceal his identity. This poem includes the lines:

I hate you until we are parted,
And ache till I meet you again!

Edith appeared to long for revenge:

Could I know that your world was just I –
And could laugh in your eyes and refuse you,
And love you and hate you and die!

Yet she denied that her poetry drew on her own experiences and insisted: 'Right or wrong I could never bring myself to lay my soul naked before the public. My published poems are nearly all *dramatic lyrics*.'[66]

Edith realised Shaw was withdrawing, yet she still valued his opinion as a critic and asked him to review *Lays and Legends*, her first collection of poems. He explained that, as he was finishing *An Unsocial Socialist*, he could do nothing before December and only then if she were 'hard pressed for it'. He asked if he might 'read the book for pure pleasure'. Before he received it, he sent her a playful yet insightful mock review:

The author has a fair ear, writes with remarkable facility and with some grace, and occasionally betrays an incisive but shrewish insight. On the other hand, she is excessively conventional; and her ideas are not a woman's ideas, but the ideas which men have foisted, in their own interest, on women. It is needless to add that she is never original; and it is probable that if she ever writes a sincere poem, she will suppress it.[67]

In an unsolicited and, ultimately, unpublished review he wrote for the *Pall Mall Gazette*, Shaw declared 'the book is eloquent and talks to you, sometimes like an angry and unreasonable wife, sometimes like a restless and too sensitive girl, often like a noblehearted and intelligent woman'.[68]

It is unclear if Hubert knew of the relationship between Edith and Shaw. Given his persistent infidelity, he had little justification for feeling aggrieved. Yet when he happened upon them in the British Museum one day, Shaw described him as looking 'rather sulky'. Certainly he maintained a friendship with Shaw, with whom he had much in common. In one fascinating letter, Shaw congratulated Hubert and himself on a shared determination to write rather than follow the 'sacred second-hand principles' that obliged men to pursue lucrative careers. He did acknowledge that this obliged his mother and Hubert's 'clever and interesting wife' to earn a living.[69]

Although Edith continued to meet Shaw at the British Museum, he grew distinctly cooler. In May 1887 he reacted angrily when she insisted on accompanying him home. 'My mother was out, and she went away after an unpleasant scene caused by my telling her that I wished her to go, as I was afraid that a visit to me alone would compromise her,' he wrote in his diary on 11 May 1887.[70] They did meet occasionally that summer, but generally in the company of others. By September Shaw had stopped writing at the British Museum since he found it 'impossible to work amid acquaintances who kept constantly coming to chat with me'. He did return on 30 September 'to hunt up some information for Mrs Bland'.[71]

In *Daphne in Fitzroy Street*, Daphne declares of her relationship with Mr Henry:

> 'It is all over. Thank God, I do not love him any more!' 'But, oh,' she told herself, 'if only he would love me again, and try once again to make me love him! That is what I really want. That's what would make the world really good again. If only I could hurt him as he hurt me. What's the use of my not loving him when I can't tell him so?'[72]

Shaw always played down the significance of their relationship, yet he conceded that Edith had talked of leaving Hubert for him. 'No two people were ever married who were better calculated to make the worst of each other,' he told Doris Langley Moore.[73] Edith was not the only one who put her life into her fiction. 'If a man is a deep writer,' Shaw proclaimed, 'all his works are confessions.'[74] Nowhere is this more evident than in his *An Unfinished Novel*, written during the summer of 1887. Although Shaw insisted he had abandoned it 'from want of time', it seems more likely that his thinly disguised critique of the Bland marriage was dangerously revelatory.[75]

In the preface he wrote six decades later, he declared 'the lover is the hero and the husband only the wife's mistake'.[76] The Maddicks are a discontented husband and wife, parents to three young children, who endure a fraught relationship exacerbated by genteel poverty. Dr Maddick, who is a surrogate for Hubert, is vain and conceited, a flashy dresser and a flirt. His enigmatic, athletic wife, who is young, freckled and more beautiful on examination than on first sight, wears an expression of 'suppressed resentment and quick intelligence'.[77] Although she is 'imperfectly educated', she makes up for this by being a voracious reader. Kincaid, the young doctor who enters their lives, is, like Shaw, rigorous in keeping 'a record of his movements'. He is attracted by the intensity and variety of Mrs Maddick's emotions – 'her restless suspicion, her shyness, her audacity, her impulsive frankness, her insatiable curiosity, base jealousy and vulgar envy'.[78]

When Mrs Maddick asks Kincaid if he believes in love at first sight, he demurs. 'I am not in love' he insists, 'and so… the subject bores me.' 'I wish you would discuss it with me,' she persists.[79] In a telling exchange, she explains:

'Mr Maddick and I open one another's letters because we have perfect confidence in one another.' He started at her voice: rage, tears, and defiance were struggling in it. He looked up, and saw that her large eyes were wet, and her cheeks red.[80]

When Kincaid wonders why they don't use alternative addresses, she responds: 'He does; but I do not,' and explains:

'There are reasons why a man should open his wife's letters – at least he would if he were half a man. Some men are not. I should despise my husband if he cared so little for himself and for me as to let me get what letters I pleased.'[81]

It would seem that Edith hoped for more commitment from Shaw, but he hid behind his 'scruples' and insisted that he was reluctant to cuckold his friends or lead women 'into trouble'.[82] Yet his entanglements were generally with married women. 'I was not attracted by virgins as such,' he explained in *Sixteen Self Sketches*:

I preferred fully matured women who knew what they were doing. All my pursuers did not want sexual intercourse. Some were happily married, and appreciated our understanding that sex was barred. They wanted Sunday husbands, and plenty of them. Some were prepared to buy friendship with pleasure, having learnt from a varied experience that men are made that way. Some were enchantresses, quite unbearable as housemates. No two cases were alike.[83]

George Bernard Shaw married Charlotte Frances Payne-Townshend, a wealthy Irishwoman, fellow Fabian and champion of women's rights, on 1 June 1898.* Naturally, he considered himself captured prey that had been pounced on when at his most vulnerable: 'I should never have married at all,' he told Wilfrid Scawen Blunt, 'if I had not been dead at the time.'[84] He had fallen off his bicycle and agreed to recuperate in her home. In truth, they got on terribly well. According to Beatrice Webb they were 'constant companions, pedalling round the country all day, sitting up late at night talking'.[85]

Shaw wrote of Charlotte:

She, being also Irish, does not succumb to my arts as the unsuspecting and literal Englishwoman does; but we get on together all the better, repairing bicycles, talking philosophy and religion... or, when we are in a mischievous or sentimental humour, philandering shamelessly and outrageously.

When it came to sex, they reached a mutually satisfactory understanding:

As man and wife we found a new relation in which sex had no part. It ended the old gallantries, flirtations, and philanderings for both of us. Even of those it was the ones that were never consummated that left the longest and kindliest memories.[86]

---

* She was related to Thomas Courtney Townshend, Shaw's old employer in Dublin.

CHAPTER 8

THE MOUSE MOVES IN

Edith's letter to Ada Breakell, in which she described George Bernard Shaw as 'one of the most fascinating men I ever met', also contained playful speculation about Alice Hoatson, who had, to an extent, replaced Ada in her affections: 'Miss Hoatson pretends to hate him [Shaw],' she declared, 'but my own impression is that she is over head and ears in love with him.'[1] In another letter she told Ada that 'Hamlin', the 'refined' man in 'The Copper Beeches', a story she had written with Hubert for the *Weekly Dispatch*, was based on Frank Podmore; 'I think he is in love with Alice Hoatson,' she ventured. 'I don't fancy she will have him.'[2]

Perhaps such speculation was motivated by her desire to see her new friend find happiness. Yet Shaw showed no interest in Alice and Podmore, who later left an unhappy marriage, was almost certainly gay.[3] It may have suited Edith to believe that Alice's attentions were occupied elsewhere, since this would leave her less susceptible to Hubert's charms. Ironically, if Alice's account of their first meeting in January 1882 is to be believed, Edith had been particularly anxious for her to meet Hubert at the time. Although Alice had accepted her invitation to visit the following Sunday, Hubert was absent and they did not meet until May 1882.

Whatever Alice thought about her new friend's husband during those early months, her attachment to Edith was undeniable. They complemented each other in temperament; while Edith was impulsive and brimful of fun, Alice was passive and accommodating. So deep was Edith's affection for Alice that she insisted they must be related. She pestered her friend Oswald Barron, who was a journalist and a scholar of heraldry, to search for some connection in their ancestry. Barron, like many young men, was susceptible to her considerable charm and agreed to do so, but he found no evidence of a blood-tie. Over time, Alice developed a more ambivalent attitude towards Edith. Decades later, she described her to Doris Langley

Moore as 'without exception, the dearest, naughtiest, most cruel, most kindly, affectionate creature God ever sent into this world'.[4]

Once Edith had written affectionate verse for Ada Breakell. Now she directed her pen towards Alice, who inspired one saccharine little ditty she included in her Gothic poem 'The Moat House':

My sweet, my sweet,
She is complete,
From dainty head to darling feet;
So warm and white,
So brown and bright,
So made for love and love's delight.
God could but spare
One flower so fair,
There is none like her anywhere;
Beneath wide skies
The whole earth lies,
But not two other such brown eyes.[5]

Oddly, this little confection is nested inside an otherwise cautionary tale that documents the fall of an innocent young novice who had entered into a free union with her callous lover. She bears her lover's child but he abandons her to make an advantageous marriage. There are obvious parallels with Hubert's abandonment of Maggie Doran.

At the time he met Alice, Hubert was still in the habit of spending several nights a week at his mother's home in Woolwich. He may have been meeting Maggie there. Alice would stay over on those nights, and Hubert's departure at about half-past ten, while the children slumbered overhead, became the signal for Edith and her to resume their work on the various poems, stories and illustrated cards for which Edith had secured commissions. When Alice tried her hand at illustrating cards, Edith would outline her drawings in order to improve them. Heads bent companionably over their task, they worked into the small hours, grinding out stories and verse in order to meet their deadlines.

At times they must have felt like Albert-Next-Door's uncle in *The Story of the Treasure Seekers*, 'pegging away at one of the rotten novels he has to write to make a living'.[6] In *The Wouldbegoods*, the fictional Alice declares: 'People aren't obliged to like everything they write about even, let alone read.'[7] Like Len in *The Red House*, they 'worked hard, hard, hard, and earned enough to keep body and soul and the two of us together in our microscopic house'.[8] Sometimes they would fortify themselves by sipping weak gin. 'One tablespoonful in water was our allowance,' Alice told Doris Langley Moore, 'but sometimes Edith would say, "O mouse just one more and we can get this batch done. Mack wants it all at once."'[9]

The 'Mack' Edith mentioned was illustrator and editor Robert Ellice Mack, who collaborated with her on a series of anthologies for children. She would write stories and verse to accompany the 'sheaves of illustrations' he sent.* They worked on 'Songs and Sketches', a lavishly illustrated series brought out by high-end publisher Griffith, Farran & Company, which contained original verse by E. Nesbit and 'Caris Brooke', a pseudonym she shared with her half-sister Saretta, alongside poems by Swinburne, Keats, Byron, Arnold and others, among them Philip Bourke Marston.[10]

Alice was invited into the Bland's inner circle. In 1884 she joined the Fabian Society and in June 1885 she was appointed acting secretary. She always insisted that Edith had pestered her to move in with them. Yet there was no room for her in their tiny terraced home in Lewisham, which doubled as the 'bandbox' starter house in *The Red House*, 'squeezed in between two more portly brethren' in the 'dusty avenue of little villas'.[11] In any case, Alice was reluctant to leave her widowed mother. Like Edith, she had lost her father when she was a child.

In March 1886 Edith and Hubert signed a six-month lease on 5 Cambridge Drive, a spacious semi-detached house with a garden located just off the Eltham Road in Lee Green. Edith may have been anxious to leave Elswick Road. In February she had been delivered of a stillborn child. More than four decades later, in the long, and rather self-serving account she gave Doris Langley Moore, Alice, who nursed her friend through this loss, recalled how 'E. went nearly mad about this'.[12] She expressed deep frustration at Edith's unwillingness to relinquish the tiny corpse and took credit for having persuaded her friend to allow her dress the 'poor mite'. She placed the baby in a 'long fish basket' and surrounded it with flowers. 'Then I took it to E.,' she wrote:

---

* Mack haggled with Beatrix Potter over the purchase of illustrations of Mr Jeremy Fisher, writing 'we certainly cannot make a booklet of it as people do not want frogs now'. When Potter held firm, Mack agreed to the price she asked.

She had promised to let me take it away in a quarter of an hour. <u>By that time I ought to have known the worth of her promises!</u> Well I didn't. For one hour and a half I struggled to get it from her while Hubert came to know what had happened to me. At last she let him take it; he looked so wretched, he could not hide his misery.[13]

Alice's instinct to align herself with Hubert in the face of Edith's perfectly reasonable grief might appear odd were it not for the fact that they had embarked on a love affair by then. As Edith grieved the loss of her fourth child, Hubert's fifth, Alice was carrying his sixth.

In a bid, perhaps, to distract her friend from the sorrow that had engulfed her, Alice presented Edith with a green-bound notebook with 'For Verses' embossed on its cover. She had little opportunity to fill it. Within weeks of losing her baby, she contracted measles from one of her children and fell dangerously ill. It was Annie Besant who took Paul, aged five, and Iris, aged four, into her home. Baby Fabian, who was just fifteen months old, stayed with his mother. Once she recovered, Edith was caught up in a whirl of intimate train journeys, liaisons in the vegetarian restaurants of London and long suburban walks. She appeared oblivious to Alice's burgeoning pregnancy. In any case, as an unattached woman from a respectable family, Alice would surely have concealed her condition.

Late in September 1886 the Bland family moved around the corner to 8 Dorville Road. Local boy Eric Bellingham Smith, who was five at the time, left a vivid description of this house.[*]

It was violently bedaubed with paint, round porch, front door, etc., and stood out between its brick coloured neighbours. Inside there was quite a nice bright little sitting room and round it as seats were square-covered boxes with colour cloth or cretonne on them. I lifted one of those covers and underneath was Tate Sugar.[14]

In *The Red House* Chloe admits: 'The divan is only orange-boxes filled with straw, and covered with those old green curtains – you know – the ones that were so faded.'[15]

Little Eric sat in on lessons Paul and Iris received from Alice and donned the miniature boxing gloves Hubert bought him so he could

---

[*] It was demolished in the 1970s.

spar with Paul. He remembered seeing Edith just once, when he caught a glimpse of her wearing a full-length black cloak over a sunshine-yellow dress. She was exceptionally busy by then, churning out novelty books for children and short stories or verse for magazines. She was also collaborating with Hubert on novels and short stories. Yet poetry remained her passion. A profile in *The Strand Magazine* confirmed: 'Her own emphatic view is that there is not better training for any kind of writing than the writing of verse.'[16]

Her first collection of poetry, *Lays and Legends*, was published in November 1886 on the recommendation of Longmans, Green and Company's reader Andrew Lang, who was also literary editor of *Longman's Magazine*. Lang was a Scottish poet, novelist and critic who is best remembered for his enormously popular series of fairy tales for children. He believed *Lays and Legends* 'might please a fairly large public', but suggested it should be 'judiciously weeded' since 'socialistic ideas' were repeated 'pretty often'.[17]

Edith's poems mirrored preoccupations with the instability of her marriage and her passion for socialism. 'A Last Appeal' features a rousing refrain:

Food that we make for you,
Money we earn:
Give us our share of them –
Give us our turn.

The collection sold well and won critical acclaim, although the reviewer at *Vanity Fair* expressed surprise at one revelation:

E. Nesbit has been a puzzle to us for some time. In reading the magazines we found from time to time verses of singular beauty, and the beauty was allied with a strength quite masculine. In this new volume we find evidence that the writer is a woman.[18]

Reviewers often assumed E. Nesbit was a man. She was described in *The Graphic* as 'a man of rare poetic gifts and of true honest purpose'. Like Lang, their critic took fright at her overtly left-leaning verse:

We would fain ask him to reconsider the use he makes at times of his talents. He must know the hollowness of the socialistic cry and that all this clamour for what some are pleased to call 'Freedom' – that is unbounded licence – is simply pernicious nonsense.[19]

Edith was fully aware of this confusion. She told her friend Berta Ruck:

All the reviewers took me for a man, and I was Mr Nesbit in the mouth of all men until I was foolish enough to dedicate a book to my husband, and thus give away the secret.[20]

The confusion persisted for years. Reviewing *Five Children and It* in 1905, at the height of her fame, one critic who described her as 'one of the most delightful present-day writers for children,' added: 'He has a wonderful understanding of child nature and his stories usually amuse grown-ups.'[21]

An astute self-publicist, Edith sent a proof copy of *Lays and Legends* to Oscar Wilde, a published poet and an acknowledged leader of the Aesthetic Movement. He replied with characteristic generosity:

Any advice I can give you is of course at your disposal. With regard to your next volume – but you do not need to be taught how to tune your many-chorded lyre, and you have already caught the ear of all lovers of poetry.[22]

He published several of her poems in *The Woman's World*, which he edited at the time, and described 'Mrs Nesbit [sic]' as 'a very pure and perfect artist'.[23] In 'Poet's Corner', which he wrote for the *Pall Mall Gazette* in November 1888, he noted the socialist influences in her poetry: 'Socialism, and the sympathy with those who are unfit seem, if we may judge from Miss Nesbit's remarkable volume, to be the new theme of song, the fresh subject-matter for poetry.' He detected in her work 'not merely the voice of sympathy but also the cry of revolution', and he quoted from her 'remarkably vigorous' 'Two Voices':

This is our vengeance day. Our masters made fat with our fasting,
Shall fall before us like corn when the sickle for harvest is strong.[24]

Just as Wilde included Edith on the list of women he considered to have 'done really good work in poetry', pioneering publisher John Lane declared that he counted himself fortunate 'to have published the works of five great women poets of the day – Mrs [Alice] Maynell, Mrs Marriott Watson, Miss E. Nesbit, Mrs Tynan Hinkson, and Mrs Dollie Radford'.[25]

One of Edith's staunchest supporters was Algernon Charles Swinburne, a man regarded as one of the most accomplished lyric poets of the time. In a letter to Philip Bourke Marston dated 15 November 1886, Swinburne asked what his connection was to the author of *Lays and Legends* since these poems reminded him 'in some of their finer characteristics rather of your own than of any other contemporary's'. Her poem 'Two Christmas Eves' struck him as 'the sort of poem that Charlotte Brontë might have written if she had had more mastery of the instrument of verse'.[26] Swinburne threw his considerable weight behind *Lays and Legends*. He arranged for Jerome K. Jerome to review it in *Home Chimes* under the heading 'The Discovery of a new poet'.[27]

Through his final years, when alcohol addiction had impaired his already fragile health, Edith maintained a close friendship with Philip Bourke Marston. In a final letter to critic Thomas Purnell, Philip asked that he take an interest in 'the poems of E. Nesbit, the sister of her who had departed'.[28] In December 1886, while confined to his death bed, he told William Sharp: 'I think few lives have been so deeply sad as mine, though I do not forget those who have blessed it.'[29] He died on 13 February 1887, and Swinburne eulogised him in the *Fortnightly Review*. Louise Chandler Moulton listed Edith, Iza Duffus Hardy, and South African novelist Olive Schreiner among 'the group of literary friends who cheered with their sympathy and appreciation the last sad years of Marston's darkened life'.[30]

Edith felt 'sick and sad' when she heard the news. She confided in Shaw:

Philip's death is the best thing that could have happened to him but it's saddening to come to the end of a fifteen years' friendship – and to feel that you can do nothing for your friend now, ever any more.[31]

By then her personal life was in turmoil. Weeks before the publication of *Lays and Legends*, Alice Hoatson moved to 8 Dorville Road. She became 'mouse' to Edith's 'pussycat' and played 'auntie' to the Bland children.

In the account she gave Doris Langley Moore, Alice claimed that she had been seriously ill and Edith had offered to nurse her in her home. In truth, she was in the final stages of pregnancy. When her daughter, Rosamund, was born in October 1886, she refused to disclose the identity of her father and Edith agreed to raise the child as her own. On 12

September 1900, when she was almost four years old, the little girl was christened Rosamund Edith Nesbit Bland.

Shaw recalled that Alice had attended a meeting of the Fabian Society on 19 November 1886, the date chosen as Rosamund's birthday. Afterwards she walked to Charing Cross station, accompanied by several others. In fact Rosamund had been born three weeks earlier. In *The Prophet's Mantle*, which was published long before Rosamund arrived, 'Alice Hatfield' who is a single woman, takes refuge with a sympathetic family when her unplanned pregnancy can no longer be ignored. The real Alice was fortunate to have been given the opportunity to keep her reputation intact while also having a hand in her daughter's upbringing.

Although accounts differ as to when Edith first learned that Hubert was Rosamund's father, she was not kept in the dark for long. May Bowley, a family friend, told Doris Langley Moore: 'I think privately, knowing them intimately as I did, that if Mr Bland was Rosamund's father, she must have happened with Mrs Bland's consent.' She cast Hubert in a heroic light and declared: 'I have often heard him express the opinion that every woman had a natural right to a child whether she were married or not.' She acknowledged that Edith and Hubert had an 'unusual' marriage, but she was adamant that they were 'good companions' who remained 'on excellent terms'. She remarked on the 'absence of jealousy' between Edith and Alice and noted that Alice 'made a useful "auntie" who helped out in any way required of her and mended for all the children'.[32]

This rather jolly description of domestic harmony clashes with alternative accounts. Rosamund believed that Edith had always had her suspicions and that she discovered the truth six months after her birth. In her version, Edith had pestered Alice for the truth until she broke down and confessed. This provoked 'a hell of a scene' after which Edith had insisted on Alice and her child being 'ejected then and there onto the street'. She only relented when Hubert threatened to join them. Lingering tensions erupted from then on.

Rosamund insisted that Edith 'could not have borne losing' Hubert since he had a 'tremendous hold' over her. She believed that he was 'absolutely irresistible to the women he paid court to, not only before the event of capture, but after'. He took 'infinite trouble to please' and he 'endowed every affair with the romance of his own imagination'. Since he was unwilling to relinquish either lover or wife, he used 'every art of which he was capable to keep them both'. Yet hostilities were never far from the surface, and friends recalled a household bubbling over with tension. 'Scenes as usual,' Shaw noted in his diary after one trying evening when only Edith and Alice were present.[33]

When it came to dealing with Edith, Rosamund believed that Hubert was 'absolutely the only person who had any influence on her moods and who could control her tantrums and bring her round to reason'. She recalled regular outbursts when:

> There would be a stormy scene at meals ending in a hysterical outburst, when she would rush from the table and retire into her study with a violent slam of the door, leaving a shattered family staring uncomfortably at their pudding plates. Daddy would say 'Oh, God!' and make for his study, also slamming the door. But always after a short while one would hear him go up to her room and beg to be let in. She would open the door and one could hear a murmur of affectionate phrase – 'Now Cat dearest, don't go on like that. Your old Cat loves you and you love your poor old Cat, don't you? There, kiss your old Cat and come and have your pudding.'[34]

Rosamund agreed with May Bowley that Edith must have known about the affair. She even suggested that it was Edith who had persuaded Alice to seduce Hubert 'in order to get him to give up another lady whom E.N. loathed'. This, Rosamund insisted, was a pattern she witnessed through-out her childhood and adolescence.

In 'The Prince, Two Mice and Some Kitchen-maids' from *Nine Unlikely Tales* (1901), Edith wrote about a prince who was in danger of falling in love with a witch who has taken the shape of a cat. When a timid little kitchen maid lures the cat away by changing into a mouse, the prince turns his attention to her; 'My love and my Lady,' he declares, holding the mouse to his cheek.[35] He plans to marry the mouse and turn her into a princess. When they discover she must remain a mouse, he agrees to become a mouse too. At that moment they are transformed into prince and princess, but they remain terrified of cats and banish them from their kingdom.

In 'The Unfaithful Lover', a story from *The Literary Sense* (1903), Ethel's lover kisses another woman who then sends him a letter making it clear she believes he is now committed to her. When he confesses to Ethel, she forgives him and declares: 'It was hateful of you, and I wish you hadn't, but I know you're sorry, and I'm sorry; but I forgive you, and we'll forget it, and you'll never do it again'. Yet she feels a 'sharp, sickening pinch of jealousy and mortification' and is unable to move on: 'How can I ever trust you?', she cries. 'Even if we were married I could never be sure you weren't kissing some horrid girl or other.' She ends their relationship but never marries and mourns her loss for the rest of her life.[36]

Rosamund's account is unreliable. She was inclined to side with her father and she insisted he had told her he loved her more than his other children. When she was a very young woman, he wrote *Letters to a Daughter*, an oddly intimate collection of essays addressed to her. She was hard on Edith, who she described as 'unreasonable and fiendish'. Yet she was no kinder to Alice, characterising her as 'a little unsophisticated mouse' who was in awe of her flamboyant friend, an observation supported by Alice's insistence that she was happy to play 'satellite' to Edith's 'comet'.[37]

Helen Macklin, who was a longstanding friend of Edith's and dedicatee of *Lays and Legends*, contradicted Rosamund's account. She suggested that Edith had fallen seriously ill shortly after Rosamund was born and that Alice had nursed her through this crisis. As her strength returned, Edith, who had her suspicions, had begged Alice to disclose the identity of Rosamund's father, which she did. Although Macklin agreed that Edith was prone to 'varying moods' and most likely resented the ménage she found herself in, she insisted that her kind-hearted friend would never have contemplated turning Alice and Rosamund out of what had become their home. Macklin considered Hubert to be 'very conceited'. If Edith ever wished to leave him a note or attract his attention to a letter, she claimed, she would 'stick it in the frame of the looking glass where he would be sure to notice it'. She did admit that Hubert, although serially unfaithful, was always contrite and filled with 'deep repentance and regret'.[38]

Although Edith may have been unhappy with their unconventional arrangement, it was Hubert who prevailed. Prolific popular novelist and raffish man-about-town Edgar Jepson,[*] who knew him well, described him as 'a truly patriarchal figure and head of a patriarchal household'.[39] In *Letters to a Daughter* Hubert declared, 'men do not love women. Or if they love them they love them as the hawk loves the pigeon, or you love chocolate almonds.'[40] He had oddly transient notions of marriage; 'Romance, in-loveness, cannot survive six weeks of the appalling

---

[*]   Edith encouraged him to publish his first book, *Sibyl Falcon*, in 1895.

intimacy of marriage,' he declared. 'The thing that should follow is friendship, friendship of a peculiar, a unique sort; friendship touched with tenderness, mixed with memories, coloured by emotion.'[41]

Edith may have acquiesced, but she found an outlet for her marital frustration in her poetry. 'Bridal Ballad', which she included in the second edition of *Lays and Legends* (1892), tells the tale of a wife who poisons her husband on their wedding night as a punishment for his infidelity. His dying words reveal his sympathy for her murderous act:

And if God judge thee as I do,
Then art thou justified.
I loved thee and I was not true,
And that was why I died.

More revealing are her companion poems 'The Husband of Today' and 'The Wife of All Ages', which she composed during the early years of their marriage. In 'The Husband of Today', written when she was pregnant with Iris, a straying husband assures his wife that the fleeting passions he enjoys can never undermine the 'love that lights life', since only his fancy is fired and not his soul.

THE HUSBAND OF TODAY

Eyes caught by beauty, fancy by eyes caught;
Sweet possibilities, question, and wonder –
What did her smile say? What has her brain thought?
Her standard, what? Am I o'er it or under?
Flutter in meeting – in absence dreaming;
Tremor in greeting – for meeting scheming;
Caught by the senses, and yet all through
True with the heart of me, sweetheart, to you.
Only the brute in me yields to the pressure
Of longings inherent – of vices acquired;
All this, my darling, is folly – not pleasure,
Only my fancy – not soul – has been fired.
Sense thrills exalted, thrills to love-madness;
Fancy grown sad becomes almost love-sadness;
And yet love has with it nothing to do,

Love is fast fettered, sweetheart, to you.
Lacking fresh fancies, time flags – grows wingless;
Life without folly would fail – fall flat;
But the love that lights life, and makes death's self stingless
You, and you only, have wakened that.
Sweet are all women, you are the best of them;
After each fancy has sprung, grown, and died,
Back I come ever, dear, to your side.
The strongest of passions – in joy – seeks the new,
But in grief I turn ever, sweetheart, to you.

In 'The Wife of All Ages' his disillusioned wife gives her answer. She dismisses his entreaties and insists that his 'meeting, scheming, longing, trembling, dreaming' is born of love and nothing less. Were their roles reversed, she suggests, he too would have little patience for such fine distinctions. Although she accepts that she will never be 'the only one' and realises she should withdraw, she believes she is bound to him for all time:

THE WIFE OF ALL AGES

I do not catch these subtle shades of feeling,
Your fine distinctions are too fine for me;
This meeting, scheming, longing, trembling, dreaming,
To me mean love, and only love, you see;
In me at least 'tis love, you will admit,
And you the only man who wakens it.
Suppose *I* yearned, and longed, and dreamed, and fluttered,
What would you say or think, or further, do?
Why should one rule be fit for me to follow,
While there exists a different law for you?
If all these fires and fancies came my way,
Would you believe love was so far away?
On all these other women – never doubt it –
'Tis love you lavish, love you promised me!
What do I care to be the first, or fiftieth?
It is the *only one* I care to be.
Dear, I would be your sun, as mine you are,
Not the most radiant wonder of a star.

And so, good-bye! Among such sheaves of roses
You will not miss the flower I take from you;
Amid the music of so many voices
You will forget the little songs I knew –
The foolish tender words I used to say,
The little common sweets of every day.
The world, no doubt, has fairest fruits and blossoms
To give to you; but what, ah! what for me?
Nay, after all I am your slave and bondmaid,
And all my world is in my slavery.
So, as before, I welcome any part
Which you may choose to give me of your heart.

Little wonder the critic at *The Graphic* declared: 'There is a note of quiet sadness in all her verses.'[42]

As the *Dictionary of National Biography* confirms, the publication of Edith's poetry 'brought recognition and friendship, but not affluence'.[43] She continued churning out less fulfilling work to pay the bills run up by a growing household. New opportunities arose in 1888, when Robert Ellice Mack was appointed London editor for innovative German printer-turned-publisher Ernest Nister, with responsibility for sourcing authors and illustrators for the books Nister printed in Nuremburg. A distribution agreement with American publisher E.P. Dutton meant Edith's books reached a huge new readership. Yet, as her reputation was not yet fully established, her stories and verses were often published anonymously.

Alice continued to help Edith with her various projects. It was she who wrote as 'Uncle Harry' for S.W. Partridge & Company, producing books with mawkish titles such as *Childhood's Happy Days* and *Holiday Hours in Animal Land*. Her *Playtime Pictures and Stories* was praised in the *Primitive Methodist Magazine* as 'just the thing to send boys and girls into raptures'.[44] With her rival so firmly inserted into the household, Edith turned her attention elsewhere.

Chapter 9

'How Was Her Fancy Caught?'

As Edgar Jepson observed, the Bland home was 'a house of youth'. Neither Edith nor Hubert 'seemed to have no use for the old' he explained, adding 'they seldom encouraged the middle-aged and never the dull'.[1] When Cecil Chesterton, who was more than two decades younger than Hubert, recalled their first meeting, he remarked:

> I was very young, but he, who was interested in almost everything, was especially interested in youth. 'The respect due to youth' was a favourite phrase of his used quite seriously. He was fond of maintaining that the young were almost certain to be more in the right than the old, that the freshness of their point of view was more important than experience. He preached this view continually, and with something of exaggeration, I think; but it was a generous exaggeration, and it helped to keep the man himself perpetually young.[2]

Naturally, Hubert proclaimed: 'I adore youth, especially youth in frilled petticoats.'[3]

Although far less predatory, Edith too surrounded herself with handsome young men and enjoyed intensely romantic friendships with several of them. Whether these developed into full-blown love affairs is a matter of speculation. Friends described her as prudish. Berta Ruck, her close confidante for many years, insisted she was 'naturally chaste'. Novelist and fellow Fabian H.G. Wells remarked on her 'anti-sexual feeling', but they had fallen out by then.[4] Whatever her inclination, it seems unlikely that Hubert would have tolerated such dalliances since he held women to a high moral standard.

Just as Edith's relationship with Shaw was reaching its unsatisfactory conclusion, she became involved with poet Richard le Gallienne, who was

almost eight years her junior. The earliest recorded reference he made to
her is in May 1888, in a letter he wrote from his native 'Darkest Liverpool'
to his friend and close collaborator John Lane. Noting their shared admiration for the late Philip Bourke Marston, Le Gallienne wondered if 'Miss
Nesbit of the Lays and Legends' was related to Mary Nesbit.[5]

Richard was the eldest of ten children born to brewery worker John
Gallienne – the 'Le' was a later addition, and his wife Jane, née Smith. He
inherited his love of poetry from his mother, who read verse to him throughout his childhood. In adolescence he was articled to a firm of accountants,
but the profession held little attraction for him and he was far more interested in literature. One colleague remembered him as 'a great reader'.[6] With
encouragement from the poet Oliver Wendell Holmes, he arranged for *My
Ladies' Sonnets*, his first literary work, to be printed privately in 1887. When
Lane got hold of a copy, he declared it the work of a genius and sent a postcard to 'Richard Le Gallienne Esq., Poet, Birkenhead', but the post office
returned it marked 'unknown'. In September 1887, when Le Gallienne
came to London in search of literary work, he sought Lane out.

Lane was said to have had 'an almost romantic affection for le
Gallienne'.[7] He described him as 'a young man of undoubted genius,
who was bound to set the Thames on fire, and whose face was the face
of a Greek god'.[8] In December 1888 Le Gallienne failed his final accoun-
tancy exams and headed for London where Lane took him on as a reader
and adviser. When Lane established the Bodley Head imprint with
Elkin Mathews the following year, the first book they published was Le
Gallienne's *Volumes in Folio*. It established his reputation as a poet of note.

In the characteristically florid account he gave Doris Langley Moore,
Le Gallienne insisted that his first memory of Edith was meeting her in
1889, in Hampstead where he had lodgings. This was possibly at the
home of Charlotte Wilson. He remembered that she was sitting in an
armchair with two of her children at her side. He was attracted by her
vaguely androgynous appearance, which suggested comradeship and
independence to him. 'I fell head-over-heels in love with her in fact,' he
recalled. 'I was hers from that moment, and have been ever since.' He left
a lovely, although undoubtedly highly embellished description:

> She was quite unlike any other women I had ever seen, with her tall lithe
> boyish-girl figure admirably set off by her plain 'socialist' gown, with her
> short hair, and her large, vivid eyes, curiously bird-like, and so full of

intelligence and a certain half-mocking, yet friendly humour. She had, too, a comradely frankness of manner, which made me at once feel that I had known her all my life; like a tomboyish sister slightly older than myself. She suggested adventure, playing truant, robbing orchards and such-like boyish pranks, or even running away to sea.[9]

Edith and Richard moved in similar circles. In *The Romantic '90s*, he recalled how Lane's 'charming "teas"' were graced by the 'boyish, bird-like charm of "E. Nesbit"'.[10] It seems certain she would have noticed this striking young man whom journalist Frederick Rogers described as 'handsome, fragile in appearance, affected, refined, and with flashes of fine manliness now and again'. Rogers insisted that 'it was impossible to know him and not to like him'.[11] Another friend, J. Lewis May, wrote of 'his chiseled Grecian features, his raven hair' and portrayed him as something of a Romantic:

Le Gallienne, I think, was the only one of the poets who sported a velvet jacket in public. He wore, like the scholar gipsy, a hat of antique shape and a 'soft, abstracted air'. His coat was of sage-green velvet, his shirt and collar a la Byron, of some soft grey material; his tie, the hue of willow leaves in the wind, was loosely flowing.[12]

It is clear from the opening paragraph of his essay, 'Woman as a Supernatural Being', that Richard had oddly idealised notions of women:

The boy's first hushed enchantment, blent with a sort of religious awe, as in his earliest love affair he awakens to the delicious mystery we call woman, a being half fairy and half flower, made out of moonlight and water lilies, of elfin music and thrilling fragrance, of divine whiteness and softness and rustle as of dewy rose gardens, a being of unearthly eyes and terribly sweet marvel of hair.

His flowery declarations contain echoes of Hubert's essentialism too:

Though she may work at his side, the comrade of his sublunary occupations, he never, deep down, thinks of her as quite real. Though his wife, she remains an apparition, a being of another element, an Undine. She is never quite credible, never quite loses that first nimbus of the supernatural.[13]

Yet for all his ethereal notions, Richard's good opinion of Edith owed much to her status as an acclaimed poet. He was keen to court her good opinion and presented her with a copy of *Volumes in Folio*, inscribed 'To E. Nesbit Esq.,' which was a jibe at her ambiguous name. In her note of thanks, she gave him advice born of bitter experience:

> If I were a mentor giving advice to young poets – I think I should say: 'do not publish too many *slight* books – but wait a year or two and then chose the *best* of your work – and give the world something worthy of your highest dreams.[14]

She offered to introduce him to Shaw, a literary hero of his, and she suggested they persuade him to feature an opera Le Gallienne was working on in his music column for the *Star*.

It is widely believed that Edith fell passionately in love with Richard Le Gallienne. Doris Langley Moore described how she threatened to leave with him after one particularly intense row with Hubert and ended up grappling on the stairs with Alice.[15] She inspired several of the love poems he included in his collection *English Poems* (1892). Yet while he was compiling it, on 22 October 1891, he married Mildred Lee. They had met in Liverpool years earlier while he was training as an accountant and she was working as a waitress in a nearby café. Sweet-natured and delicately pretty, she inspired many of the poems in *Volumes in Folio* and their marriage appeared happy. Frederick Rogers declared that 'their devotion to each other was a pleasant thing to see'.[16]

An intriguing account of this poetic love triangle was left by Arthur James Bennett, a chartered accountant turned journalist who knew Le Gallienne from youth. Bennett established a monthly one-penny paper, which he named *The Dawn* after Le Gallienne's fictional newspaper in *The Romance of Zion Chapel* (1898). He wrote much of the content himself, including *Harold Wolfgang*, a meandering serial novel that includes a 'sentimental episode' between Robert du Mervyn and 'Mrs. Rusk, wife of Alfred Rusk… a famous Fabian'. She is 'a clever poetess and a very charming woman'. In a key scene, du Mervyn's wife weeps over 'passionate verses' her husband has written for Mrs Rusk, who is described as 'the unintended interloper'. The poem Bennett had in mind was most likely Le Gallienne's 'Why Did She Marry Him?', included in his collection *English Poems*.[17]

Why did she marry him? Ah, say why!
How was her fancy caught?
What was the dream that he drew her by,
Or was she only bought?
Gave she her gold for a girlish whim,
A freak of a foolish mood?
Or was it some will, like a snake in him,
Lay a charm upon her blood? Love of his limbs, was it that, think you?
Body of bullock build,
Sap in the bones, and spring in the thew,
A lusty youth unspilled?
But is it so that a maid is won,
Such a maiden maid as she?
Her face like a lily all white in the sun,
For such mere male as he!
Ah, why do the fields with their white and gold
To Farmer Clod belong,
Who though he hath reaped and stacked and sold
Hath never heard their song?
Nay, seek not an answer, comfort ye,
The poet heard their call,
And so, dear Love, will I comfort me –
He hath thy lease, that's all.

Since Le Gallienne wrote a 'Books and Bookmen' column for the *Star* as 'Logroller', it was Shaw, who wrote music criticism for that newspaper as 'Corno di Bassetto', who was asked to review *English Poems*. His scathing review appeared under the heading 'Bassetto on Logroller' on 27 October 1892. Quoting from 'Neaera's Hair', which opens 'Let me take thy hair down, sweetheart', Shaw wondered: 'Can any man of experience believe that the author of this passage is a strict monogamist?' When he reached a series of poems called 'Love Platonic', he warmed to his theme. 'Platonic Indeed!' he humphed before coming straight to the point:

But the worst is to come. One of the ladies is undoubtedly married. The poem entitled 'Why Did She Marry Him?' will set a good many of Mr Le Gallienne's domesticated friends speculating rather dubiously as to which of them is the subject of it. At any rate, since she did marry him, Mr Le Gallienne's duty is plain.

Responding to 'The Lamp and the Star', a poem Edith is believed to have inspired, he exclaimed:

> I wonder what people would say of me if I wrote such things! It is all very well for Mr Le Gallienne to call his poems 'Platonic,' and to pitch into the 'Decadent Poets' in his virtuous intervals; but if he came round watching my windows in that fashion, I should have a serious talk with Madam di Bassetto on the head of it.

Having highlighted Le Gallienne's moral failings, he proceeded to eviscerate the remainder of his collection.[18] When challenged on the ferocity of his review, he showed no remorse but countered that it had whipped up controversy and improved sales, which was true. Le Gallienne appeared to take it well. He responded with a playful poem that was published in the *Star*, but he told his mother that Shaw was a 'vulgar-minded man'.

Less than three years into her marriage, in May 1894, Mildred Le Gallienne died from typhoid fever, leaving behind a daughter, Hesper, who was not yet six months old. This loss blighted her husband's life. Frederick Rogers, who was certain he never recovered, wrote 'for the young author the world was never the same again'.[*] This tragedy signalled a cooling in his relationship with Edith. He included a qualified and oddly dispassionate critique of her poetry in 'Women Poets of the Day', which he wrote for the *English Illustrated Magazine* in April 1894. He described her as 'Mrs Bland who, until recently has followed the woman's fashion of writing as a man under the now well-known disguise of "E. Nesbit"'. Declaring her 'one of the most instinctive of our living poets' he went on to carp:

> Her great lyrical gift tempts her, one fears, to write too fast. She has the 'fatal facility'. She does not keep her conceptions long enough in soak. She

---

[*] In 1897 Le Gallienne married Danish writer Julie Nørregaard, but their relationship failed and she left, taking Hesper and their daughter Eva with her. In 1903 he left England for America. In 1911 he married Irma Hinton, former wife of American sculptor Roland Hinton Perry. He retired to France and died in Menton on the French Riviera in 1947.

seldom gives us the loaded, authoritative line. But if she lacks 'art,' she has vitality; and some of her love-songs, and perhaps especially her exquisitely tender lullabies, are of that poetic stuff which, to quote Mr Stevenson, 'delighted the great heart of man'.[19]

Yet in his collection *Vanishing Roads and Other Essays* (1915), he recalled:

A beautiful poem [The Mermaid] by 'E. Nesbit' which has haunted me all my life, a poem I shall beg leave to quote here, because, though it is to be found in that poet's volume, it is not, I believe, as well known as it deserves to be by those who need its lesson.[20]

He included it in *The Le Gallienne Book of English Verse* (1922) and claimed he could quote it from memory. Ironically, Edith had written it with Shaw in mind.[*]

Whether she had any intention of leaving Hubert for Richard Le Gallienne, or anyone else for that matter, remains a matter for speculation. What is certain is that the constant presence of Alice in the household and Hubert's appetite for 'youth in frilled petticoats' gave her cause for unhappiness. In 'The Bibliophile's Reverie', a poem that was published towards the end of 1887, the year she discovered Hubert was Rosamund's father, she included the line: 'The Marriage Service… Well my dear, you know/Who forgot first.'[21] Yet Edgar Jepson recalled: 'Though it may have been ravaged by these secret storms, the Blands' was a very pleasant and stimulating house to go to, and they must have been the most hospitable creatures in the County of London'.[22] He continued:

I was under the impression that the patriarchal Bland household lived in admirable harmony, and only once was I aware of strain. I took it that this came from the fact that Bland and Mrs Bland had arranged to go their own ways – an arrangement not uncommon at the end of the last century among both the fashionable and the advanced – and that the arrangement was working as it usually does; with pleasant smoothness as long as only the lady goes her own way, with considerable roughness as soon as the man also goes his. Today that arrangement would be called Modern, but in those days it was called *fin-de-siècle*.[23]

---

[*] By coincidence, Edith and Richard were among the dozen poets selected for the *Modern Poets Calendar for 1897*; she was June while he was September.

Le Gallienne was not the only young man who entered Edith's orbit at this time. When Hubert was travelling home by train one evening in 1887, he spotted a young man in the same carriage reading a book by political theorist Herbert Spencer, a man he admired. He engaged this young man in conversation and they realised they were slightly acquainted. Several years earlier, Noel Griffith, a chartered accountant in his early twenties, had audited a set of accounts for the London Hydraulic Power Company while Hubert was secretary there.* They chatted amiably about the socialist movement and, keen to continue this conversation, Hubert invited Griffith to call on him the following Sunday.

Once again, Edith's life was brightened by the attention of an admiring young man. When Griffith turned up, Hubert took him upstairs to meet her since she was in bed recovering from a miscarriage. She captivated him with her bright eyes and unruly masses of shiny brown curls. The next time he called, he brought her flowers. Griffith was welcomed into their vibrant circle. In November 1889 he joined the Fabian Society. Maggie Doran joined six months later and Griffith was certain she was still involved in a sexual relationship with Hubert. Yet he believed Edith was reasonably content in their marriage and that it was Alice who found it difficult to cope.

The Blands enjoyed playing mentor to the enthusiastic young artists and writers who gathered in their home. At mealtimes, everyone present was invited to grab a plate and pile it high with mostly vegetarian fare. Iris remembered her mother as a good home manager who fed everyone well on cheap lentils, beans and suet pudding.[24] In May 1888 their bohemian household featured in a column published in the *Star* under the heading 'Gossip – Mostly About People':

E. Nesbit, the gifted poetess of *Longman's Magazine* and the *Weekly Dispatch*, is known among her friends, literary and otherwise, as Mrs Edith Bland, wife of Hubert Bland. She is a tall woman of somewhat over 30, with dark hair and eyes. Although her features are not precisely regular, their expression is full of charm when they are lit up by a smile or animated by any absorbing topic. Mrs Bland has a soft, melodious voice, and her manner may best be described by the French term *enlinerie* [sic]. She dresses in Liberty's fabrics. Mr Hubert Bland is a tall, broad, portly man, with a large

---

* According to the census of 1891, Griffith was later appointed actuary with the Bloomsbury Savings Bank at 30 Montague Street.

head. He is dark, wears a moustache and imperial, and is a little under 40. The Blands used to live at Blackheath, but now reside at Lee, in Kent. They have two children [sic], a boy and girl, the former of whom now bears the familiar name of Fabian Bland.[25]

Poor Paul never seemed to make much of an impression.

By then, Edith was acknowledged as one of Britain's leading women poets. Hubert too was earning a reputation as a writer. He had assumed sole editorship of the Fabian Society periodical *To-day* in 1886 and he also contributed book reviews and short articles to the *Daily Chronicle*. He wrote fiction too, a weekly story for the *Stock Exchange Journal* and various collaborations with Edith as Fabian Bland. They continued to struggle with plots. In 'Only a Joke', which they wrote for *Longman's Magazine* in 1889, they poked fun at this perennial problem, writing: '"Oh, plots are simple enough: I could think of a dozen in half an hour." The person who does not write fiction always says so.'[26]

In 1889 Hubert was chosen as one of seven contributors to *Fabian Essays in Socialism*, a landmark collection that was edited by Shaw. His essay, 'The Outlook', exposed societal inequalities in galvanising language:

> For years and decades the squirearchy retained an influence in the House of Commons out of all proportion to its potency as an economic force; and even at this moment the 'landed interest' bears a much larger part in lawmaking than that to which its real importance entitles it.[27]

He may have looked like a Tory, but his instincts were socialist and he was convinced that the means of production should be nationalised. In 1891 he was invited to write a weekly column as 'Hubert of the Chronicle' for the socialist-leaning *Manchester Sunday Chronicle*. He became enormously popular and his four thousand words across two columns provoked a huge correspondence. The *Daily Chronicle* declared of him: 'Philandering, philosophising, or shooting folly as it flies, Hubert you invariably comport yourself with manners.'[28] A commentator in the *Manchester Evening News* declared that the key to his success was 'the gift, which he shared with very few other writers, of being able to make the most recondite subject to be "understood of the people"'.[29] Another praised his ability to tackle 'a bewildering variety of topics, and always with vivacity and humour, allied with culture'.[30]

Ada Chesterton, who remarked that Hubert's 'public ranged from bish-ops to stable-boys', believed the secret to his success lay in his ability to interest 'the working men of the Industrial North' in the most erudite of topics. She recognised that he had 'a supreme gift of exposition, and could write on philosophic, scientific or economic theories in language so lucid, so simple and so touched with humour that the most unlettered, as the most cultured reader, could enjoy and understand'.[31] Cecil Chesterton, her husband, remarked that Hubert seized upon ideas 'with all the zest of a hungry tiger seizing its prey', and was not satisfied until he had 'torn every scrap of truth that there was out of it'.[32] As a contributor to *Fabian Essays in Socialism*, he was required to lecture. He adapted his columns as spoken word performances and discovered he had a talent for making complex and challenging ideas accessible to any audience. He became enormously pop-ular in working-men's clubs across the Midlands and the north of England. As Ada Chesterton remarked: 'Hubert did not frequent the bars of Fleet Street, but, like G.B.S., he was a familiar figure on the platform.'[33]

When Edith's second collection of poems, *Leaves of Life*, was published in 1888, Shaw reviewed it for *The Star* and declared it a 'very charming little book'.[34] The *Overland Monthly* described it as 'a confusion of love and radicalism, both very fervent, both very honest and loyal, and both put into poetry of considerable excellence'.[35] Influential literary critic William Archer regarded it as 'chiefly notable for the vigorous rhetoric of some of her revolutionary chants'. He noted, 'many of her poems breathe a deeply-felt sympathy with the toilers of the earth and a burning sense of the inequality of social conditions'.[36]

Edith's radicalism brought her into contact with controversial South African novelist Olive Schreiner, whom she met in in 1885. Schreiner had come to London to train as a doctor, but debilitating ill health put paid to that ambition. Her interest in socialism and her liberal views on gender equality, sexuality, birth control, marriage and the emancipation of women, led her to seek out radical thinkers, among them Eleanor Marx and Charlotte Wilson. She developed 'a tender regard' for Edith and described her as 'one who understands how one's heart goes out much further than one's hands can reach in this short life'.[37] 'You would love Mrs Bland <u>very</u> much,' she told socialist poet and philosopher Edward Carpenter. 'She's quite genuine.'[38]

Edith was grateful for Schreiner's friendship. 'You took me out of my world into another,' she told her.[39] In October 1888 poor health and low spirits prompted Schreiner to leave for northern Italy and Edith lost a useful ally. Schreiner told her friend Henry Havelock Ellis:

> Mrs Bland ('E. Nesbit') was so kind to me before I left London. I don't think I should have got away without her. She came the last morning to finish packing my things and see me off. Do you know, she's one of the noblest women? I can't tell you about her life, because I mustn't, but it's grand. The last night she lay by me on the bed and drew me very close to her and pressed her face against mine, and do you know, I have felt it ever since.[40]

She was aware of turbulence in her friend's marriage and her sympathies lay firmly with Edith. A passionate supporter of women's rights, she had taken issue with Hubert's à la carte morality; she wrote him a long letter on the subject. Hubert, who disliked being challenged, mocked her in one of his essays:

> The Emancipated Woman too had her points – sharp as needles they were. Let loose by Miss Olive Schreiner from an African Farm, she had a lurid career in Europe. She irritated, bewildered, fascinated, and finally bored us.[41]

Schreiner returned to South Africa in 1889. Shortly afterwards she sent Edith a postcard via Charlotte Wilson, since she had lost her address. 'It's just to tell you that I never forget you,' she assured her. 'Please send me a line.'

CHAPTER 10

'A CHARMING LITTLE SOCIALIST AND LITERARY HOUSEHOLD'

When the three-year lease on 8 Dorville Road was up in September 1889, the Bland family moved to 2 Birch Grove, a substantial house situated just a few minutes' walk from Lee station. That same month, an article in the *Glasgow Evening Citizen* described '"E. Nesbit" the Poetess'. She had just turned thirty-one:

> Mrs Bland herself is a very pretty woman, with soft brown eyes, and a delicacy of look, dress and carriage which belongs to the old mythic days, which, in her costume at least, Mrs Bland revives. She delights in soft greens and browns.[1]

That same month, readers of 'General Gossip of Authors and Writers,' in American magazine *Current Opinion*, learned:

> E. Nesbit, whose beautiful and passionate poems have of late attracted so much attention, is tall, slender, and her dark flowing hair makes her look like the pictures of the Italian angels. She dresses in a most aesthetic fashion and is a picturesque figure in London literary society. Her real name is Mrs Edith Bland, wife of Hubert Bland, and she is a vigorous socialist and member of the Fabian Society. She is about thirty years of age, and lives at Lee, one of the suburbs of London.[2]

Margaret Dilke, wife of radical Liberal politician Ashton Wentworth Dilke, described the impact the arrival of the Bland family had on this most conventional of neighbourhoods:

> Passing from art to literature, there is a charming little socialist and literary household down at Lee in Kent, tenanted by Mr and Mrs Hubert

Bland, both of them original members of the [Fabian] Society. This prim suburb, mostly given over to British Philistinism in its most bourgeois manifestation, was terribly scandalised at first by the pleasant *sans-gêne* of its socialist neighbours. Mrs Bland was observed personally instructing her domestic in the mysteries of colouring the doorstep with red chalk, and the merry little Bland children in aesthetic pinafores were seen daily running about the garden with bare feet! The gossips of Lee were deeply agitated, but the Bland household went peacefully on its way. Both husband and wife write articles, reviews and stories, the latter often in partnership; but Mrs Bland, under her maiden name of E. Nesbit, has published moreover a great deal of very charming verse.[3]

Edith's neighbours were a conventional bunch. Anne Robenson, an elderly widow in her seventies, lived with her daughter Mary, who was in her forties and also widowed, and Mary's young daughter Maud at number three. William Venn, a notary in his twenties, lived with his wife Mabel at number six. John Stap, a ship owner's clerk in his sixties, lived with his wife Rebecca and their four grown-up children at number four. Charles Kingsford, a financial agent in his forties, lived with his wife Anne and their six daughters at number seven. The only other unusual household was number five, where two young Canadian men lived, one a medical student and the other a physician.

Ada Jane Moore, who was twenty-five, lived at 1 Birch Grove, directly across from the Blands. She shared her home with her husband William, a cotton broker who was almost twice her age, her stepson Arthur, aged fourteen, and her own children, James, aged five, and new-born Dorothy. Of her new neighbours, Ada declared:

No rumour nor gossip was considered too bad to be believed about them. They rode bicycles in bloomers, they were absolutely unconventional and careless, they outraged 'Mrs Grundy' in every way and were condemned and generally disliked by the very respectable neighbourhood of Lee.

She described 'little Fabian', aged four, as 'the most amazing child – odd and tiresome and a terror'. He would accost 'City Gents' on their way to the train station and beg them for halfpennies. 'Imagine the disgust of the neighbourhood,' Ada exclaimed.[4] Rosamund, who was known affectionately as Rom, was 'easily the most attractive' of the children. Ada considered her 'a real darling with her soft dark eyes and pretty ways'. She could be precocious too, Ada reported: 'Sitting on the knee of a man-visitor she said gravely, lifting her skirt, "Do you know I have real lace on my drawers".'

Edgar Jepson confirmed that the Bland children were 'to an extent, the children of the House of Bastable'. He described how Fabian and Rosamund, whom he called 'an amazingly pretty child', had scandal-ised the neighbourhood when they 'made posies of flowers from their garden, took off their shoes and stockings, and in their shabbiest clothes sold the posies to native residents on their way to catch the business trains to London'.[5] Edith allowed her children to go barefoot and dressed them in the loose-fitting, aesthetic clothing she favoured. Her fictional children often struggle with garments they describe as 'tight under the arms' or 'prickly round the neck'. The incident with the posies, and others like it, provided her with inspiration for a series of stories that would ensure her literary legacy. The first of her Bastable books, *The Story of the Treasure Seekers*, appeared in 1899, when she was in her early forties, but early versions were published anonymously in *Nister's Holiday Annual* between 1894 and 1896. In one episode, Oswald Bastable puts on his oldest clothes and heads to Greenwich Station, where he sells yellow chrysanthemums 'in penny bunches'. A similar episode appears in *Harding's Luck* (1909) when Dickie Harding sells posies to earn money.

Ada Moore believed the Bland children 'ran wild', but she insisted that Edith was 'a tender mother and devoted to the children who were considered neglected'. 'I doubt if they were,' she added. Edith could certainly be exceptionally affectionate. Like Mother in *The Railway Children*, she 'made up funny pieces of poetry for their birthdays and for other great occasions, such as the christening of the new kittens, or the refurnishing of the doll's house, or the time when they were getting over the mumps'.[6] She wrote a poem for Paul to celebrate his recov-ery from typhoid fever. When Iris recovered from measles, she recited a poem that described how their pets cheered her return downstairs. Another of the comic verses Edith wrote for Iris prompted the nick-name 'That'. When Iris was twelve or thirteen, she decided that she no longer wished to be called by the various pet names she had been given. Edith wrote:

They often call me bunny
Or sometimes kitten cat
My proper name is Iris
So please to call me that.[7]

Ada Moore told Doris Langley Moore that Edith was 'always the
spirit of originality, freedom and difference... a smoker of cigars who
just went her own way and was the centre of a group of people who
did likewise'. She cared little for the good opinion of her strait-laced
neighbours. 'The Blands' aloofness was the right attitude for people
interested in ideas to assume when living in suburbs,' Edgar Jepson
declared. 'Though civil to their neighbours, they were never intimate
with them; they believed that the native residents would bore them by
a lack of understanding.' He regarded Edith as 'an uncommonly clever
and often amusing woman', and admired the 'vivacity and intelligence'
of Hubert's conversation.[8]

Members of the Blands' unorthodox circle were perfectly willing to
travel to 2 Birch Grove for regular 'at homes' at which they would discuss
politics into the small hours, or play hide-and-seek, charades and other
lively games. Sometimes Edith would play the piano so they could dance.
Many of these visitors were enthusiastic members of 'It', a monthly
debating society that Edith had a hand in establishing; 'we had nearly
every literary man and women we knew meeting here once a month',
Alice bragged. Occasionally a discussion paper would be circulated in
advance, but more often than not, as Alice confirmed, they would 'just
talk on any subject under the sun'.[9] On 18 January 1896 Shaw noted in
his diary that he had addressed '"It" on "Great Men: Are They Real?"'.
'It' was a great success for a time, but it was disbanded after Harold Cox,
future Liberal MP for Preston, caused a scandal by reading a paper on
'Nudity in Art & Life'. Noel Griffith claimed that Edith was outraged,
but Shaw insisted Cox meant no harm. This incident was reported in *The
Sphere*: 'Mr Cox once astonished an audience by advocating, with apparent seriousness, a dispensation from clothes.'[10]

Jepson believed that Edith 'rather queened it over the young writers
and painters she gathered round her and directed their lives with a ruth-
less precision'.[11] Prominent among her protégés was Oswald Barron, who
was almost a decade younger than her and wrote a daily column for the
London Evening News as 'The Londoner'. According to Jepson:

The Londoner, one of the earliest and the most intelligent of Mrs Bland's young men, was an uncommonly witty and amusing talker and helpful to her in the matter of the stories of the House of Bastable – indeed the hero of them was drawn from him.[12]

Edith paid Barron the highest tribute by naming Oswald Bastable after him and dedicating the first of her novels for children:

TO OSWALD BARRON
WITHOUT WHOM THIS BOOK COULD
NEVER HAVE BEEN WRITTEN

THE TREASURE SEEKERS IS
DEDICATED IN MEMORY OF
CHILDHOODS
IDENTICAL BUT FOR THE ACCIDENTS
OF TIME AND SPACE

Barron was living in rooms at Temple when they met but he moved to Grove Park in 1896, where he shared a house with Jepson and Italian journalist Olindo Malagodi.* Jepson admitted that they moved there 'in order to be near the Blands'.[13] All three were in their mid-twenties and were members of the Fabian Society.

For a time Barron behaved like a member of the Bland household. When he was collaborating on ballads and short stories with Edith, she would confine him to her study until they came up with something worthwhile. She was keen to promote his career and asked John Lane if she might visit some Saturday afternoon to introduce 'my friend Mr Oswald Barron, who collaborates with me in prose and verse'. Barron, she explained, was 'learned in archaeology and things like that'. 'I think you will like him,' she assured Lane, 'and I am sure he will like you.'[14] They dedicated their short story collection, *The Butler in Bohemia* (1894), to Rudyard Kipling and their one-act farce, *A Family Novelette*, was performed in New Cross Public Hall in February 1894.

Barron had a vivid imagination and plots came easily to him. Hubert paid him half a crown each for ideas for his weekly *Stock Exchange Journal* stories. Edith protested that he was 'robbing the poor boy'.[15]

---

* Malagodi trained as a journalist in England and became a prominent Italian liberal journalist and writer, and eventually editor of *La Tribuna* in Rome.

It is thought that Barron suggested the plot for *The Railway Children*. He certainly inspired Edith's mystery *The Secret of Kyriels* (1889) when he suggested, during a day trip to Scotney Castle in Kent, that 'Old Cyrals', a knot of houses to the southwest of Brenchley, might be a corruption of the Breton name Kyriels. The novel features Christopher Surtees, a scholarly man with a deep love for history and genealogy. Fellow Fabian Adeline Sergeant, a prolific poet and novelist, gave her opinion on an early manuscript titled *Kyriel's Bridge* and assured Edith that it was 'certain to achieve success'. She predicted: 'Your name is so well known as a writer of lovely verse and striking short stories, that you will indeed be made welcome in the ranks of novelists!'[16] The *Literary World* described *The Secret of Kyriels* as 'an old-fashioned sensational novel of the *Jane Eyre* school' and informed readers that Edith showed 'unusual literary ability'.[17] A review in *Book News* lauded 'a superabundance of ingenuity not only in the construction of the plot but in the conception of the characters'.[18] Yet sales were disappointing and it did not endure.

Many people believe Edith and Oswald were lovers, but their relationship cooled after 1899 when he married the aristocratic Hilda Leonora Florence Sanders. They may have named their daughter Yolande, who was born in 1906, after a character in *The Red House* (1901). Afterwards, Barron devoted increasing time and energy to the study of heraldry. In 1901 he was elected a Fellow of the Society of Antiquaries. He founded and edited a scholarly periodical, *The Ancestor*, the following year. Although Barron always refused to discuss his relationship with Edith, it seems he inspired a sequence of poems she wrote early in 1898 under the title 'Via Amoris'. She told her agent William Morris Colles that she was particularly fond of three: 'After Death', which is a lament for a lost love, and 'Via Amoris' and 'The Poor Man's Guest', both narrated by someone who did not seek love but was overwhelmed by it.

Although Edith's first two poetry collections were critically and commercially successful, she struggled to interest any publisher in a third. She was enormously grateful when D'Arcy Wentworth Reeve, a wealthy member of the Fabian Society, paid for *Lays and Legends* to be reissued and funded a second series under the same title. She presented him with a first edition of *The Poetical Works of Dante Gabriel Rossetti*, which she inscribed 'D'Arcy Reeve from E. Nesbit. Je suis ici en bien d'amie'. In 1892 a notice in *Current Literature* confirmed 'E. Nesbit (Edith Bland), after a long illness is working on her new book, Lays and Legends, Second Series, the first series having run through three editions.'[19]

Reeve called to see Edith in January 1892, and was shocked to find her struggling with bronchitis, a condition that plagued her throughout her life. In *The Red House* H.O. says of Noël, Edith's fictional alter ego: 'Wait till you see his poetry! It comes of his having bronchitis so often, I think.'[20] When Reeve gave her £300 for a holiday, she travelled with Alice to Antibes in the south of France.*

Their trip started disastrously when they boarded the wrong train in Paris. On reaching Dijon at ten o'clock that night, they were ordered to disembark without warning. They had retired for the night and they struggled to gather their belongings. Edith spoke excellent French but she had lost her voice. When she begged for light to pack by, the conductor simply repeated: 'Depechez vous tout de suite, le train parti.' They stood on a platform in Dijon Station, half-dressed and clutching armfuls of whatever they could 'gropingly find' in the minutes available. Most of their money and several items of value remained on the departing train.[21]

Never one to waste a plot, Edith included this incident in her novel *Dormant* (1911). Anthony Drelincourt laments: 'I have lost my watch and my purse, and I feel that I have caught the cold of my life.' He explains:

> At Lyons the train stopped – stopped going for good, I mean. It was 'All Change.' A very wet night. I got into my clothes as well as I could. But before I was dressed, the officials turned the lights out, and dragged me and my odds and ends onto a swimming black platform. Then the train went away. And I found I had lost my watch and my purse.[22]

Edith and Alice reached Marseilles at seven o'clock the following morning, shivering with cold and desperately hungry. As it was too early to call on the British Consul, they found a café and ordered coffee and buttered rolls, which Edith was too ill to eat. When the unsympathetic Consul advised them to take the matter up with his counterpart in Toulon, they caught a train to that city. They stayed for four days in 'a dilapidated hotel... with a general air of poverty and neglect', then headed for Antibes. Edith was so desperately ill that she struggled to walk unaided.

---

* Her decision to visit this relatively unexplored resort may have been influenced by Grant Allen's article 'Cap d'Antibes' (*Longman's Magazine*, March 1890). Hubert indicates as much in his essay 'In the South' while suggesting that Allen had not visited the town when he wrote it.

Days later, Hubert joined them, accompanied by sisters Ada and May Bowley, whom he had bumped into in Paris.* On learning that they had been ill with influenza, he had persuaded them to travel south. May left an account of their time in Antibes, a 'quaint little Mediterranean town – all white walls, red roofs, soldiers and smells'. Locals, unused to such exotic visitors, turned out to stare at Edith and Alice in their loose aesthetic dresses. They mixed well with fellow tourists, described by May Bowley as a 'party of painters, romancists, rhymers, journalists – all happy, all idle, all rejoicing in the fair jewels of sea and sun and sky'. Since Alice and Hubert took early morning swims together, the proprietors of their hotel decided they must be brother and sister.[23]

There was a group of French army officers stationed in the town and Hubert appeared to have no objection to Edith strolling about 'with the arm of a French army officer round her waist'.[24] They were invited to a local dance and one officer provided a room where the women could change. Edith found it unbearably stuffy and joked that there must be a corpse under the floorboards. She forced open a window that had been painted shut and was leaning out as far as she could when the room's occupant returned. She inadvertently started a trend when she told a dance partner who trod on her toes repeatedly that it was customary in England to dance side by side.

In an article she wrote for the *Daily Chronicle*, Edith described how they would sit 'on Myrtle bushes' reading 'pleasant books' and gazing out towards the island of Corsica, a 'little shadow on the skyline':

> And when we were hungry and thirsty, we ate and drank, French bread which is long, and French butter which is perfect, and little French oranges which they call Mandarins, and French galantine which is a mystery.[25]

She hired a guitar and carried it 'slung round her shoulders', a habit that may have inspired her story 'The Girl with the Guitar'.[26] She also fell in love with a 'very artistic green tea service' but she packed it carelessly at the bottom of her suitcase and it reached England in pieces.[27]

In an essay titled 'In the South', Hubert left an account of the people they met during their stay:

---

* The Bowley sisters worked as illustrators for Raphael Tuck and Sons and supported their family. May was involved in Conan Doyle's fairy investigations. She also illustrated E. Nesbit's *Children's Shakespeare* and *Royal Children of History*. They were inseparable and neither ever married.

Chatting to them [the locals] on the ramparts, when the setting sun is tinting with rose colour the snow-capped peaks of the Maritime Alps and turning the little bay into one wondrous gleaming opal, you shall hear more good things in twenty minutes' talk than in a week of Kensington drawing-rooms, even when Oscar Wilde and his followers are of the guests.[28]

He criticised local Frenchmen for staring at the women, but could not resist pointing out:

And yet here there is some excuse for male staring, for the companion of most of my walks is worth more than a passing eye-blink. She is pretty, dainty, piquant, and altogether pleasant to look upon. She dresses in a blue skirt and blue jacket with a bright yellow blouse, and she wears a little round scarlet cap set jauntily on her head at a provoking angle. As she herself says, she looks like a paroquet – but then, as I tell her, a paroquet is a nice, decorative little bird.[29]

They paid just five francs a day to stay at the 'white-walled' Hotel du Commerce, which stood 'on the summit of a hilly promontory'. Hubert was certain that the six-course breakfasts there were far superior to those provided at the nearby and considerably more expensive Grand Hotel du Cap, where Grant Allen was staying, although he did admire the waitresses there:

At the Grand Hotel the waitresses are things of beauty in Swiss costumes – blue silk aprons, muslin sleeves, velvet bodices, silver chains and neat ankles. What matter then, if the wine they pour out be thinner than that served by the single fat waiter here?[30]

When Allen dined with them one evening, May Bowley reported that he was 'very afraid of typhoid in consequence of the very conspicuous wells of Antibes'. She also reported that he 'held forth, with rather bad taste, on the inferiority of women'.[31]

While they were there, Hubert christened Edith 'our poet' and she celebrated their stay in a rondeau she sent to her young friend and fellow Fabian Bower Marsh.

RONDEAU DE L'HOTEL DU COMMERCE

For five francs a day, five francs a day,
For *diner* and for *déjeuner*,
For little rooms whose windows high
Shew us blue hills, blue sea, blue sky,
And snowy mountains far away,
In Toulon and Marsailles our stay
Was bleak with bills – and life was grey.
But now we pay – the Mouse and I –
Five francs a day.
Here life flowers daily, glad and gay
With *citron, rose* and *oranger*,
We watch the bright blue days go by,
And think of you at home – Ah, why
Are you not also here, to pay
Five francs a day?[32]

She also presented Marsh with a watercolour sketch she made of a stone archway in Antibes. They had been friendly for a couple of years by then and she had a habit of presenting him with inscribed editions of her books on his birthday. She also invited him to join her on several holidays, one to Whitstable and another boating on the Medway. Noel Griffith remembered him joining them for a day in Rottingdean when he spent most of his time chasing Edith's runaway dog. Most significant was the trip they took to Halstead, where she brought him to her childhood home. Whatever the nature of their relationship, it ended when he married Gertrude Holroyd on 20 August 1901.

Edith made little money from her poetry and she needed to accept whatever paid work she was offered in order to meet her financial commitments. In 1892 her first full-length book for children, *Discovery of America: The Voyage of Columbus*, a lavishly illustrated narrative in verse, was brought out by Raphael Tuck and Sons in a guinea edition to commemorate the four-hundredth anniversary of that event. The following year, A.D. Innes published two volumes of her Gothic horror stories, *Something Wrong* and *Grim Tales*. She also wrote *The Marden Mystery*, which was brought out in a very limited run by Chicago-based self-publishing specialist S.J. Clarke in 1894. No surviving copy can be found, but its theme seems to have been the early days of the socialist movement and it is thought to have had chapters in common with *Something Wrong* by Fabian Bland. In March 1896 it won seventh prize, a sum of $600, in a competition for 'stories of mystery' sponsored by the *Chicago Record*.

In 1894, the Bland family moved to Three Gables, a substantial house in Baring Road, off Grove Park in Lewisham, and May Bowley described a dance her sister attended there. The company was 'very mixed'. When refreshments failed to turn up, Edith and Alice distracted guests with lively duets on the piano, and the housemaid danced with Hubert and several of their male guests. One 'young lady from the East End' suggested to Miss Bowley 'let's sit here and have a nice talk about the fellers'.[33] To cap it all, the cook was drunk:

> Mrs Bland got her up to bed and then searched the room and found a bottle of whiskey – This she hid in my sister's room – not altogether to her content as she thought the cook might come in search of it in the night; but Mrs Bland said it would never occur to the culprit to look in the room of a visitor.[34]

When deadlines loomed, Edith would hang a 'keep out' notice on her door. Money was tight and she often needed to write a story or poem to settle a particular debt. As often as not, she would divert this money to pay for some entertainment or donate to a charitable cause. In the title story from *The Butler in Bohemia*, a family throws an extravagant dinner party at which nothing on the table is paid for while tradesmen demand the settlement of long overdue debts.

She continued to write poetry. John Lane published several of her poems in *The Yellow Book* and brought out *A Pomander of Verse* in 1895. The following year Lane published *In Homespun*, a collection of tales written in Kentish dialect, as part of his avant-garde Keynotes series.[*] That same year she was appointed to the panel of poetry critics at *The Athenaeum*. She reviewed *The Wind Among the Reeds* by a young poet named William Butler Yeats, and declared: 'Mr Yeats's sketches are full of charm; his poems are full of lyric sentiment; a slight voice sings, but it sings truly, sweetly and with a clean and fresh sincerity.' Her *Songs of Love and Empire* was published in 1897 to coincide with the jubilee of Queen Victoria. She dedicated it to Hubert:

---

* The series included nineteen volumes of short stories and fourteen novels. The first of these, and the work that gave its name to the series, was George Egerton's extraordinary *Keynotes*, a collection of her short stories.

> To you the harvest of my toil has come
> Because of all that lies its sheaves between;
> You taught me first what Love and Empire mean,
> And to your hands I bring my harvest home.

She was also invited to contribute to 'The Wares of Autolycus,' an unsigned daily column in the *Pall Mall Gazette*. This was a great honour since only leading women writers were invited to contribute.

Given her output at this time, and her prominence as a poet, it seems extraordinary that *The Spectator* would declare, in 1906, 'Nesbit always writes with a facile and graceful pen, but her real forte is not in short stories for grown-up people, but in stories for children.'[35] Yet her celebrated stories for children were taking shape. The first story to feature the Bastable children, 'The Play Times', appeared anonymously in *Nister's Holiday Annual* in 1894. She reworked it as 'Being Editors' in *The Story of the Treasure Seekers*.

Another Bastable story, published in *Father Christmas*, a supplement to the *Illustrated London News*, in December 1897, was attributed to 'Ethel Mortimer' since Edith had a story, 'The White Messengers', in the main paper. Although she believed that her stories had been 'miserably mutilated' in *Father Christmas*, they did hint at wonderful things to come: 'I can't tell you about that now,' Oswald Bastable declares in one, 'but it will all be printed in a book some day, and then you can get someone to buy it for you for Christmas.'[36]

It was not until 1898 that six episodes of *The Story of the Treasure Seekers* appeared between the *Pall Mall Magazine* and the *Windsor Magazine*. Edith turned forty that summer and she described her birthday party in a letter to her mother:

I had a very nice birthday. Fabian made a bonfire in the evening and decorated the garden with Chinese lanterns. I had some pretty presents – a moss agate brooch, a gold ring (fifteenth century), gloves, table centres, a silver watch chain, a book, a pair of little old flint-lock pistols and some beautiful flowers.[37]

In *The Red House* she described: 'A garden hung with soft-tinted Chinese lanterns glowing amid gleams of green leaf-lights and deeps of black-leaf-shadow, a company… placated by good drink.' She was a youthful, vivacious woman and she commented, wryly, to her mother 'I am forty, as you say: but I never feel forty. When I am ill I feel ninety – and when I am happy I feel nineteen!'[38] When *The Story of the Treasure Seekers* appeared in book form in 1889, *The Athenaeum* gave it a muted welcome:

> *The Story of the Treasure Seekers* (Fisher Unwin) describes the adventures of some children who endeavour to supplement their father's limited means by various expedients. Falling on good luck generally in the shape of 'tips,' they are left finally installed in the good graces and luxurious home of a regular fairy-tale uncle. It is evident that E. Nesbit knows children, their ways and habit of thought, thoroughly; and assisted by two clever illustrators like Mr Gordon Browne and Mr Lewis Baumer, she has made an attractive book of her young people. They seem very grown-up at times, but that is perhaps a distinctive charm of the modern child. Two little protests only as to this pleasing performance. One regrets to find the children paid five shillings by an editor for retailing personalities about an old man of their acquaintance, and also to find them using the word 'beastly' so much.[39]

This reviewer identified the key to Edith's success, a childlike quality that she retained throughout her life, which enabled her to empathise with children in a way few of her peers have managed, before or since.

CHAPTER 11

'DRAMATIC ENTERTAINMENT AT NEW-CROSS'

In *Memories of an Edwardian* and Neo-Georgian, Edgar Jepson described Edith as 'as generous a creature as I ever came across', adding:

> Not only was her purse always at the service of her hard-up friends and all the distressed who crossed her path, but there was no end to the pains she would take to get them work and straighten out their affairs and keep them on their feet.[1]

As her finances improved she stayed true to her socialist credentials and was determined to do something for people who lived in heartbreaking destitution right on her doorstep. In 1889 social scientist Charles Booth, aided by a team of researchers, among them his cousin Beatrice Webb, a leading Fabian, compiled *Life and Labour of the People in London*. Booth revealed that the closure of the docks in 1869 had created a poverty rate of sixty-five per cent in the district that lay adjacent to the riverside at Greenwich, an area that included Deptford in the borough of Lewisham, where Edith lived.

In *Harding's Luck* (1909), Edith described the Lewisham district of New Cross, home to her protagonist Dickie Harding, in stark terms: 'its dirty streets, its sordid shifts, its crowds of anxious, unhappy people, who never had quite enough of anything'. Deptford also provided the backdrop for 'After Many Days', a story for *Longman's Magazine* in which she described the desperate state of the tenements that were populated by 'groups of dirty-faced children who played on the stairs and on the landings'.[2] She wrote a letter to the *Daily Mail* that was described as a 'powerful plea for the underfed children in our elementary schools'.[3] Not content with merely highlighting this crisis, Edith donated generously, even when she could ill afford to do so. When tradesmen presented their bills, she would cry: 'How can I let the Deptford children starve to pay butchers, bakers, etc.!'[4]

In January 1895 an article in the *Kentish Mercury* titled 'Humanitarian Work in Deptford' brought one area that was experiencing unspeakable destitution to the attention of readers:

Hughes Fields have long since ceased to be fields in anything but name. Dingy-looking houses of a terrible sameness, peopled for the most part with riverside labourers, cattle market men, and costermongers who eke out a precarious livelihood, and generally 'do the best they can'.[5]

Yet the children who lived in this district had not been abandoned entirely:

It is the school which serves this poverty-stricken spot that has been chosen by Mr and Mrs Hubert Bland for a number of years now as the object of their benevolence. Though the people are the poorest of the poor they are not lacking in those little graces which go to sweeten even the roughest of lives.[6]

The London School Board had designated Hughes Fields primary school a 'specially difficult school'. Pupils were withdrawn as soon as they were capable of earning a wage and the attendance rate was just sixty-five per cent. It was reported that one kindly school inspector purchased food for the children out of his own pocket. The dire poverty they endured was highlighted in an appeal carried in the *Blackheath Gazette*:

In this very poor school a large proportion of the children are either shoe-less or very badly shod and clad, even during this inclement weather, and the teachers would gladly welcome any gifts of old boots and clothing – no matter how old they may be.[7]

Edith opened *Harding's Luck* with a lament for the urban sprawl that had replaced 'once green fields':

Dickie lived at New Cross. At least the address was New Cross, but really the house where he lived was one of a row of horrid little houses built on the slope where once green fields ran down the hill to the river, and the old houses of the Deptford merchants stood stately in their pleasant gardens and fruitful orchards. All those good fields and happy gardens are built over now. It is as though some wicked giant had taken a big brush full of yellow ochre paint, and another full of mud colour, and had painted out the green in streaks of dull yellow and filthy brown; and the brown is the roads and the yellow is the houses. Miles and miles and miles of them, and not a green thing to be seen except the cabbages in the greengrocers' shops, and here and there some poor trails of creeping-jenny drooping from a dirty window-sill.[8]

She had strong views on education and held the teachers who worked in deprived schools in high regard. In *Wings and the Child*, she explained:

There are no words to express half what I feel about the teachers in our Council Schools, their enthusiasm, their patience, their energy, their devotion… The hard thing to do is to live for your country – to live for its children. And it is this that the teachers in the Council Schools do, year in and year out, with the most unselfish nobility and perseverance. And nobody applauds or makes as much fuss as is made over a boy who saves a drowning kitten. In the face of enormous difficulties and obstacles, exposed to the constant pin-pricks of little worries, kept short of space, short of materials and short of money, yet these teachers go on bravely, not just doing what they are paid to do, but a thousand times more, devoting heart, mind, and soul to their splendid ambition and counting themselves well paid if they can make the world a better and a brighter place for the children they serve. If these children when they grow up shall prove better citizens, kinder fathers, and better, wiser, and nobler than their fathers were, we shall owe all the change and progress to the teachers who are spending their lives to this end.[9]

She understood the constraints these teachers faced when dealing with overwhelming inequality:

When we think of what the lives of poor children are, of the little they have of the good things of this world, the little chance they have of grow- ing up to any better fate than that of their fathers and mothers, who do the hardest work of all and get the least pay of all those who work for money – when we think how rich people have money to throw away, how their dogs have velvet coats and silver collars, and eat chicken off china, while the little children of the poor live on bread and tea, and wear what they can get – often enough, too little – when we think of all these things, if we can bear to think of them at all, there is not one of us, I suppose, who would not willingly die if by our death we could secure for these children a fairer share of the wealth of England, the richest country in the world.[10]

Edith's ideas were exceptionally progressive and she advocated radical change to the school curriculum. 'The teaching in our schools is almost wholly materialistic,' she claimed. 'We teach children about the wonders of gases and ethers, but we do not explain to them that furnaces ought to consume their own smoke, nor why.'[11] She regarded education as 'the unfolding of a flower, not the distorting of it'.[12] 'If I had my way,' she insisted, 'children should be taught no facts unless they asked for them. Heaven knows they ask questions enough. They should just be taught the old wonder-stories, and learn their facts through these.'[13]

She believed that every child, regardless of their circumstances, deserved at an absolute minimum 'good food, warm clothes, fresh country air, playthings and books, and pictures'.[14] Rather than rely on the state to provide these basic necessities, she undertook to distribute them herself. She organised her first Christmas party for the pupils of Hughes Fields primary school in 1888, and maintained this tradition for ten years. Just twenty children attended the first party, which was held at 8 Dorville Road. When Edith discovered they had earned their invitations through good behaviour, she insisted on including every child. Attendance rose to five hundred, then one thousand, necessitating a change of venue to the school building itself. The *Kentish Mercury* reported on the party she hosted in January 1896:

Following her usual custom, Mrs Hubert Bland, of Lee, assisted by several friends gave a tea and entertainment on Saturday afternoon to between 300 and 400 of the poorest and wretchedest of the little ones who attend the Hughes' Fields Board Schools, Deptford. The whole of the children were first mustered in the infants' class-room, and eventually divided into batches and served with tea – which included a plentiful supply of bread and butter and cake – in the four classrooms... each child was made the recipient of a warm garment and a toy.[15]

She raised funds and hosted working parties every Saturday for three months leading up to each party, at which family, friends and neighbours made warm, practical clothing; they knitted hats and comforters, and, on one occasion, made trousers for the boys from blue corduroy that had been supplied by Saretta's husband, John Deakin. Edith's neighbour Ada Moore described these gatherings:

> I shall never forget our Saturdays during the winter of 1890-1 (I think). We worked at all kinds of things for the very poor of Deptford for some hours, then a supper of, probably, herrings, cheese and bottled stout, followed by a dance.[16]

It was 'very hard but glorious fun', Alice confirmed, 'and we enjoyed every minute of it'.[17]

Edith shared her views on how children should be treated at Christmas with readers of the *Yorkshire Evening Post*:

> If... a committee of persons who dislike children and wished them ill were to meet for the purpose of discussing how best to treat children worst, that committee could hardly have devised any more pernicious scheme than the orgy of excitement and food which we offer to our children on and about the Feast of Christmas.[18]

Several of Edith's stories draw on this charitable work. In 'The Town in the Library in the Library in the Town' from *Nine Unlikely Tales*, 'Mother' helps the elderly poor by organising 'Christmas presents, tea and snuff, and flannel petticoats and warm capes, and boxes of needles and cottons and things like that'. Like their real-life counterparts, 'Rosamund' and 'Fabian' are required to help, but an outbreak of measles has confined them to the library at home. There, they find Christmas treats and toys that have been hidden away and they get up to all sorts of mischief.[19]

One year, Fabian stole sweets intended for pupils of the Hughes Fields school. He denied it, but he was found out and punished severely. In her story 'The Criminal', Edith described how wretched and remorseful he was. She evoked the Christmas spirit:

> It was Christmas time. The house was alive with children, and filled with a rosy mist of open secrets... In the drawing-room, too, were the presents

that were not secrets – the gifts of sweets and toys and clothes for the poor little children, who had no nice homes and kind mothers, the children who, on Christ's birthday, at least, were remembered.

It is clear that she was addressing Fabian, although he is not named:

There, also, on a chair, were the little bags of sweets that you yourself had helped to tie up with red wool for the poor little children with no nice homes and no kind mothers. There were a great many bags, and you looked at them and wished you were a poor little child, so that you might have one for your own.[20]

Inevitably, he is caught:

There was a pulsating, confused horror, then, of people who said they had seen you open the window; there was the red of the sweets on your hands, the stickiness on your little lips that lied and trembled. They said things to you about stealing and prison and thieves – many words many times repeated. They told you how much worse it was to rob the little children, who had no nice homes and kind mothers, than it would have been to take something from your sisters' tables or your own. And they told you how wicked it was to tell lies. And you had no answer to give. You were very little, you had indeed done this thing, and you were sorry. They beat your little hands that had stolen, and they told you that it hurt them more than it hurt you. Then they put you in the schoolroom, and locked you in, and went away.

Edith realises her resilient child, with the passage of time, has forgotten this humiliation, and it is she who feels desperately remorseful for what he has endured:

I do not think that you forgive or do not forgive. I do not believe that you remember now that quiet room which was your prison, the long hours when for the first time you knew yourself alone. But you remember the sunny garden where you played, were noisy, were happy. You remember, perhaps, hours when your mother was not your gaoler; when she held you not in prison but in her arms that loved you – hours when you were not alone. These other things… it is your mother who has them to remember.[21]

One young man who threw himself enthusiastically into the planning of Edith's parties was writer and illustrator Laurence Housman, younger brother to poet A.E. Housman and a graduate of the Lambeth School of Art. They met after Edith wrote to him in October 1892 to tell him how much she had enjoyed his poem 'The Corn-Keeper'. He mentioned this in *The Unexpected Years* (1937):

> One of my kindest and most generous friends in those early days was E. Nesbit, who, when I began contributing to *Atalanta* wrote asking that we might meet. She was an able and energetic writer of stories for children; but her prose was better than her poetry, and this she did not know. It was, indeed, rather an offence to hint it; and when, after some years of happy association, I said that some poem she had written was 'good verse', she replied with a quiver of indignation mixed with triumph, 'That is the *first* time you have ever praised my poetry!' I did not know that I had been so honest; it was difficult – she hungered for appreciation, and I liking her so much – to remain quite sincere without seeming to be unkind.[22]

At that time Housman was living in Kensington with his sister Clemence, an accomplished engraver and novelist. Like many of Edith's friends, he had lost a parent in early childhood. His mother died when he was just six. His experience of poverty in childhood prompted an interest in socialism and he too joined the Fabian Society. Many of Housman's stories explore issues of social justice and reform. Witty, sociable and brimful of exuberance, he was popular in literary circles and became a regular visitor to Edith's home. On one occasion he was persuaded to participate in a mock breach of promise trial. Oswald Cox, brother of Harold, dressed as a baby to play the defendant and insisted he was underage; playwright Alfred Sutro played defending counsel; and Oswald Barron acted as the judge. Housman, who played prosecuting council, admitted 'I was quite incapable, in those days, of speaking, except conversationally and I hated the job and did it badly.'[23]

He was happier accompanying Edith to John Lane's legendary tea parties, which were 'thronged with literary and artistic notabilities'.[24] They also attended the annual 'Crab and Cream' suppers held at the Temple, where they feasted on dressed crabs set out along a long table in the centre of the room, followed by Devonshire cream and strawberry jam, all washed down with wine and Benedictine. He joined in enthusiastically when the Blands developed a passion for badminton. Alice Hoatson told Doris Langley Moore that they 'became quite respectable players', although, on one occasion, Housman hit Edith on the nose with his racket and cut her quite badly, an incident he commemorated in a hand-drawn birthday card for her.[25]

They collaborated professionally too. Housman designed the title page for *A Pomander of Verse* (1895) and illustrated 'The Ballad of the White Lady' for the *English Illustrated Magazine*.[26] Like Oswald Barron, he had hundreds of ideas for stories and verse, which he was happy to share with her. He allowed her to use an abandoned storyline involving a phoenix that laid an egg in a letterbox. This became *The Phoenix and the Carpet*. When she sent him a copy accompanied by a note of thanks, he replied:

> It is delightful to find how fruitful small suggestions – mere pegs or stems on which to hang a story – become under the genial breath of your invention. It is so long ago since I proposed the carpet and the phoenix as properties for a magic plot to be woven around, that I had forgotten all about them.[27]

From 1892 onwards Edith decided to stage a Christmas drama for the children of Hughes Fields primary school. Early performances were little more than tableaux, but before long she was writing and producing plays, sewing elaborate costumes, and rehearsing her cast once or twice a week during the months of October, November and December. Housman became one of her most enthusiastic volunteers and he found that she could be very demanding: 'Hew me in pieces before the Deptford board-school children, and have done with me,' he complained playfully.[28] In January 1895 he played the king in *Sleeping Beauty*, and he was the slave of the lamp in *Aladdin* the following year.

Another enthusiastic volunteer was Francis Edward (F.E.) Marshall Steele, general secretary of the Lewisham and Lee Liberal and Radical Club. Steele, a talented orator, made his living teaching elocution and editing books of recitation. The *Blackheath Gazette* reported that the Lewisham Liberal Club was 'full to overflowing' on Sunday 10 October 1897, 'when Mr Marshall Steele gave several of his well known and popular recitals'.[29] He encouraged Edith to write verses and recite them as 'Miss E. Nesbit'. Noel Griffith remembered them reciting duologues and solos 'professionally' at working men's clubs, private functions, parties and 'smoking concerts'. A favourite duet of theirs was 'Un Mauvais Quart d'Heure', a dialogue by 'Fabian Bland'.

The *London Daily News* reported on an event in St James's Hall in December 1889, and declared that Steele was 'possessed of the first essential in a public reciter, a musical and sympathetic voice'. On that occasion he was accompanied by 'Miss E. Nesbit, a lady who has assisted him for some time past in entertainments given by them in the suburbs of London and elsewhere'. The reviewer described how 'Miss Nesbit, whose delicate and refined manner suffers rather by contrast with that of her more robust companion, gave one or two of her own beautiful compositions, including "The Ballad of Splendid Silence".' It seems the night was a great success: 'Both performers were frequently applauded by a fairly large audience, which included one or two well-known rep-resentatives of Literary London.'[30] In April 1891 they performed at a fundraiser for *Freedom*, an anarchist newspaper that had been established by volunteers, among them Russian dissident Pyotr Kropotkin and for-mer Fabian Charlotte Wilson.

Steele found it almost impossible to make a decent living. When Iris stayed with his family she was shocked by how poor they were. Edith was keen to help out but she needed to do so without embarrassing her friend. She wrote to John Lane offering:

> Mr Steele and I will come and recite for you. – We will do a dialogue called 'Un Mauvais Quart d'Heure,' – by Fabian Bland – if you like. Miss E. Nesbit is my reciting name – and Mr Marshall Steele's name is here written out in full.[31]

She also arranged for him to replace her when she gave up writing political poems for the *Weekly Dispatch*. She even encouraged him to write children's books for the publishers who had brought out her early books. Although he wrote several slight books for children, he never came close to emulating her success.

Edith dedicated *A Pomander of Verse* 'To My Friend Marshall Steele' and he wrote 'E. Nesbit: an appreciation' for *Harper's Bazaar*. He declared:

> She has an artist's conception of the short story; she never overloads it, she rigidly excludes from it all that is unnecessary, and she chooses for its

theme one episode, not a series of episodes which would provide material for a novel of the old three-decker dimensions.[32]

He also insisted: 'With the single exception of *The Jungle Book*, no children's book of recent years has had success to compare with that of *The Wouldbegoods*.'[33] Every year Steele would write a poem for Edith on her birthday. Friends believed he was desperately in love with her. He certainly threw himself enthusiastically into the production of her Christmas plays.

On 16 February 1894 a notice in the *Kentish Mercury* informed readers:

In aid of the fund for feeding and clothing poor children at Hughes' Fields Board Schools, Deptford. A Dramatic performance will be given at the New Cross Public Hall on Wednesday February 21 at 8 p.m. When the following original plays will be acted: A Family Novelette by E. Nesbit and Oswald Barron, and Cinderella, A fairy play in five scenes by E. Nesbit. Seats 3s, 2s, 1s, and 6d.[34]

Edith had decided that, since so much effort was expended on her Christmas plays, a second performance should be staged as a fundraiser. The *Blackheath Gazette* carried this report:[35]

DRAMATIC PERFORMANCE AT NEW CROSS HALL

At the New Cross Hall on Wednesday evening a dramatic performance was given in aid of the dinner funds of the Hughes Fields Board Schools. The entertainment comprised a farce entitled 'A Family Novelette,' the characters being represented by Mr Marshall Steele, Miss Ada Breakell, Miss Rhondda Knight, Mrs E. Nesbit, Mr Willis Utley, and Mr Noel Ledbrook. Some of the situations were extremely laughable, and, despite the fact of the dialogue dragging at times, the production gave great satisfaction. The fairy play, in five scenes, and entitled 'Cinderella,' by E. Nesbit, formed Part II of the programme. The parts were all well delineated, the very juvenile 'Herald' and the still more juvenile 'Fairy Godmother' acting with a confidence and style which would have done credit to much older folk. The proceedings were interspersed with pianoforte selections. The Hughes Street Board School Dinner Fund is now in the third year of its existence, during which period, owing mainly to the untiring efforts of

Mrs Bland and her helpers, something over 60,000 meals have been provided for the poor children who attend their schools. Clothing has also
been supplied in numerous cases, and it is to be hoped that the entertainment of Wednesday evening will be the means of materially adding to the
resources of such a praiseworthy movement.

The *London Daily News* also carried a glowing review:

A Dramatic performance was given last night at the New-cross Public
Hall, in aid of the dinner fund of the Hughes' Field School. It owed
nearly all its success to the labours of Mrs Hubert Bland. This lady,
better known as Miss E. Nesbit, was the sole author of one of the
pieces played, and the part author of the other. She played in one of
them, and, with Mr Marshall Steele, was a stage manager for the entire
performance. The first piece, in which her name was associated with
that of Mr Oswald Barron in the authorship, was a new and original
farce called 'A Family Novelette.' It turns on the imaginative extravagance of an amiable pair, whose minds are so steeped in cheap serial
fiction that they try to shape their lives by its laws. Their niece Angelica
(Miss Rhondda Knight) has formed an attachment to an artist, but they
think it incumbent on them to throw a baronet in her way. Their goodness of heart, however, makes them repent of the distresses incidental
to their scheme; and, though the niece does accept the baronet in the
end, it is certainly not their fault. This game of cross purposes between
the heart and the head was very happily conceived, and was of the
essence of comedy. Miss Nesbit and Mr Marshall Steele sustained parts
in this piece with great effect. The fairy play of Cinderella[*] that followed was wholly from Miss Nesbit's pen. The story was delightfully
told, in verse of great beauty, especially in the lyrics. It was delightfully
played, mainly by a troop of small children, among whom a whole
contingent of little 'Blands' held a conspicuous place. Where they
occasionally failed in self-possession, their infantine embarrassment
was only a charm the more. They were reinforced in the cast by Miss
Alice Hoatson and Miss Olive Steele, two young ladies who played the
wicked sisters with great spirit and effect.[36]

---

[*]   *Cinderella* by E. Nesbit was published in play version in 1909 with songs to popular
tunes, in a series designed for schools.

It was 'a bitterly cold night', but it was confirmed in *The Sketch* that they performed in front of a full house. Iris played Cinderella and 'looked the part exactly'. It was also reported that 'a tiny child, Miss Rosamund Bland, looked elfish enough for the Fairy Godmother and spoke her lines admirably'. Fabian was the herald: 'His self possession was wonderful, and he sang a capital song with so much "go" that an encore was instantly demanded.' Paul played 'Second Gentleman' and had a love scene with Marshall Steele's daughter Enid. Edith accompanied them all on the piano, play original songs she had composed with Marshall Steele and Oswald Barron. She also donned 'a snowy cap and expansive white apron' to played the housemaid in *A Family Novelette*.

In January 1886 the play was *Aladdin* 'in five acts, written by "Miss E. Nesbit" and Marshall Steele'.[37] Steele adapted *Sleeping Beauty* the following year and oversaw its staging. The *Kentish Mercury* reported: 'The play went very prettily, and its absurdities were happily hit off to the immense delight of the youngsters.' The purpose of the evening was not forgotten:

Before the play started we were taken into a classroom at the end of the corridor, where there was an array of dolls all beautifully dressed, scrap books, and sweetmeats, and, still more to the point, articles of clothing. All these things, which were afterwards handed over to the children, had been made or collected by Mrs Bland, Miss Hoatson and Mrs Steele, a labour of love which takes up many weeks during the year... Presently the children began to file into the big class-room to witness Sleeping Beauty [which had been performed in New Cross Hall the previous Spring and raised £29 for the dinner fund].[38]

Hubert's name is rarely mentioned in connection with these entertainments. In fact he was immensely supportive and utterly committed to the cause. In Fabian Tract Number 120, which was titled *After Bread Education: A Plan for the State Feeding of School Children*, he condemned the desperate conditions that prevailed in England's most deprived schools, writing: 'No one who has made even the most cursory study of the condition of children in elementary schools can doubt the existence of quite an appalling amount of underfeeding.'[39] Within a year, the reforms he had advocated were carried into law, a proud testament to his eloquence and compassion. Edith ended her connection with the Hughes Fields School in 1898. According to Alice, Rosamund had contracted a dose of scarlet fever and as a result 'everything was moved to a near by neighbour who ran the treat for us'.[40] Edith would probably have stepped down regardless. In spring 1900 she left London to move into a magical new home.

CHAPTER 12

'THE MEDWAY, WITH THE PSAMMEAD'

In 1906 an admiring article in the *Saturday Evening Post* described Edith, who was forty-eight by then, as 'the author of some of the very cleverest of recent stories'. It was reported that she 'kept up her badminton and whist, pulls a strong oar in a boat and swims quite as well as she rows'.[1] That same year *The Bookman* declared: 'she is an enthusiastic "outdoor" woman, and takes great delight in swimming and boating'.[2] An active, athletic woman, she walked and ran, and was a strong swimmer and an adventurous cyclist, just like her character Diana Redmayne from 'The Hermit of "The Yews"', a story included in *Man and Maid* (1906). She was keen to inspire other women. In an article titled 'Rational Exercise and Women's Dress', in which she insisted 'athletics is the natural foe of tight lacing', she declared:

> Rowing, running, jumping – if girls went in for these with half the enthu-siasm of their brothers the Gordian knot of the stay lace would be cut once and for all. They say most women run like cows. How can it be otherwise when their hips are constricted so that all their movement comes from the knees only? How can one jump when one's lungs are so compressed that one loses one's wind in the mere spurt preliminary? But here again, let our advanced women say what they will, man has the game in his hands. Let men cease to admire the pinched-up waist, let them encourage athletics among their sisters and sweethearts, and they will have stronger, better, sweeter women for their wives, and healthier mothers for their children.[3]

Edith's good friend Berta Ruck remembered her as 'a carpenter, handy with a boat, a swimmer'. She wrote: 'I forget how many miles she had once tramped bare-foot for a bet – that was before I met her.'[4] Stories of her prowess were occasionally conflated. One newspaper reported: 'Adventure is in Mrs Bland's blood for she ran away as a child to Germany and once walked barefoot from Whitstable to Canterbury for fun.' Boating holidays on the Medway and seaside trips to the Kent coast in the company of a willing band of young acolytes provided her with opportunities to indulge in such activities.

Edgar Jepson declared: 'Wherever they [Edith and Hubert] went, too, their own circle went with them.' Several times each year they would leave London with friends to walk, cycle or swim in the sea. In Dymchurch Edith liked to 'cycle down to the seafront in a billowing garment bearing some resemblance to a tea-gown'.[5] The children accompanied them on seaside holidays to Deal, Sheerness, Whitstable or Dymchurch, but river holidays, lasting a week, or sometimes just a weekend, were strictly for adults. Edith adored boating and she used the promise of an impending trip as an incentive to meet her deadlines. In one couplet, she promised:

And I will earn, working like mad,
The Medway, with the Psammead.[6]

Another begins:

How can I work? The stupid task
That heartless publishers may ask
Is all too hard for me to do,
Dear Medway, since to you, to you,
My thought flies, falling like an arrow,
Amid your meadowsweet and yarrow.[7]

Noel Griffith often made up a foursome with Edith, Hubert and Alice on boating holidays. He told Doris Langley Moore that he realised how unconventional the Blands' marriage was when he accompanied them to Whitstable. Rather than wearing bathing suits, Alice and Edith would tuck their shifts up and dive straight into the sea. When Alice emerged from the sea, Hubert commented approvingly on her figure and invited him to do the same. He regarded Hubert as 'very hot-blooded... abnormally sexual, too much so for the tastes of his wife'.[8]

Edith's relationship with Griffith is difficult to decipher. In the account he gave Doris Langley Moore, he described her as 'a mixture of sensuality and intellectuality' and suggested, albeit coyly, that her response to Hubert's flagrant infidelity was to take lovers of her own. He indicated that he was one of them. They were certainly very close, and Edith named Noël Bastable after him. Griffith was a regular member of Edith's Medway boating parties. He described how they would hire a double-sculling boat, then 'start at Maidstone after buying stores'. They would row to East Peckham, near Yalding, and spend a shilling each on a room in some riverside pub. Languid days were filled with rowing, walking and swimming. They collected their lunch from some riverside hostelry and ate it at some beauty spot that took their fancy along the way. He remembered 'lots of good laughter and lots of good talk', the talk 'being very much of the socialist state of the future'.[9]

Edith wove memories of these treasured days into her stories and poems. She put a Lord Yalding and a Yalding Castle into *The Enchanted Castle*, and a Lady Yalding into *Man and Maid*. In *Five Children and It*, Uncle Richard takes the children 'on the beautiful Medway in a boat'. In *Salome and the Head* (1909), Edith described how: 'They had lunch together in that flat meadow away to the left by Oak Weir, among the roots of the great trees that reach down to the backwater where the water-lilies are.'[10] A similar lunch is included in *The Incredible Honeymoon*:

At Oak Weir they put the boat through the lock, and under the giant trees they unpacked the luncheon-basket they had brought from the Midlothian – how far away and how incredibly out of the picture such a place now seemed! – and sat among the twisted tree roots, and ate and drank and were merry like children on a holiday.[11]

During their real holidays, as dusk fell, Edith would play her guitar, often strumming a song of her own composition. Her 'Medway Song' opens with a nod to her friend Laurence's older brother, A.E. Housman:

MEDWAY SONG
(Air: Carnaval de Venise)

Let Housman sing of Severn shore,
Of Thames let Arnold sing,

But we will sing no river more
Save this where crowbars ring.
Let others sing of Henley,
Of fashion and renown,
But we will sing the thirteen locks
That lead to Tonbridge town!
Then sing the Kentish river,
The Kentish fields and flowers,
We waste no dreams on other streams
Who call the Medway ours.
When on the level golden meads
The evening sunshine lies,
The little voles among the reeds
Look out with wondering eyes.
The patient anglers linger
The placid stream beside,
Where still with towering tarry prow
The stately barges glide.
Then sing the Kentish river,
The Kentish fields and flowers,
We waste no dreams on other streams
Who call the Medway ours.
On Medway banks the May droops white,
The wild rose blossoms fair,
O'er meadow-sweet and loosestrife bright,
For water nymphs to wear.
And mid the blowing rushes
Pan pipes a joyous song,
And woodland things peep from the shade
As soft we glide along.
Then sing the Kentish river,
The Kentish fields and flowers,
We waste no dreams on other streams
Who call the Medway ours.
You see no freight on Medway boats
Of fashions fine and rare,
But happy men in shabby coats,
And girls with wind-kissed hair.

The world's a pain forgotten,
And very far away,
The stream that flows, the boat that goes –
These are our world to-day.
Then sing the Kentish river,
The Kentish fields and flowers,
We waste no dreams on other streams
Who call the Medway ours.

William Archer noted that Edith had 'a real love for English nature and a keen eye for it'.[12] Nowhere is this more evident than in her descriptions of the lovely Kent countryside lying either side of the lazy River Medway. In *The Wouldbegoods*, she wrote:

We went along the towing path; it is shady with willows, aspens, elders, oaks, and other trees. On the banks are flowers – yarrow, meadow-sweet, willow herb, loose-strife, and lady's bed-straw.[13]

Long passages in *The Incredible Honeymoon* describe the beauty of her beloved Medway, and in *Salome and the Head* she wrote:

The Medway just above the Anchor (at Yalding, Kent) is a river of dreams. The grey and green of willows and alders mirror themselves in the still water in images hardly less solid-seeming than their living realities. There is pink loosestrife there, and meadow-sweet creamy and fragrant, forget-me-nots wet and blue, and a tangle of green weeds and leaves and stems that only botanists know the names of.[14]

The real Anchor was a quaint fourteenth-century pub that stood just over the river from the medieval Twyford Bridge and weir. Australian-born poet and nature writer Walter James Turner described it in *The Englishman's Country* (1945) as a 'beautiful inn with its nooks and corners answering no particular scheme of architecture'. Its origin, he explained, was as a bargeman's inn, but it became 'a favourite anchorage for anglers, who have miles of water, swift or slow to yield them sport'.[15]

Edith stayed in several of the pubs and inns that punctuated the riverbank. She wrote in *Salome and the Head*:

If you go to Yalding you may stay at the George, and be comfortable in a little village that owns a haunted churchyard, a fine church, and one of the most beautiful bridges in Europe. Or you may stay at the Anchor, and be comfortable on the very lip of the river.

Her protagonist, Templar, chooses to stay at the Anchor and Edith describes its proprietor as a 'just man'. She may have been referring to John William Freeman, who explained at a hearing to decide on the license in 1909, that he needed to engage rooms at cottages nearby to accommodate extra visitors during the summer season.[16] Edith stayed there many times and she included a description of breakfast there in *Salome and the Head*:

At the Anchor you breakfast either in a little room whose door opens directly on that part of the garden which is adorned by two round flower-beds edged with the thickest, greenest box you ever saw – this is next door to breakfasting in the garden itself – or you *do* breakfast in the garden. Once upon a time you used to breakfast in a hornbeam arbour, but now that is given over to bargees. The landlord of the Anchor is a just man, and apportions the beauty of his grounds fairly among his clients.

The morning being a prince of mornings, even for June, Mr Templar ate his eggs and bacon in the garden, drank there his three cups of tea, and there leaned back and smoked the after-breakfast pipe. There were birds singing in the alders opposite; the river, decorated with sunlight, looked warm and brown, like the shallow pools whose warmness quite shocks you when you dangle your feet in them from seaweed-covered rocks.[17]

Her couple from *The Incredible Honeymoon*, Edward and Katherine, stand 'on the landing-stage of the Anchor, looking down on a sort of Sargasso Sea of small craft that stretched along below the edge of the Anchor garden'.[18] They take to the water on the very next page and Edith uses this as an opportunity to condemn the hideously utilitarian architecture that was encroaching on this beloved landscape, a theme she returned to again and again:

A few strokes took them out of sight of the Anchor, its homely, flowered garden, its thatched house, its hornbeam arbor; they passed, too, the ugly, bare house that some utilitarian misdemeanant has built next to it, then nothing but depths of willow copse, green and grey, and the grassy curves of the towing-path where the loosestrife grows, and the willow herb, the yellow yarrow, and the delicate plumes of the meadow-sweet.[19]

The George in Yalding, a riverside inn that dated back to 1642, provided an alternative to the Anchor. In *Salome and the Head*, Templar enjoys a drink there:

> But he walked up to Yalding and leaned on the bridge and looked down into the mysterious shadowy depths that by daylight are green-water-meadows; saw two white owls fly out from the church tower; heard the church clock strike nine; had a drink at the George and a pleasant word with the George's good landlord; and went back over the broad, deserted green space, tree-bordered, which Yalding calls the Leas, to that other bridge which is almost as beautiful as Yalding's, and so to bed in a little bungalow close to the water, and there fell asleep with the sound of the weir soothing him like a lullaby.[20]

In 1905 Edith sent a note to H.G. Wells, who was due to join them: 'I can't remember whether you were told that our inn at Yalding is the *George* – it would be dreadful if you were to seek us vainly at the *Bull* or the *Anchor*.'[21]

She was staying at the Rose and Crown on Banbridges Road in East Peckenham when she wrote to her mother: 'the river is always beautiful, and soothes me as nothing else does'.[22] Iris was with her and had just completed her first term at the Slade School of Fine Art. The Rose and Crown became the bargees pub in 'Coals of Fire', a story from *In Homespun*.[23] In *The Railway Children* (1906), she wrote:

> There is a nice old-fashioned room at the Rose and Crown where Bargees and their wives sit of an evening drinking their supper beer, and toasting their supper cheese at a glowing basketful of coals that sticks out into the room under a great hooded chimney and is warmer and prettier and more comforting than any other fireplace *I* ever saw.[24]

Boating holidays were glorious but they were arduous too. 'On the Medway life is real, life is earnest,' she explained in *The Incredible Honeymoon*. 'You mostly pull a hundred yards, anchor and fish; or if you do go farther from harbour you open your own locks, with your own crowbar.'[25] They spent much of their time opening and closing locks; 'the Medway strings them quite thickly on her silver thread', Edith observed. She identified them by name in *The Incredible Honeymoon*:

> Thus the two passed through Stoneham Lock and the next and the next, and then came to the Round Lock, which is like a round pond whose water creeps in among the roots of grass and forget-me-not and spearmint and wild strawberry. And so at last to Oak Weir Lock, where the turtledoves call from the willow wood on the island where the big trees are, and the wide, sunny meadows where the sheep browse all day till the shepherd calls them home in the evening – the shepherd with his dog at his heels and his iron crook, polished with long use and stately as a crozier in a bishop's hand.[26]

She was drawing on backbreaking experience when she described the strength and skill required to open each one. 'The locks on the Medway are primitive in their construction and heavy to work,' she explained:

> There are no winches or wheels or artful mechanical contrivances of weights and levers and cables. There are sluices, and from the sluice-gates posts rise, little iron-bound holes in them, holes in which the urgent nose of the crowbar exactly fits. The boatman leans indolently against the tarred, unshaped tree trunk whose ax-wrought end is the top of the lock gate; the tree trunk swings back above the close sweet-clover mat that edges the lock; the lock gates close – slow, leisurely, and dignified. Then the boatman stands on the narrow plank hung by chains to each lock gate, and with his crowbar chunks up the sluice, with a pleasant ringing sound of iron on iron, securing the raised sluice with a shining iron pin that hangs by a little chain of its own against the front of the lock gate, like an ornament for a gentleman's fob. If you get your hand under the pin and the sluice happens to sink, you hurt your hand.[27]

Yet the rewards were rich once you sailed through:

> Slowly the lock fills with gentle swirls of foam-white water, slowly the water rises, and the boat with it, the long gates unclose to let you out – slow, leisurely, dignified – and your boat sweeps out along the upper tide, smoothly gliding like a boat in a dream.[28]

With a poet's sensibility, Edith let her prose soar to lyrical heights as she described the untamed beauty that lay beyond each lock gate:

The quiet river, wandering by wood and meadow, bordered by its fringe of blossoms and flowering grasses, the smooth backwaters where leaning trees touched hands across the glassy mirror, and water-lilies gleamed white and starry, the dappled shadows, the arch of blue sky, the gay sunshine, and the peace of the summer noon all wrought in one fine spell to banish from their thoughts all fear and dismay, all doubts and hesitations.[29]

She must be describing herself when she writes of Katherine in *The Incredible Honeymoon*:

She was very much interested in the opening of the lock gates and deplored the necessity which kept her in the boat, hanging on to the edge of the lock with a boat-hook while he wielded the crowbar.[30]

Edith was an exceptionally strong swimmer. When Hubert dropped the crowbar while attempting to open the sluice-gates of Yalding lock, without hesitation she swam down to retrieve it.

Holidays were not always taken on the river. On at least one occasion, Edith stayed near the coastal village of Rottingdean on the Sussex South Downs, near where Rudyard Kipling lived. She gave chapter four of *The Incredible Honeymoon* the title 'The South Downs' and placed Edward Basingstoke in this lovely corner of England:

He climbed the cliff above Cuckmere and sat in the sunshine there, where the gulls flashed white wings and screamed like babies; he watched the tide, milk-white with the fallen chalk of England's edge, come sousing in over the brown, seaweed-covered rocks; he felt the crisp warmth of the dry turf under his hand, and smelt the sweet smell of the thyme and the furze and the sea, and it was all good.[31]

While she was in Sussex Edith joined in with companionable cross-country hikes and took jaunts along country lanes in a hired dogcart. When she bumped into Scottish balladeer John Davidson, a regular at John Lane's tea parties, they organised a cricket match and he made her laugh by removing his toupee and hanging it from the stumps. The incorrigible Max

Beerbohm suggested he wore it, not from vanity, but because he believed no one would employ him if he were bald.[32] She befriended another young cricketer, one with considerably more talent. Dr Edwin Percy Habberton Lulham was a medical doctor and a fast bowler for Sussex and England. While tending to their medical needs, he took striking photographs of the Sussex traveller community. He was an accomplished lecturer and he also wrote poetry as Habberton Lulham. He presented Edith with an inscribed copy of his *Songs from the Downs and Dunes* (1908).*

Hugh Bellingham-Smith, an accomplished artist and graduate of the Slade, was another young man who joined Edith's party for a day or two. It was his little brother, Eric, who had shared lessons with Paul and Iris, and sparred with Paul in the drawing room of 8 Dorville Road. Their parents were prominent members of the Fabian Society who lived in Lee. Edith told Ada Breakell that Henry Bellingham-Smith was 'interested in social questions and dried fruit − married − very much'. Frances Bellingham-Smith was, she reported, '*very* youthful and gushing'.[33] Later in life Hugh earned a reputation as an accomplished if unremarkable landscape painter. He is believed to have painted a full-length portrait of Edith for the Blackheath Art Club, but there is no trace of it. He also illustrated several books of her verse, among them *All the Year Round* and *In the Springtime*. He moved to Paris in 1890 to study at the *Académie Julian*, and they lost touch.

Edith also travelled north to visit Saretta, who lived in the Derbyshire Peak District with her family. They lived for a time just outside the village of Hayfield in a cottage named 'Paradise', nestled in the valley of the River Sett. Local legend had it that English cleric and theologian John Wesley named this cottage while he was preaching there during the 1740s because he admired the view so much.

Saretta introduced Edith to the Woodcock family who lived at Aspenshaw Hall, a rambling old house that was filled with dogs, roaring fires and relaxed attitudes. Fanny Woodcock told Doris Langley Moore that her family was 'dazzled, amazed and amused by their visitor, who would stretch out with the dogs on the hearthrug'. She described how her 'hair was cut short and her uncorseted figure was clothed in a flowing wool gown'. Edith never played up to her status as a celebrated author, nor did she hint at any difficulties in her family life. Instead, Fanny Woodcock remembered that 'her manner was as gay and careless as a child's' and described her as:

---

* That book is now in my possession.

An exceptionally handsome, tall, slender, young woman with a figure at once strong, graceful and supple; eyes dark but bright and very watchful, beautiful eyebrows and a fine, broad forehead half-covered by a fringe of naturally curly brown hair; a narrow, delicate nose which faintly and most attractively misses regularity; a firmly modelled mouth, rather thin, but sweet in its expression – the upper lip and the chin somewhat shorter than is common. All the forms of the face are definite to the point of sharpness, and this, with the alertness of her glance, and the quick movements of her head, suggests to almost everyone who sees her the epithet 'bird-like'.[34]

Edith borrowed a pony from the Woodcocks and rode along local tracks, up over hills, and through fields criss-crossed with drystone walls. She put the people and places of Derbyshire into her stories. A house called Three Chimneys became home to *The Railway Children*. Some people believe that the trains that steamed along the Sett Valley can be found on its pages too. References to 'Old Mills' and 'Aspenshaw Farm' scattered throughout her early stories must relate to the nearby industrial town of New Mills and to Aspenshaw Hall.

In 1891 John and Saretta moved to the tiny village of Boothstown in Worsley, seven miles west of Manchester. Edith stayed with them in 1893, arriving in the middle of a miners' strike. The local economy was utterly dependent on deep mining, which had come to the region with the sinking of Mosley Common Colliery during the 1860s. When coal prices dropped, colliery owners attempted to maintain their profits by reducing the miners' wages. The Miners Federation responded by calling for a living wage and organising a lock-out, which lasted for much of that summer. Edith volunteered at the local soup kitchen.

That was also the year she chanced upon her favourite holiday destination, the coastal village of Dymchurch in Kent.[35] She was there when she dedicated *The Phoenix and the Carpet*:

TO
My Dear Godson
HUBERT GRIFFITH
and his sister
MARGARET

This Hubert, who was born in October 1896, was the son of Noel Griffith and his wife Georgina 'Nina' Freeling.* Edith wrote a charming poem under her dedication:

TO HUBERT
Dear Hubert, if I ever found
A wishing-carpet lying round,
I'd stand upon it, and I'd say:
'Take me to Hubert, right away!'
And then we'd travel very far
To where the magic countries are
That you and I will never see,
And choose the loveliest gifts for you, from me.
But oh! alack! and well-a-day!
No wishing-carpets come my way.
I never found a Phoenix yet,
And Psammeads are so hard to get!
So I give you nothing fine –
Only this book your book and mine,
And hers, whose name by yours is set;
Your book, my book, the book of Margaret!
E. NESBIT
DYMCHURCH
September, 1904

---

* In adulthood Hubert Freeling Griffith (1896-1953) became a journalist, playwright and drama critic. He also joined the RAF. Margaret and he also had a brother, Owen, who was born in 1907.

CHAPTER 13

'ISN'T IT A DEAR LITTLE PLACE?'

The summer of 1893 was unusually hot and England was gripped by drought from April to August. Edith was keen to escape the oppressive suburbs, so she took Paul, aged thirteen, and Iris, aged eleven, to the coastal town of Hythe on the edge of Romney Marsh. She loved the spectacular Kent coastline and it is celebrated in her beautifully illustrated seafaring tale, *The Pilot*, which was published that year. Hythe had been one of the original Cinque Ports granted limited autonomy in exchange for defending the country against invasion. By 1893 it was a bustling seaside resort with shingle beaches, an esplanade, bathing machines and donkey rides. It was packed with holidaymakers so they escaped the hordes by taking an excursion to Dymchurch, a tiny fishing village five miles down the coast.

Dymchurch was built on reclaimed land and a sea-barrier originally constructed by Roman invaders has been maintained there ever since. The name derives from Deme, an Old English word for judge or arbiter, and in medieval times it was the administrative seat of Romney Marsh. As the head magistrate was called the 'Leveller of the Marsh Scotts' a tax known as a 'Scott-tax' was levied on residents to fund the upkeep of the sea wall. People who lived just beyond the boundaries and therefore not liable for this tax were said to have got away 'Scott free'.

Edith fell in love with this unspoiled village. Her first impressions can be gauged from Katherine's reaction in *The Incredible Honeymoon*:

They sped on; through Dymchurch, where the great sea-wall is, and where the houses are built lower than the sea, so that the high tide laps against the sea-wall level with the bedroom windows that nestle behind its strong shelter.

It was she who spoke then 'Isn't it a dear little place?' she said.

In Dymchurch a staunch Martello tower stands sentinel behind the sea wall, one of seventy-four built along the south coast between 1805 and 1812 to repel a French invasion. Katherine describes it in *The Incredible Honeymoon*:

Wouldn't you like to live in a Martello tower? They have one beautiful big room with a Norman-looking pillar in the middle, and a down-stairs part for kitchens, and an up-stairs, where the big gun is, that you could roof in for bedrooms. I should like a Martello! Don't you want to buy one? You know they built them to keep out Napoleon – and the canal as well – but no one uses them now. They just keep fishing-nets in them and wheelbarrows and eel-spears.

Her companion, Edward, suggests that it is haunted:

A soldier's ghost walks there; the village people say 'it's one of them there Roman soldiers that lived here when them towers was built in old ancient Roman times'.[1]

During the seventeenth and eighteenth centuries Dymchurch was a haven for smugglers. In *The New Treasure Seekers*, an old man relates this dark history to the Bastable children:

'There used to be lots of smuggling on these here coasts when my father was a boy,' he said; 'my own father's cousin, his father took to the smuggling, and he was a doin' so well at it, that what does he do, but goes and gets married, and the Preventives they goes and nabs him on his wedding-day, and walks him straight off from the church door, and claps him in Dover Jail.'[2]

When Edith first arrived the village had a windmill, but it stopped working in 1882 and it was demolished in 1905. One of the first places she rented was Mill House on Mill Street. She used it in *The New Treasure Seekers* as the home of Miss Sandal, and Oswald Bastable describes it to readers:

It is before you come to the village, and it is a little square white house. There is a big old windmill at the back of it. It is not used any more for grinding corn, but fishermen keep their nets in it.[3]

That first summer Edith took rooms in a house on Marine Terrace. Once she had settled in, she sent for the rest of her family. Hubert's beloved mother, Mary Ann Bland, had died on 7 August, at the age of seventy-four, and it would seem that he welcomed the opportunity of a seaside holiday. In late October he sent a note to Edward Pease asking if he might be excused from the next Fabian meeting: 'We are having a very good time down here, shrimping, eeling, swimming, etc.,' he wrote.

Edith enjoyed the seclusion she found in Dymchurch. Yet two years after she chose it as her favourite holiday destination, in 1895, the wealthy Stoakes-Jones family commissioned a development that included the Arcade Gift Shop and a cluster of holiday houses, the first to be built in the village. She explored the surrounding countryside by bicycle and dogcart, and took inspiration from that secluded landscape. Several of the stories she included in *Grim Tales* are set in and around Romney Marsh. The exceptionally chilling 'Man-size in Marble' unfolds in St Eanswith's Church in the village of Brenzett, which lies just eight miles inland. Her eerie, animated marble knights were suggested by the tomb chest of John Fagge and his son, which dominates the North Chapel. One of these figures rests on his elbow as if he is about to rise.

The horror genre was popular with magazine editors and Edith sold dozens of stories that she later collected in book form. She had a talent for the Gothic. A review in *The Spectator* likened her style in *Something Wrong* to that of Poe 'whose influence, indeed, seems, with or without the author's consciousness, to have affected the whole book'.[4] She also used the genre to help her explore deep-seated fears and phobias that had endured since childhood. Since she was determined not to pass these on to her children, she kept a human skull on the top of the piano and scattered several human bones about the house.

Edith put Dymchurch into several of her stories, and she usually renamed it 'Lymchurch'. 'Tomorrow,' says a wise woman in *The House of Arden* (1910), 'the French shall land in Lymchurch Bay.'[5] In *Oswald Bastable and Others*, Lymchurch is home to Miss Sandal:

It was the seaside so, of course, there was a beach, and besides that the marsh – big green fields with sheep all about, and wet dykes with sedge growing, and mud, and eels in the mud, and winding white roads that all look the same, and all very interesting, as though they might lead to almost anything that you didn't expect. Really, of course, they lead to Ashford and Romney and Ivy Church, and real live places like that. But they don't look it.[6]

It also features in her collection *Man and Maid* (1906) and in one story, 'The Millionairess', she included a description of the beach:

> The tide was low, the long lines of the sandbanks shone yellow in the sun – yellower for the pools of blue water left between them. Far off, where the low white streak marked the edge of the still retreating sea, little figures moved slowly along, pushing the shrimping nets through the shallow water.

In 'The Millionairess', Rosamund 'watched the seagulls and shrimpers from under the sea-wall of Lymchurch' while Andrew Dornington, a young poet seated beside her, celebrated the landscape in verse:

> Now the vexed clouds, wind-driven, spread wings of white,
> Long leaning wings across the sea and land;
> The waves creep back, bequeathing to our sight
> The treasure-house of their deserted sand;
> And where the nearer waves curl white and low,
> Knee-deep in swirling brine the slow-foot shrimpers go.
> Pale breadth of sand where clamorous gulls confer
> Marked with broad arrows by their planted feet,
> White rippled pools where late deep waters were,
> And ever the white waves marshalled in retreat,
> And the grey wind in sole supremacy
> O'er opal and amber cold of darkening sky and sea.

This fictional Rosamund is staying in 'a little house behind the sea-wall'. Its door 'opened straight from the street into the sitting-room, after the primitive fashion of Lymchurch'. Andrew Dornington is at The Ship, a genuine Dymchurch inn. He observes: 'The trees, still gold in calmer homes, stood almost leafless in wild, windy Lymchurch.'[7]

In 'Rack and Thumbscrew' from *Man and Maid*, Milly describes Lymchurch as 'a glorious place to work', adding: 'Father did reams down there.'[8] Edith too found she could work well in Dymchurch. She was not alone. Romney Marsh was a magnet for writers: Henry James, whose writing she emulated in *The Literary Sense*, lived just sixteen miles away in Lamb House in Rye. Joseph Conrad lived all over Kent. Edgar Jepson remembered meeting him in Dymchurch 'one hot summer when he came from his home in the hills above the marsh, bringing his family, to spend the day with [author and journalist] Perceval Gibbon'.[9] In 1901 Ford Madox Ford moved to Winchelsea, just a twenty-mile cycle along the narrow lanes leading from Dymchurch. It was also in 1901 that H.G. Wells moved his family into Spade House, a house built to his specifications in Sandgate near Folkestone. He celebrated the area in his novel *Kipps*:

> There were glorious days of 'mucking about' along the beach, the siege of unresisting Martello towers, the incessant interest of the mystery and motion of windmills, the windy excursions with boarded feet over the yielding shingle to Dungeness lighthouse... wandering in the hedgeless, reedy marsh.[10]

Edith returned to Dymchurch every summer for more than a decade, and her improved finances allowed her to rent ever better holiday homes. In 1899 she received her first commission from *The Strand Magazine* when she was invited to write 'The Book of Beasts', a series of seven stories about dragons. An eighth dragon story was published in their Christmas number. A very generous thirty pounds per story was added to when she collected and published them as *The Book of Dragons* in 1901. She dedicated it:

> To Rosamund
> chief among those for whom these tales are told
> The Book of Dragons is dedicated in the confident hope
> that she, one of these days, will dedicate a book
> of her very own making
> to the one who now bids
> Eight dreadful dragons
> Crouch in all humbleness
> at those little brown feet.

It was also in 1899 that T. Unwin Fisher published *The Story of the Treasure Seekers* on the recommendation of their reader, Edward Garnett. He was a mentor to Joseph Conrad and a key influence on the work of D.H. Lawrence, but he had foolishly turned down James Joyce's *Portrait of the Artist as a Young Man* on behalf of the publisher Duckworth in 1915. Although *The Story of the Treasure Seekers* would become a classic of children's literature, it did not have an easy start. While individual chapters appeared in *Pall Mall Magazine* and *Windsor Magazine*, it was rejected by several publishers, among them Edith's old collaborator Robert Ellice Mack who was working for Edinburgh-based publisher Thomas Nelson and Sons by then.

Perhaps she frightened them off with her terms. She told her agent William Morris Colles, the first of several to represent her, that she wanted fifty pounds plus a royalty of 16.5 per cent. A former solicitor and leader writer for *The Standard*, Colles was described by publisher William Heinemann as 'a big, burly, bearded lawyer with a wheezy infectious laugh – a sort of well-spoken, decent-minded, entirely reputable nineteenth-century Falstaff'. He had founded the Authors' Syndicate, which he operated under the auspices of the Society of Authors.[11] His impressive client list included William Somerset Maugham and George Gissing and, briefly, H.G. Wells and Arnold Bennett. Yet he was generally regarded as ineffective. Edith soon replaced him with James Brand Pinker.

Ultimately, Edith prevailed and *The Story of the Treasure Seekers* was published by Christmas 1899. There should have been a second cause for celebration as that year came to a close. In the spring of 1899, Edith, who was forty-one, had discovered she was pregnant. She decided to look for a home in the countryside where she could raise what was to be her last child. In *My School Days*, she had written longingly of a country childhood:

> Oh, those dewy mornings – the resurrection of light and life in the woods and fields! Would that it were possible for all children to live in the country where they may drink in, consciously or unconsciously, the dear delights of green meadow and dappled woodland! The delight in green things growing, in the tender beauty of the evening light on grey pastures, the glorious splendour of the noonday sun on meadows golden with buttercups, the browns and purples of winter woodlands – this is a delight that grows with ones growth, a delight that 'age cannot wither nor custom stale', a delight that the years who take from us so much can never take away – can but intensify and make more keen and precious.[12]

On a lovely spring day she was wandering along a country lane in the Well Hall district north of Eltham in the Royal Borough of Greenwich, verdant with chestnut, hawthorn, lilac blossom and Queen Anne's lace. There she stumbled upon a dilapidated eighteenth-century house that stood half a mile from the rural village of Eltham and three miles from Woolwich. It had thirty panelled rooms, a great hall and vaulted cellars.*

Edith adored it. She bought out the five-year lease that had been due to run until September 1899 and moved in that May. As soon as she arrived, she began working on *The Red House*, a celebration of her new home that was published in 1902. Len and his wife, Chloe, travel 'through green lanes where hawthorns were budding in pink and pearl' to reach a dilapidated mansion he has inherited:

The house was hidden almost – at any rate transformed, transfigured – by a network of green leaves and red buds; creepers covered it, all but. And at the side there was jasmine, that in July nights would be starry and scented, and wisteria, purple-flowered and yellow-leaved over its thick gnarled boughs, and ivy. And at the back where the shaky green veranda is over-hung by the perilous charm of the white balcony, Virginia creepers and climbing roses grew in a thorny maze. The moat was there, girdling the old lawns with a belt of silver and on it a sad swan and a leaky boat kept each other company. Yellow laburnums trailed their long hair in the water, and sweet lilac bushes swayed to look at their pretty plumes reflected in it. To right and left stretched the green tangled mysteries of the overgrown gardens.[13]

Just after they moved in, Sidney Webb told his wife Beatrice:

The Blands are living in a queer and ramshackle old house, somewhat baronial in 18th-century style, right out in the country, with a moat, swans, wild ducks & rabbits on their own 4½ acres of ground. It is an odd but attractive rough place, which they have on 5-year lease.[14]

One American visitor who remarked on the age of the house was surprised by Edith's response: 'It is not really old,' she said, 'this part of the house was built in 1740, and the original walls are only five-hundred years old.' Her visitor felt 'impossibly youthful'.[15]

In 'Mr Alden's Views,' a column for the *New York Times*, American journalist W.L. Alden confirmed:

---

* The house was demolished in 1931 and the grounds form Well Hall Pleasaunce – a tranquil garden in a bustling urban setting.

I suppose there is no objection to mentioning what every one in London knows, that 'E. Nesbit' is Mrs Bland, and that the story of the 'Red House' is in many respects a truthful narrative. I have seen the 'Red House' in question and a very attractive place it is, although I have the suspicion that the young people found it rather damp.[16]

Berta Ruck, who was a frequent visitor, also confirmed that Edith's 'lovely shabby old house with three ghosts and a moat' was exactly as she had described it in *The Red House*.[17]

The house was in poor repair and significant renovations were required to make it habitable. The oak staircase collapsed while they were moving in, confining them to the ground floor. Blocked gutters and broken leads led to flooding in the parlour; precious books and ornate Turkish carpets were destroyed. Edith filled the house with heavy oak furniture, a decision Edgar Jepson attributed to the influence of Oswald Barron who 'collected old oak, a horrible practice, in which she aided him'.[18] Her favourite feature was a moat spanned by a fifteenth-century bridge leading to an island lawn, the original site of a Norman manor house occupied by Margaret Roper, eldest daughter of Sir Thomas More.* In summer it was used for swimming and boating. In winter it made a wonderful skating rink. A red-brick Tudor barn with high chimneys and gables stood on the north side of the moat. There were sheds and stables too, and two Tudor cottages, North Lodge and South Lodge, which they let to their friends.

Edith loved the story of how Margaret Roper had kept her father's head in the original house, pickled in spices. There are echoes of this macabre tale in *Salome and the Head* (1909). She believed the house was haunted and told Andrew Lang she had evidence of a ghost in the garden. He responded:

The ghost in the garden is usually the ghost in the house. Possibly if you tried a planchette he might communicate. At all events nothing is lost by experiment.[19]

---

* When Sir Gregory Page bought the property in 1733, he pulled down the old Roper mansion and built Well Hall outside the moat. Later it was occupied by a man named Arnold, watchmaker to George III. It was let to a Major Nicholls in 1818, and it operated as a preparatory school from 1880 to 1890.

Apparently one of Edith's ghosts played the spinet, but always in the next room, while another had a disconcerting habit of standing behind her and sighing softly as she worked.

One of the first people to visit Well Hall was American writer and utopian feminist Charlotte Perkins Gilman. While visiting London she attended a meeting of the Fabian Society, and described them as 'that group of intelligent, scientific, practical and efficient English socialists'. She was struck by the odd costume adopted by several members, 'knee-breeches, soft shirts, woolen [sic] hose and sandals'. Of Edith she wrote: 'Mrs Hubert Bland asks to be introduced and asks me to dinner.' This signalled 'the beginning of a most pleasant friendship with a delightful family'.[20] In *The Living of Charlotte Perkins Gilman* she described her 'delightful visit' to Well Hall:

> The earlier mansion, built for Margaret Roper by her father, Sir Thomas Moore [sic], had been burned, and replaced by this one which they said 'was only Georgian'. Behind the house, just across a little vine-walled bridge, was a large rectangular lawn, surrounded by thick-grown trees and shrubs, outside which lay the moat that once guarded the older building. Here, in absolute privacy, those lovely children could run barefoot, play tennis and badminton, wear any sort of costume; it was a parlor out of doors. We all joined in merry games, acted little plays and fairy-tales, and took plentiful photographs.[21]

Since Edith had developed an interest in photography, she may well have taken these 'plentiful photographs'. Prominent in several is Martha, the bulldog she immortalised in her Bastable stories. Martha also appears in 'Fortunatus Rex & Co.' from *Nine Unlikely Tales*. An old lady who wishes to protect her orchard demands that the king provide her with 'a fierce bull-dog to fly at the throat of any one who should come over the wall':

> So he got her a stout bull-dog whose name was Martha, and brought it himself in a jewelled leash.
> 'Martha will fly at any one who is not of kingly blood,' said he. 'Of course she wouldn't dream of biting a royal person; but, then, on the other hand, royal people don't rob orchards.'[22]

As 1899 came to a close Edith gave birth to a child, but it was stillborn or died shortly after delivery, and they buried the tiny corpse in their new garden. At the end of *The Red House*, Chloe and Len welcome 'a very, very small usurper'. a 'pussy-kitten' into their new home, who makes her entrance as 'a fat, pink fist thrust out from beneath the pink eider-down'. There was a real baby at Well Hall too. On 6 October 1899 Alice gave birth to a healthy baby boy. They celebrated his birthday on 21 October and named him John Oliver Wentworth Bland, but he was nicknamed the Lamb. Once again Hubert was the father and Edith agreed to raise him as her own.

John was considerably younger than the other Bland children. Paul, who was nineteen by then, worked at the London Stock Exchange. Iris, aged eighteen and a talented artist like her mother, was studying at the Slade School of Art. Fabian and Rosamund, who were fourteen and thirteen, were both at school. Edith dedicated *Five Children and It*, which was published in 1902:

> TO JOHN BLAND
> My Lamb, you are so very small
> You have not learned to read at all.
> Yet never a printed book withstands
> The urgence of your dimpled hands.
> So, though this book is for yourself,
> Let mother keep it on the shelf
> Till you can read. O days that pass,
> That day will come too soon, alas!

She populated *Five Children and It* with her own children. Cyril took Paul's middle name; Iris became Anthea, the Greek word for blossom; Fabian was Robert; and Rosamund became Jane, who was known affectionately by the family nickname Pussy. In *Five Children and It*, the Lamb is called Hilary, but he is really John, 'the original little tiresome beloved Lamb', and 'they called him that because "Baa" was the first thing he ever said'.[23]

The real-life Lamb was a precocious child with an abiding interest in science. It was said of him that he read books on biology and cell life from the age of five.[24] A chemist in Eltham, who had started out as a junior apprentice in a shop on Well Hall Parade, remembered weighing a young Bland child in the shop's wicker scales. This can only have been John. This man described the Bland family as 'distinguished but very friendly and ordinary'. He found the children polite, intelligent, friendly and bright, and he was struck by how Edith treated them all equally.[25]

On 25 October 1899, when John was less than three weeks old, Edith received news that her half-sister Saretta had died at the age of fifty-five. She dedicated 'In Memory of Saretta Deakin', a moving elegy, to Saretta's daughter Dorothea. Edith too had a health scare that year. Confined to bed with what she assumed was lumbago; she was horrified when her doctor diagnosed stomach cancer and insisted on an operation. While this was being arranged she left her bed to entertain visitors, among them Laurence Housman, who knew of her diagnosis and testified that she 'carried us through the evening with colours flying, apparently in the happiest spirits possible'.[26] Happily, she had been misdiagnosed. She confided in Housman that the whole affair made her realise she had no fear of death, a discovery that satisfied her enormously.

Shaken by the experience and the loss of her half-sister, she headed for Dymchurch were her spirits were always restored.

CHAPTER 14

'MY SON; MY LITTLE SON, THE HOUSE IS VERY QUIET'

At eleven o'clock on the morning of Thursday 18 October 1900, while Fabian Bland, aged fifteen, was digging in the garden, the family doctor arrived at Well Hall accompanied by his anaesthetist. It seems Edith had forgotten they were expected, since she had to be roused from her bed. She summoned Fabian and instructed him to wash and change his clothes. As he had been suffering from a series of debilitating colds for some time, the decision had been taken to remove his adenoids, a procedure considered routine at the time and performed in the patient's home under general anesthetic. It seems entirely possible that no one thought to remind Fabian to fast beforehand. This may explain why he never came round after the operation.

When the medics were finished, they left Fabian sleeping and instructed the family to wake him after a time. Although Edith, Hubert and Alice tried for hours, they could not rouse him. Demented with grief, Edith swathed his lifeless body in blankets and hot water bottles in an attempt to warm him back to life. Eventually she allowed the coroner to be called, and while she waited she placed sixteen lit candles around his body to mark the sixteenth birthday he would never reach.[1] Fabian's death certificate attributes his death to 'Syncope following administration of chloroform properly administered for performance of necessary operation'. This finding is generally used to explain a temporary loss of consciousness that results from insufficient blood flow to the brain. In Fabian's case this loss of consciousness was permanent.

The tragedy ripped the family asunder. Three decades later, Paul could recall how his mother was 'absolutely distracted' with grief. Rosamund, who was thirteen at the time, told Doris Langley Moore that she discovered Edith was not her mother that day because she shouted at Hubert: 'Why couldn't it have been Rosamund!' Helen Macklin, who was visiting and stayed on to comfort Edith, offered a contradictory version of events. She admitted that Edith had told her Rosamund was not her child that night, and that she seemed unsettled by her presence, but she swore that Rosamund suspected nothing for some time to come. Rosamund's future husband, Clifford Dyce Sharp, supported this version since he believed that his wife only discovered that Alice was her mother in 1906.

Iris learned of the tragedy when Hubert met her off the train from London. Although Hubert's relationship with Fabian had been fraught, probably because they were both strong-willed and irrepressible, he was devastated by the loss of his son. In *Letters to a Daughter*, he wrote:

> This autumn weather, this dismal lingering death of summer, oppresses my soul, and one should be in high fettle to talk intelligently of love. Now I am not that to-day as I look out of the library window and see those big funereal cedars lords of all, the whole garden subdued to their sombre humour. Day and night the piteous leaves of all the other trees are falling, falling like slow rain-drops; and at twilight they sound upon the garden paths as the footsteps of ghosts might sound – creepy, creepy.

When he picked a rose, its pink petals 'turned livid as the lips of a corpse; it exhaled, not perfume, but an odour of death'. Even the birds are affected by his enveloping sorrow:

> The birds flutter about aimlessly, they seem to feel there is nothing left for them to do in a world full of sadness, no nests to be builded, no broods to be reared; and they haven't the heart to sing... Oh, the deathly chill of an empty and tidy nursery.[2]

Edith too found solace in writing. She addressed Fabian directly in 'The Criminal':

> My son; my little son, the house is very quiet, because all the other children grew up long ago, and went out into the world. The lamp has just been lighted, but the blinds are not drawn down now. Outside the winter dusk is deepening the shadows in the garden where, in the days when the sun shone, you used to shout and play.[3]

It would appear that grief drove a wedge between them. In her blank verse drama *Absalom, or In the Queen's Garden*, Edith appears to suggest that Hubert found consolation with another woman. When Maacah, one of three consorts of King David, learns that their son Absalom has been slaughtered in battle, she is desperate for the king to seek comfort with her, but he turns to one of the others instead.[4]

Shortly before Fabian died, the *Illustrated London News* had commissioned ten new Bastable stories from Edith, which they planned to run between November 1900 and July 1901. An eleventh was requested for their Christmas issue. It was then that Laurence Housman suggested she write about a society for being good. When T. Fisher Unwin published these stories as *The Wouldbegoods* in September 1901, Edith dedicated it:

TO
MY DEAR SON
FABIAN BLAND

It was the first in a series that won her acclaim and secured her literary legacy. She paid tribute to Fabian in her Bastable stories. He had earned the nickname 'Bloodthirsty Bill' at St Dunstan's College in Catford because he was frequently in trouble and showed little respect for authority. In 'Bill's Tombstone', chapter three of *The Wouldbegoods*, a mother believes her son has been killed but he turns up, very much alive: 'She met him at the gate, running right into him, and caught hold of him, and she cried much more than when she thought he was dead.'[5] Fabian's most prominent role is as Robert in her Psammead series, and the illustrator H.R. Miller used his own son, who had also died young, as a model for this character. He also informed Richard in *Harding's Luck* (1909), Edith's favourite of her novels. When Dickie, a boy from Deptford, travels back in time and becomes Richard, a kindly nurse declares:

There are certain children born now and then – it does not often happen, but now and then it does – children who are not bound by time as other people are. And if the right bit of magic comes their way, those children have the power to go back and forth in time just as other children go back and forth in space – the space of a room, a playing-field, or a garden alley. Often children lose this power when they are quite young. Sometimes it comes to them gradually so that they hardly know when it begins, and leaves them as gradually, like a dream when you wake and stretch yourself. Sometimes it comes by the saying of a charm.[6]

As Fabian had not been doing well at St Dunstan's, he was sent to Loretto, a strict boarding school just outside Edinburgh, but he returned home after six desperately unhappy months. He died shortly afterwards. When the children in *The Wouldbegoods* dress up to play at foxhunting, H.O. wears 'the old red football jersey that was Albert's uncle's when he was at Loretto'. When they misbehave, Oswald tells readers: 'My father said, "Perhaps they had better go to boarding-school." And that was awful because we know father disapproves of boarding-schools.'[7]

After Fabian died Edith buried herself in her work. She retreated into her little study at the top of the house, which she had furnished with 'her desk, her chair and one large crock, kept always full of flowers'.[8] Berta Ruck remembered seeing 'great childish bunches of buttercups and blue-bells'.[9] She appears to have used her own study as a model for Mother's workshop in *The Railway Children*:

> One day when Mother was working so hard that she could not leave off even for ten minutes, Bobbie carried up her tea to the big bare room that they called Mother's workshop. It had hardly any furniture. Just a table and a chair and a rug. But always big pots of flowers on the window-sills and on the mantelpiece.[10]

Hubert had a study on the ground floor and Berta Ruck remembered hearing him hit a punchbag he had installed there over and over.[11]

Edith would work feverishly when deadlines loomed. She filled page after page of the glossy, coloured paper she favoured before flinging each one to the floor until her desk became an island in a sea of unedited work. At the end of each session, she would gather these pages together to revise them. Such industriousness made 1901 the most lucrative year of her writing career. The three major books published that year were *The Wouldbegoods*, *Thirteen Ways Home* and *Nine Unlikely Tales*, the stories from each of which had been published in magazines and periodicals earlier. The reviews she was receiving for her adult books make it clear that her talent lay in writing for children, as this damning review of *Thirteen Ways Home*, published in *The Athenaeum*, makes clear:

Thirteen Ways Home, by E. Nesbit (Treherne & Co.), consists of some pretty little stories of the unexpected sort, which mostly end in a happy marriage after not too disquieting obstacles. There is really very little to say about them. We imagine most of them have already appeared in monthly magazines, and it is almost a pity they did not stay there, as they were hardly worth preserving in more permanent form.[12]

She borrowed from other writers when writing her stories for children. When *Five Children and It* was serialised in the *The Strand Magazine*, she paid tribute to F. Anstey, whose story *The Brass Bottle*, featuring a genie that grants wishes, had been serialised in the same publication two years earlier:

'It's like "The *Brass Bottle*",' said Jane.
'Yes, I'm glad we read that or I should never have thought of it.'[13]

Unlike Anstey, she had the ability to write from the perspective of a child and was brilliant at weaving magic and fantasy into their everyday lives. She opened *Five Children and It* by explaining: 'Grown-up people find it very difficult to believe really wonderful things, unless they have what they call proof. But children will believe almost anything, and grown-ups know this.'[14]

She also took inspiration from her own life. 'The Blue Mountain', one of the stories from *Nine Unlikely Tales*, features her grandfather Anthony Nesbit and her nephew, also Anthony, son of her brother Alfred Anthony Nesbit, who had died in tragic circumstances in 1894. During his life, Alfred had made his name but not his fortune as an inventor and was lauded as 'an analytical and consulting chemist of great attainments'.[15] An ink he had developed to prevent the fraudulent alteration of cheques and postage stamps was praised in *Scientific American* but was never put to commercial use.[16] Similarly, his experiments on the action of coloured light on carp were reported in the *Journal of Science* in June 1882.[17] His most celebrated experiment, perhaps, was his system for dyeing flowers, which was featured in *The Globe* under the heading 'Painting the Lily' in July 1882.[18] It was his ingenuity that made it possible for Oscar Wilde and his friends to wear green carnations to the opening night of *Lady Windermere's Fan* on 20 February 1892. In September 1913, almost two decades after his death, Edith wrote a letter to *The Globe* that was published under the heading 'Chemicals and Flowers':

Sir, – In your issue of to-day, under the head 'Chemicals and Experiments,' you state that Mr Leonard Bastin has been writing about methods of changing the colour of flowers. The discoveries treated of were made by my brother, Anthony Nesbit, in 1882, in which year flowers coloured by him were sent to Queen Victoria, and a bouquet of flowers coloured by him was presented to the then Princess of Wales, at the Savage Club. The discoveries were made in the course of experiments dealing with the veining of flowers and are chronicled, if my memory serves me, in the 'Daily Telegraph,' January 1883, among the scientific discoveries of the year. My brother is dead, and so I venture to write to claim for him the little sprig of laurel which crowns the discovery of these pretty and interesting experiments.[19]

On Christmas Eve 1879 Alfred had married Zara Ann Rogerson Tuxford, the daughter of George Parker Tuxford in whose Barnes home his father had died. Their first child, John Caleb Anthony Nesbit, was born in 1881, making him almost exactly the same age as Iris. A daughter, Zara Antonia, born in 1884, was close in age to Fabian. On 15 September 1891 a notice in the *Bankruptcy Gazette* confirmed that 'A.A. Nesbit, Analytical Chemist' had been declared bankrupt. Two years later, on 7 September 1893, he was admitted to Gray's Inn Road Workhouse but discharged after just four days. Six months later, on 19 March 1894, he died of 'pulmonary tuberculosis exhaustion'. He was just thirty-nine years old.

Edith often included chemists and inventors in her stories. One of the characters in *The Red House* is an 'experimental chemist'. A clever young chemist in *Dormant* (1911) inherits a title, a fortune and a family mystery. John Rochester in *The Lark* (1922) 'knows all about chemistry and dyes and engines and dynamite and all sorts'. He declares, 'rather bitterly', 'I shall invent something some of these days, and then you can have all the social and financial advancement you want.'[20] Her Mr Bastable is an absent-minded inventor whose business failure prompts his children to seek a family fortune. They visit a workhouse on Christmas Day in *The Wouldbegoods*. Rather than encountering hardship there, Matron invites them to tea and ushers them into 'a very jolly room with velvet curtains and a big fire, and the gas lighted'. The food is excellent and entertainment is laid on. In contrast, in *The Incredible Honeymoon* she wrote of 'the great terror of the poor – the living tomb which the English call the Workhouse'.[21]

Since Alfred's family was left penniless, Edith did what she could for them. In May 1896 she wrote to the Reverend C.H. Grinling, secretary of the London (Woolwich) branch of the Charity Organisation Society, to explain that 'all the money we can spare has to go to my sister-in-law and her children'.[22] She also helped Zara find literary work. Anthony trained as an analytical chemist and Antonia was a teacher at a London County Council school, but after a time they all left for Australia where they had family.

Edith dedicated *Oswald Bastable and Others* (1905) to 'my dear niece Anthonia Nesbit'. By then, her fortunes were improving and much of her income came from *The Strand Magazine*. Yet her relationship with this publication developed slowly. Although her dragon stories, serialised in 1899, had been popular with readers, the magazine commissioned just three stories from her in 1900 and none at all in 1901. This all changed in 1902 when she submitted nine interlinked stories that featured a magical sand fairy and five children who bore an uncanny resemblance to her own.

Harold Robert (H.R.) Miller, a young Scottish graphic artist who had trained as a civil engineer, was asked to illustrate *Five Children and It*. His ability to render her characters so perfectly, her Psammead in particular, astounded Edith. She suggested they must be connected through some form of telepathy, but he assured her that his precision owed much to her detailed, evocative descriptions. Miller was the perfect collaborator since he could accommodate her chronic tardiness and complete half a dozen elaborate drawings in just a couple of days. She always apologised profusely and promised to alter her story to fit his drawings. They had worked together for several years before they met for the first time at a party she hosted to introduce him to their young fans.

Fabian's death cast a pall over the Blands' home, but after a time they opened it to their friends once more. After all, as Edgar Jepson put it, Edith and Hubert were 'the most hospitable creatures in the County of London'.[23] H.G. Wells described Well Hall as 'a place to which one rushed down from town at the week-end to snatch one's bed before anyone else got it'.[24] Berta Ruck regarded it as 'a place of infinite hospitality, a house of call for an infinite variety'. She insisted that she 'could turn up at any time without invitation'.[25] One evening each week was devoted to political speeches and thirty to forty invited guests would be seated in rows in the grand hall as if they were at a public event. Berta Ruck remembered meeting Laurence Housman, Noel and Nina Griffith, and Cecil Chesterton, who she described as 'cherubic and argumentative'.[26] In *The Chestertons* (1941) Cecil's wife Ada described their visits to what she described as 'the head-quarters of enthusiastic youth, artists, writers, flaming socialists and decorous Fabians':

Every Saturday evening Well Hall, a huge old house, rambling and romantic, was thrown open. We used to crowd into the long, low drawing-room and listen to a challenging speech on some vexed topic. H.G. Wells, Orage,* and some of the Fabian Executive would turn up fairly regularly and contribute to the discussion. Names that later became notable in Fleet Street were familiar, Ivor Heald, the white-headed boy of the [Daily] Express, and Allan Ostler,† both of them brilliant and both killed in the Great War. Oliver Onions was another habitué, with his wife Berta Ruck.

Ada thought very highly of Edith and wrote of her:

She was a wonderful woman, large hearted, amazingly unconventional but with sudden strange reversions to ultra-respectable standards. Her children's stories had an immense vogue, and she could write unconcernedly in the midst of a crowd, smoking like a chimney all the while.[27]

If guests arrived at the front of the house they would find a placard informing them: 'The Front Door is at the Back!' This was because the front door opened directly into the long hall where dinner was served and draughts were not welcome. Those who arrived early would often

---

* Alfred Orage, editor of the *New Age*, to which Edith contributed regularly.
† Allan Ostler M.C., R.A.F., was a Yorkshire-born war correspondent with the *Daily Express* and the *Standard*. On 16 October 1918 he was killed in action, aged thirty-three, while serving as an observer. He had accompanied the Turkish Army to cover the Balkan War in 1912-13. Edith was very friendly with his younger sister Margaret. She sent her inscribed books and dedicated *The Enchanted Castle* (1907) to her when she was sixteen:
TO MARGARET OSTLER WITH LOVE FROM E. NESBIT
Peggy, you came from the heath and moor,
And you brought their airs through my open door;
You brought the blossom of youth to blow
In the Latin Quarter of Soho
For the sake of that magic I send you here
A tale of enchantments, Peggy dear,
– A bit of my work, and a bit of my heart…
The bit that you left when we had to part.

find Hubert and Edith hard at work. Mary Milton, the doctor's daughter, remembered Hubert striding out of his den, immaculate in evening dress, his indispensable monocle pressed firmly in place. Edith would then appear at the top of the stairs, 'radiant' in a vibrant, flowing silk dress paired with Turkish slippers. Along her arms jangled dozens of silver bangles, each one presented to her by Hubert to celebrate her finishing a book. She wore them always, even when bathing.

Ada Chesterton left a vivid description of Edith:

> She was a very tall woman, built on the grand scale, and on festive occasions wore a trailing gown of peacock blue satin with strings of beads and Indian bangles from wrist to elbow. Madame, as she was always called, smoked incessantly, and her long cigarette holder became an indissoluble part of the picture she suggested – a raffish Rossetti, with a long full throat and dark luxuriant hair, smoothly parted.[28]

Edith would serve her guests a late dinner at their long table in the great hall, which she had covered with dozens of roses from her garden and adorned with elaborate silver candelabra. When her bank balance was healthy, she would hire foreign chefs who kept the kitchen maids on their toes by creating a 'ballroom atmosphere in the kitchen'.[29] Nina Griffith described these dinners as 'chancy' and recalled two Swiss chefs who conjured up exquisite dishes, among them a dessert of tiny white sugar chalets, each with a real light inside. When money was scarce, guests were served simpler fare, a gigantic soup-tureen of haricot beans followed by a block of cheese and apples from the orchard. There was always plenty of wine, red and white, served in exquisite Venetian bottles.[30]

Afterwards everyone retired to the drawing room, which had been cleared for dancing. Edith would accompany her guests on the piano, playing Sir Roger de Coverley, an English country dance, or perhaps the Lancers, which was a variant of the quadrille. She would finish with an energetic Gallop. Berta Ruck described how 'cigarette in mouth, coloured Liberty draperies streaming over the piano stool, [she] would sit at the piano playing for Rosamund to sing'. Sometimes they would exaggerate some 'sloppy English drawing room ballad, such as "Love's Old Sweet Song"'.[31]

There were games too. Edith was particularly fond of charades. Another favourite of hers was 'Subjects and Adjectives', where players would choose a noun from one hat and two adjectives from another before writing a verse using all three. They also played whist, piquet, patience and chess. Boisterous games included hide-and-seek and devil in the dark, which was abandoned because it caused too much damage to their furniture. Of course, there was always talk, lots of it, and it continued late into the night. Then trains would be missed and guests would be obliged to stay the night. Next morning they would eat breakfast with Paul before he left for his job in the City.

The children were encouraged to invite their friends. As Nina Griffith reported, 'the children were never shut away, and gave their opinions as definitely and dogmatically as the rest of us'.[32] She remembered that Hubert in particular was perfectly happy to defer to youth. Berta Ruck remembered how Edith would 'cuddle [John] on her lap, smile, and join animatedly in the general conversation'.[33] 'It is as well to live with three generations at once,' she declared, 'your own, your elders and the younger ones.'[34] One young guest recalled 'very lively' gatherings during which they acted out plays Edith had written and wore elaborate costumes she had made for them. Another young woman found these gatherings excruciating, particularly when everyone was asked to 'give a song': 'I *hated* them,' she insisted. 'I also hated Mrs Bland. She snubbed the girls and flattered the boys.'[35]

Invitations were reciprocated, and Arthur Ransome remembered one gathering at G.K. Chesterton's flat near Battersea Park in 1904:

Here I met E. Nesbit and her husband, the rather florid Hubert Bland, with his monocle dangling from a broad silk ribbon, a confident, blustering creature for whose work both Chestertons had an exaggerated respect and I had none, though I had a great deal for the works of his wife.[36]

Towards the end of 1900, shortly after Fabian died, Hubert was received into the Catholic Church. He insisted that he was a lapsed Catholic who had returned to the fold, but it seems he was brought up non-conformist, possibly Plymouth Brethren. In any case, he demonstrated little interest in organised religion. In 1888, when he stood as a school board candidate for Finsbury division, he had advocated 'the entire omission of religious teaching of every kind from the curriculum of rate aided schools'.[37] Cecil Chesterton, who was also a Catholic convert, believed Hubert 'was Catholic because he felt that if one were to have a religion it must be a religion at once traditional and dogmatic'.[38]

They both joined the Church Socialist League when it was established in 1906. Hubert wrote 'Socialism and the Catholic Faith' for the Catholic Socialist Society and this pamphlet was mentioned by Sean O'Casey in his play *Drums Under the Window* (1945):

> Socialism Made Easy, a penny a copy, only a penny the copy; tuppence each, Can a Catholic be a Socialist? only tuppence each, the truth for tuppence; Hubert Bland's great work, Can a Catholic be a Socialist?[39]

Edith had been raised in the Anglican faith but she too converted to Catholicism shortly after Hubert. The faith was fashionable at that time and neither observed it closely, nor instilled it in their children. They did welcome several Catholic clergymen into their circle, notably the charismatic Monsignor Robert Hugh Benson, former Anglican priest and son of an Archbishop. He had converted in 1903 and was ordained a Catholic priest in 1904.

Benson, like Edith, wrote prolifically across several genres: historical, horror, science fiction, children's stories, plays, apologetics, newspaper articles and devotional works. His visits to Well Hall were so frequent that they converted a tiny room adjoining his usual bedroom into an oratory. It was he who introduced them to the extraordinary Frederick William Serafino Austin Lewis Mary Rolfe. Rolfe, the eldest son of a piano manufacturer, left school at fourteen but managed to secure employment as a teacher in several London grammar schools. He too converted to Catholicism and thought of becoming a Catholic priest. Sometimes he abbreviated his name to Fr. Rolfe, although it seems he was dismissed from a seminary at Oscott, near Birmingham, and the Scots College in Rome. He returned to England where he made a poor living as, variously, an artist, a photographer, an historian and a translator.

Rolfe was openly homosexual and enjoyed an intense but ostensibly chaste friendship with Benson. Before their friendship ended abruptly in 1906, they had exchanged letters several times a day. Afterwards they satirised each other viciously. Rolfe wrote books as 'Baron Corvo', and sometimes 'Frank English', 'Frederick Austin', 'A. Crab Maid', and various other unlikely monikers. Critic J. Lewis May described him as a 'strange, erratic creature, half-imposter, half-genius'. He wrote for *The Yellow Book*, and John Lane collected his stories as *Stories Toto Told Me* in 1898. Reports suggest that when he came to Lane's office to discuss a further series, he infested a chair with fleas, a legacy of time spent in a Welsh workhouse. May confirmed this:

> Corvo, I have heard it said, was not infrequently verminous, and after his departure it was found necessary to treat with abundant doses of insecticide the armchair on which he had reposed.[40]

Lane described Rolfe as 'a gaunt figure shrouded in a tattered mackintosh which might hide anything or nothing'. Yet he spoke with 'an arctic highness which strangely contrasted with his frightfully shabby garb'.[41] Rolfe in turn described Lane as 'a tubby little pot-bellied bantam, scrupulously attired and looking as though he had been suckled on bad beer'.[42]

Rolfe claimed to own original material relating to the Borgias. Grant Richards published his *The Chronicles of the House of Borgia* in 1901, and Rolfe invited Hubert to invest thousands of pounds in some related scheme. Hubert turned him down, but Edith and he did attempt to persuade Richards to publish Rolfe's satirical novel *Nicholas Crabbe, A Romance* even though it contained a description of Richards as a 'scorbutic hobbledehoy' and a 'bumptious young thing [with] a silly noddle'. It was so inflammatory and its characters were so identifiable that it was not published until 1958, decades after he died.

During visits to Well Hall Rolfe struck up an unlikely friendship with John Bland, who remembered him as 'a man of charming manners to a child, who knew all about magic and charms, who wore strange rings and told fascinating histories'. Every year on his birthday John would receive a letter from Rolfe. He described these as 'so unlike any others I ever received both in substance and in script'. He even modelled his handwriting on Rolfe's beautiful script, which had been likened to that of a mediaeval manuscript.[43] Rolfe moved abroad when John was still a child and his final years were marked by extremes of poverty and affluence. He died in Venice in 1913.

It's clear that Edith and Hubert had a habit of taking in odd waifs and strays. As Nina Griffith told Doris Langley Moore:

> Invariably, in the midst of the most distinguished gathering, one would find some weak or wounded creature who was taking shelter at Well Hall – a baby rescued from poverty or illness (who surprisingly appeared at late dinner), a poor relation waiting for a job, a painter seeking recognition, a

timid girl whom someone there believed in and encouraged to write stories. No one who knew the Blands could resist seeking their comfort and
their counsels in distress.[44]

The census of 1901 recorded Edith's old friend Ada Breakell living in the
lodge at Well Hall with her younger sister Annie, a district nurse.* Ten years
earlier, in 1891, Maggie Doran had shown up in the census record for their
home at 2 Birch Grove. In 1898 she had taken over her late father's business
and the Beckenham Directory lists 'Doran, M. and Co., Dyers' operating
out of his old premises, 31 High Street, Beckenham.[45] A short time later she
contracted pleurisy and Edith took her in once more. She was nursed by Iris
until she was transferred to the Cottage Hospital in Eltham where she died
on 25 March 1903. She was forty-seven years old and she had never married.
    Edith's mother, Sarah, had died the previous year at the age of
eighty-four after a long and trying illness. In his letter of condolence,
Laurence Housman paid tribute to the 'quiet charm' of this 'sweet and
beautiful character'. Once again Edith sought refuge in Dymchurch.
Edgar Jepson recalled:

> In the summers we still went to Dymchurch, where we always found the
> Blands. In those days Dymchurch was just a village. No strangers came to
> it for weeks on end, and if you wished to go to any place from it, you had
> to walk, drive, or bicycle… In those summers there was very good lawn
> tennis and bridge at the house of the Squire.[46]

Berta Ruck described these holidays too: 'We bathed, we tramped, we
played rounders with her on the sands'.[47] She dubbed the houses they
rented 'an annexe to Well Hall'. The little weather-boarded cottage on
the High Street, which they shared with the village post office, became
'Well Cottage'.
    She received a series of heartwarming letters from another writer who
took inspiration from the coastal Kent landscape. In 'Dymchurch Flit',
which he included in his fantasy *Puck of Pook's Hill* (1906), Rudyard Kipling
would write of Old Hobden's wife, one of the 'Marsh folk', who hails
from 'Dymchurch under the Wall'.[48] Edith admired Kipling enormously.
Oswald Barron and she had dedicated *The Butler in Bohemia* to him. When

---

* Ada Breakell died in Wimbledon on 14 November 1943. She had never married and
she left her estate of £788 to her unmarried sister Maria.

she reviewed A.E. Housman's *A Shropshire Lad* (1896) for the *National Observer*, she remarked of his poems: 'one or two have yielded a little to the wide and wonderful influence of Mr. Kipling'.[49] In November 1896 she had invited Kipling to contribute to a magazine for children she was planning to edit.* It came to nothing. She filled her Bastable stories with references to Kipling. In *The Story of the Treasure Seekers* Oswald declares of the detective stories of Émile Gaboriau: 'Of course they're not like Kipling but they're jolly good stories.' When the children meet a poet who 'didn't talk a bit like a real lady, but more like a jolly sort of grown-up boy in a dress and hat', she declares: 'I am very pleased to meet people who know their Jungle Book.' Their father tells them that this woman 'wrote better poetry than any other lady alive now'.[50] Edith enjoyed inserting herself into her books. She is Mrs Bax in *The New Treasure Seekers* (1904), who has short hair and gold spectacles, and smokes cigarettes surreptitiously.

In *The Story of the Treasure Seekers*, at the end of a chapter titled 'The Divining Rod', Oswald declares:

> But that is another story. I think that is such a useful way to know when you can't think how to end up a chapter. I learnt it from another writer named Kipling. I've mentioned him before, I believe, but he deserves it![51]

In *The Wouldbegoods* he describes Kipling as 'a true author and no rotter'. When the children play *The Jungle Book*, he insists: 'I shall be Mowgli. The rest of you can be what you like – Mowgli's father and mother, or any of the beasts.'

Edith must have been delighted when Kipling expressed his admiration for her children's stories. In March 1903 he wrote to her from South Africa, where he was living at the time:

> Dear Mrs Nesbit-Bland,
> Your letter of the 15th Feb comes out to me here but not the Red House [her novel]. I will go into Cape Town and get it from the bookseller.
> It has been on the tip of my pen to write to you again and again – on the "Would-be-goods" *several* times because I laughed over them riotously; but more particularly about the Psammead yarns.

---

* The magazine was rejected by the publisher Edith had in mind. A successful children's magazine was launched some time later by Scottish journalist and educator Arthur Mee, but she never contributed to it.

My kiddies are five and seven (they can't read thank goodness!) and they took an interest in the psammead stories – a profound and practical interest. Their virgin minds never knew one magazine from another till it dawned upon Elsie that 'a thing called the Strand', 'with a blue cover and a cab' was where the Psammead tales lived. Since which as the advertisements say I knew no peace. I have been sent for Strands in the middle of the month, I have had to explain their non-arrival; and I have had to read them when they came. They were a dear delight to the nursery and they were discussed and rediscussed in all possible lights. You see *we* have a sandpit in our garden and there was always a chance of a Psammead.

I wish I could tell you what a joy it gave them and how they revelled in the fun of it. A kiddie laughing at a joke is one of the sweetest sights under Heaven and our nursery used to double up and rock with mirth. They were very indignant when the series came to an end. They profoundly disapproved of Little Red Indians story. Why, I cannot say. It is a matter beyond me. They like best the magic gold and the attempt to buy horses and carriages, and next to that the growing up of the Baby.

In another year I shall give 'em the Would-be-goods again. They've had bits of it but it doesn't appeal, like the Psammead, to their years. If it isn't impertinence to say so I've been watching your work and seeing it settle and clarify and grow tender (this sounds like a review but it isn't). With great comfort and appreciation.

Very sincerely yours,
Rudyard Kipling[52]

He wrote from Sussex the following year, to enthuse about *The Phoenix and the Carpet*:

Dear Madam,
I take the present of yr book about Carpets in a kind spirit though it has not done me much good personally and the trouble and Fuss in the past on account of forgetfulness when I was ordered to buy serial Strands at the Station which is all of three (3) miles uphill you should have known to have appreciated. My orders were that any time I went that way to bring back a Strand and you know owing I presume to Sir G. Newnes's stinginess the Publication only comes out once a month but that didn't matter to them worth a cuss on account of their Innocence and I had to explain that too. Besides they couldn't read… they got the Governess to read to

them and me afterwards (not more than three times) and their mother just all the time… it came to fighting over looking at the pictures and splitting the Strand down Sir George Newnes's back cover… so when the book came all in one piece… I no sooner had got it than both the two of them found out by watching the Post I suppose and they have Jumped it and took it off already and God knows I am sorry for the Governess first and me after and their mother too because it will all have to be read over again. They done just precisely the same about the Psammead whose title should not have been Five Children and It because everyone calls him by his Christian name… a name is just as important to a Book as a Baby and it is born more frequent… The consequence is they are highly delighted in the School Room though they say they knew it all before and they want a lot more of the same sort quick. I am to tell you this and – I am to send you their love.

I am yrs respectfully,
Rudyard Kipling[53]

They never met, and her view of him soured in 1906 when she convinced herself that he had plagiarised *The Story of the Amulet* in his *Puck of Pook's Hill*. She complained indignantly to H.G. Wells, who had set his novel *Kipps* in and around Dymchurch, and asked for his opinion on the matter. Ironically, they would fall out a short time later. It seems she based her accusation against Kipling on his inclusion in *Puck of Pook's Hill* of a sharp-tongued fairy and two time-travelling children. His timing seemed suspicious too. While *The Story of the Amulet* was serialised in *The Strand* from May 1905, *Puck of Pook's Hill* started seven months later, in January 1906. Yet experts suggest that Kipling was a slow writer and began *Puck of Pook's Hill* as early as September 1904.

Although he had praised Kipling in a lecture he delivered to the Fabian Society, Hubert took Edith's side. In 'The Decadence of Rudyard Kipling', which appeared in the *Manchester Chronicle* in 1910, he wrote of 'the obvious, the lamentable, the almost inexplicable decline of his [Kipling's] literary power'. He admitted that he had read little of *Puck of Pook's Hill*, but insisted that he had read its sequel, *Rewards and Fairies*, with 'puzzled dismay'. He was particularly disparaging about Kipling's child characters and described them as 'two little sawdust-stuffed dolls, one in knickerbockers and the other in skirts'.[54]

From 1904 to 1911 Edith rented Sycamore House, a substantial Georgian dwelling that had once been the Rectory. Since it was let unfurnished, she filled it with second-hand odds and ends sourced from a local dealer. It became 'the Other Place'. If visitors were plentiful, she would rent 'Well Cottage' too.

It was while she was in Dymchurch that Edith invented her terrifying Ugly-Wuglies when a scene they were acting out required more characters than they had people. She painted paper faces and mounted them on coat hangers that were hung with clothes, just as her children did in *The Enchanted Castle*:

> The seven members of the audience seated among the wilderness of chairs had, indeed, no insides to speak of. Their bodies were bolsters and rolled-up blankets, their spines were broom-handles, and their arm and leg bones were hockey sticks and umbrellas. Their shoulders were the wooden cross-pieces that Mademoiselle used for keeping her jackets in shape; their hands were gloves stuffed out with handkerchiefs; and their faces were the paper masks painted in the afternoon by the untutored brush of Gerald, tied on to the round heads made of the ends of stuffed bolster-cases. The faces were really rather dreadful. Gerald had done his best, but even after his best had been done you would hardly have known they were faces, some of them, if they hadn't been in the positions which faces usually occupy, between the collar and the hat. Their eyebrows were furious with lamp-black frowns – their eyes the size, and almost the shape, of five-shilling pieces, and on their lips and cheeks had been spent much crimson lake and nearly the whole of a half-pan of vermilion.[55]

Edith must have cut a dash as she cycled down to the seafront in her billowing Liberty frocks. She would perch on a rain barrel chatting to the vicar, her amber cigarette holder clenched between her teeth, or wander arm-in-arm with Mrs Fisher, the woman who cleaned her house. She organised fundraising theatricals for local causes and petitioned for the first dustcart for the village. This dustcart was given a heroic role in *The New Treasure Seekers*:

> We heard afterwards that poor, worthy Mr Sandal had climbed a scaffolding to give a workman a tract about drink, and he didn't know the

Edith Nesbit as a child, 1862.

The Vault of Mummies, or Skeletons from St Michael's Tower, Bordeaux, 1885,
by Leon Augustin Lhermitte (1844-1925). Charcoal on paper.

"WE FOLLOWED HER ON TIPTOE, AND ALICE SANG AS SHE WENT."

An illustration from *The Story of the Treasure Seekers*; being the adventures of the
Bastable children in search of a fortune by E. Nesbit. Illustration by Gordon Browne.

Fabian Essays - Cover for a collection of essays on Socialism by the Fabian Society's members.

Fabian Bland, undated
(shortly before his death
in 1900).

Hubert Bland,
photographed by
Frederick H. Evans,
c. 1895-1900.

The house at Well Hall where E. Nesbit lived for two decades.

Alice Hoatson
and John Bland,
undated.

Portrait of George Bernard
Shaw, 1889. held in the
New York Public Library
Henry W. and Albert A.
Berg Collection of English
and American Literature.

Edith Nesbit with her son John Bland. Unnamed photographer in *The Tatler*, 10 February 1904, p. 241.

E. Nesbit holding chicks.

proper part of the scaffolding to stand on (the workman did, of course) so he fetched down half a dozen planks and the workman, and if a dust-cart hadn't happened to be passing just under so that they fell into it their lives would not have been spared.[56]

Kathleen Waters, a young visitor, left a description of Edith at this time:

[She] sat at breakfast… hung with beads and jingling silver bangles, and glowing in a flowery crimson dress like a poppy: and those young men about her all talking and arguing. We had our picnic at Hythe Canal and returned home in the evening – only to learn that there was no dinner! Our hostess had forgotten to order it. Quite unperturbed even by the appearance of several extra visitors, she disappeared while we went to dress, and when we came down, there was a perfect meal ready – an omelette about a yard long and some delicious strange drink with excellent coffee to follow. At about 10 o'clock we all bathed by moonlight.[57]

CHAPTER 15

'ALWAYS SURROUNDED BY ADORING YOUNG MEN'

According to Ada Chesterton, Edith was 'always surrounded by adoring young men, dazzled by her vitality, amazing talent and the sheer magnificence of her appearance'.[1] These would-be disciples vied eagerly for her attention, since they realised that her patronage could benefit their literary careers. She spurned those she thought insincere. Edgar Jepson observed of Alfred Sutro, a partner in a firm of wholesale merchants who had ambitions to be a writer:

> It even seemed to him that to round off his Literariness he ought to become one of Mrs Bland's young men, and he set about becoming one. But she did not see eye to eye with him in the matter. Indeed she spoke to me of his effort with indignation; I gather that she thought it monstrous pretentiousness.[2]

Sutro succeeded as a playwright and was elected, with Edith, to the dramatic sub-committee of the Society of Authors.

Edith showed no such reticence in befriending Richard Reynolds. This Liverpool-born son of a Brigadier General was nine years her junior and a brilliant scholar with a first in Classics from Balliol College, Oxford. A committed socialist, he joined the Fabian Society in 1890 and was appointed secretary. He worked as a barrister and a journalist before taking a job as a schoolmaster. Friends believed that he was passionately in love with Edith for more than a decade. It is possible that she named Richard Bastable, father of the Bastable children, as a tribute to him, since they attended the same college. She put a Richard into *Harding's Luck* too.

It was Reynolds who had come to Edith's aid when Paul contracted typhoid in October 1898 and needed to be kept in isolation. She had agreed to his suggestion that Iris and Rosamund stay in his rooms at Temple, even though they were obliged to sleep on his floor. Reynolds lived at Well Hall for several months. He was there for the census of 1901 but left for Birmingham a short time later to take up a position as schoolmaster at King Edward's School. During the long school holidays he spent time with Edith in Dymchurch. He accompanied her on boating holidays too and she mentioned him in a poem she sent to Iris's friend Douglas Kennedy in June 1902:

Dorothy, dearest of my nieces –
Her dearness breaks one's heart to pieces;
Iris, most aged of two dear daughters,
Shall dream beside the Medway waters;
And there with Esmond gay will be
Reynolds and Kennedy and me!

Although Kennedy was confined to a wheelchair, he loved boating and accepted her invitation to join them. She appears to have taken an almost motherly interest in him and he told Doris Langley Moore that she sent him 'hundreds of letters'.[3] He may have informed her lame boy, Dickie Harding, in *Harding's Luck* (1909). Her decision to allow Dickie escape his disability by travelling back in time to live as able-bodied Richard indicates a troubling sympathy with ideas underpinning eugenics and seems horrifically patronising now. It seems certain that Kennedy informed Denny in *Salome and the Head*, since he relies on a wheelchair and lives in a house on the banks of the Medway.

The 'Dorothy' Edith mentioned in the first line of her poem was Saretta's daughter Dorothea Deakin, of whom she was exceptionally fond. She dedicated *The Literary Sense* (1903) to 'Dorothea Deakin with the author's love'. Dorothea was twenty-five years old at the time they went boating, slim, raven-haired and strikingly attractive. She had aspirations to be a writer and collaborated with Edith on two one-act plays, *The King's Highway* and *The Philandrist, or The London Fortune-teller*, which were performed in the Woolwich Freemason's Hall on 13 May 1905. In 1906 Edith asked her agent James Brand Pinker to place Dorothea's novel *Georgie*, and it was picked up by the Century Company in New York.

When Dorothea's novel *The Wolves of Shiloh* was serialised in the *London Daily News*, an accompanying profile informed readers that she 'began writing when she was only sixteen', adding 'the young authoress says that she owed much to "E. Nesbit" in mastering the art of story-writing'.[4] Her story 'Candle-light', published in *Lippincott's Monthly Magazine* in May 1914, was prefaced by a short poem by Edith.[5] She made little impact. The *Gloucester Journal* described her as 'a magazine writer with a pretty style and some originality'.[6] She was included in *The Oxford Companion to Edwardian Fiction* but was merely credited with having 'published some fairly tedious comedies of village or country house life'.[7]

Edith treated Dorothea like a third daughter. In March 1904 she took her to Paris with Iris and Rosamund. Iris was a talented artist and planned to enrol in the life classes offered by the Académie Colarossi. When she showed her work at an Arts and Crafts Exhibition in Hampstead in 1906, the *Hampstead and Highgate Express* commended: 'Miss Iris Bland, daughter of the novelist E. Nesbit, whose exhibit consists of exquisite stenciling on Chiffon.'[8] Rosamund too had reason to be in Paris. A tantalising snippet in *The Writer* informed readers: 'In 1904 a bust of her [Rosamund] appeared in the Paris Salon. It shows a noble, thoughtful face marked by both intellect and beauty'.[9] Although the catalogue for 1904 includes several busts of young girls, it does not indicate which one is Rosamund.[10]

Rather than book into a hotel, Edith took a furnished flat in Montparnasse where, according to Berta Ruck, a succession of visitors enjoyed 'wolf-sized tea out of those two-handled Breton pottery cups with *brioches*, and cherry jam spread over holey French bread, and many slabs of *patisserie*'.[11] Berta, who was just a little older than Iris, was studying at the Académie Colarossi. They became friends and she described Iris as 'a dark-eyed, witty slip of a girl in a green gown'.[12] She must have been thrilled when she discovered Edith was her mother since she and her siblings were 'enraged E. Nesbit fans' who bought *The Strand Magazine* for her stories alone.[13] When they met, she christened Edith 'Duchess' after the character in *Alice in Wonderland*, and described her as 'A woman of great vitality and super-abundant energy. Tall, fresh-faced, brown-haired, with brown eyes that both saw and spoke.'*

Berta left a description of Edith at that time:

---

* According to Ruck, Edith referred to her eyes as 'green'.

E. Nesbit was then a tall, richly-coloured, handsome woman, who held her brown head well in the air, and who dressed (even in the rigidly-corseted Naughty Nineties) in flowing waistless Liberty robes, hand-embroidered at yoke and cuffs. She swept about... trailing long scarves on the ground or throwing black lace ruffles from her competent and freckled hands, but on her this fashion (or lack of it) was never a pose. It was 'her', just as her long cigarette-holders were, or her twinkle, or her demand of 'Does anybody know what I'm going to write a story about next? My God! Has nobody got a plot for me? Cat? Mouse? Rabbit?' (these were nicknames of her family), and her intent widening of the eyes as she listened to some suggestion for the story, and her hollow groan at the end of it, for she, like most story-tellers, realised the irritating truth that no *proffered* plot is going to be of use... Yet she continued to demand suggestions, to listen and to turn away in that blank-eyed, groaning despair. She loved thus to dramatise the details of daily life. She herself called this trait 'The Literary Sense' and brought out a book of short stories on that motif. But it was more than literary in her; it was the love of a bit of 'good theatre'. 'Drama, drama keeps women *going*,' I heard her say once. Of her one feels it was perfectly true. Her bright, greeny-brown eyes were full of enormous curiosity and *zest* for life; the storytelling side of it was only one facet.[14]

Edith offered this young woman some liberating advice: 'If you aren't a lady, don't try to be one,' she said, 'much better stay a free and happy bounder.'[15] Berta witnessed her shifting moods, her 'dramatic storm-and-brilliance quality', and recalled:

She could be morose as a gathering thunder-cloud. She could flash into a *prima donna*'s rage. Having spread panic, blight and depression over the entire household of which one member had displeased her, she would withdraw behind an emphatically-closed door, and there stay, leaving those who loved her to the darkness that can be felt. When she emerged – a sunburst! The entire landscape and population would bask in that genial all-pervading warmth, charm and sympathy that streamed from her – for one half-hour of which I would exchange the life-long friendship of any of your even-tempered, well-balanced, impersonal, tepid, logical Laodiceans.[16]

She detailed the 'vivid contrasts' that characterised Edith's extraordinary personality:

She was wise – and frivolous; she was kind… and so intolerant. She didn't dissect her aversions, but when she said of someone: 'Dear I don't *like* them!' it was *finis*. She was a brave socialist of pioneer views – and how artfully she included propaganda in her children's stories. But I have heard her complain that some illustration made her characters look 'as if they weren't children of *gentle folk*'![17]

Another friend of Iris's attended the Académie that spring. Arthur Watts was a handsome young man from Kent who turned twenty-one while they were there. Edith nicknamed him 'Oswald in Paris' after Oswald Barron. She dedicated *The New Treasure Seekers*:

TO
ARTHUR WATTS
(OSWALD IN PARIS)
FROM
E. NESBIT
Montparnasse, 1904

Watts, who was a talented artist and would win acclaim for his work with *Punch*, took to sending her illustrated letters signed 'Oswald'. He illustrated several of her stories, among them 'The Power of Darkness' and 'The Third Drug' for *The Strand Magazine*.[*]

At some point Hubert joined them. Novelist Arnold Bennett, who lived in the city, noted in his diary that he bumped into him with 'his Liberty-clad daughter Rosamund' at the studio of Miss Thomasson, an American painter friend of his. Although H.G. Wells had offered her an introduction to Bennett, Edith was absent that day and they did not meet during that trip. Noel and Nina Griffith joined them in April and they went to the Trocadero Museum to watch free-spirited American dancer Isadora Duncan perform to Beethoven's Seventh Symphony in front of an immense and wildly enthusiastic crowd.

While she was sitting in the public room of a Paris hotel, Edith heard someone strumming on a mandolin. She sent Rosamund to borrow matches from him and report back. It was Herman Webster, an artist

---

[*] Watts lived overseas for long periods and lost touch with the Bland family. He was killed in July 1935 when a KLM flight from Milan to Amsterdam via Frankfurt crashed in the Italian Alps. He had been rushing home to be with his second wife who had given birth to their third child days earlier.

who was studying at the Académie Julian. They christened him 'Monsieur Trente-Sept' after the number of his room. Webster took Rosamund to a concert and introduced her to American novelist and playwright Justus Miles Forman, aged twenty-nine, who was also studying in Paris.* Berta Ruck remembered him as 'a young man of parts, good looks and charm' who was 'writing a novel about a haunted man'.[18]

While her daughters and niece returned to England in May, Edith left Paris for Grez-sur-Loing, near Fontainebleau, accompanied by Herman Webster, Justus Miles Forman, Berta Ruck and Arthur Watts. They took rooms at an old farmhouse in the village and Edith covered Watts' expenses since he had no money. He had travelled there by motorcycle and he would rattle up and down the dusty white roads around Grez with one or other of them in his side-car. Their days were spent messing about on boats and barges, riding in a donkey cart and eating outdoors. Each evening they would talk, or play music and games, on a terrace overlooking the river. Berta left a lovely account:

In the evenings we supped out of doors with a lamp on the table, round which the moths fluttered and blundered. I see us now – the Duchess, with her inevitable cigarette in its long holder, her elbow on the table, the Inn cat lying asleep on the trail of her sweeping, peacock-blue robe. Mr Webster strumming his mandoline. Mr Forman fastidiously, Arthur scare-crowishly, turned-out, and myself dressed by the Duchess in a bright green silken tea-gown of her own – 'Here's a picturesque rag, Berta,' she said. 'You have it. I hate blouses and skirts, especially in a place like this. And wear a red rose in your black plaits and look as much like a [the artist Alphonse] Mucha... as you can.'[19]

Three of Webster's first etchings, small pastoral studies made in and around Grez and in the Forest of Fontainebleau, were accepted by the Salon de La Société Nationale des Beaux-Arts and he was recognised as an emerging talent. Edith had an unpleasant encounter with an alcoholic English musician who claimed he had set one of her poems to music and Forman included a similar scene in his novel *Tommy Carteret* (1905), which

---

* Forman was among the 1,198 passengers who perished when the *Lusitania* was torpedoed on 7 May 1915. He was thirty-nine and had been travelling in the hope of selling his only play, *The Hyphen*. Before boarding he had received an anonymous phone call warning him that the *Lusitania* would be blown up, but he disregarded it as a practical joke. His body was never identified.

he dedicated 'To Rosamund Bland'. In it, a young woman 'was singing a song by E. Nesbit, called "The Past"'.[20]

While she was there Edith worked on *The Incomplete Amorist*, which is set largely in Paris and which she discussed at length with Forman. As Berta Ruck recalled:

> He and the Duchess would go out and talk shop together by the hour in a crazy row-boat they had moored under the willows of the little forget-me-not bordered stream.[21]

One dashing, green-eyed character in *The Incomplete Amorist* is named 'Eustace Vernon'. In a studio in Paris, her protagonist, a young Englishwoman named Betty Desmond, is confronted with:

> The strange faces, the girls in many-hued painting pinafores, the little forest of easels, and on the square wooden platform the model – smooth, brown, with limbs set, moveless as a figure of wax.

One exchange goes: '"Go to Grez" said the other, not without second thoughts. "It's a lovely place – close to Fontainebleau."' She included images of the river in *The Incomplete Amorist* too: 'A turn of the river brought to sight a wide reach dotted with green islands, each a tiny forest of willow saplings and young alders.' Betty spots a boat moored under an aspen and decides to row to the islands. 'As she stepped into the boat, she noticed the long river reeds straining down stream like the green hair of hidden water-nixies.'[22]

During this time Edith developed a very close relationship with Berta, who took to calling her 'mother'. Her character 'Bobbie' in *The Railway Children* is Roberta, which was Berta's full name. Just as Berta was the oldest child in her family, Edith explained in *The Railway Children*: 'Roberta was the eldest. Of course, Mothers never have favourites, but if their Mother *had* had a favourite, it might have been Roberta.' Chapter seven opens:

> I hope you don't mind my telling you a good deal about Roberta. The fact is I am growing very fond of her. The more I observe her the more I love her. And I notice all sorts of things about her that I like.[23]

She also has Bobbie recite a poem that is almost identical to 'Birthday Talk for a Child (Iris)', a poem she included in *The Rainbow and the Rose* (1905). The original goes as follows:

DADDY dear, I'm only four
And I'd rather not be more:
Four's the nicest age to be −
Two and two, or one and three.
All I love is two and two,
Mother, Fabian, Paul and you;
All you love is one and three,
Mother, Fabian, Paul and me.
Give your little girl a kiss
Because she learned and told you this.

Edith dedicated *The Rainbow And The Rose* to Eleanor Ruck, Berta's mother, in commemoration of a delightful week she spent with the family in Caernarfon in Wales:

To Eleanor Ruck
Seven roses for seven days!
Now they're over, I go my ways;
With me the thought of the good week goes −
Every day was a rainbow rose.
The white rose blows in your own dear heart,
And the black in mine, now we have to part.
E. Nesbit
Bryn Teg October 31 November 6

She told Berta she 'put some of Caernarfon in The Incredible Honeymoon'.[24] One character, Colonel Bertram, was modelled on Berta's father, Colonel Arthur Ashley Ruck, who was Chief Constable of Caernarvonshire. While she was staying with them, he arranged for Edith to tour a Welsh prison. This experience appears to have affected her greatly. As she left, she turned to one convict and declared 'I wish you well'. In 'Cheaper in the End', the remarkably progressive essay she wrote for Cecil Chesterton's magazine, the *New Witness*, she declared 'we want more money spent on schools and less on jails and reformatories'.

She believed education was the key to avoiding incarceration and she explained her reasoning:

> It cannot be put too plainly that the nation which will not pay for her schools must pay for her prisons and asylums. People don't seem to mind so much paying for prisons and workhouses. What they really hate seems to be paying for schools. And yet how well, in the end, such spending would pay us! 'There is no darkness but ignorance' – and we have such a chance as has never been the lot of men since time began, a chance to light enough lamps to dispel all darkness. If only we would take that chance! Even from the meanest point of view we ought to take it. It would be cheaper in the end. Schools are cheaper than prisons.[25]

The first instalment of *The Railway Children* appeared in the *London Magazine* in January 1905. When the book version was published the following year, Edith dedicated it:

> To my dear son Paul Bland,
> behind whose knowledge of railways
> my ignorance confidently shelters

Paul, who was in his mid-twenties by then, had inspired ten-year-old Peter. He says to his mother:

> Wouldn't it be jolly if we were all in a book and you were writing it? Then you could make all sorts of jolly things happen… and make Daddy come home soon.

She responds:

> Don't you think it's rather nice to think that we're in a book that God's writing? If I were writing a book, I might make mistakes. But God knows how to make the story end just right – in the way that's best for us.

This, her most popular book, marked a shift in tone from the magical to the natural. Three 'ordinary suburban children' move with their mother from London to Yorkshire after their father has been imprisoned on a false charge of selling secrets to the Russians. A review in *Kindergarten* magazine declared:

The background of the father's imprisonment seems rather tragic for a child's book, but it is not made prominent and would, perhaps, be scarcely felt by the younger readers who will enjoy the healthy experiences of the children.[26]

The reviewer suggested that the book unfolded 'as though it might have been suggested by the Dreyfus tragedy'.[27] That political scandal was playing out in the British press as Edith was writing *The Railway Children*; Captain Alfred Dreyfus, the French artillery officer who had been convicted of treason for passing French military secrets to the German Embassy in Paris in 1895, was officially exonerated in 1906. Edith knew several Russian dissidents who lived in London. Among them was Ukrainian socialist revolutionary Sergei Stepniak, who had founded the Society of Friends of Russian Freedom in April 1890 but was killed by an oncoming train on 23 December 1895. She was also acquainted with Russian aristocrat turned anarchist Pyotr Kropotkin, who founded the Freedom Press with Charlotte Wilson. He appears in *The Prophet's Mantle*.

In *The Railway Children* Edith expressed sympathy with Russian dissidents by including a member of this movement who arrives from Siberia where he had been imprisoned for writing 'a beautiful book about poor people and how to help them'. Mother tells her children:

But you know in Russia you mustn't say anything about the rich people doing wrong, or about the things that ought to be done to make poor people better and happier. If you do, they send you to prison.

Edith put a Russian émigré into *Daphne in Fitzroy Street* too, a Mr Vorontzoff who is 'very unkempt and very shabby' and had been imprisoned and tortured in Russia. He had come to London to campaign for the oppressed but he finds the city 'so rich – so rotten'. Realising that the wealthy care little for the plight of the poor, he decides to mount 'an exhibition of paintings in which I will show, to the eyes of the half-blind, the slime of misery on which they build their palaces'.[28] Daphne realises that her compatriots are immune to terrible headlines from Russia:

The things that we read of every week in our daily papers, the things that do not take away our breakfast appetites. But 'Further Outrages in South Russia,' 'Massacre of Jews at Odessa,' 'Three Hundred Peasants

Shot down by Cossacks,' 'Children Tortured by Russian Officials' – these in cold black and white are powerless to stir jaded nerves.[29]

In 1906, Edith signed her name to 'The British Memorial to the Russian Duma', a statement of support for the Russian legislative chamber. In June 1907, she wrote a letter to the *Manchester Courier* that was published as 'Great Britain and Russia':

> The persistent rumours of a proposed alliance with the Russian Government are causing alarm and uneasiness in decent men of every shade of political opinion. An alliance with the Russian Government means, in plain words, an alliance with men in power who have not scrupled to use that power to crush with every circumstance of abominable cruelty the people of their country.

She urged readers to write to the newspapers and to their M.P. in order to 'compel our Minister to pause, to reconsider, to retreat from a position that threatens so unbearably the honour of England'.[30]

When *The Railway Children* was serialised in an American newspaper, the *Saturday Evening Post*, in 1914, Edith was paid an exceptionally high fee. Her old friend Justus Miles Forman, who had returned to his native country by then, wrote to congratulate her. She had a talent for negotiating excellent terms and she could be uncompromising when her work was used without permission. In 1904, when a young journalist named Alphonse Courlander published a story that included a song she had written about a bluebird, she wrote to him and asked for his publisher's address so she could send them an invoice. She convinced them to pay her twenty pounds and invited Courlander to tea to thank him for his cooperation. Afterwards she took an interest in his career and befriended his wife, Elsa.

This was not the first time she had asserted her rights. In a letter published in the *St James's Gazette* on Saturday 24 April 1897, she complained about a poem of hers that had appeared in the *Weekly Sun*. 'No acknowledgement of its source was appended and the name affixed was E. Nesbitt (the name I believe of another writer),' she explained. When the editor had refused to pay her, she threatened him with her solicitor and received payment by return of post.[31] In February 1907 the *Yorkshire Post* reprinted, without permission or payment, a poem she had translated for the *Daily Chronicle*. She instructed her agent James Brand Pinker to write to the editor:

Mrs Nesbit [sic] will be glad to know what fee you propose to pay for the use of the poem, and she thinks it should not in any case have been published in an incomplete form, without the fact being explained.

Pinker received an unsatisfactory response and published the exchange in *The Author*, explaining that he did so:

To draw attention to the extraordinary attitude towards authors who make the very reasonable request that they should be remunerated for the use of their property, and that such property should not be annexed without acknowledgement of the source from which it is taken.[32]

Edith's steely determination spilled over into other aspects of her life. When some troublesome tenants refused to leave one of the cottages at Well Hall, she let the adjoining cottage to Sergeant William Birbeck and his wife Marjorie, and the unwanted tenant left shortly afterwards. In *The Red House*, when Len and Chloe want to get rid of Prosser, a bricklayer's labourer, and his wife, a 'slatternly drab of a dusty-haired woman', they let the neighbouring cottage to a policeman. The newly vacated fictional cottage is let to 'a journalist, or an author, or something'. In real life, Edith let her cottage to Sidney Lamert, who was managing editor of a London broadsheet, *The Sun*. Like his fictional alter ego, he left his home each day 'to fight with beasts in the newspaper offices of Fleet Street'. Both men were war correspondents; Lamert covered the Boer War for the London *Daily Express*.* It was he who recommended that Fabian be sent to Loretto School.

Edith often included real people in her novels and stories. Laurence Housman believed either he or Lamert had inspired Father in *The Phoenix and the Carpet*. She included two real magicians in *The Railway Children*, and hinted at an exciting new project:

I don't suppose they had ever thought about railways except as means of getting to Maskelyne and Cooke's, the Pantomime, Zoological Gardens, and Madame Tussaud's.

---

* Afterwards Lamert worked for the London *Financial News* and edited the *Money Market Review*. He was appointed Chairman and Managing Director of Thomas de la Rue and Company Limited, a specialist printing company. He developed an interest in politics and was unsuccessful in contesting the Buckrose (Yorkshire East Riding) constituency as a Liberal candidate in 1929. He married Elizabeth (née Sheepshanks) and they had a daughter Margaret.

John Nevil Maskelyne and George Alfred Cooke were hugely popular stage magicians. They often worked with a third magician, David Devant. Towards the end of 1906 Edith was supervising rehearsals for a Christmas performance of *The Magician's Heart*, a play in three scenes, in St Georges Hall, Langham Place. A version of 'The Magician's Heart' is included in *The Magic World* (1912). According to the *Pall Mall Gazette*, this play 'tells of the adventures of a wicked magician who casts a spell over a beautiful princess and made her ugly'. Readers were informed that 'Messrs Maskelyne and Devant have produced new tricks, illusions and magical effects to accompany it'.[33] Devant played 'Professor Taykin' in the play and Edith made his most famous trick, 'The Mascot Moth', the centrepiece. A review in *The Morning Post* declared:

> Mr Devant brings before us all the wonders of E. Nesbit's fairy story: it is like reading about the 'Phoenix and the Fairy Casket' or 'The Amulet' with the authoress's imaginings rendered in living pictures.[34]

She put Devant into *The Story of the Amulet* too:

> Though the eyes of the audience were fixed on Mr David Devant, Mr David Devant's eyes were fixed on the audience. And it happened that his eyes were more particularly fixed on that empty chair. So that he saw quite plainly the sudden appearance from nowhere of the Egyptian priest.[35]

He also appears in *The Enchanted Castle* with his partner Maskelyne:

> They were alone in the room. The jewels had vanished and so had the Princess. 'She's gone out by the door, of course,' said Jimmy, but the door was locked. 'That is magic,' said Kathleen breathlessly. 'Maskelyne and Devant can do that trick,' said Jimmy.[36]

Many of Edith's young friends had married by the end of the first decade of the new century. So too had her daughters Iris and Rosamund, although neither relationship would be successful. While Iris chose poorly, Rosamund was pushed into marriage to avoid a disastrous affair with a family friend. Edith's intense relationship with Richard Reynolds had lasted ten years and appeared to have a sexual dimension. When he decided to marry her niece Dorothea, friends and family believed she did all she could to prevent this. She did not succeed. Dorothea was thirty-four when they married on 21 December 1910, at Saint Mary's Church in Finchley. Her new husband was a decade older. Dorothea suffered from poor health and in 1922 Reynolds left his job at King Edward's School in Edgbaston to move with her and their three daughters, Diana, Hermione, and Pamela to Anacapri on the island of Capri, where Dorothea died two years later.* Edith, who was ill herself by then, wrote:

> Poor Dorothy is dead at Lugano after years of suffering. Seems hard that she should be taken from her three little children and I should be left a withered tree.[37]

CHAPTER 16

'ERNEST, I'VE COME TO STAY'

When Graham Wallas,* a fellow Fabian, introduced Edith to science fiction writer H.G. Wells in 1902, she was amused to discover that, although
familiar with her work, he had always assumed she was a man. To per-
petuate the joke, Wells took to calling her 'Ernest' every time they met.
On one memorable occasion, he turned up at Well Hall, suitcase in
hand, and announced, 'Ernest, I've come to stay.' Wells, the son of a
lady's maid and a gardener-turned-shopkeeper, had endured a miserable,
impoverished youth blighted by depression and an overwhelming sense of
doom. On reading Darwin's theories, he became convinced that evolution
would lead inevitably to extinction. He was exceptionally clever and was
awarded a scholarship to the Normal School of Science (now Imperial
College London) to train as a science teacher. When ill health cut his
teaching career short, he turned to journalism instead.

In 1891 Wells married his cousin Isabel, but the marriage ended when
he left her for one of his students, Amy Catherine Robbins, whom he
nicknamed 'Jane'. They lived together for a time and were married in
1895. Wells was plagued by ill-health but in 1901, after he was treated by
a doctor in Kent, he felt so much better that he moved to the coastal village of Sandgate with Jane and their two young sons. He was delighted to
learn that Edith and Hubert could often be found in nearby Dymchurch,
just a few miles along the coast. He knew them from the Fabian Society,
which he joined in 1903, and he later described them in *Experiment in
Autobiography*, although he had fallen out with them by then:

---

* Wallas, a social psychologist and educationalist, who would co-found the London
School of Economics, makes an appearance in *Wings and the Child* when Edith describes
encountering 'the Discobolus whom we all love and who is exactly like Mr Graham
Wallas in youth'.

E. Nesbit was a tall, whimsical, restless, able woman who had been very beautiful and was still very good-looking; and Bland was a thick-set, broad-faced aggressive man, a sort of Tom-cat man, with a tenoring voice and a black ribboned monocle and a general disposition to dress and live up to that.[1]

Jane and he were invited to Well Hall and learned to play badminton there. Wells recalled:

She [Edith] ran a great easy-going hospitable Bohemian household at Well Hall, Eltham, an old moated house with a walled garden. Those who loved her and those who wished to please her called her royally 'Madame' or 'Duchess,' and she had a touch of aloof authority which justified that.[2]

Edith thought highly of Wells as a writer and valued his opinion on her work. He wrote to congratulate her on *The Literary Sense*, which he liked 'immensely', but he was less impressed with *Thirteen Ways Home*, since he found it too sentimental. She hated to be criticised and chided in response:

Love is not always the detestable disintegration that you pretend to think it. Sometimes, and much oftener than you admit, it is 'nice straight cricket'. Anyhow one wishes it to be that – you do, too.

She closed this letter by scolding: 'But it is a dreadful thing, and one of the curses of middle age to forget how to be sentimental.'[3]

In December 1904, in a letter he addressed to 'Steamed Lady', Wells expressed huge admiration for *The Phoenix and the Carpet* and assured Edith that the Phoenix was the greatest of her characters. 'Your destiny is plain,' he wrote:

You go on every Xmas never missing a Xmas, with a book like this, and you will become a British Institution in six years from now. Nothing can stop it. Every self-respecting family will buy you automatically and you will be rich beyond the dreams of avarice, and I knock my forehead on the ground at your feet in the vigour of my admiration of your easy artistry.[4]

In 1905 Wells gave Edith a presentation copy of *The Time Machine* inscribed 'To E. Nesbit from H.G. Wells and thank God for her'. After his *A Modern Utopia* was serialised in the *Fortnightly Review*, she assured him: 'I've read your Utopia again. I don't disagree as much as I thought.'[5] She mentioned his *The Time Machine* in her story 'The Dwellers', which she wrote in April 1909 after they had fallen out:

> Why not cave dwellers, who had gone on unsuspected by the busy world – like in Mr Wells' 'Time Machine' – lurking underground. I did wish then that I hadn't read the 'Time Machine'.[6]

In happier times she put him into *The Story of the Amulet*:

> 'Why do you call him "Wells"?' asked Robert, as the boy ran off. 'It's after the great reformer – surely you've heard of HIM? He lived in the dark ages, and he saw that what you ought to do is to find out what you want and then try to get it. Up to then people had always tried to tinker up what they'd got. We've got a great many of the things he thought of. Then "Wells" means springs of clear water. It's a nice name, don't you think?'

Just as she had asked Kipling, Edith asked Wells, an accomplished cartoonist, if he would contribute an illustrated piece to the children's magazine she was planning. They were exchanging playful letters at the time. In one she confessed to her dislike of housework:

> Directly I got home the horrors of housekeeping clawed me, and I've lived in a wild whirl of misery ever since… It is most horribly hard on women who work; that they should have, as well, to constantly fight with beasts at Ephesus – I mean in the kitchen.[7]

On one occasion she asked Wells if she might bring Berta Ruck and Richard Reynolds to meet him. Berta was particularly keen since she admired him hugely and regarded him as 'the determined fighting champion for better things on earth'. She remembered: 'I knew him when his zenith was approaching. He was beginning to be acclaimed as a prophet who would leave his imprint on the generations.'[8]

When Wells turned up unannounced during the summer of 1905, Edith was delighted. He stayed for a week and sat in her lovely garden working on a first draft of his novel *In the Days of the Comet*; it was published the following year. Once his day's writing was done, he joined energetic games of badminton. This was a habit of Edith's too. Berta Ruck confirmed that she would write a chapter of three to five thousand words, send it to be typed, then head outdoors to do 'some quite hefty gardening' or play 'a hard game of badminton'.[9]

While Wells was with them, Edith organised evening tableaux and charades themed on the titles of his books. He read fairy tales to John, aged six, flirted with nineteen-year-old Rosamund, and stayed up until two or three in the morning chatting with his hosts and fellow guests. Richard Reynolds was there, as was Marshall Steele's daughter Enid, and a young man named Horace Horsnell, who was known affectionately as 'Jimmy'. Horsnell was working as Edith's secretary at the time, a role he occupied on and off for eight years.[*] They knew each other because he had shared rooms with Arthur Watts, 'Oswald in Paris'. Edith dedicated *Daphne in Fitzroy Street* to him.

Wells invited Edith to visit Spade House on her way to Dymchurch later that year; 'Miss Ruck and Enid and Reynolds count as *Blands*,' he assured her. Since Jane and he could not accommodate the full party, he suggested they come in 'ones and twos and threes' like a 'circulating library'. He set aside, for the full month of September, a bedroom with two beds, which he christened 'the Well Hall room'. He even planned to 'erect a sort of badminton'.

Rosamund was showing an interest in writing at the time, and Wells threatened playfully to 'go thoroughly into the sorrows of an incipient literary career' while she was there. Turning to Iris, he admitted, 'I never *have* talked to Iris.'[10] Although Iris was artistic, she was far less flamboyant than her half-sister. Ada Chesterton commented on this:

> With such magnetic personalities in the family Paul Bland and his sister Iris were overshadowed, but Rosamond [sic], the other sister, was too dominant to be obscured. Dark and comely, with a full figure and lovely eyes, she was very attractive, and many of the older men completely lost their heads over her.[11]

Ironically, it was Rosamund, or 'Rom', who was most like Edith. In 'To A Child (Rosamund)', a poem from *The Rainbow and the Rose*, Edith called

---

[*] Horace Horsnell became a playwright, drama critic and author in his own right, and wrote as 'H.H. of the *Observer*' for a time. He wrote supernatural fiction and is profiled in *Shadows in the Attic: A Guide to Supernatural Fiction, 1820-1950*.

her 'my little lovely maid'. Everyone assumed they were close and several people remembered Rosamund singing sweetly to Edith's accompaniment, their lovely melody floating out through the balconied window of the upstairs drawing room and across the rose garden. When Berta Ruck learned the truth, she exclaimed: 'You're so like her!... How could one have thought – ! I should have said the most like of all her children,' to which Rosamund responded serenely: 'I know. Convenient... that we've all got these brown eyes.'[12]

Edith was horrified by Wells's threat. 'Don't, please don't discourage Rosamund,' she begged:

> She *must* earn her living. If Hubert and I were to die she'd have to earn it at once: I want her to be able to earn it by writing – and not to have to go into a shop or be a humble companion.[13]

Opportunities for young women were limited at the time, and she encouraged Rosamund's precocious talent. In 1908 a profile in *The Writer* informed readers: 'Miss Bland began to write at an early age, and there are in existence verses of hers accompanied by her own illustrations executed at the age of five.'[14] When she was fifteen she collaborated with Edith on *Cat Tales* (1902), a slight picture book published by Nister in London and Dutton in New York. Although it is attributed to 'E. Nesbit and Rosamund E. Bland', Edith's name is considerably more prominent on the cover. Rosamund also wrote stories as 'Rosamund Edith Nesbit Bland', but she never came close to emulating Edith's success.

In October 1905 Wells returned to Well Hall accompanied by Jane. Edith was completing the final chapters of *The Railway Children* at the time. She was halfway through *The Story of the Amulet*, which was being serialised in *The Strand Magazine*, and she was working on *The Magician's Heart* too. Shortly afterwards, she wrote to tell them: 'I have finished The Railway Children which has sat on my bent and aged shoulders for nearly a year!!!!!!!' Perhaps that's why 'Jimmy' Horsnell could accept Jane Wells' invitation to come to Spade House and help her type up her husband's work. He worked for them on and off for years.

Edith, Iris and Rosamund planned to visit the Wells's in December 1905, but they postponed when Iris fell ill with suspected appendicitis. Once she was well, she asked if she might visit her fiancé John Austen Philips and Edith went with her. When they finally got to Spade House in January, Edith was out of sorts. She apologised for having been a 'dull guest' in her thank-you letter. When the Wells came to Well Hall in early spring, Rosamund was staying with the Steele family. She wrote to tell them 'the only thing I have to look forward to is my visit in April'. Iris wrote too. In an intriguing postscript, she asked Jane not to reply, since she was 'so much disliked at head quarters now-a-days' that she would 'surely answer back' if she was asked awkward questions.[15]

There was always some drama playing out. As Wells wrote of Edith and Hubert:

The two of them dramatized life and I had as yet met few people who did that. They loved scenes and 'situations.' They really enjoyed strong emotion.

He observed that, when the Blands were around, 'rumour moved darkly and anonymous letters flitted about like bats at twilight'.[16] Recalling 'an atmosphere of talk, charades, mystifications and disputes', he remarked:

All this E. Nesbit not only detested and mitigated and tolerated, but presided over and I think found exceedingly interesting. Everywhere fantastic concealments and conventions had been arranged to adjust these irregularities to Hubert's pose of ripe old gentility. You found after a time that Well Hall was not so much an atmosphere as a web.[17]

Wells was an unapologetic and open advocate for free love and, like Hubert, had numerous affairs, some more significant than others. Apparently Hubert spoke often to him of his illicit romances. Wells wrote:

He would give hints of his exceptional prowess. He would boast... He was, he claimed to me at least, not so much Don Juan as Professor Juan. 'I am a student, an experimentalist,' he announced, 'in illicit love.'

He believed Hubert enjoyed the deception:

It had to be 'illicit' and that was the very gist of it for him. It had to be the centre of a system of jealousies, concealments, hidings, exposures, confrontations, sacrifices, incredible generosities – in a word, drama. What he seemed most to value was the glory of a passionate triumph over openness, reason and loyalty – and getting the better of the other fellow. The more complex the situation was, the better it was fitted for Bland's atmosphere.[18]

Tensions came to a head after Wells became involved with Rosamund, a liaison he attempted to justify in *H.G. Wells In Love*:

In that hothouse atmosphere of the Bland household at Dymchurch and Well Hall I found myself almost assigned as the peculiar interest of Rosamund, the dark-eyed sturdy daughter of Bland and the governess Miss Hoatson. Rosamund talked of love and how her father's attentions to her were becoming unfatherly. I conceived a great disapproval of incest, and an urgent desire to put Rosamund beyond its reach in the most effective manner possible, by absorbing her myself.[19]

This accusation was highly damaging and Wells cited no evidence to support it. Yet Hubert did have an oddly intimate relationship with his daughter; he dedicated *Letters to a Daughter* to her, writing 'we have been as intimate as most fathers and daughters; more intimate I fondly think'.[20] He was clear about the nature of this intimacy, and explained:

His daughter is the only women in all the world for whom a man five-and-twenty years her senior can feel no stir of passion, no trace of that complex emotion that modern novelists and people of that sort are so pleased to call sex-love; the only woman from whom he cannot possibly evoke passion in return.[21]

Exactly what happened between Rosamund and Wells remains unclear. Accounts suggest that, sometime during the summer of 1908, Hubert, accompanied by Clifford Dyce Sharp, a young Fabian, intercepted them at Paddington station. They may have been eloping or simply heading to Paris for the weekend. There is some suggestion that Rosamund may have been disguised as a boy, which would indicate it was all a bit of a lark. Various reports suggest that Hubert hauled Wells off a train and punched him. Certainly, in *Letters to a Daughter*, he had promised to 'punch a man who tried to take you away from me'.[22] Wells played the whole thing down and denied any genuine interest in Rosamund, but he confided in Violet Hunt, another of his lovers: 'I have a pure flame for Rosamund who is the Most – Quite!'[23]

According to Alice, Edith was incandescent with rage and sent an abusive letter to Jane Wells. Wells commented on this too:

Miss Hoatson, whose experiences of life had made her very broad-minded, and who had a queer sort of liking for me, did not seem to think this would be altogether disastrous for her daughter; but presently Mrs Bland, perceiving Hubert's gathering excitement in the tense atmosphere about us, precipitated accusations and confrontations. Bland stirred up her strain of anti-sexual feeling. She wrote insulting letters to Jane, denouncing her tolerance of my misbehaviour which came rather oddly from her.[24]

He gave his version of what had transpired:

Rosamund was hastily snatched out of my reach and, in the resulting confusion, married to an ambitious follower of my party in the Fabian Society, Clifford Sharp – and so snatched also out of the range of Hubert's heavy craving for illicit relations. It was a steamy jungle episode, a phase of coveting and imitative desire, for I never found any great charm in Rosamund... in that damned atmosphere that hung about the Blands, everyone seemed impelled towards such complications; it was contagious...[25]

This episode provoked a breach between Wells and the Blands, and he labelled them 'the strangest of couples'.[26] Dismissing Hubert as 'a tawdry brain in the Fabian constellation', he observed:

The incongruity of Bland's costume with his Bohemian setting, the costume of a city swell, top-hat, tail-coat, greys and blacks, white slips, spatterdashes and that black-ribboned monocle, might have told me, had I had the ability then to read such signs, of the general imagination at work in his *persona*, the myth of a great Man of the World, a Business Man (he had no gleam of business ability) invading for his own sage strong purposes this assembly of long-haired intellectuals. This myth had, I think, been developed and sustained in him, by the struggle of his egoism against the manifest fact that his wife had a brighter and fresher mind than himself, and had subtler and livelier friends.[27]

He declared that Edith possessed 'a certain essential physical coldness' and sneered that 'most of her activity went into the writing of verse, rather insincere verse, rather sentimental stories for adults and quite admirable tales for children'. Yet, his excruciating analysis of her marriage does include a degree of sympathy:

> In the end she became rather a long-suffering lady, but her restless needle of a mind, her quick response, kept her always an exacting and elusive lady. It was I am convinced because she, in her general drift, was radical and anarchistic, that the pose of Bland's self-protection hardened into this form of gentlemanly conservatism.[28]

Although Wells could see that Edith accommodated Hubert's behaviour, he insisted that cracks lay close to the surface of their relationship:

> She acquiesced in these posturings. If she had not, I suppose he would have argued with her until she did, and he was a man of unfaltering voice and great determination. But a gay holiday spirit bubbled beneath her verbal orthodoxies and escaped into her work. The Bastables are an anarchistic lot. Her soul was against the government all the time.
>
> This discordance of form and spirit lay on the surface of their lives. Most of us who went to them were from the first on the side of the quicksilver wife against the more commonplace, argumentative, cast-iron husband. Then gradually something else came into the *ensemble*. It came first to the visitor at Well Hall as chance whisperings, as flashes of conflict and fierce resentment, as raised voices in another room, a rush of feet down a passage and the banging of a door.[29]
>
> I found these two people and their atmosphere and their household of children and those who were entangled with them, baffling to an extreme degree. At the first encounter it had seemed so extraordinarily open and jolly. Then suddenly you encountered fierce resentment, you found Mrs Bland inexplicably malignant; doors became walls so to speak and floors pitfalls. In that atmosphere you surprised yourself. It was like Alice through the Looking Glass; not only were there Mock Turtles and White Queens and Mad Hatters about, but you discovered with amazement that you were changing your own shape and stature.[30]

When Shaw attempted to mediate, Wells dismissed him as 'an unmitigated middle Victorian ass'. In an excoriating letter, he railed:

You play about with ideas like a daring garrulous maiden aunt, but when it comes to an affair like the Bland affair you show the instincts of conscious gentility and the judgement of a hen. You write of Bland in a strain of sentimental exaltation, you explain his beautiful, romantic character to me – as though I don't know the man to his bones. You might be dear Mrs Bland herself in a paroxysm of romantic invention. And all this twaddle about 'the innocent little person' [Rosamund]. If she is innocent it isn't her parents' fault anyhow.[31]

Naturally Shaw had the perfect riposte. He described Wells as 'the most completely spoilt child I have ever known'.[32]

The debacle with Rosamund damaged the relationship between Wells and Shaw, but the campaign Wells launched to reform the Fabian Society cracked it wide open. Although Wells appeared sincere, Ford Madox Ford claimed he had boasted: 'Fordie, I'm going to turn the Fabian Society inside out and then throw it into the dustbin.' Ford was aghast at such disingenuousness and wrote:

Never would he think of becoming anything so detrimental as a politician. He was just going to upset the society for a lark because it was so dull and pompous and because he wanted to introduce some imagination into its methods... and because he wanted to study the methods of politicians. Then he would pull out and write political romances with all the local colour correct.[33]

If it was a lark, Wells certainly went to great lengths to pull it off. If he was to be successful, he needed to displace the Fabian executive, the 'Old Gang', and Hubert was its longest standing member. Wells, who was so compelling on the page, was also a notoriously poor public speaker. In *The History of the Fabian Society*, Edward Pease noted that he deployed a 'low monotonous voice, addressed to a corner of the hall'. This left him 'severely handicapped in his contest with the skilled debaters of the "Old Gang"'. Undaunted, he launched his campaign by delivering two key lectures early in 1906. His delivery may have been poor, but his content was provocative. The first, 'The Misery of Boots', contained overt criticisms of Sidney and Beatrice Webb but was hailed as a brilliant critique. The second, 'Faults of the Fabians', which fired up an increasingly heated debate, was summarised by Pease:

On February 9th the great controversy began by the paper entitled 'Faults of the Fabians,' read by Mr Wells to a members' meeting and subsequently issued as a private document to all the members of the society. It was couched altogether in a friendly tone, expressed cordial appreciation of the record of the Society, but criticised it for lack of imaginative megalomania. It was "still half a drawing-room society," lodged in "an underground apartment," or "cellar," with one secretary and one assistant.[34]

A special committee was established in response. During 1906 and 1907 debates were conducted at members-only meetings. Since Shaw led for the Executive, the controversy narrowed to Wells versus Shaw.

Many Fabians welcomed this push for reform. The special committee agreed that the Society's Basis should be rewritten, its name should be changed, its executive should be enlarged, new members should be recruited and candidates should be put up for Parliament. Flushed with success, Wells argued that this amounted to a vote of no confidence in the existing executive. He hoped to win Hubert's support, but Shaw warned Hubert to tread carefully so he merely pointed out that, rather than initiating grassroots reform among young Fabians, Wells was representing middle-aged members of the special committee. Although Wells was appointed to the Executive and his ideas were given a fair hearing, he felt he was making no real impact. He broke with the Fabian movement two years later. Shaw summed up the whole affair:

To Fabian socialist doctrine he [Wells] could add little; for he was born ten years too late to be in at its birth pangs. Finding himself only a fifth wheel in the Fabian coach he cleared out; but not before he had exposed very effectively the obsolescence and absurdity of our old parish and county divisions as boundaries of local government areas.[35]

One legacy of all this upheaval was the establishment, at Wells's suggestion, of an educational and social group that was dubbed the Fabian Nursery. It was open to members aged twenty-eight and under, who were encouraged to attend parties, dances, country rambles, musical entertainments and lectures. Rosamund was appointed secretary and Clifford Dyce Sharp was treasurer. When they married in September 1909, Ada Chesterton declared 'Clifford Sharp carried off the prize'. Although she acknowledged that he was a 'good-looking boy, with shining fair hair and very good nose... almost a Georgian type, with an inborn chivalry for women', she confessed to finding him 'painfully priggish and pompous'. She observed that he 'gave little promise at that time of his future brilliance, though he was very controversial even then'.[36]

Beatrice Webb thought Rosamund 'a charming little person... with literary tastes and housewifely talents', but she regarded Sharp as 'not a sympathetic or attractive personality', and added 'he has little imagination, he is quite oddly ungracious in his manner'. Sharp had been born into a strict Nonconformist family from Surrey. He abandoned an engineering degree at University College London and worked as a journalist instead. When the Webbs founded the *New Statesman* in 1913, they appointed him editor.

By the time Rosamund was married, Wells had embarked on a tempestuous affair with Amber Reeves, another member of the Fabian Nursery. A brilliant young woman, she was a first class honours student and had co-founded the Cambridge University Fabian Society (CUFS), the first to enlist women from its founding. She had a daughter with Wells before she too was married off to a suitable man, a young lawyer named Rivers Blanco White. 'I did not arrange to marry Rivers,' she insisted, 'he arranged it with H.G., but I have always thought it the best that could possibly have happened.'[37]

Beatrice Webb condemned this 'sordid intrigue with poor little Amber Reeves', and insisted that, had her parents known of his attempted seduction of Rosamund, they never would have allowed her relationship with Wells to develop.[38] She had good reason to feel ill disposed towards Wells. As Shaw explained, he had 'caricatured, abused, vilified and lampooned her again and again'.[39] In *The New Machiavelli* (1910), Wells's alter ego Dick Remington has an affair with 'Isabel Rivers', who is a blending of Amber and Rosamund. Beatrice is caricatured as aggressive, domineering Altiora Bailey, a character she described as 'really very clever in a malicious way'.[40] In early editions Wells lampooned the Blands as the spiteful and intrusive Booles, 'queer rivals and allies and under-studies of the Baileys', but he wrote them out later, or melded them with the Baileys. At one point Remington declares of Mr Boole:

I particularly recall a large, active, buoyant, lady-killing individual with an eyeglass borne upon a large black ribbon, who swam about us one evening. He might have been a slightly frayed actor in his large frock-coat, his white waistcoat, and the sort of black-and-white check trousers that twinkle. He had a high-pitched voice with aristocratic intonations and he seemed to be in a perpetual state of interrogation. 'What are we all he-a for?' He would ask only too audibly. 'What are we doing he-a? What's the connection?'[41]

He characterised Mrs Boole as 'a person of literary ambitions' and 'a vulgar careerist aiming only at prominence'. Remington declares that she 'writes a poor and slovenly prose and handles an argument badly'. He describes how the Booles 'set themselves industriously with all the loyalty of parasites to disseminate a highly coloured scandal':

Boole, I found was warning fathers of girls against me as a 'reckless libertine,' and his wife, flushed, roguish, and dishevelled, was sitting on her fender curb after dinner, and pledging little parties of five or six women at a time with infinite gusto not to let the matter go further.[42]

Wells includes 'a youngster named Curmain' in *The New Machiavelli*. This man acts as supplementary typist and secretary to both Remington and Mrs Boole. He is described as a 'tall, drooping, sidelong youth with sandy hair, a little forward head and a long thin neck', and he is almost certainly Jimmy Horsnell. When Remington learns that Curmain has passed letters he received from his young lover Isabel to Mrs Boole, he remarks that she 'wasn't ashamed to use this information in the service of the bitterness that had sprung up in her since my political breach with the people to whom she had attached herself'.[43]

Clifford Sharp edited the *New Statesman* for many years, but was dismissed in 1930 on account of his chronic alcoholism. Afterwards he would turn up and sit behind his old desk, drinking whisky and drafting copy. He was a morose drunk. Leonard Woolf described him as 'a curiously chilly and saturnine man'.[44]

After Sharp lost his job, Rosamund, who was deeply in debt and desperate for work, took on some copywriting for an advertising agency. In this capacity she asked Wells to recommend a brand of cigarettes. In her letter, she recalled:

I remember I give you promise on the seashore at Dymchurch *twenty-two* years ago that I would tell you if ever I was stranded. You told me then that Clifford Sharp would be no good to me. How terribly, terribly right you were.[45]

She wrote in a letter dated 3 September 1930: 'Dear H.G. Clifford came home the other night & thrust a page of "The Tatler" under my nose, saying "There's H.G. for you." And it really was.'[46]

Rosamund separated from Sharp in 1932, but she took him back a few months later and they lived off her tiny income. Poor Sharp made strenuous attempts to give up alcohol but died of complications related to his alcoholism in 1935. In September 1933 Rosamund had written to Wells:

> By degrees I got used to the idea that I didn't exist except simply as a thread on which all sorts of odds and ends are stuck together… Yet I am glad so many of your bits stuck.[47]

She dedicated *The Man in the Stone House* (1934), her semi-autobiographical novel, 'to my first love and to my last love'. This odd, unsettling book, set on Romney Marsh, documents a love affair between a teenage girl named Monday Wallace and a much older man who resembles Wells. He is 'the hero and fascinated villain of all her daydreams'.[48] This man tells her: 'I'm by way of being an author and I came here to write a book, a book which requires a good deal of thinking about.'[49] He wonders if he is 'guilty of forcing a bud into too early a blooming'. Rosamund wrote: 'Her love for him was only a child's love, he believed but there was sex in it, for all that. Sex flowing in the right channel, to mature later, when the right time came.'[50]

CHAPTER 17

'I WANT THE PLAIN NAKED UNASHAMED TRUTH'

In April 1905 Edith had written a disconsolate letter to her agent, J.B. Pinker:

> I wish you could get me an order for a serial for grown-up people, something like the *Red House*. I don't think it is good for my style to write *nothing* but children's books.[1]

In 1907, as she was approaching her fiftieth birthday, she took charge of a project she ran with a group of talented, imaginative young men who were in their mid-twenties. One was Francis Ernest Jackson, a poster designer and lecturer in lithography at the Central School of Arts and Crafts. Jackson was keen to produce a college magazine and he discussed this possibility with a colleague, Graily Hewitt, who was a calligrapher. They recruited a mutual acquaintance, Welsh artist Gerald Spencer Pryse, to help them. Pryse, a recent recruit to the Fabian Society and a friend of Arthur Watts, suggested they consult Edith on editorial content.

Edith had an interest in calligraphy and illumination. She invited the men to Well Hall and undertook to find contributors for this new magazine, which they named *The Neolith*. Pryse was appointed art editor, Jackson agreed to oversee technical production, and Hewitt took responsibility for calligraphy. They agreed to run the business as a cooperative and to take an equal share of any profit, and they each put up capital of ten pounds to pay for advertising and other expenses. Since they needed a London base, Edith agreed to rent a flat in Royalty Chambers, adjacent to the Royalty Theatre on Dean Street. She described it in her novel *Dormant* (1911):

If you mount the steps of the Falstaffe Theatre under the glass roof here the pink geraniums and white daisies make a light that you can see from the end of the street, you will find between the box office and the pit entrance a door, and beside it the legendary 'Falstaffe Chambers'. When the theatre is closed, as it quite often is, the ragged children of Soho play about the entrance, and on the lower steps of that staircase elderly little girls sit nursing heavy babies and scolding their little brothers, and the door of Royalty Chambers serves them as shelter, ambush, and hiding place. It is an untidy doorway, through whose door, mostly open, the wind blows dust and straws and scraps of paper. If, picking your way through the clusters of infants, you go up a flight of stone steps, you pass, on your right, the fine rooms where the Management does its business, when it has any. Still ascending, you pass another plate on the door of Mr Ben Burt, where to his name are added the significant words 'Correspondence only'. On the floor above you find a brown door on which is whitely painted the word Monolith, and below it 'William Bats, Editor'. If you knock on the door and ask for a copy of Monolith, Mr Bats, if he be at home, will tell you that the paper has ceased to appear.[2]

Edith and Pryse collaborated on several projects. He illustrated her books *These Little Ones* (1909), *Salome and the Head* (1909) and *The Magic World* (1912), and she persuaded the editor of *The Strand Magazine* to allow him to illustrate *The Magic City*, although H.R. Miller illustrated the book version. Pryse was also responsible for the arresting images of poverty that accompanied her socialist poem 'Jesus in London'.[*] He adored her sense of fun. With Arthur Watts, he would cycle through the night from London to Dymchurch, arriving there without even a change of clothes. Edith never seemed to mind. She may have been pleased with the distraction, since Watts believed she never enjoyed writing and grew ever more stressed as deadlines approached.

During one visit the young men built a raft out of old fencing and invited Edith to sit in a wicker chair they had perched on board. When the raft capsized she ruined her new Liberty dress, but she found the whole episode very funny. She hired a car on another occasion and they set out

---

* In 1914, Pryse documented the horror of war by driving a Mercedes around France and Belgium, carrying his lithographic stones in the back. He left an account of this trip in *Four Days: an account of a journey in France made between 28 and 31 August 1914*, published by John Lane.

for London, accompanied by their five dogs: Edith's dachshunds, Max and Brenda; two greyhounds belonging to Pryse; and a bullterrier owned by Watts. It took them twelve hours to travel seventy miles because the engine kept cutting out and they had several punctures. Edith never lost her cool, even though the dogs fought continuously, and she remained in good spirits throughout.

Edith adored her dachshunds and often put them into her books. For some reason, when he illustrated *The Magic City* Pryse drew them as Dalmatians even though she described them as 'dachshunds, very long and low'. Miller did the same in the book version. These dogs were not universally loved. One friend described them as snappy, and Rosamund admitted that they were terribly spoilt. At mealtimes they would rush around the table, then jump onto Edith's lap. If she had attached their leashes to her chair, she would trip over them when she got up.

Producing *The Neolith* was an ambitious undertaking. An article in *Putnam's Monthly* confirmed that its 'projectors' saw it as 'less of a commercial enterprise than an effort to place before the public sound pictorial and literary work'.[3] They sent circulars to prospective subscribers; an annual subscription cost one pound while a single number could be bought for 7s 6d. When Edith was soliciting contributions, she asked that they be written 'in the most beautiful English'. She was adamant that she wanted no 'Yellow Book suggestiveness'. It would appear that she was disillusioned with the publishing industry, since she told socialist writer Evelyn Sharp: 'Almost everything that's printed now is lies, in one form or another,' adding, 'I want the plain naked unashamed truth.'[4]

Editorial meetings were often fraught. Jackson and Hewitt found Edith headstrong, highly strung and difficult to deal with, particularly when she burst into tears if she felt her decisions were being undermined. Hewitt described her as 'very flustered' with 'those beads and bangles and incessant cigarettes'.[5] To add to their frustration, commissions generally arrived late. Yet they managed to produce issue one, in folio size, for November 1907. Edith was given top billing on the masthead and 'The Criminal', the poignant story that had been inspired by her son Fabian, was included inside. She had persuaded Shaw to contribute 'Aerial Football: the new game', a witty short story concerning a bishop and a drunken charwoman who enter heaven together. The clergyman, poet and stained glass designer, Selwyn Image, gave her a short essay on the engraver and natural historian, Thomas Bewick. She had also persuaded G.K. Chesterton to give her one of his best-known poems, 'The Secret People'.

Edith promoted emerging writers too. One was twenty-one-year-old Gerald Gould, a graduate of Magdalen College, Oxford and author of a poetry collection titled *Lyrics*. Gould was a huge fan of her Bastable stories, which he had read while convalescing from a serious illness in 1902. He was thrilled when his friend Clifford Sharp offered to introduce him to her at Well Hall.

Like Edith, Gould was a fun-loving free spirit with a passion for socialism, who composed comical ballads. He got on brilliantly with her family and was invited to join them in Dymchurch and on impromptu boating parties on the Royal Military Canal. He described Edith reclining in a chair on the lawn:

> A majestic, ample figure, clad in a flowing robe of green, and festooned with a long and tangled scarf; her arms heavy with bangles: on her knee the inevitable box of tobacco, out of which she spun an endless chain of cigarettes: in her mouth the longest cigarette-holder in the world; at her feet, in an attitude of easy indolence, a delightfully but austerely handsome young man.[6]

She offered to mentor him and published poems he had written in three of the four issues of *The Neolith*. It seems likely that she named Gerald in *The Enchanted Castle* (1907) after him. Although he was grateful for her patronage, he believed she was too indulgent of her young protégés, some of whom had precious little talent.

Producing *The Neolith* required dedication and hard graft, but there was fun to be had too. The flat at Royalty Chambers often reverberated with the sound of games and charades, or the sea-shanties and folk songs Edith would play on a battered old piano. When they were working they had food sent up from local Soho restaurants, but they ate out when they could. They celebrated their first issue with dinner for twenty guests in Villa-Villa at 37 Gerrard Street, the former home of Edmund Burke. This lively spot was included in *Europe after 8:15* (1914):

> Their [Villa-Villa and Maxim's at 30 Wardour Street] reputations are far from spotless and English society gives them a wide berth. Because

of this they have become the meeting place of clandestine lovers. Here is the genuine laughter and the wayward noise of youth. Nine out of every ten of their patrons are young, and four out of five of the girls are pretty. Music is continuous and lively, and they possess an intimacy found only in Parisian Cafés.[7]

Afterwards they returned to the flat for games and songs. Edith accompanied them on a guitar she had borrowed from the proprietor of Villa-Villa in exchange for an invitation to their party.

Issue one of *The Neolith* was well received. The *Morning Post* declared: 'The first number reaches a standard which places it above any magazine of the kind ever produced.'[8] The *Burlington Magazine* was broadly supportive but lamented the lack of fresh writing talent. It failed to mention Edith's involvement and declared:

The NEOLITH is a novelty among artistic publications… lithography is used both for the text and plates, the stories and poems contained in it being admirable examples of modern penmanship. Of the pictures, those by Mr Sims and Mr Raven Hill best combine vitality with coherence. It was perhaps a pity that the editors should have relied so much on veteran talent. Mr Selwyn Image, Mr. Bernard Shaw, Mr G.K. Chesterton and Mr Frank Brangwyn are useful names with the public but less practised work from younger pens would have been a more realistic raison d'être.[9]

Edith persuaded several old friends to contribute to issue two. Laurence Housman and Hugh Benson gave her a story each, and Arthur Watts illustrated Andrew Lang's story 'Neolithic Decadence'. She also included a story titled 'The Highwayman', the work of Edward John Moreton Drax Plunkett, 18th Baron of Dunsany, an aristocratic young man who wrote as Lord Dunsany and was known as Eddie to his family and friends. Dunsany was born and raised in London to the second oldest title in the Irish Peerage, dating back to 1439. He kept a home in London but spent much of his time at the family seat, Dunsany Castle near Tara, in County Meath, Ireland, where he did much of his writing in a room in one of the towers, using quill pens he had cut from feathers discarded by ducks on the estate.

Dunsany was exceptionally tall at six foot four, an attribute he inherited from his statuesque mother, Ernle Elizabeth Louisa Maria Grosvenor Burton, a cousin of the explorer Richard Burton. He was also an athletic and accomplished man. At one time he was both chess and pistol-shooting champion of Ireland, and he travelled and hunted extensively. A prolific writer of short stories, novels, plays, poetry, essays and autobiography, he published in excess of eighty books during his lifetime. He was recognised as an important patron of the arts in Ireland, a donor to the Abbey Theatre, and a literary collaborator with William Butler Yeats and Lady Augusta Gregory.*

Pryse had brought Dunsany to Edith's attention when he recommended *The Gods of Pegāna* (1905), a collection of his fantasy stories. Dunsany insisted they were his first and second readers. She enjoyed the book and wrote to him on 9 October 1907: 'can you let me have a short story or article (between 800 and 1,000 words) before Christmas? (Or even shorter if you would wish it so.)' She employed her considerable charm:

> So far I have, with one or two exceptions, only asked for contributions from personal friends – but I love your book so much that I cannot bear to let go any chance, however slight, of receiving a contribution from you. If you will give me one I shall be for ever your grateful debtor.[10]

In response Dunsany sent her 'The Sword of Welleran'. She liked it but advised him that it was far too long, so he sent two shorter stories, 'The Highwayman', which appeared in issue two, and 'Three Tales', which appeared in issue four. She invited him to lunch at Royalty Chambers. There, while he was explaining his deep interest in the Greek god Chronos, governor of time, the hands of a clock began spinning erratically, the mechanism emitting an odd whirring noise. This clock may have resembled the one described in *Dormant*: 'A tall clock ticks near the door. It has a silver face, and a painted moon and sun mark the hours of day and night.'[11] Since Dunsany regarded Chronos as the most significant of the gods, he took this as a good omen. He presented Edith with a copy of *Time and the Gods* (1906), his second book, which he inscribed to 'Mrs Bland from Dunsany'.

When Edith visited Dunsany's home at Cadogan Place, she was introduced to his wife, Lady Beatrice Child Villiers. She met W.B. Yeats there at a later date and likened him to a very handsome raven. She took to

---

* Dunsany died in Dublin in 1957 after an attack of appendicitis. His wife Beatrice was supportive of his literary career, assisting him with his writing, typing his manuscripts, selecting work for his 1950s retrospective short story collection, and overseeing his literary heritage after his death.

Lord and Lady Dunsany. They were invited to Well Hall, and also to Dymchurch where they remembered playing hide-and-seek and cha- rades with fellow guests. As a committed and campaigning socialist, Edith appeared amused by this connection with aristocracy. 'Do I address you correctly on this envelope?' she asked him in one letter, 'I am inexperi- enced in correspondence with Lords.'[12]

Dunsany was not the only young man whose talent she spotted early in their career. Issue four of *The Neolith* contains a poem and short story from Richard Barham Middleton. Perhaps he reminded her of Hubert, since he was twenty-five at the time and had resigned from his post as a clerk in the Royal Exchange Assurance Corporation Bank to pursue a literary career. A popular, gregarious man, he makes a thinly disguised appearance in Arthur Ransome's *Bohemia in London*:

> A huge felt hat banged freely down over a wealth of thick black hair, bright blue eyes, an enormous black beard, a magnificent manner… a way of throwing his head back when he drank, of thrusting it forward when he spoke, an air of complete abandonment to the moment and the moment's thought; he took me tremendously. He seemed to be delighting his friends with extempore poetry.[13]

Like Edith, Middleton was passionate about poetry. He was grateful for her support, and counselled: 'I hope the Neolith will continue. It would be a pity if it were to join the dodo and the great auk after a brief but glorious career.' He advised her to advertise with *The Studio* and the *New Age*. She must have been in Dymchurch at the time as he included the line: 'Meanwhile, I hope the rushes grow green in the neighbourhood of Dymchurch.'[14] Like Edith, Middleton made hardly any money from his poetry. He fell into a deep depression as a result and left London for Brussels in 1911. When happiness eluded him there too, he poisoned him- self with chloroform that had been prescribed as a remedy for his mental anguish. He was just twenty-eight years old.

At least one writer turned Edith down. A.E. Housman told his brother Laurence:

> I don't at all want to contribute to Mrs Bland's publication… I suppose she already knows that I am morose and unamiable, and will not experience any sudden or agonising shock.[15]

Edgar Jepson, who was a useful documenter of the period, confirmed that *The Neolith* had a significant influence on literature at the time:

> Literature was quiet in the middle of the Edwardian age; then Mrs Bland founded the Neolith… The Neolith was the forerunner of the revival of literature at the end of the Edwardian Age.

He was close enough to those involved to observe the tensions that were emerging, and he held Edith largely responsible:

> I do not know what there is in lithography to make one's angry passions rise, but the editorial offices, in Soho, were the field of furious battles between Mrs Bland and her art editor. I could not understand what the battles were about; but she was used to having her own way, and naturally she had to have it. She got it.[16]

Inevitably perhaps, the task of producing such an intricate magazine overwhelmed them. Hewitt found it deeply frustrating to have to write stories and poems by hand onto transfer paper. Jackson was juggling his commitments with commissions for portraits, which paid his bills. Edith too had many calls on her time. Her time-shifting children's book, *The House of Arden*, appeared towards the end of 1908 and she began writing *Harding's Luck*, its sequel, almost immediately. That year the Fabian Society published her *Ballads and Lyrics of Socialism*, and she was also working on having *Absalom, or In the Queen's Garden*, a verse drama she had written for issue four of *The Neolith*, produced for the stage. Even though Shaw advised her on licensing and copyright, the Censor banned it on the grounds that it featured biblical characters, the same ruling that had halted Oscar Wilde's *Salomé*. As if this wasn't enough, Oxford University Press had invited her to edit their illustrated Children's Bookcase series. Her own contribution was *The Old Nursery Stories*, a clever reworking of traditional fairy tales including *Cinderella, Beauty and the Beast, Jack the Giant-killer, Puss in Boots, and Jack and the Beanstalk*.

Although she employed a secretary from time to time, it was generally some literary-minded young person she was helping and she almost always submitted handwritten manuscripts to her publishers. Her letters were handwritten too and she often closed them with a tiny drawing of a clover shape, which formed her initials. By then she was receiving dozens of fan letters, many of them addressed to Oswald Bastable esq. She was desperately short of time but answered every single one. Occasionally Paul would help her and they would clear thirty in an evening.

Edith was unfailingly kind to her younger fans and took a genuine interest in their lives. One was Kathleen Waters, whose benevolent uncle had been advised to speak with the Blands about helping poor people in London. When he called at Well Hall he left her waiting in his car, but Edith invited her inside, exclaiming: 'Fancy leaving anything so charming to sit alone in the dark!' Kathleen described Well Hall as 'a great place full of people, mostly young and all laughing and talking in the bright light'. While she was there, Edith inscribed a copy of *Fabian Essays* for her. 'She was so generous,' Kathleen remembered, 'so vital, that I imagine she swept most of her young friends up, as she did me, into the warmth of her heart, and gave them a vision to carry them through life.'[17]

The Neolith never lost money, but it occupied a considerable amount of time and energy. When they decided to discontinue it after four issues, Edith remained on friendly terms with everyone except Jackson. She kept on the flat in Royalty Chambers and continued to champion talented young men. In 1909 she read *A Room with a View*, the third novel from Edward Morgan (E.M.) Forster. She loved it so much that she invited him to lunch at her flat. Forster, who was two decades her junior and shy and awkward, knocked over a towering pile of plates while he was closing a window at her request. She responded kindly, assuring him that she had purchased them for practically nothing from a bric-a-brac stall at the Caledonian Market in Islington. Forster admired her stories. A favourite of his was 'The Town in the Library in the Library in the Town' from *Nine Unlikely Tales*. In it she explores the building of a model city, a theme she returned to again and again, most notably in *The Magic City*, which was serialised in *The Strand Magazine* from January 1910.

That same month she travelled with John to Dunsany Castle, where they stayed for ten days. Each evening they acted out charades, held writing contests and played boisterous games of hide-and-seek. Lord and Lady Dunsany helped Edith construct an elaborate model city in their parlour. Their stay was delightful, but the ferry crossing home was horrendous and was followed by a night in Holyhead in 'perhaps the worst hotel in Europe'.[18]

One day when Margaret Bondfield, future Labour Minister and a member of the Fabian Woman's Group, called on Edith, she found her playing with her children:

They were building a wonderful house with such immense attention to detail – no scamp work was allowed – and she identified herself so completely with the children that I also was drawn into feeling that to build that house securely on the best possible plan was a matter of supreme importance.[19]

Edith shared this interest with her old friend H.G. Wells. Both may have been inspired by Evelyn Sharp's 'The Palace on the Floor', a fairy story from her collection *The Other Side of the Sun* (1900). Wells would spend hours constructing railways and cities with his two young sons, and they conducted miniature wars with toy soldiers on their nursery floor. He included these games in *The New Machiavelli*. In *Floor Games*, published in December 1911, he explained that 'a large part of the fun of this game lies in the witty incorporation of all sorts of extraneous objects'.[20] Edith felt exactly the same.

Forster visited Well Hall in 1911. Edith played the pianola for him and they strolled through the orchard discussing books. At sunset he joined the party in the garden to watch her burn a cardboard model that depicted rows of factories and terraced housing. Edith detested this creeping urbanisation. In 'Fortunatus Rex and Co.' she wrote: 'The ugly little streets crawled further and further out of the town eating up the green country like greedy yellow caterpillars.' She attributed this blight to greed and lamented: 'It is curious that nearly all fortunes are made by turning beautiful things into ugly ones. Making beauty out of ugliness is very ill-paid work.' In *Wings and the Child* she warmed to her theme, protesting 'everything is getting uglier and uglier. And no one seems to care':

The hideous disfigurement of lovely hills and dales with factories and mines and pot banks – coal, cinder, and slag; the defilement of bright rivers with the refuse of oil and dye works; the eating up of the green country by greedy, long, creeping yellow caterpillars of streets; the smoke and fog that veil the sun in heaven; the sordid enamelled iron advertisements that scar the fields of earth – all the torn paper and straw and dirt and disorder spring from one root. And from the same root spring pride, anger, cruelty and sycophancy, the mean subservience of the poor and the mean arrogance of the rich.[21]

For years Well Hall had remained an idyllic oasis in the midst of this creeping sprawl, but the tramline had reached them by then and it ran right past her front gate. A young amateur artist named Albert Coumber provided a snapshot of the isolation she had once enjoyed. On a Saturday afternoon sometime around 1906, he had travelled from London, with a friend, to 'the comparatively rural district of Well Hall, Eltham'. They wandered through adjacent fields on that beautiful sunny evening and decided to sketch a cluster of redbrick outbuildings. As they approached the main house, it became clear that a soirée of some sort was underway, since guests in evening dress had wandered out onto the lawn. Spotting two girls on a balcony, Coumber blew them a kiss, which they returned.

The young men returned the following Saturday to finish their sketches. Absorbed in their work, they were startled when a 'deep female voice' asked them if they realised they were trespassing. This belonged to 'a stately lady in some sweeping garment who repeated the question in some sepulchral tones'. They offered to leave, but Edith merely sighed and responded 'we like to be asked'. She invited them to stay and examined their sketches. After they agreed to show them to her daughter, she returned with a girl who seemed 'somewhat shy and embarrassed'. Coumber suspected she was one of the girls from the balcony. This may have been Iris since she was artistic. They chatted for a while and Edith sent out tea to them.[22]

Iris married John Austen Philips, a civil servant who was six years her senior, in a simple ceremony held on 5 February 1907. He had served with the British army in South Africa and was Postmaster at Droitwich in northern Worcestershire at the time, but he had ambitions to write. He succeeded with a good deal of help from Edith. She was in her early fifties by then but had lost none of her high spirits. In March she travelled to Paris with Hubert, Alice, Arthur Watts and a young man named Ambrose Flower who she nicknamed 'Florizel, Prince of Bohemia'. He was a friend of Iris's from the Slade School of Fine Art but had retrained as an actor. As it was exceptionally hot when they visited Versailles, Edith suggested they paddle in a fountain. She hitched up her skirts and Flower rolled up his trousers, but an irate gendarme ordered them out. Later, at the Comédie-Française, Flower and she went from corridor to corridor opening every window, even when they were asked not to do so. In response, Edith gripped the curtains and pretended to feel faint while Flower assured the ushers that his friend was desperately ill and needed some air. She must have seemed an unlikely rebel. A profile in *Authors Today and Yesterday* described her at this time:

In physical aspect a stout, ageing woman who suffered from asthma and bronchitis and walked about in trailing gowns with a tin of tobacco and cigarette papers under her arm, in heart a combination of the whole Bastable family put together, in capabilities a great artist one day and no sort of artist at all the next, it is not astonishing that she inspired in many of her friends a mixture of awe, bewilderment, and devoted love.[23]

Iris gave birth to a daughter in Well Hall on 27 January 1908. It was a difficult birth and she was desperately weak afterwards. She named her daughter Rosamund Philippa Philips, but the family called her Pandora and she looked uncannily like her maternal grandmother. Edith doted on her and dedicated *Harding's Luck* to 'Rosamund Philippa Philips with E. Nesbit's love'. Iris's marriage was not a success. By 1911 she was earning a living as 'Madame Iris', an 'artistic dressmaker and designer'. She operated her business out of Edith's flat at Royalty Chambers. It may have been Iris's status as a single mother and the circumstances that required her to earn her living that in some way informed an exceptionally controversial speech her mother delivered to the Fabian Women's Group in 1908.

CHAPTER 18

'VOTES FOR WOMEN? VOTES FOR CHILDREN! VOTES FOR DOGS!'

Edith showed exceptional loyalty to her women friends. Under the terms of her will she guaranteed Ada Breakell a place in her home in perpetuity. She also acted as mentor to several young women, including Berta Ruck who recalled with embarrassment the hours she spent 'unthinkingly and unblushingly' in Edith's study, reading aloud her 'perfectly hopeless young writings':

> I wish I could adequately convey to you that delightful and gifted friend of mine as I saw her then, at Well Hall, or down at Romney Marsh, when, as a lanky girl, I used to sit quite literally among scattered sheets of manuscript paper at her feet, and used to be given advice and help, of which I shall feel the benefit of her patience... her generosity... her unconquerable frankness over anything that she considered beneath my powers as far as they went. 'Won't do, Berta! Won't *do*!' she would exclaim suddenly and would stop me to show how various details of the story were not consistent, pointing out the faults kindly but quite firmly.[1]

Yet it was Edith's failure to support women that prompted a breach with Laurence Housman, one of her staunchest friends. He admitted to admiring her 'fine generous character and her enormous energy – also her wonderful faculty of joie-de-vivre', but he justified this estrangement in a letter to Doris Langley Moore:

> After 1902 I saw less and less of her. I never liked her husband; and when my feeling toward him became active dislike, it was embarrassing to continue visiting the house. I fancy she understood the reason, and acquiesced. When the Women's Suffrage Movement started, she

disappointed me by refusing to take any part in it when it took the form
of Adult Suffrage. I felt that this was a dishonest excuse, put forward, I
guess, because her husband was a violent Anti, and she wished not to
annoy him.[2]

Housman, who was openly homosexual, campaigned bravely for gay
rights and law reform. When Oscar Wilde was impoverished and living
in exile, Housman travelled to Paris with funds his friends had collected
at the Café Royal. A staunch socialist and a committed pacifist, he was
also a tireless campaigner for women's suffrage. His sister Clemence, a
leading figure in the movement, sat on the committee of the Women's
Tax Resistance League.

Edith's views on women's rights, and the suffrage question in particular,
were generally hostile. She justified her opposition to limited suffrage on
the grounds that it was contrary to her commitment to socialism. In June
1910 she refused a request from journalist Evelyn Sharp to sign a petition
asking Prime Minister Asquith to put through the Conciliation Bill of
1910. She explained her decision:

> I am sorry I cannot sign the enclosed memorial as it does not embody my
> views. I am for adult Suffrage, but primarily my political interest is all for
> socialism, and I do not wish socialism to be endangered by an extension of
> the franchise to Conservative women.[3]

Before she sent it, she softened this note by replacing 'Conservative
women' with 'a class of women mainly Conservative'. She was not the
only socialist to rely on this argument. Her fellow socialist Gerald Gould,
a co-founder of the United Suffragists, explained:

> E. Nesbit's attitude towards Woman's Suffrage, for instance, was a rea-
> soned one; she favoured adult suffrage, but refused for political reasons to
> support the Conciliation Bill [this would have allowed the vote to about a
> million women]; whereas Hubert's contribution to the controversy was to
> exclaim with the manner of one swallowing an emetic; 'Votes for women?
> Votes for children! Votes for dogs!'[4]

This stance was confirmed when her letter to the *Sheffield Daily Telegraph*
was published on 22 January 1912:

Sir – The question of Woman's Suffrage is not one in which I take much interest. At the same time I admire the courage of the militant suffragettes. And if the right to own property be conceded to women, and the obligation to pay rates and taxes be enforced on women, I cannot see any logical loophole by which I can escape from giving women the vote.[5]

Her ambivalence peaked in 1908 when she joined the Fabian Women's Group. Many Fabian women were expressing impatience at the lack of progress on women's rights, and prominent among them was anarchist Charlotte Wilson, who had re-engaged with the society. This unrest was summarised in *Fabian Women's Group, Three Years' Work 1908-1911*, a pamphlet published in 1911:

Many ardent suffragists amongst Fabian women felt that the Society was not keeping pace with a movement to which it had recently committed itself by the insertion of a new clause on its basis.[6]

On 14 March 1908 a 'little party' of like-minded women met in the home of Maud Pember Reeves, who was Amber's mother, to 'discuss the situation'. Wilson addressed them on the need to clarify the 'real meaning and significance of the Economic Independence of women under socialism and the steps to be taken to obtain it'.[7] That day the Fabian Women's Group was established and Wilson was elected secretary. The six hundred women members of the Fabian Society (out of two thousand) were invited to a general meeting at which the group outlined its stated aims:

Firstly, to make the equality in citizenship advocated in the Fabian Basis an active part of the Society's propaganda and an active principle in its internal organisation; Secondly, to study woman's economic independence in relationship to socialism.[8]

On 4 April a 'large gathering' assembled in the studio of artist Marion Wallace Dunlop. It was agreed that, while 'natural difference' existed between men and women, this had been 'artificially exaggerated and distorted by the subjection of women'. They drafted an announcement that asserted the equality of Fabian women and launched a campaign to get more women onto the Executive. It was also agreed that they would participate in the suffrage processions that were organised by the National Union of Woman's Suffrage Societies and the Woman's Social and Political Union. A group banner was designed and May Morris presented the materials to make it.[9] By 9 May, 159 women had joined the Women's Fabian Group. During the summer of 1908 they demonstrated under a banner that read 'Women's Will Beats Asquith's Won't'.* On 5 July 1909 Marion Wallace went on hunger strike after she was arrested for militancy. By 1910 eleven members had been jailed for their activism.[10]

Edith joined the Fabian Women's Group, but she was reluctant to engage with their suffrage campaign. She did, however, accept Charlotte Wilson's invitation to deliver the first in a series of lectures on 'Women and Work'. Since its title was advertised as 'Motherhood and Breadwinning', those gathered to hear her on 29 May 1908 were astonished when she announced that, rather than addressing them as a successful writer, she would speak as the wife of Hubert Bland. Her name is not mentioned in the account of her lecture included in the Fabian Women's Group's *Three Year's Work 1908-1911:*

> Our first paper was by a socialist wife and mother who had herself gained economic independence by her arduous and brilliant work, and we asked her to take 'Women and Work' as her general subject. The special aspect of it she chose was the 'Natural Disabilities of Women'. Women, she held, are predominately creatures of sex, whose paramount need is a mate and children; and also they are heavily weighted throughout life by physical and mental disabilities unknown to men. Nevertheless, their economic independence ought to be secured if only to enable them to mate well and wisely.[11]

One audience member, who described herself as 'an English socialist woman', gave an account of this controversial lecture in an open letter she sent to *Wilshire's Magazine*:

> The Fabian women have formed a branch of their own a month or so ago, to study especially those questions which affect women, and their

---

* Alice Hoatson contributed towards a banner for the Women's Suffrage Movement, and it may have been this one, or another, which read 'Equal opportunities for Men and Women'.

meetings bid fair to be very interesting, though the first lecture, given by Mrs Hubert Bland (E. Nesbit) was a very extraordinary one, and the lecturer found her audience more or less hostile all the way through. I can't think how she could have come before an audience of 'waked-up' women and expect them to listen to her running down their sex. She took a very odd tone: of course, in a mixed audience, we should not give ourselves away, but, as we were all women together, we might as well be honest with ourselves and own that women were men's inferiors all along the line, inherently, etc., etc. She got a nice chorus of opposition: she said too that if we were honest we should own that all we have of the best we could always trace back to some man, and it did me good to hear the interruption there. 'What about our mothers?' and the call was taken up till the whole meeting was calling 'Mothers. Mothers.' in remonstrating tones. She put my back up before five minutes were over by flattering us with pretty names – 'flower of femininity' was one awful appellation she presented us with and in the same breath inviting us superior beings to join her in throwing stones at 'the average woman'. Lord save me from Mrs Bland. I wonder her socialism hasn't sweetened her imagination.[12]

A summary of Edith's lecture, produced for private circulation, confirmed that she had described women as 'predominantly creatures of sex, whose paramount need is a mate and children'. She also spoke in defence of polygamy and suggested that women should be willing to accept short-term mating, leading to motherhood, in preference to enduring marriage. She allowed that such arrangements would require women to be financially self-supporting but warned that the cultivation of the intellect led to sterility in women. One can only imagine the gasps of horror that greeted her suggestion that the world would suffer little if women's output were eradicated.[13]

The official report, although diplomatically worded, makes it clear that Edith's audience was far from supportive:

The stress laid on the inevitable disabilities of sex in the first lecture had aroused a strong feeling of opposition amongst our members, including some who were themselves mothers. It was felt that an altogether disproportionate importance had been attached to female incapacity for other vocations than motherhood. Our Studies Committee therefore decided to take natural and inevitable sex disability as a preliminary subject, with the object of discovering what women themselves are feeling about it.[14]

In response the Fabian Women's Group resolved to demonstrate that:

Women's disabilities of strength and skill were the result not of natural difference, but – in the age-old plea of feminism – of the artificial exaggeration of sex differences, arguing that this exaggeration was historical, patriarchal, and that its effects radiated adversely through domestic and industrial production.[15]

A new lecture series was organised to counteract the damage she had done. It was reported that the first speaker, physician Dr Constance Long, 'set the physiology of the matter clearly before us'. Novelist Emma Brooke, a founder member of the Fabian Women's Group, delivered the second lecture and argued that 'the ability for motherhood was in itself a cogent reason why the claim of women to full social recognition, economic and political, should be acknowledged'.[16]

George Bernard Shaw was tasked with correcting the proof copy of *Summary of Seven Papers and Discussions Upon the Disabilities of Women as Workers*. He erased Edith's name and the summary of her lecture and, in a handwritten note, directed that the final copy must omit all reference to her paper in order to avoid a scandal should the press get hold of it. An excerpt from the unedited version makes it clear that she regarded the campaign for women's suffrage as a threat to both maternity and the socialist cause. She insisted that 'the cause of mankind is greater than the cause of women' and argued:

And supposing that, by training and teaching women to use their brains, it were possible, contrary to received opinion regarding the transmission of acquired characteristics, to produce a crop of geniuses it would have to be at the expense of the mother characteristics which are women's raison d'être; and thus the cultivation of the intellectual or masculine characteristics of women would end in sterility and race extermination.[17]

The Fabian Society struggled to arrive at a comprehensive and coherent approach to the women question, a failing Ramsey MacDonald attributed to the inherent conservatism of the 'Old Gang'. A proposed tract asserting women's entitlement to the same civil and political rights as men was abandoned in disarray.[*]

Although Edith appeared to speak her own mind, Hubert exerted a considerable influence over her views. Several of the statements in her controversial lecture echoed his more forthright declarations. In 'Men's Love' he observed:

> Why is it, by the way, that when there was no 'Women's Movement' there were great women artists and that now when woman is clamorous and obtrusive, there are none?[18]

Although both were essentialists, Hubert was utterly unreconstructed. 'Women's realm is the realm of the heart and the afternoon tea-table, not of the brain and the intelligence. It is hers to bewitch man, not to convince him,' he insisted.[19] In *Letters to a Daughter*, he advised women to 'affect an ignorance' since:

> There is nothing people in general like so little in women as knowledge, and when I say people in general I mean people of both sexes. So you must never put all the goods in the shop window, or, at any rate, not all at once.[20]

He believed that men loved explaining things to young women, and he warned:

> Unexpectedly to check his enterprise by showing that you know as much as he does has pretty much the same effect upon his mind as though you were to suddenly add twenty years to your age, to discover wrinkles, or to develop a squint.[21]

He justified the exclusion of women from the legal profession by pointing out, playfully:

---

* There were exceptions. In February 1896 Beatrice Webb had written *Women and the Factory Acts*, which was published as Fabian Tract No. 67. In March 1900 Shaw wrote *Women as Councillors*, which was published as Fabian Tract No. 93. In 1927 Shaw's *The Intelligent Woman's Guide to Socialism and Capitalism* was published. Penguin Books reissued it in 1937 as the first book under the Pelican imprint, at which time Shaw amended the title to *The Intelligent Woman's Guide to Socialism, Capitalism, Sovietism, and Fascism*. In *The Socialist Woman's Guide to Intelligence: a reply to Mr Shaw*, Lilian Le Mesurier objected to his self-satisfied and condescending tone.

We feel that so irresistible are woman's attractions, so winsome her ways, so seductive and bewildering the very atmosphere she creates around her, that were a woman, a pretty woman, (and one cannot ensure, you know, that all women lawyers should be ugly), to appear in court as the counsel for the most obviously guilty prisoner the jury would promptly acquit the criminal and then wait outside on the chance of inviting the lady to luncheon at the Savoy.[22]

Turning his attention to the medical profession, he declared:

But we do not allow our young women in schools to learn physiology, for we regard it as indelicate, almost indecent, that a young woman, particularly that species of young woman that we call a young lady, should know more of her own body than her own looking glass can tell her.[23]

It is tempting to blame Hubert for Edith's illiberal views, but this does not exonerate her entirely. A letter she sent to Ada Breakell in 1884 describes an 'infinitely boring' meeting of a Women's Rights Group. She characterised one speaker, Lydia Becker, who was Secretary of the Manchester National Society for Women's Suffrage and an influential leader of the Women's Suffrage Movement, as 'hideously like a *hippopotamus*'.[24] In *A Story-Teller Tells the Truth*, Berta Ruck included an anecdote of Edith's that underlined her ambivalence to the cause:

From the start she was all for women's Causes. Yet this was a story the every-sided woman told us, at Grez, about herself when young in a house-party of the (then) Ultra Emancipated. 'They talked and they talked and they talked for hours of Women's Rights. You never' – Here E. Nesbit took out her cigarette, drew down her lips, and let that ineffable blank grimace widen her eyes – '*you* never heard so much about the Enfranchisement of Women. At last Miss—' a girlhood's friend – 'and I were able to stagger to our bedroom and take out our hair-pins and shake out our hair and I was just able to say faintly: '*Now* let's have a nice long talk ALL ABOUT YOUNG MEN!'[25]

Edith held extraordinarily traditional views on gender, although she rarely fulfilled the role of a traditional woman herself. In 'The Goodwife's Occupation Gone', she lamented the decline of the traditional household:

Homes are ceasing to exist, and housewives, as our grandmothers understood the word, are no more. Well-to-do women keep servants to relieve
them of the work of the house, and the mistress no longer finds it need-
ful or desirable to practise the household arts in which her grandmother
excelled. From the stores she can order the sheets ladies used to weave and
hem, the clothing ladies used to cut out and make, the stockings ladies
used to knit, and the kerchiefs they used to embroider. The kind of life she
lives can be sustained on machine made things and the steamroller we call
civilisation has gone over all the old occupations of women: occupations
calling for patience, energy, imagination, and a host of little kindly virtues.
It has crushed individuality out of the home, and it is crushing the home
out of the house.[26]

In 'Miss Lorrimore's Career', published in *Sylvia's Journal* in February
1894 alongside an article titled 'Women in Journalism', her Miss Lorrimore
is in possession of 'brave independence'. She makes her living as a journalist and is a better researcher than any of the male writers she meets
in the British Museum Reading Room. When she turns down a proposal
of marriage from a fellow journalist, she declares, 'I have a paper on old
maids to finish for the Globe.' But she abandons her research because it
makes her fearful. A friend remarks that he rarely sees her name in print
and that she has grown 'a bit thin and seedy looking'. She agrees to marry
her rejected admirer, declaring: 'I don't care about independence now...
I don't want independence, I want you.'[27]

Edith could be very contradictory. In 'The Slaves of the Spider' she
decried those women who were willing to be tricked into buying the latest
fashions:

Wasting time, thought, money, brains, heart and energy, not on inventing
or making, or causing to be made, beautiful garments, distinguished and
individual, but in a passionate, delirious, all-absorbing effort to wear what
other people are wearing.[28]

She interpreted this as proof of women's unfitness to wield power:

It has been said that any claim which women may make to equal rights and
political privileges can never be taken seriously so long as women follow
the fashion. And the observation is just. The long, glittering line of Oxford

Street alone, with its shop after shop devoted entirely to different kinds of clothes and ornaments for women, shouts a negative to the Woman's Rights question. Our fashion papers, blossoming week by week with the exotic flower of some new absurdity; our daily Press, with its woman's page, and its serious treatment of a thousand feminine fripperies; the very existence, the prosperous existence, of these things proves more convincingly than a whole library of anti-feminist tracts that the great mass of women are not as yet fitted for the use of power and responsibility; and, what is more, that they do not really desire these.[29]

When war was declared in 1914 Edith castigated the frivolity of women who 'could find no more engrossing thoughts than lace petticoats and new skirts six yards round'. She contrasted this with the 'example men had set to the world by their magnificent valour and the splendour of their endurance', and she warned of austere times to come when regret would bite hard.[30]

Edith held young women, her own daughters included, to an impossible and undesirable standard. Yet she allowed her fictional girls far more latitude; they could be brave and resilient. In *The Magic City* (1910) her adult Pretenderette, a nasty, spiteful nursemaid, appears to lampoon the suffragette movement. Yet an edict decrees: 'Girls are expected to be brave and the boys, kind.' In *The House of Arden* (1908) Elfrida is consistently braver than her brother Edred. One passage is particularly insightful:

Elfrida did not understand. How should she? It's almost impossible for even the most grown up and clever of us to know how women used to be treated – and not so very long ago either – if they were once suspected of being witches. It generally began by the old woman's being cleverer than her neighbours, having more wit to find out what was the matter with sick people, and more still to cure them... from 'wise woman' to witch was a very short step indeed.

She included this radical exchange in *The Railway Children*:

'*Can* girls help to mend engines?' Peter asked doubtfully.

'Of course they can. Girls are just as clever as boys, and don't you forget it! How would you like to be an engine-driver, Phil?'

'My face would be always dirty, wouldn't it?' said Phyllis, in unenthusiastic tones, 'and I expect I should break something.'

'I should just love it,' said Roberta, – 'do you think I could when I'm grown up, Daddy? Or even a stoker?'[31]

Her women protagonists do occasionally earn their living, but they generally follow conventional courtship plots and aspire to marry a suitable young man. In 'The Girton Girl' her Laura Wentworth, who is 'handsome and learned', likens marriage to slavery but marries a young man she saves from drowning. The closest Edith came to writing an emancipated woman was Sandra in *Salome and the Head*. She flees a dysfunctional marriage and supports herself as an interpretive dancer. Edith based her on the scandalous Maud Allan, who was billed as 'The Salomé Dancer' when she toured England in 1908.

In contrast, Edith used her horror stories to critique traditional marriages and allowed women to occupy more fluid gender roles. In 'Man-Size in Marble' a young husband courts disaster by dismissing his sensible wife's legitimate concerns. In 'Hurst of Hurstcote' a controlling husband commands the soul of his deceased wife to remain in her body until he too is dead. In 'From the Dead' another husband, who is overtaken by masculine instincts, chastises his wife too harshly. She haunts him after she dies.

Edith may have been inconsistent on the woman question, but her support for socialism never waivered. She shared Hubert's concern for exploited working-class women whom they wished to restore to what they regarded as their rightful place in the home. In his essay 'To the Emperor of Japan' Hubert railed:

In spite of the deep-rooted conviction of ours as to woman's sphere (we always call it woman's sphere) being purely domestic, many hundreds of thousands of women in England are working outside of that sphere, working in factories and fields for their living, working in garrets and cellars for a pittance that will not provide a living or anything like a living, that pregnant women within a few days of their childbearing are compelled to daily labour, the severity of which inflicts upon them and their offspring lifelong injury, that in the streets of all our great cities thousands of women are nightly offering their bodies for sale.[32]

When writing for children, Edith seemed keen to deliver a strong message of social justice. With good reason, she regarded her young readers as far more open to reform than their parents. One clear message in *The Story of the Treasure Seekers* (1899) is that: 'Poverty is no disgrace. We should honour honest poverty.' In *The New Treasure Seekers* she encouraged children to recognise the inequities in English society and to empathise with those less well off. When her children attempt to explain government policy they generally expose its inherent flaws.

In *The House of Arden* Richard condemns a social system that obliges mothers to work while leaving their children in inadequate care. In *The Story of the Amulet*, the Babylonian Queen warns that the 'slaves' she encounters in Victorian London appear to have been so badly treated that they must be on the verge of revolt. The children counter this by arguing that democracy and voting rights render these workers free. Yet they cannot explain why misery persists in a system that is touted as fair. When they attempt to house an orphan child who is destined for the workhouse, the Psammead points out: 'You've got your country into such a mess that there's no room for half your children – and no one to want them.'

The past offers no solutions, since tyranny is endemic to human nature; she makes this clear in her descriptions of the harsh, hierarchical Egyptian regime. Solutions can only be found in a reformed future that is built on socialist ideals. In *The Story of the Amulet* (1906) her children travel forward in time to a verdant, utopian London where school is delightful, mothers and fathers share the burden of childcare, and everyone dresses in comfortable clothing. In *The Magic World* (1912), when the enchanted crows that inhabit 'Justnowland' are changed back into men, they vow 'in future we shall not be rich and poor, but fellow-workers, and each will do his best for his brothers'.

In *The Railway Children*, which was published in the year that the Labour Party entered government as an independent political force, Edith promoted a sense of individual responsibility and community. Her children are far more visionary and ambitious than her adults and they reflect the Fabian belief that socialism transcends class since it benefits everyone. Since they lack awareness of rigid class boundaries, they teach the adults to let go of their notions of charity and hierarchical inequality in order to concentrate resources where they are needed.

In *The Wonderful Garden* (1910) an old woman is being put out of her rented home:

'Gentlefolks,' said the woman bitterly; 'got a grand 'ouse of their own up in London. But they gone and took a fancy to my little bit, 'cause it looks so pretty with the flowers I planted, and the arbour my father made, and the roses as come from mother's brother in Cambridgeshire... "Such a sweet pretty cottage to stay in for week-ends," they says; an' *I* may go to the Union and stay there, week in, week out, and much they care. There's something like it in the Bible, only there ain't no prophets now like there was of old to go and rebuke the folks that takes away poor folks' vineyards and lambs and things to make week-end cottages of.'[33]

She expects little sympathy from her landlord: 'He's all right,' she points out, 'he's got the castle and he's got his mansion in Belgrave Square; I can't expect him to bother about me and my little house.' Yet the children are horrified. They petition the landlord and persuade him to change his mind. Edith included utopian thinking in this book too. When Mr Noah takes Philip to see their factories, he expects ugliness but finds instead:

Pleasant, long, low houses, with tall French windows opening into gardens of roses, where people of all nations made beautiful and useful things, and loved making them. And all the people who were making them looked clean and happy.[34]

Philip wonders why real-life factories are so unpleasant:

'That's because all your factories are *money* factories,' said Mr Noah, 'though they're called by all sorts of different names. Every one here has to make something that isn't just money or *for* money – something useful *and* beautiful.'[35]

Although Edith delivered her socialist message very effectively, she never hectored and she was not above poking fun at socialists and utopian thinkers. In *The New Treasure Seekers*, Eustace Sandal, an amalgam of Fabian Society members Edward Carpenter and Henry Salt, is:

A vegetarian and a Primitive Socialist Something, and an all-wooler, and things like that, and he is really as good as he can stick only awfully dull... Well he has great magnificent dreams about all the things he can do for other people, and he wants to distil cultivatedness into the sort of people who live in Model Workmen's Dwellings, and teach them to live up to better things.[36]

CHAPTER 19

'A CURTAIN, THIN AS GOSSAMER'

In a passage in *The Enchanted Castle* (1907) Edith explained how magic gives rise to endless possibilities:

> There is a curtain, thin as gossamer, clear as glass, strong as iron, that hangs forever between the world of magic and the world that seems to us to be real. And when once people have found one of the little weak spots in the curtain which are marked by magic rings, and amulets, and the like, almost anything may happen.[1]

The Bastable stories and *The Railway Children* were rooted in reality, but many of her most celebrated stories enmesh the magical with the mundane. When conjuring up fantastic creatures, like her Psammead, she relied on her extraordinarily vivid imagination or accepted ideas from friends. When writing *The Story of the Amulet*, the third book in her Psammead trilogy, serialised in *The Strand Magazine* between May 1905 and April 1906, she drew heavily on the magic of Ancient Egypt.

This story opens with her fictional children finding the Psammead in a pet shop near the British Museum. With his help they acquire one half of a magic amulet that allows them to travel through time. She dedicated this brilliant book:

TO
DR WALLIS BUDGE
OF
THE BRITISH MUSEUM
THIS BOOK IS DEDICATED
AS A SMALL TOKEN OF GRATITUDE FOR HIS
UNFAILING KINDNESS AND HELP IN
THE MAKING OF IT

Seeking inspiration for her time-travelling story, she had visited the British Museum, where she spotted a notice informing visitors that Ernest Alfred Thompson Wallis Budge, Keeper of Egyptian and Assyrian Antiquities, was available to answer queries. She knocked on his door and explained that she was a children's writer in search of inspiration. Budge, a portly, ruddy-cheeked man from Bodmin in Cornwall, who was one year older than Edith, recalled her visit as 'a very pleasant break in the day because she was "quick on the uptake," and had a delightful sense of humour'.[2] When he learned of her interest in magic, he suggested she set her book in Ancient Egypt where pharaohs and kings kept storytellers as members of their households; he told her that their best-loved tales concerned sexual intrigue spiced with magic. He advised her to mull over his advice and to return if she wished to know more. She was back within the week.

Ernest Alfred Thompson Wallis Budge was an extraordinary man. His mother was the daughter of a waiter in a Bodmin hotel and his father was never identified. As a child he was sent to live with relatives in London. Although he was exceptionally bright, he was obliged to leave school at the age of twelve to work as a clerk with W.H. Smith. His thirst for knowledge undimmed, he studied Hebrew and Syriac, a form of Aramaic, with a volunteer tutor who introduced him to pioneering Egyptologist Samuel Birch, Keeper of Oriental Antiquities at the British Museum. Birch's patronage was invaluable. He gave Budge access to rare books and precious stone tablets, and he asked his assistant, the Assyriologist George Smith, to help him with the ancient Assyrian language, which he studied for almost a decade. During his lunch break, Budge would sneak into St Paul's Cathedral to study in solitude. Such dedication attracted the attention of the organist John Stainer, who raised funds so Budge could study the Semitic languages – Hebrew, Syriac, Ethiopic and Arabic – at Cambridge University.

Budge published dozens of works on the ancient Near East during his tenure at the British Museum, and he travelled to Egypt and the Sudan to acquire antiquities, often by controversial means. Edith was delighted when he agreed to help her. He translated aloud from Babylonian and Egyptian texts that she incorporated into her story, and he read early drafts of *The Story of the Amulet*. His input is evident throughout. It was Budge who informed Edith's description of an Assyrian banquet:

They did enjoy the banquet. They had a beautiful bath, which was deli-cious, were heavily oiled all over, including their hair, and that was most unpleasant. Then, they dressed again and were presented to the King, who was most affable. The banquet was long; there were all sorts of nice things to eat, and everybody seemed to eat and drink a good deal. Everyone lay on cushions and couches, ladies on one side and gentlemen on the other; and after the eating was done each lady went and sat by some gentleman, who seemed to be her sweetheart or her husband, for they were very affec-tionate to each other. The Court dresses had gold threads woven in them, very bright and beautiful. The middle of the room was left clear, and dif-ferent people came and did amusing things. There were conjurers and jugglers and snake-charmers, which last Anthea did not like at all. When it got dark torches were lighted. Cedar splinters dipped in oil blazed in copper dishes set high on poles.

Then there was a dancer, who hardly danced at all, only just struck attitudes. She had hardly any clothes, and was not at all pretty. The chil-dren were rather bored by her, but everyone else was delighted, including the King. 'By the beard of Nimrod!' he cried, 'ask what you like girl, and you shall have it!' 'I want nothing,' said the dancer; 'the honour of having pleased the King may-he-live-for-ever is reward enough for me.'

And the King was so pleased with this modest and sensible reply that he gave her the gold collar off his own neck.

Budge showed Edith the amulets in the museum's collection, including one that was strikingly similar to the amulet 'made of a red, smooth, softly shiny stone' that her children find. He also suggested that she use this 'Tyet' amulet, the Isis knot, since it allowed the bearer to access regions of the underworld. He described it in his book *Egyptian Magic* (1901):

This amulet represents the buckle of the girdle of Isis, and is usually made of carnelian, red jasper, red glass, and of other substances of a red colour; it is sometimes made of gold, and of substances covered with gold.[3]

Budge told Edith that each amulet was associated with a Hekau, a word of power:

By pronouncing certain words or names of power in the proper manner and in the proper tone of voice he [a priest] could heal the sick, and cast out the evil spirits which caused pain and suffering in those who were diseased, and restore the dead to life, and bestow upon the dead man the power to transform the corruptible into an incorruptible body, wherein the soul might live to all eternity. His words enabled human beings to assume divers forms at will, and to project their souls into animals and other creatures; and in obedience to his commands, inanimate figures and pictures became living beings and things which hastened to perform his behests.[4]

He invented a word of power for her, which he wrote out in hieroglyphics: 'Ur Hekau Setcheh' translates as 'Great of magic is the Setcheh', the Setcheh being a mythological serpent demon. He also suggested elements of her plot: the 'arrival and conquest of the copper-users', the inclusion of ancient Assyria as a location, and the name Rekh-mara for her Egyptian priest. It was Budge who drew her attention to the bas-relief of an eagle-headed god, which she cast as Nisroch. This god releases her children from a dungeon:

'UR HEKAU SETCHEH,' she [Anthea] cried in a fervent voice. 'Oh, Nisroch, servant of the Great Ones, come and help us!' There was a waiting silence. Then a cold, blue light awoke in the corner where the straw was – and in the light they saw coming towards them a strange and terrible figure. I won't try to describe it, because the drawing shows it, exactly as it was, and exactly as the old Babylonians carved it on their stones, so that you can see it in our own British Museum at this day. I will just say that it had eagle's wings and an eagle's head and the body of a man.[5]

Playfully, she included her own name:

'What was the name the Queen said?' asked Cyril suddenly. 'Nisbeth – Nesbit – something? You know, the slave of the great names?'
    'Wait a sec,' said Robert, 'though I don't know why you want it. Nusroch—Nisrock—Nisroch—that's it.'[6]

Budge is in her book too. He shares some characteristics with her 'learned gentleman' and both value the ability to speak ancient languages. She also pokes gentle fun at his proclivity for writing prolifically on topics that interested him:

He had not had many adventures with children in them, and he wondered whether all children were like these. He spent quite five minutes in wondering before he settled down to the fifty-second chapter of his great book on 'The Secret Rites of the Priests of Amen Ra'.[7]

Several of the learned gentleman's pronouncements might have come directly from Budge's mouth:

'It's quite possible,' the learned gentleman replied. 'Such charms have been found in very early Egyptian tombs, yet their origin has not been accurately determined as Egyptian. They may have been brought from Asia. Or, supposing the charm to have been fashioned in Egypt, it might very well have been carried to Babylon by some friendly embassy, or brought back by the Babylonish army from some Egyptian campaign as part of the spoils of war. The inscription may be much later than the charm. Oh yes! it is a pleasant fancy, that that splendid specimen of yours was once used amid Babylonish surroundings.'[8]

The real Budge appears briefly on the steps of the British Museum when the Babylonian Queen arrives to retrieve her jewellery: '"But we don't wish to use harsh measures," added the nice one, who was really very nice indeed, and seemed to be over all the others.'

Although Budge had been married for years, it has been suggested that there was a romantic element to his friendship with Edith. She appears to have confided in him about her unhappiness at Hubert's serial infidelities. He told Doris Langley Moore that she felt unfulfilled and disillusioned when they met and that she had 'worries and domestic troubles'. He even hinted strongly that she asked him to take her away, as she had once asked Richard Le Gallienne. It seems she wept when he refused. 'She was a great woman,' he declared, 'and I valued her friendship highly.'[9] Edith's story 'The Kiss' may reveal the true nature of their relationship. Neville Underwood sets eyes on a young woman writer for the first time:

Their first meeting was in the long gallery among the Egyptian and Assyrian antiquities at the British Museum. Enthusiast though he was, he was tired, as human souls are tired, with the cold reserve of carved stone – the imperturbable mystery of these old kings and gods who had kept for thousands of years, amid the shifting sands of the desert, their immemorial secrets. His eyes ached with the close scrutiny of minute and delicate detail. Then suddenly his eyes rested on her, fair and laughing and full of the joy of life, and his soul rejoiced because there was still youth in the world, and secrets that no kings and gods had power to keep from the sons of men who walk the earth to-day.[10]

Underwood helps this young woman with a book she is writing on ancient Egypt. They fall in love and he discovers that she wears an amulet that is the counterpart of one he wears around his neck. Whatever the nature of the real relationship, it came to an end when Budge left on one of his long archaeological tours to Egypt.[11]

Magic fascinated them, but the extent to which they participated in the occult and paranormal practices that were popular at the time is unclear. Budge was certainly perfectly happy to have the public believe that artifacts in the British Museum were cursed. Both of them believed in ghosts, and several of Budge's friends were members of the Ghost Club, a secretive organisation that promoted belief in the spirit world and conducted paranormal investigations. He never joined this club but he was welcome as a guest. One friend remembered what a 'marvellous storyteller' he was:

Like Scheherazade, he could keep a company at dinner spellbound till dawn with tales of his experiences both East and West. They would range from adventures on Nile and Tigris to the most thrilling of ghost stories.[12]

Several members of the Fabian Society, Frank Podmore in particular, took a keen interest in the paranormal and participated regularly in séances or investigated hauntings. Others, including Edith, were more sceptical and took no part in these activities. Yet in a letter to Ada Breakell, dated March 1884, she mentioned that she had read 'an intensely interesting book… called *Esoteric Buddhism* by Sinnett'. He was Alfred Percy (A.P.) Sinnett, a theosophist and disciple of the Russian mystic Madame Helena Petrovna Blavatsky, founder of the occult Theosophical Society. In *The Lark* one of Edith's characters lends his house 'to a Theosophist Brotherhood'. The former Fabian Annie Besant was president of the Theosophical Society and Edith submitted a poem, 'Torch-bearers', to *Lucifer*, a Theosophic magazine that Blavatsky and Besant edited.[13] Yet she expressed scepticism about Besant's conversion. Edgar Jepson explained:

Her [Edith's] interest in the occult had brought her into close contact with Mrs Annie Besant, in the days when it had been made quite clear to that good woman that she was not going to become the supreme ruler of the Fabian Society, and she was turning her attention to Spiritualism, in which there seemed a possibility of undisputed sway. Mrs Bland told me that it was truly entertaining to observe the firmness with which Mrs Besant insisted that spiritualistic phenomena should come and saw to it that they did come, and then the ease with which she persuaded herself that they had come wholly of themselves. It is plain therefore that Mrs Besant was fortunate in presently discovering Theosophy, and that her decision to rule in Theosophy rather than serve in socialism was sound.[14]

This scepticism creeps into *The Story of the Amulet* too:

A journalist, who was just leaving the museum, spoke to Robert as he passed.

'Theosophy, I suppose?' he said. 'Is she Mrs Besant?'

'*Yes*,' said Robert recklessly.

The journalist passed through the gates just before they were shut.

He rushed off to Fleet Street, and his paper got out a new edition within half an hour.

MRS BESANT AND THEOSOPHY: IMPERTINENT MIRACLE AT THE BRITISH MUSEUM.[15]

Edith's reputed membership of the Hermetic Order of the Golden Dawn, the foremost occult organisation of the day, is intriguing. The founding principles of the order were drawn from new interpretations of ancient texts, particularly those written by mystic and philosopher Hermes Trismegistus. By 1896 more than three hundred men and women, drawn predominantly from the middle classes, had joined this shadowy organisation. Among them were Arthur Conan Doyle, Aleister Crowley, W.B. Yeats, Constance Wilde, Bram Stoker, Florence Farr and Maud Gonne, who resigned on the grounds that her fellow members were inherently dull. 'They looked so incongruous in their cloaks and badges at initiation ceremonies,' she complained.[16] Most biographical accounts suggest that Edith was a member of Golden Dawn, yet evidence to support this is rarely cited. The organisation was of course secretive by nature, yet eyewitness accounts never mentioned her as they did others and her name does not appear on the rolls.[17] Budge too never joined the order even though his translation of *The Book of the Dead* (1895) had particular significance for members.

There is no doubt that Edith was drawn to darkness, and the magic in her stories often takes a dark turn. Quentin falls asleep at Stonehenge in 'Accidental Magic'. When he wakes in 'the great and immortal kingdom of Atlantis', surrounded by blue-robed priests, he realises he has been chosen for sacrifice. He is a curious boy and questions his mother:

> 'I say, mother, tell me some more about Atlantis.' Or, 'Mother, tell me some more about ancient Egypt and the little toy-boats they made for their little boys.' Or, 'Mother, tell me about the people who think Lord Bacon wrote Shakespeare.'[18]

This last question intrigued Edith for more than a decade and consumed vast quantities of her time, energy and money. She had always loved Shakespeare's plays and her attempts to explain them to her children prompted her to adapt them into stories. In her introduction to *The Children's Shakespeare*, she is huddled with Iris and Rosamund before a roaring fire at an inn in Stratford-upon-Avon. They are poring over a volume of *Collected Works* the innkeeper has lent them. Edith 'with eyes fixed on the fire was wandering happily in the immortal dreamland peopled by Rosalind and Imogen, Lear and Hamlet'. She is roused by a 'small sigh':

> 'I can't understand a word of it,' said Iris.
> 'And you said it was so beautiful,' Rosamund added, reproachfully. 'What does it all mean?'
> 'Yes,' Iris went on, 'you said it was a fairytale, and we've read three pages and there's nothing about fairies, not even a dwarf, or a fairy god-mother.'
> 'And what does "misgraffed" mean?'
> 'And "vantage," and "austerity," and "belike," and "edict," and–?'
> 'Stop, stop,' I cried, 'I will tell you the story.'
> In a moment they were nestling beside me, cooing with the pleasure that the promise of a story always brings them.

Iris asks her mother:

Why don't you write the stories for us so that we can understand them, just as you told us that, and then, when we are grown up, we shall understand the plays so much better?[19]

It is not known at what point Edith became fascinated by a theory that suggested a group of writers and thinkers led by Sir Francis Bacon had written Shakespeare's plays. She also subscribed to a belief that they had embedded an elaborate philosophic system in the texts.* Prominent figures who thought likewise included Friedrich Nietzsche, Henry James and the German mathematician Georg Cantor. Mark Twain explored this in *Is Shakespeare Dead?*, while her old friend Andrew Lang wrote *Shakespeare, Bacon and the Great Unknown*.

Edith decided she would try to decipher, using mathematics, the coded information embedded in Shakespearean texts that confirmed Bacon as their author. Just as she had recruited Budge to explain ancient Egyptian magic, she approached mathematician Edward Neville da Costa Andrade, who would one day become a distinguished physicist.† Andrade had submitted several poems to *The Neolith*, which Edith had chosen not to publish, but they became friends anyway. When Berta Ruck met him at Well Hall, she described him as 'rather bewildered-looking'.[20]

It must have frustrated a man as mathematically gifted as Andrade to have to explain complex logarithms to a woman he regarded as having 'no mathematical capabilities at all'.[21] He was certain that Shakespeare had written his plays and regarded her investigations as 'dreary nonsense'. He believed that she had received encouragement from a 'monstrous regiment of quacks'.[22] Yet he was fond of her and he worried that this pursuit had 'completely stopped her creative work'. He may have hoped to debunk her notions and persuade her to abandon this project by gently working through the mathematics with her.

---

* This theory gained currency midway through the eighteenth century after the publication in 1857 of *The Philosophy of the Plays of Shakespeare Unfolded* by Delia Bacon. It was perpetuated by William Henry Smith, author of *Was Lord Bacon the Author of Shakespeare's Plays?* in 1856.

† Andrade was later appointed Professor of Physics at University College London and Director of the Royal Institution Davy-Faraday Research Laboratory. In 1958 he was awarded the Royal Society Hughes Medal. Edith dedicated *Wet Magic* to him.

In pursuit of her proof Edith purchased numerous books on ciphers and secret codes. Several were rare and costly, including an original 1614 edition of Napier's *Mirifici Logarithmorum Canonis Descriptio*. She even studied Latin to help her with her quest. Yet it was doomed by her innumeracy. In an attempt to explain complex logarithms, Andrade resorted to using matches and sand. He recalled:

> She was by nature quite incapable of mastering the means of mathematical symbols and arguments and for a long time based theories on the supposition that the incommensurable number e was 2.7182, whereas these are but the first five figures of a number that can be worked out to as many as thirty decimal figures.[23]

When challenged on its validity, Edith would describe her work as a 'mental narcotic – such as some people find playing patience'. In the grip of her obsession she would spend whole days working on ciphers, ignoring stories she was contracted to complete, or rushing through them to get them out of the way. In her eagerness to prove her theory she would pounce on random sequences of letters. She insisted that sections of *Sonnet CV* could be deciphered as 'I am F.B.' or 'I am Fras B.' or 'I am Hog' or 'F. Ba is W. Sha'. She also searched for significant dates – 1616, the year of Shakespeare's death, or 1623, the year *Mr. William Shakespeare's Comedies, Histories, & Tragedies*, commonly referred to as the 'First Folio', was published. She also explored the theories of occult Baconians who credited Rosicrucian mysteries to him.

She broadened her investigations to include Elizabethan and Early Jacobean texts such as Spencer's *Faerie Queene* and Burton's *Anatomy of Melancholy*. She even scoured the authorised version of the Bible in the hope of uncovering clues concealed within the text. Andrade told Doris Langley Moore:

> In the end it grew, as far as I could make out, into a theory that some mysterious collection wrote Shakespeare's plays, Bacon's essays, Burton's 'Anatomy of Melancholy', the Authorised Version, Spenser's 'Faerie Queene', and many other books.[24]

Gripped by Baconian mania, she wrote to her brother Harry in Australia in 1912, to ask him if he was a Baconian or a Shakespearean.

She explained:

> I have been investigating the question of ciphers in the works of
> Shakespeare – and have found several – but I don't know enough about
> figures to get very far. I wish you were here to help me![25]

In a follow-up letter she expressed frustration with the logarithms she
was using: 'The Shakespeare Cipher I am after involves the use of Logs not
Briggs but Napier's,' she wrote. 'I can get no book dealing with Napier's
Logs to the base E i.e. $1/2.2121396$ – and so on. And I am quite incapable
of learning such things from books even if there were one, which I don't
believe there is.'[26]

No one was safe from her quest. One young visitor to Well Hall
remembered being handed a magnifying glass and asked to find a pig
in an old engraving or print of Shakespeare.[27] In 1914 Edith turned to
George Seaver, a young classics tutor she had hired to coach thirteen-
year-old John for his school entrance exam. He described his first
sighting of her:

> Presently the door was flung open and a tall lady in a trailing black silk gown
> and somewhat careless disarray stepped – or rather swept into the room.
> Her countenance was round and ruddy, her bird-like eyes and curly hair
> were brown, her freckled wrists jingled with silver bangles, other trinkets
> hung from necklaces about her dress; she carried a long cigarette-holder in
> one hand and under her arm a tobacco-tin and papers; with nimble fingers
> she rolled her own cigarettes and smoked incessantly. She might have been
> a gipsy queen.[28]

Seaver admired Edith enormously and he hated to see her wasting
her time, and what he recognised as a genuinely deep knowledge of
Shakespeare's work, on what he regarded as 'naïve ingenuity in fitting
facts to theories'. Other friends tried to dissuade her too. John Squire,
a reviewer for literary magazine the *New Age*, spent hours attempting to
convince her that she was wasting her time. On one occasion he sat up
with her until two o'clock in the morning while she laboured over some
Baconian 'proof' that was dependent on her erroneous calculation that 4
x 13 = 42. He pointed out her error and was dismayed when she seemed
surprised rather than disillusioned.

George Bernard Shaw learned of her obsession when she asked to borrow his first folio facsimiles of Shakespeare. When she asked him for money to fund her investigation, he gave her a cheque for £100. He did likewise the following year but warned her to sort out her finances and to accept the commissions she was missing out on. She wrote to assure him of her commitment and he sent her a postcard with the perfect riposte:

> Have you ever considered (this is a belated reply to yours of 8th May) how utterly impossible it is that Shaw of Dublin could have written his wonderful plays. Is it not clear that they were written by Sidney Webb L.L.B. Shaw was an utterly ignorant man. His father was an unsuccessful business man always on the verge of bankruptcy, just like old Shakespear [sic] or John Dickens. Shaw had a very narrow escape from the police for setting fire to a common [in Dalkey in Dublin at the age of twelve]. He was a disgrace to his school, where he acquired little Latin & less Greek. He got no secondary education & came to London an unknown & obscure provincial. And this is the man to whom people attribute the omniscience, the knowledge of public affairs, of law, of medicine, of navigation &c&c&c, which informs the plays and prefaces of G.B.S. Absurd! Webb, the L.L.B, the man who carried all before him in examinations in his boyhood, the upper division civil servant of the Foreign and Colonial Offices, the author of Industrial Democracy &c, was clearly the man. I could pile the case much higher if there was room.
>
> G.B.S.[29]

It would seem those few who supported her had questionable motives. Prominent among them was Edmund Vivian Tanner, brother of the celebrated actress Mrs Patrick Campbell, who was born Beatrice Stella Tanner. Tanner used the alias Max, and Edith named one of her dachshunds after him. He claimed to have collaborated with Sir Edwin Durning-Lawrence on *The Problem of the Shakespeare Plays* (1910), which experts dismissed. Andrade considered him a charlatan and described him as 'a long-haired man whom she [Edith] maintained at her expense in Dean Street'.[30] When she took a lease on a flat at 42 Rathbone Place in 1912 she allowed him to stay there too. She even paid him a small allowance. Tanner, who suffered from tuberculosis, is thought to have inspired Great Uncle Charles in *The Wonderful Garden*:

He was more shadowy than you would think anybody could be. He was more like a lightly printed photograph from an insufficiently exposed and imperfectly developed negative than anything else I can think of. He was as thin and pale as Mrs Wilmington [his housekeeper], but there was nothing hard or bony about him. He was soft as a shadow – his voice, his hand, his eyes.[31]

It may have been Tanner who encouraged Edith to believe she had made a breakthrough. She told A.P. Watt, her new agent:

I know it sounds mad, but I have found the Shakespeare cipher. I have told no one but you. The discovery ought to be worth thousands of pounds. I can't leave my work. Do trust my word. I have imagination but I am not a fool or a liar. *Come and see.* You will be very glad if you *do* come. It is wonderful yet simple and you can work it yourself. I am willing to trust you with the secret, and I think you will come at once and receive it… *It comes out as definitely as the result of an addition sum.* You will see. You will see… Try not to think about history or literature or the *improbability* of cipher being there. It *is* there.[32]

She offered to write a series of articles on her discoveries. Like several others, she had become convinced that Elizabeth I had been married in secret to the Earl of Leicester and had two sons by him – Francis Bacon and the Earl of Essex.

Although she was sincere in her pursuit, she could send herself up too. She included playful references to her obsession in several of her books. William Bats from *Dormant* is a Baconian. In *The Magic City* her gaoler, Mr Bacon-Shakespeare, 'has written no less than twenty-seven volumes, all in cypher' on the subject of a crochet mat that no one can unravel since he has forgotten the cypher. One exchange between Katherine and Edward from *The Incredible Honeymoon* goes as follows:

'You aren't a Baconian, are you?' she asked, looking at him rather timidly across the teacups. 'But you can't be, because I know they're all mad.' 'A good many of them are very, very silly,' he owned, 'but don't be afraid – I'm not a Baconian, for Baconians are convinced that Bacon wrote the whole of Elizabethan and Jacobean literature off his own bat. I only think there's a mystery. You remember Dickens said the life of Shakespeare was

a fine mystery and he trembled daily least something should turn up.'
'And nothing has.' 'Nothing. That's just it. There's hardly anything known
about the man.'[33]

Edward insists he is not a Baconian, but he tells Katherine: 'I'm pretty
sure that whoever wrote "Hamlet", that frowsy, money-grubbing provin-
cial never did.'[34] One character in *The Incredible Honeymoon*, 'a tall, gaunt
man in loose, ill-fitting clothing with a dispatch case in one hand and three
or four note-books in the other', has given up his job as an accountant and
spent eighteen years decrypting ciphers. He tells Edward and Katherine
that Shakespeare's grave contains no body, and he cites 'the evidence of
facts as well as of ciphers'.[35]

As to what Hubert made of all this, he wrote in *The Happy Moralist*:

The well-meaning and industrious pedants who spend time and temper in
wrangling as to whether Shakespeare was Bacon and Bacon was the son
of Queen Elizabeth… doubtless have a place to fill in the universal scheme
of things; but their place, we may be sure, is not among the artists. And
yet in saying so much I am falling perhaps into the very error I set out to
condemn; for if more pleasure is to be got from combing a folio through a
magnifying glass in order to discover a possible cypher than with Romeo
wooing Juliet on her balcony, who am I that I should scoff?[36]

Edith was very vocal in stating her position. When an exchange of
letters was published in the *Sheffield Daily Telegraph* during 1911 and 1912,
she took the side of the Baconians. Writing of Shakespeare's grave, she
wondered:

Whether the person occupying the grave (or enjoying the fame) is the person entitled to occupy the grave (or enjoy that fame). The problem is to
find out who is in that grave (enjoying that fame), to find out whether the
grave (or fame) is occupied by a great and noble man, or whether, as some
of us fear, a very costly and beautiful monument has been erected – by
regrettable error – over the body of a dead donkey.[37]

In 'An Iconoclast in Stratford', which she wrote in 1921, she declared:
'I cannot find the slightest shadow of evidence that Shakespeare was
born in this house.' She insisted that Stratford 'lives on the open-mouthed

credulity of its visitors'. Yet she seemed cured of her Baconian obsession, since she declared:

> Is there not Shakespeare's true shrine, his glorious works, which, as he himself foresaw, 'marble and the gilded monument of princes' shall not outlive? About the authenticity of such relics as Hamlet and Lear there is no doubt; they bear in them the signet-stamp of immortal genius. Can we not honour the man who wrote them, without wasting enthusiasm on rings that he never wore and snuff boxes that he never touched? And if we must have some material object for our devotion there is always the grave-stone in the chancel of Stratford church under which lies Shakespeare's last secret. We can at least lay our garlands there with clean hands and with honest hearts.[38]

CHAPTER 20

'I AM NOT HURT'

Hubert Bland, although powerful and imposing, was plagued with chronic heart trouble for much of his adult life, a condition no doubt aggravated by his enthusiasm for cigarettes. Sometime around 1910, when he was in his mid-fifties, he turned down an invitation to lecture on the grounds that he never knew when 'one of these brief heart attacks is coming on'.[1] A major attack in November 1910 brought him so low that he was obliged to rest completely over Christmas. By January he was well enough to travel with Edith to the Headland House Hotel in the busy fishing port of Looe in Cornwall, where they took the sea air for a month.

He seemed much recovered when they returned home, but his eyesight, never dependable, had begun to fail badly. He was diagnosed with retinal disease in both eyes. When a heavy fall detached the retina in his relatively good eye, doctors warned him that he would almost certainly go blind. As he was desperate to avoid this, he agreed to undergo an expensive course of treatment, but it had little effect. Lecturing became impossible and he resigned his position as honorary treasurer of the Fabian Society, a post he had held since its formation in 1884. He did continue with his weekly column in the *Sunday Chronicle* and he reviewed novels for his son-in-law Clifford Sharp at the *New Statesman*, but he depended on Alice to read and take dictation for him.

By the spring Edith was desperate for a holiday, but she seemed reluctant to return to the 'Other House' in Dymchurch. Perhaps it seemed haunted by memories of the time she had spent there with Richard Reynolds, who was married to her niece by then. Instead she rented Crowlink Farmhouse, which she described to Harry as 'an old farm house near the sea – very lovely'.[2] Large enough to accommodate a dozen guests at a time, it was perched high above the Seven Sisters on the cliffs of the West Sussex coast and had once been a smugglers' retreat. She wrote it into *The Incredible Honeymoon* as 'Crow's Nest Farm':

Then over the crest of the hill, in a hollow of the downs there was the dark-spread blot of house and farm buildings ... The path that led to the door had its bricks outlined with green grass, a house-leek spread its rosettes on the sloping lichened tiles of the roof, and in the corner of the window the toad-flax flaunted its little helmets of orange and sulphur colour.[3]

Edith decided that Crowlink was haunted and nailed charms over the lintels to ward off malevolent spirits. She loved the early spring solitude of her new surroundings, which she described in a letter to Lady Dunsany:

It is a lonely little house on the downs, not a sound all day but the wind and the sea, and on sunny days, the skylarks. The quiet is like a cool kind hand on one's forehead. There are no flowers now, except the furze which as you know only goes out of flower when kisses go out of season.[4]

During the six years that followed she fled to Crowlink as often as possible. When she could not get there, she sublet it to friends. One was historical novelist Maurice Hewlett, who needed a retreat after he separated from his wife, Hilda, in 1914. This breach was caused in part by her obsession with aviation; in 1911 she had become the first woman in England to gain a pilot's licence.

During the summer of 1911 Edith stayed in Birmingham with Dorothea and Richard. He drove her to Edgbaston so she could take three young fans out for the day. They were Mavis and Cecily Carter, cousins in their mid-teens, and Kathleen, or Kay, Mavis's ten-year-old sister. They went to the Lord Leycester Hospital, an historic group of medieval timber-framed buildings on Warwick High Street dating mainly from the late fourteenth century. Then on to Warwick Castle, Guy's Cliffe, and Stratford-upon-Avon, where Edith complained about having to pay sixpence to visit Shakespeare's church.

Mavis had been the first to discover Edith, when she received a copy of *Five Children and It* for her ninth birthday. She was captivated by it and shared her enthusiasm with Cecily and Kay. They decided to write to Edith to thank her for writing it. Mavis explained:

The first letter went astray and daring greatly we wrote again. This time we received a prompt reply written in her own broad, generous but difficult-to-read handwriting that I was soon to know so well. 'My dears,' she wrote,

'I *did* reply to your first letters. I wonder what happened to mine? Perhaps it got put in a drawer and slipped over the edge and was lost forever, or perhaps bad boys put lighted fuses in the pillar box in which it was posted... its fate would remain a mystery like that of the Man in the Iron Mask, or what became of the little Dauphin?[5]

In her letter Cecily, with the impudence of youth, had included a list of authors whose work she preferred. Edith commended her choices and advised her to add Mrs Ewing to her list. From then on the girls sent Edith a letter on her birthday every year. Her responses were unfailingly warm. She dedicated *The Wonderful Garden* 'to Cecily, Kathleen and Mavis Carter'. She told Kay that she wished for a magic carpet so she could bring them all to her. When she put Mavis and Kay into *Wet Magic*, her last serial for *The Strand Magazine*, she had them reading Kingsley's *The Water Babies*, one of the books they preferred to hers.

In the autumn of 1910 Mavis, aged fourteen, was sent to boarding school in Folkestone. Her mother sent Edith a photograph accompanied by a note telling her how happy she was to be in a school near Dymchurch, where they knew Edith spent her holidays. A telegraph arrived the following day, inviting them to lunch at 'the Other House'. Mavis recorded her memories of this day:

I remember well driving from Folkestone along the coast, punctuated by the old Martello towers erected in the days when Napoleon was expected to invade our shores. The old horse clip-clopped along and my heart was beating in anticipation. We (my mother and I) arrived at a shabby lovable house near the sea, and she stood at the door to welcome us. I can see her still so vividly – of medium height and fullish figure, her brown untidy curly hair piled up and held with tortoiseshell combs. Her kind and beautiful brown eyes looked at one, over spectacles tilted to the very tip of her well-shaped nose – they looked with such penetration I remember. She wore flowing frocks of 'Liberty' browns and flames, hanging from a yoke with flowing sleeves, and I rather think amber beads; and a longish cigarette holder completed the picture, for she was always smoking.[6]

To put the young girl at her ease, Edith had organised for a basket of kittens to be brought to the house. For lunch she served roast chicken with bread sauce, followed by chocolate pudding. The day was a great success and they resolved to meet any time Edith was in the Midlands, but they mostly communicated by letter. Edith became a trusted adult friend who was always ready with encouragement or advice. When Mavis confessed that she had difficulty controlling her temper, Edith replied with eight pages of reassurance that began: 'My dear, *I* know what it is to have a temper, I've had a long and hard struggle with mine.' When Edith undertook to write a column describing her childhood for the *Daily Chronicle*, she consulted Mavis on what she thought readers might enjoy. When she asked her to let her know if she ever skipped or disliked any parts of her books so she could write better stories in the future, Mavis assured her that she loved every word.

Edith had a reputation for not taking criticism well, but she was in the habit of asking trusted friends for their opinion on her work. She sent a proof copy of her supernatural novel *Dormant* (1911), which she had completed at Crowlink, to Lady Dunsany and asked her to check if she had 'made footmen or butlers do anything foreign to their beautiful natures'. She also asked for permission to dedicate it:

To Lady Dunsany

From

E. Nesbit

They had grown close. When Edith charted the moat at Well Hall, she included a 'Lady Beatrice's Haven'. She also chose the name 'Dunsania' for 'a great tract of country' within her boundary walls.

Edith's books were selling poorly by then and sales of *Dormant* were disappointing. When she declined Harry's invitation to invest in a newspaper he hoped to establish in Brisbane, she explained that they were 'awfully hard up at present'. She sent him an unpublished poem and asked him to return it if he did not use it. 'I am frightfully busy,' she told him, 'Rehearsals of my play every day.'[7] The play she was referring to was *Unexceptional References*, a slight one-act comedy licensed to the Royalty Theatre in Dean Street. Since it was performed just once, as a matinee, on 10 December 1912, she certainly wasn't going to make her fortune from it.

That same month the first instalment of *Wet Magic* appeared in *The Strand Magazine*, along with her story the 'The Sleuth Worm', the first of her work to appear in the magazine that year. Edith attributed her absence to 'the muddleheadedness of an agent' but it seems more likely that she had nothing ready. She was still spending far too much time on her Baconian investigations and she had been in such a hurry to finish her previous serial, *The Wonderful Garden*, that her illustrator H.R. Miller needed to work from chapter summaries and drawings she had dashed off. She did promise to alter any aspect that was at odds with his illustrations.

This decline in sales had been of concern in 1910 when Macmillan published *The Magic City*. Desperate to promote it, Edith suggested mounting a small exhibition in Selfridges. H.R. Miller helped her with this project and remembered that the store manager had been horrified to discover how many bricks she had taken from the toy department. When he refused to allow her to take any more, she took umbrage and left. She took her project elsewhere. In a letter to Harry, she explained that she was building 'a "Magic City" of bricks and dominoes and odds and ends, at Olympia for the Children's Welfare Exhibition'. In preparation, she erected a section measuring ten feet by six in her Rathbone Place flat. This time Sir Frederick Macmillan offered to pay for the bricks.

The Children's Welfare Exhibition was held at London's Olympia from 31 December 1912 to 11 January 1913. Thousands of visitors, including politicians and several members of the Royal Family, attended debates, discussions and lectures on children's literature, health and psychology. Edith's booth was open on one side and the three enclosing walls were painted sky blue. On a raised surface she had constructed a city with elaborate palaces and towers, delicate bridges and lush gardens, all fashioned from common household items: cotton reels, biscuit tins, saucepan lids and chessmen. She hung illustrations from *The Magic City* on the walls and offered copies for sale.

While she was there, Edith chatted with fans and read fairy tales in a session chaired by G.K. Chesterton. Afterwards she responded to numerous letters requesting instructions for building a city like hers by writing *Wings and the Child*. She included an account of the Children's Welfare Exhibition:

Let me remember how many good friends I found among the keepers of the stalls, how a great personage of the *Daily News* came with his wife at the last despairing moment, and lent me the golden and ruby lamps from their dining-table, how the Boy Scouts 'put themselves in four' to get me some cocoa-nuts for roofs of cottages, how their Scout Master gave me fourteen beautiful little ivory fishes with black eyes, to put in my silver paper ponds, how the basket-makers on the one side and the home hobbies on the other were to me as brothers, how the Cherry Blossom Boot Polish lady gave me hairpins and the wardens of Messrs W.H. Smith's bookstall gave me friendship, how the gifted boy-sculptor for the Plasticine stall, moved by sheer loving-kindness, rushed over one day and dumped a gorgeous pre-historic beast, modelled by his own hands, in the sands about my Siberian tomb, how the Queen of Portugal came and talked to me for half an hour in the most flattering French, while the Deity from the *Daily News* looked on benign.[8]

It was pointed out to her that poor children could not build her magic city, so she built 'a Poor Child's City of cardboard, treacle-tins, jam-jars and clothes pegs, all painted and polished and cemented until people exclaimed at its beauty and marvelled at its ingenuity'.[9] All this effort did little to improve sales of her book. She never worked with Macmillan again and wrote a letter of complaint:

> I am still not at all well; the failure of *The Magic City* has quite knocked me over. You know, really, I am a person who has never quite grown up, (that is why I am able to write for children!) and I feel this blow as though I were a disappointed child.[10]

Unfortunately *Dormant* and *Ballads and Verses of the Spiritual Life*, both published in 1911, fared no better. Equally disappointing were sales of *The Magic World*, a collection of twelve stories published in 1912. Edith was frantic by the time the final instalment of *Wet Magic* appeared in *The Strand Magazine* in August 1913. She confided in Harry:

> Things are pretty black for us – Hubert has practically lost his sight – he is undergoing a very expensive treatment which *may* do some good, but so far has done very little, if any. I am getting very tired of work, and the expenses of life don't seem to get less. I wish everyone had a small pension at 50 – enough to live on. I have had a novel [*The Incredible Honeymoon*] in hand for some time, but I have been too worried to get on with it. I am now going into the country for a few weeks, in the hope of getting some work done.[11]

Edith retreated to Crowlink with her dogs. She also took her new secretary, who she described as 'a quiet youth who types what I write and in the evenings plays chess with me'. She was 'trying to get well and do a little work', she told Lady Dunsany, but she resented the demands placed upon her:

> I am getting very tired of writing stories and wish I need only write verse, and set down the things I think. Any success my stories have had is due I think to a sort of light-hearted outlook on life – and now that Hubert's eyes have failed him a steam-roller seems to have gone over all ones hopes and ambitions, and it is difficult to remember how it felt to be lighthearted.[12]

She returned to Well Hall with a plan, which was explained in the *Pioneer* newspaper:

> Passers-by, catching glimpses of the garden, often came to ask if flowers were sold. In the old days the flowers were given away. But these enquiries suggested a new industry.[13]

Edith described her glorious flowers in her final novel, *The Lark* (1922):

> The peonies were out now – great balls of splendid crimson – and the white balls of the guelder rose, sheaves of violet and purple flags, the wide graceful arches of Solomon's seal, armfuls of lilac sweet as Spring herself, tall tulips rosy and white and gold, the yellow stars of the leopard's bane – oxslips, cowslips, and always forget-me-nots.[14]

Berta Ruck remarked of Edith, 'if I know her generous heart the flowers would have been made up in enormous bunches and the fruit would be heavily overweight!'[15] Sure enough, her prices were keen. She refused to accept any payment for a beautiful wreath of narcissi and white lilac that she made for a shabbily dressed woman who enquired about flowers for her daughter's funeral; she even pinned original verses among the blooms. It was only when war came that her takings improved. At the height of hostilities she was making twenty-five shillings a week.

By spring 1914 Hubert had lost his sight entirely. Edith left him with Alice and Ada Breakell and travelled to Crowlink with her son John. With them went his friend Stephen Chant, and Cecil Gould, who was Gerald's younger brother.* On the afternoon of 14 April Hubert finished dictating several book reviews and a letter to the editor of *The Chronicle* to Alice, rose unsteadily to his feet and announced 'Mouse, I feel giddy.' She ran to support him and shouted for Ada to phone for the doctor. As Hubert fell to the floor he reassured her that he was not hurt. He died almost instantly. Since Rosamund was convalescing in Dymchurch after a serious illness, Alice phoned Clifford Sharp, who arrived with Iris. It was he who organised for a death mask to be made. She then sent Edith a telegram urging: 'Come at once Hubert very ill.' They were having supper when it arrived. Edith ordered a car from nearby Eastbourne and they drove home in complete silence. They arrived at two in the morning and learned that Hubert had been dead for several hours by then. Unable to comprehend her loss, Edith attempted to warm Hubert back to life by covering him with eiderdowns and hot water bottles. It took a doctor opening a vein to convince her that he was gone.

On 19 April 1914 *The Chronicle* carried a report headed 'Sudden End to a Great Writer's Career'. It was attributed to a young journalist named St John Ervine, who was a member of the Fabian nursery and had been suggested by Clifford Sharp. Although Ervine admired Hubert enormously, he barely knew Edith and he appears to have sourced much of his information from Marshall Steele's daughter Enid, who disliked her intensely.† This odd eulogy made no mention of Hubert's wife and promoted Alice instead. Describing his first sighting of Hubert, Ervine wrote:

> He was striding down Walbrook, talking loudly in his curious, thin, tinny voice to a lady whom I afterwards learned to know as his devoted friend and, when his eyes failed him, secretary, Miss Alice Hoatson.[16]

In response, Alice described Ervine's obituary as 'the most insulting and impossible laudation – meant as praise no doubt, but dreadful to me, and to Edith too'.[17]

Edith's tribute to Hubert was to compile *Essays by Hubert Bland: 'Hubert' of the Sunday Chronicle*, which she dedicated to 'the readers who loved Hubert'. In a touching epilogue she commended the qualities she admired most in her late husband:

---

* She dedicated *The Magic City* to Barbara, Maurice and Stephen Chant. Cecil Gould was killed in action in 1916.

† It seems this animosity was mutual, since Edith used her name for the nasty aunt in *Wet Magic*.

Hubert wrote as he spoke and he spoke as he thought. He never did for money or for fame sell himself. He had, in the highest degree, the quality of intellectual honesty. He would not deceive himself, nor would he suffer others to be deceived. His was the large tolerance of one who understands the weakness and the strength of the soul of man. He hated the Pharisees, the Prigs, the Puritans, and those who grind the faces of the poor. All men else he loved.[18]

She praised his bravery in facing blindness 'like a man' and reconstructed his final moments: 'Hubert worked to the last, he died working, and his last words when he felt the hand of death upon him were "I am not hurt".'[19] Whether she felt regret that these words were not directed at her, she did not disclose.

In keeping with her rather macabre nature, Edith kept Hubert's death mask wrapped in a silk handkerchief on a shelf beside the fireplace in her living room. She would show it to people of whom she was particularly fond.[20] Although their marriage had been turbulent, she missed the man she described as her 'close and constant companion and friend for thirty-seven years'.[21] Berta Ruck insisted that 'they were interested in each other to the end'. She suggested that Hubert had provided Edith with the drama she needed in her life.[22] It is true that she sometimes seemed more amused than upset by his womanising. She told May Bowley that she had once called on a 'Mrs M.', an attractive young married friend, only to find her 'becomingly arrayed as an interesting invalid with a sprained ankle, lying on a sofa, while Mr Bland sat by her side reading poetry to her'. She observed that it was 'his turn to look rather foolish'.[23] Toleration for such behaviour was higher at that time. As Edgar Jepson wrote of Hubert:

During the ten years, or more, that we were on friendly terms I never knew him to have more than two, or perhaps three [mistresses] at a time, and no one can say that was excessive for the days of Edward the Peacemaker.[24]

The *Liverpool Echo* reported on the terms of Hubert's will:

The testator left the balance of his property upon trust to his youngest son, John, stating: 'This I do because my wife is happily able to earn a good income, and my other children are provided for.'[25]

Further detail was provided in the *Yorkshire Post and Leeds Intelligencer*:

He bequeathed his household effects to his wife ('E. Nesbit'), expressing the hope that she will give any of his books which she may not care to keep for herself to such libraries or persons as she may consider will make good use of them, and that she would make gifts of mementos of his personal effects to intimate friends. The balance of his property he left upon trust for J.B.[26]

Shortly after he lost his father, Edith took John, aged thirteen, to Paris where they spent time with her friend Alphonse Courlander, Paris correspondent for the *Daily Express*, his wife, Elsa, and their daughter, Rosemary. Edith fell desperately ill while they were there and crippling stomach pains confined her to her hotel room. When Alice arrived to take them home, she found her bedbound and surviving on a diet of bread and milk. In England she was diagnosed with a duodenal ulcer and admitted to Guy's Hospital for an operation. Money was so scarce that she could not afford to hire a car to take her there. As Hubert had instructed Alice to go to Shaw for help should she ever need it, she asked if she might borrow his car. He told her it was in for repair and gave her five pounds to hire one. Edith was exasperated when she returned change to him of more than three pounds.

On 22 September 1914 the *Hull Daily Mail* reported that 'E. Nesbit (Mrs Hubert Bland), the well-known writer for children, has undergone a serious operation at Guy's Hospital, London and is still very ill'.[27] Her temperature had dropped so dramatically that doctors warned Iris there was little hope of her surviving. Ignoring their advice, Edith insisted that Iris feed her half a teaspoon of Brand's Essence of Beef every hour. She was discharged shortly afterwards.

Her long convalescence was not helped by tragic news that reached her on 23 October. When war was declared on 28 July 1914, shortly after she left Paris, her friend Alphonse Courlander spoke of travelling to the front. Yet he had been traumatised by his experiences covering the Balkan Wars of 1912-13. Hamilton Fyfe, a journalist friend, described his state of mind: 'A delightful fellow he was, amusing, quick-witted, but not well-equipped to withstand the panic which seized the city as the Germans came nearer every day.' Courlander's response was catastrophic:

One morning he made up his mind to leave for London [where his wife and daughter were by then]. Then, as he sat in the train, the shame of abandoning his post came vividly before him and he jumped out. But the next morning he went to the station again and this time he stayed in the train. In London he was badly received. He killed himself.[28]

Courlander was just thirty-three years old when he took his own life. Elsa, his widow, stayed in London, where she helped Alice nurse Edith back to health.

The Bland family was caught up in hostilities too. Paul joined the special constabulary and Iris was appointed as an overseer at the Woolwich munitions factory, where she was joined by several members of the Well Hall staff who found jobs filling shells. Clifford Sharp was recruited by the Foreign Office and took Rosamund to Sweden on a covert diplomatic mission. Although Edith detested war, she was unwavering in her patriotism. She composed war poetry and compiled *Battle Songs, Chosen by E. Nesbit*. True to her kind and contradictory nature, she also sheltered an elderly German friend to save him from internment. She chastised Alice for applauding the shooting down of a zeppelin, reminding her that people were being burned alive before their eyes. When Edward Andrade was sent to the front, she wrote to express her hope that war would be over by summer:

> But with this war going on the world seems so unreal that doing any writing seems futile. It feels like beginning an epic on the morning of the Last Day, with the last trumps sounding in your ears.[29]

She lit a candle for Andrade on Easter Sunday and placed his badge in front of a statue of St Anthony. He visited her at Well Hall whenever he had leave. She told Mavis Carter that she was struggling to finish *The Incredible Honeymoon* because the 'horrible war' had added to 'the desolation and the feeling that nothing is worthwhile'. She described it as 'a nightmare of horror, the whole thing'.[30] In a gloomy letter to Harry, in which she accepted that she would probably never see him again, she wrote: 'If I could live without writing I should like never to write another line.'[31] Yet all was not bleak. She welcomed cheery visits from Enid Bagnold, future author of *National Velvet*, who came to tea on her motorcycle several times when she was working as a Voluntary Aid Detachment at the Royal

Herbert Hospital. As a teenager Bagnold had lived on nearby Shooters Hill. She had been so keen to meet a writer that she had taken walks in the hope of bumping into Edith or Hubert.

Edith's financial woes were alleviated somewhat in 1916 when Maurice Hewlett, her tenant at Crowlink, organised for her to receive a Civil Pension of sixty pounds 'in consideration of the merits of her writings in prose and poetry, and of her straitened circumstances'.[32] This was supplemented with tiny subventions she received from the Royal Literary Fund, although these did little to help her meet her commitments. Her seaside holidays were put on hold and her dinner parties curtailed. Even so, Elsa Courlander insisted that she looked 'as much a chatelaine as ever, and there was still a baronial air hanging over the frugal feasts'.[33]

When G.K. Chesterton asked Edith to assist his friend Reginald Brimley Johnson* with the production of a children's newspaper, he explained 'I thought of you not only as the ablest children's novelist I know, but also more generally as one who understands the heroic simplicity of all revolutions of the right sort'.[34] She found Johnson to be a 'gracious, generous, and vivid personality' and agreed for her name to be included in his prospectus, but the scheme fell through due to lack of funding.

Since it was her habit to write late into the night, she was usually first downstairs during air raids. She would organise card games to keep family and guests occupied. One favourite was racing demon, a fast and furious form of patience that they played by the light of a flickering candle. As trams on the line from Woolwich to Eltham were obliged to stop outside Well Hall during these air raids, she would take coffee to those on board. She was standing on the top of the tram, surrounded by family, passengers and guests, when she witnessed the zeppelin being brought down. She was reduced to tears.

War seemed interminable, and she missed Hubert desperately. Berta Ruck confirmed this:

> E. Nesbit often told me of her loneliness after her husband's death; her children were grown up and John, who later became a doctor, seemed to be the only one at home and her devoted slave.[35]

---

* A biographer, critic and editor who specialised in writing about nineteenth-century English literature and literary figures.

She confided in Edward Andrade. 'Nothing seems worthwhile, some-how,' she told him. 'It is like doing work on the sea shore when you know the tide is coming in that will wash away you and your work together.'[36] A prayer she composed expresses her longing for companionship:

> God give me a garden of roses,
> And, someone to walk with there[37]

It was during these bleak days that she grew close to the man who would bring her great happiness during the years that remained to her.

CHAPTER 21

'A HANDYMAN OF THE SEA'

Edith had chosen Well Hall for its seclusion but the tramline had run past her gate since 1905 and a branch of the Woolwich Co-operative stores had opened across the road from her in 1906. Now war accelerated development. The Royal Arsenal at Woolwich lay four miles due north and extended over 1,300 acres. At the height of production, eighty thousand people were employed there and local housing for munitions workers was supplemented with wooden detached hutments as war rumbled on. In June 1917 an article published in the *Woolwich Pioneer and Labour Journal*, a weekly newspaper produced by the Woolwich Labour Party from 1904 to 1922, documented the impact of war on Well Hall:

> The first change came with the cultivation of all available land: the old orchard, long left to run wild in tangled beauty, was let out in allotments to working men. Gone are the pretty weeds and wild roses and lace-flowered elder trees; the old orchard now looks like a patch of French ground, intensively tilled.[1]

When the government began requisitioning unused land in 1916, Edith, in a panic, organised for her gardener to let their paddock in allotments. In 'The Voyage of the Hut', which she wrote for *The Graphic*, she admitted that she saw opportunity in adversity:

> In the first year of the war a garden suburb and a sprawling Alpine-looking village of huts for munition-workers sprang up about us. And workmen passing saw our good green garden, and came in, by ones and twos and half-dozens, to ask whether we sold flowers.[2]

She described to Edward Andrade how she would 'stand all Friday and Saturday making up bundles of flowers to sell to working men' and admitted: 'It's a queer life, but I think it's the best that could befall me just now.'[3] *The Pioneer* newspaper confirmed:

The doors of Well Hall were besieged on Friday and Saturday by crowds of working men ready to spend shillings and half crowns on big bunches of sweet old-fashioned flowers, to take home to their mothers and wives… From this to the sale of vegetables and plants was an easy step.[4]

Edith also sold flowers, fruit and vegetables to the military hospitals. When her customers enquired about the availability of freshly laid eggs, she advertised for a poultry expert. She hired Lillian Steele Evans, a separated mother of four in her mid-forties who had studied poultry rearing for six years. In autumn 1915 Evans sent her children, two boys and two girls, to boarding school and moved into the cottage that stood to the right of the entrance gate to Well Hall. In 'The Voyage of the Hut' Edith described the impact of her arrival:

The few quiet casual hens who laid our breakfast eggs gave place to 'intensively' kept birds, many of them, and incubators infested the cellars, once sacred to nut-brown ale, to the red wine and the white. And children came to the door a hundred times a day for a pennorth of apples, a ha'porth of parsley, or an egg, 'and mother says can she have a very small one, cheap?'[5]

The *Leeds Mercury* published an article titled 'Popular Novelist becomes Poultry Expert' and illustrated it with a photograph of Edith holding a chick and staring directly into the camera with a characteristically forthright expression.[6] She approached her new business with admirable professionalism; converting outbuildings and printing headed writing paper:

E. Nesbit Bland
Garden Produce,
Poultry,
New-laid Eggs

In 'Poetess and Poultry Culture' the *Sevenoaks Chronicle and Kentish Advertiser* reported: 'Saturdays are market days for Mrs Bland, and on that day all Eltham flocks to her for eggs, roses and home-made jams.'[7] She told Edward Andrade they sold more than one thousand eggs in one week alone. Demand was so strong that Lillian Evans offered classes in poultry keeping to local women. Her daughter Joan left a vivid description of spending her Christmas holidays at Well Hall:

That first night we assembled for supper in the dining room, the old Hall, where a long oval table was placed lengthwise in front of a roaring fire. The table looked gay; there was the smell of food and the chatter of voices; everything radiated warmth. But we were bewildered. Grown-ups gathered; there were other P.G.s [paying guests] beside ourselves, and we children, seven to nine strong, as always, congregated at the far end of the table. And then E. Nesbit appeared on the stairway. She was fifty-seven at this time, rather stout, and dressed in a flowing sort of dress not unlike today's Caftan, with a kind of longish oriental coat. She wore Turkish slippers and quantities of jangling bangles – she always wore those – reaching almost up to her elbows. Her face was small, her voice warm and soft. Her wispy hair was parted in the middle and knotted in a kind of bun at the back. She wore large spectacles and carried under her arm a box – she was seldom without it – in which was a tin of tobacco, cigarette paper, and a long quill cigarette holder.[8]

It struck Joan that the children were invited to join in with adult games and conversations on equal terms. There were sing-songs around the piano and the carpet was rolled back for dancing. She remembered that Edith 'excelled at rhyming games, patience, and chess, and she loved to play whist'.[9] When deadlines obliged her to stay up all night, she could be 'as cantankerous as her own cantankerous Psammead'. Yet she was generally good-tempered. She 'liked to be embraced, and embraced us often and called us "dear"'.[10] Like Edith, Joan was prone to bronchitis. When she felt ill, Edith would sit beside her and tell her a story or allow her to help with sewing and mending.

Joan Evans described Alice as a 'diminutive, vivacious, and competent little woman, with her big brown eyes and mop of grey hair'. She was 'the pivot of all the functional and complicated household finances'.[11] The older Bland children were not much in evidence by then but John, a day pupil at St Paul's School, became like a brother to Joan and her siblings. He could be 'a real loner and very sullen', Joan remembered. When his humour was good, he would perch little Margery Evans on his shoulders, grab Pandora's hand and invite Joan to clutch on to his coat tails before taking them all around London.[12]

Mavis Carter recorded her memories of Well Hall in wartime:

> I remember well one happy Sunday at Well Hall when I arrived to find all and sundry making jam – a glorious mixture of improbable people from every walk of life, all stirring away, while E. Nesbit, who had invited me to lunch, said gaily, 'We've settled *not* to have any lunch as it's war-time!' and handed me instead a spoon for stirring. Oh how hungry I was! Later we all ate by candlelight and adjourned to the panelled drawing room where she sat at the grand piano and played little old-fashioned lilting waltzes while we young things danced or sang songs of her inventing, set to the traditional old tunes, and her son John, aged about seventeen (the lamb of *The Five Children and It*) gave his celebrated imitation of Sir Henry Wood conducting his orchestra at the Queen's Hall 'Proms'.[13]

When Paul Bland joined up as a sapper with the London Electrical Engineers in 1916, he was stationed at a garrison at Newhaven. By then he was engaged to Gertrude Nebel, a primary school teacher of German descent. Edith and she were terrified that he would be posted overseas. That July, Edith travelled to Newhaven to see him. She stayed in a 'horrid inn' which she described in a letter to Edward Andrade:

> My bedstead is enormous, modern and made of brass and iron – but I think the bed dates from one of the early Ptolemys. It has a pyramid in the middle and slopes to the sides so that you can only remain in it by curling around the pyramid and holding on to the one pillow with your eyelashes. The sitting room is what William Morris might have seen in a nightmare. It is difficult to understand how so much plush and walnut and of such a quality could have been brought together in one *real* room.[14]

She struggled with a chest ailment while she was there and drank Worcester sauce to ease it since this was the only warming substance she could find in the coffee room.

While Paul was away, Edith rented his room to paying guests. She had already converted the maid's sitting room into a bedroom since she was working in the Woolwich Arsenal. In her novel *The Lark*, Jane and

Lucinda, two enterprising young women, sell produce from their garden and take in 'Pigs – P.G.'s, you know, Paying Guests'.[15] They don't enjoy having strangers in their home: "'I'd no idea it would be like this," said Jane. "It's perfectly ghastly. You're never free of them. All day long and the evenings too.'"[16] Edith too seemed unable to settle on whether her guests should be treated as customers or friends. She stuck up reminders and notices in rhyme with instructions she wished them to follow.

When the novelist Peter Blundell and his wife were working in the Woolwich Arsenal they stayed at Well Hall. The gardener objected to the way they treated the garden as their own, picking choice fruit that was intended for sale.* Blundell told Doris Langley Moore that Edith 'never tired of doing her utmost to entertain us [P.G.s] and keep us happy'. He remembered dancing in the drawing room and recalled that Edith 'could dance well although easily fatigued'. John Lane had told him that, when she was young, she was 'the handsomest woman I had ever met'.[17] Blundell thought her 'still beautiful' even though she was in her late fifties by then. He left a description:

I can see her now with her ample figure rather untidily dressed in black, her grey masses of hair done rather sketchily, a cigarette in a holder stuck in the corner of her wide, generous mouth, the round, ruddy low-browed face and the grey-blue [sic] eyes behind the big spectacles, eyes that shone with a wish to make everybody happy.[18]

For a time Well Hall prospered as a result of the war. In June 1917 *The Pioneer* reported:

And now the green lawns of Well Hall are dotted with poultry coops; prize bred ducks swim in the old moat; prize-bred hens range by its banks, and the egg business grows and grows. New-laid eggs sold not just for immediate eating, but in quantities, to be laid down in water-glass, so that people may be sure of fresh eggs in the winter, when eggs are dear and scarce. Day-old chicks are to be bought, of approved breeds, that will be hens and laying hens by Christmas. Young fowls for table form another branch of the trade.[19]

---

* Blundell, whose real name was F.N. Butterworth, may have known Edith through the Authors' Club, since he was secretary for a time.

As war dragged on, rationing led to a shortage of chicken food and, consequently, poor laying rates. An outbreak of fowl disease, which was exacerbated by the thieving habits of foxes and water rats from the moat, finished the business off.

Lillian Evans found a job filling shells at the munitions factory, but Edith and Alice continued to sell produce from the garden; Alice supervised sales of fruit and vegetables while Edith took charge of flowers. In the early years they used the dining hall, which Edith described as 'a big room with a chequered marble floor … dark with old oak, and bright with old brass and china'. She noted the challenges they faced:

> Our hall, which is also our dining room, opens straight into out-of-doors. The hall was piled with heaps of cabbages, carrots, onions, jars of chrysanthemums, baskets of potatoes, boxes of apples. We lived through that winter in one perpetual draught. Seventy-five pocket-handkerchiefs in one week and two cases of bronchitis impelled us to change.[20]

Such hardship prompted her to transfer their activities into 'a little wooden shop, set up on the front lawn at Well Hall'.[21] Measuring thirty feet by thirteen by twelve, it was little more than a hut. A white fence enclosed it and a little white gate fronted the garden boundary of Well Hall, facing out towards the tramlines and the Co-operative store. Edith planted roses against the sides and installed a gas heater. To attract customers she erected a coop with three hens and a cock. 'My own darling boy,' she told Paul, 'we opened the hut-shop and did splendidly, taking nearly £5 for eggs and vegetables and flowers.' She was filled with enthusiasm: 'I was on my feet today from 8.30 to 8.15 so I am pretty tired,' she confessed, 'but I am very well.'

Her article, 'The Voyage of the Hut', was subtitled:

> A tale of the difficulties attending to the removal of a wooden hut, designed to house a flower, fruit and vegetable business of War-time growth, and of how they were surmounted through the instrumentality of a handyman of the sea.

In it, she described the arrival of this hut in June 1916.[22] The 'handyman of the sea' she mentioned was Thomas Terry Tucker, a local marine engineer known affectionately as 'Skipper'. They had been friends for several years and Edith was very grateful for his help: 'Mr Tucker keeps up my spirits and prevents my worrying over trifles,' she told Paul.[23] She wrote in a letter to Harry: 'I have a sailor friend who can find anything, and can do everything. Also, he knows everything.'

They made a good team, as *The Pioneer* reported:

Last February [1917], Mr T. Tucker, of the Woolwich Ferry, entered the partnership with E. Nesbit; and the crowds of friends who have known Mr Tucker in the social and political worlds will not be surprised to hear that he is entering into the business of poultry farming, gardening and floriculture with the indomitable energy and 'go' which always characterises his varied activities. With four such partners success should be assured, especially in a business which set out to supply fresh fruit, fresh flowers, fresh eggs, and fresh vegetables – the best of everything and nothing but the best.[24]

Tucker was two years older than Edith. He had left school early after his father died and went to work as a rivet boy in Sir Alfred Yarrow's yard, where torpedo boats were built. Afterwards he joined the merchant navy. In February 1898 he was appointed first class engineer with the Woolwich Ferry. He and his wife, Sophia, a former machinist, lived for a time in a house on the newly constructed Corbett Estate on the other side of Well Hall Road.* They had no children. Tommy and Sophia were committed socialists and Labour activists. He attended Fabian lectures and Sunday meetings at Poplar Town Hall while she was a driving force in the Woolwich Labour Movement and an original member of the Well Hall Women's Guild. She joined strike committees and worked tirelessly with strike leaders, and she also provided assistance to South London's poorest families. When the London County Council replaced the London Schools Board in 1904, Tommy, who was a member of the Woolwich Labour Party, was appointed one of eighteen school managers allocated across three local schools. He was also selected as a Labour Party candidate for the River Ward in the Woolwich Borough Council elections in 1909 and again in 1912.

After Hubert lost his sight, Tommy took to visiting him almost daily to talk politics and share gossip from socialist circles. He nursed Sophia through her final, difficult illness until her death on 14 January 1916. They had been married for thirty years. When Sophia was laid to rest in

* Archibald Cameron Corbett purchased the Eltham Park Estate and from 1900 to 1914 developed it with well-constructed suburban housing.

the churchyard of St John's at Eltham, close to Fabian Bland, Edith and Alice sent wreaths made with flowers from their garden. Now that they were both alone, Edith's friendship with Tommy intensified. He had been an invaluable source of support ever since she lost Hubert. In 1915 he had helped her with a fundraising event in aid of *The Pioneer* newspaper that was held in the grounds of Well Hall.

As *The Pioneer* newspaper operated at a loss, the women members of the Labour Party who were responsible for distributing it banded together to ensure its survival. They formed the Women's Pioneer Campaign Committee and established a 'Pioneer fund'. One young member, Mabel Crout, who would become Dame Mabel Crout later in life, asked Edith's permission to hold a garden fête at Well Hall. She described their meeting as 'an eye opener'. Edith, dressed in a black gown with an extended train and smoking a cigarette in a very long holder, granted permission on condition that her granddaughter Pandora could perform a dance on the day. An article in *The Pioneer* on 28 May 1915 confirmed that 'Mrs. Hubert Bland has very kindly consented to allow a Garden Party to be held in her grounds at Well Hall on June 26'.[25]

Edith agreed to open her grounds at four o'clock. The entrance fee was set at 6d and tickets were sold from the office of *The Pioneer* or could be bought at the gate on the day. Tommy Tucker undertook to sell one hundred tickets and also offered to lend 'the necessary crockery and a piano'. Additional revenue would be raised by selling refreshments: 'home-made dainties' and 'ices and cooling drinks'. Attractions included an exhibition of dancing by Miss Mary Hope and her pupils; dancing on the lawn accompanied by the Misses Bevan on cello, piano and violin; palm reading; and 'games and competitions of an original character'.[26]

The afternoon was a great success. *The Pioneer* carried an account of 'a delightfully enjoyable gathering' in lovely surroundings. It reported: 'In addition to rendering assistance in many other ways, Mrs Bland delighted those present with some skilfully and tastefully executed pianoforte solos.' She also presented competition winners with autographed books and awarded prizes for races on the lawn; a boys' and a girls' handicap race, an egg-and-spoon race, and a men's blindfold race, during which participants were 'guided by ladies'. John oversaw boating trips on the moat and Pandora, accompanied by Rosemary Courlander, 'enacted a beautiful fairy scene'. As proceedings came to a close, Councillor E.J. Mayers offered eloquent thanks:

For the loan of the grounds and for the manifold assistance which she [Edith] had rendered, also for her labours in many ways in the past and in the present, in the direction of promoting the desires of the people for a nobler life.

Edith responded with 'a graceful little speech' and three cheers were raised before those gathered sang a hearty rendition of Auld Lang Syne.[27] A second garden party was held the following year. *The Pioneer* reported:

The event of first importance will be the launching of the lifeboat on the moat, in which they [children in attendance] will all be required to assist, then exploratory expeditions will be made in the lifeboat all round the moat.[28]

Attractions included a baby show, a recital by the cinema orchestra, fortune-telling from the 'Queen of Sheba' and races on the lawn. Pandora won the race for girls aged eight to ten, and also danced 'graceful classical Greek dances' on the lawn. So central was Tommy Tucker to proceedings that he was rechristened 'Admiral Tucker, the Lord High Everybody of the Day'. As the event reached its conclusion, Will Crooks M.P. proposed 'a hearty vote of thanks to Mrs Bland for distributing the prizes and lending her grounds'. Edith insisted that she deserved no thanks since 'it had been the greatest pleasure to her to see them all there, and their thanks were due to the ladies and Mr Tucker for all the work they had done'. Afterwards 'dancing on the lawn in the gathering twilight, to the fine music of the cinema orchestra, brought the programme of events to an end'. *The Pioneer* declared the event 'probably their greatest public success so far recorded'.[29]

Yet life was difficult for Edith. She told Harry that she had endured a 'horrible three years' since Hubert's death and she likened these years to 'shivering in a sort of Arctic night'. Yet, even though she called him 'the best man I have ever known', when Tommy had proposed marriage to her six months earlier she had turned him down. Undaunted, he declared his intention of 'devoting the rest of his life' to her. When she discovered that he had turned down a job worth an extra £100 a year in order to stay near her, she decided 'perhaps life would be less wretched if one joined hands with a good friend and chum who believed that one could make him happy'.[30] She talked it over with family and close friends before she accepted his proposal, and she prayed to his late wife, Sophia, asking that she bless their marriage.

Tommy and Edith were married in St Peter's Roman Catholic Church in Woolwich on 20 February 1917. This surprised Iris, since Edith had expressed anger that the Pope had remained neutral during the war, particularly after Germany invaded Belgium.[31] By the time they arrived back at Tommy's little house, they were so tired that she placed her head on his shoulder and they both fell happily asleep. They made Well Hall their home but kept Tommy's house, which they nicknamed 'the Hutch', as a 'little refuge from P.G.s'.

Edith told Edward Andrade that everyone was 'very much surprised' at her second marriage, 'but no one more surprised than I am', she added. She attributed its success to the fact the Tommy was not a literary man, although she recognised that her second husband shared several character-istics with her first: 'his sane socialist view of life, his sense of humour, and his love for me'. She likened her second marriage to 'a consolation prize for all sorts of failures' and admitted that 'the knowledge that I have a friend and comrade to sit on the other side of the hearth where life's dying embers fade is incredibly comforting'.[32] She signed a letter to Harry 'E.N. Bland-Tucker' and described her newfound contentment:

He is the soul of goodness and kindness, and he never blunders in matters of sentiment or emotion. He doesn't blunder in anything, for the matter of that, but you know in those matters how fatally easy it is to go wrong. After the cold misery of the last three years I feel as though someone has come and put a fur cloak round me. Or like one shipwrecked on a lonely island, and I have found another shipwrecked mariner to help me build a hut and make a fire. He is a widower and I knew his wife and he knew Hubert so we can talk about *them*. His name is Thomas Terry Tucker and his whole life seems to have been spent in doing good. Also he is fond of laughter, and likes the same kind of jokes that please me. I am very, very happy. I feel as though I had opened another volume of the book of life (the last volume) and it is full of beautiful stories and poetry.[33]

Tommy took over the management of Well Hall and ensured that pay-ing guests occupied just two or three bedrooms. One was Russell Green, editor of the influential literary and artistic magazine *Coterie*. During the autumn of 1920 Edith spotted an advertisement he had placed in the *New Statesman* seeking accommodation outside London. She offered him a tiny bedroom that overlooked the back lawns. He recalled a crumbling iron-railed balcony and a moat choked with briars and brambles.

Green, who stayed for three months, regarded the household as 'a psychological kaleidoscope'. He described Edith, aged sixty-two, as looking her full age with grey hair and gold-rimmed glasses. Yet she was 'sprightly and sharp' and possessed a 'fairy godmother charm'. She was often in the company of little girls aged between six and ten. He detected 'a hint of hardness in the pressure of her lips', which suggested to him 'a very strong and unrebuttable will'.[34] Edith seemed unconcerned by aging. She told Berta Ruck that she 'never wished to change the outward appearance, or rather the selfness of my body with all its defects'. She found it terribly funny when one old suitor who called to see her exclaimed in obvious distress: 'But what has become of all your good looks – your pretty hair, your lovely eyes, your soft little hands?'[35]

When war ended in November 1918 Edith's first thought was for Paul. 'Thank God for this day!' she wrote in a note to his wife Gertrude. 'Now our boy is safe!' They got on well but Gertrude seemed rather in awe of her and called her 'Mrs Tucker' until she read a couplet Edith had scribbled on her trademark coloured paper:

> Gertrude, holding Paul's dear hand,
> Do not call me 'Mrs Bland'.
> Call me Jane or Peg or Sue
> Anything but what you do![36]

They settled on MIL and DIL. Sometimes Edith signed her letters 'MII', which was her shorthand for Mother Two.[37] She dedicated her poetry collection *Many Voices* 'To my dear Daughter in law and Daughter in love, GERTRUDE BLAND'.

Tommy had worked for the duration of the war and Edith hoped he would now retire, but he continued to work until May 1921. Occasionally she would accompany him on the ferry. He was 'skipper' and she was 'cook', which was upgraded to 'mate'. She would grill them a steak or make coffee in the galley. She told Edward Andrade:

> I feel fur-wrapped from the cold of old age. Wrapped, indeed, in furs of price, for he is (as my gardener said of him) an 'only' man. There is no one like him. I grow fonder of him every day.[38]

Edith considered Tommy 'a born *observer*' who was blessed with 'words to clothe his thoughts and observations'. 'If we had time,' she told Harry, 'I am sure we could do some good writing work together.' They did collaborate on stories, articles and sketches for the *Saturday Westminster Gazette*, the *New Statesman* and the *New Witness*.* Edith wrote up several of his nautical tales and included one, 'Tammy Lee's Jack', in *Five of Us and Madeline* (1925), her last book for children, which Rosamund edited posthumously.

Money was shockingly tight by then and Edith took a loan from Edward Andrade. She also sold some of her precious possessions, letters from Kipling and postcards from Shaw. With Hubert no longer there to keep them together, Alice moved out of Well Hall and went to stay with her sister in Yorkshire, although she did eventually return to London, where she shared a flat with Lillian Evans for a time. Edith was delighted when children's writer Olive Hill approached her for advice and agreed to move into Well Hall to help her out.

Yet it was clear they simply could not generate enough revenue to make Well Hall pay. It was time to give it up for a more modest home. In *Wings and the Child* she described how the wild and lovely spot she had moved to as the last century came to a close had changed over time:

Once the road from Eltham to Woolwich was a grassy lane with hedges and big trees in the hedges, and wild pinks and Bethlehem stars, and ragged robin and campion. Now the trees are cut down and there are no more flowers. It is asphalt all the way, and here and there seats divided by iron rods so that tired tramps should not sleep on them.[39]

---

* A weekly paper established by Cecil Chesterton in 1912. When Cecil joined the British Army in 1916, his brother G.K. agreed to fill in as editor. Cecil died in a French military hospital in 1918 and G.K. was left in charge.

CHAPTER 22

'TIME WITH HIS MAKE-UP BOX
OF LINES AND WRINKLES'

On 2 February 1922, before she left Well Hall, Edith decided to write
her will. She was sixty-three by then and in reasonable health, although
she was plagued by bronchial complaints that left her gasping and
wheezing. She made Tommy her executor and asked a couple called
Elliot, paying guests who would take over the lease on Well Hall, to
act as her witnesses. Under the terms of her will, her estate was to be
divided between Tommy, Paul and Iris, although she did not anticipate
leaving much since publishers had lost interest in her stories and poems.
Turning to her adopted children, she wrote: 'Rosamund is well provided
for by her marriage and John had his full portion of his family's money
in legacies from his father and aunt.'[1]

It seems she was favouring her natural children, but there was a certain
brutal logic to her thinking. John was an undergraduate at Cambridge at
the time and had a bright future, while Rosamund's husband, Clifford
Sharp, was well remunerated as editor of the *New Statesman*. In John's case,
her instincts were correct. He obtained a medical qualification from the
Society of Apothecaries in 1924 and registered with the department of
pathology at St Bartholomew's Hospital in London. He was promoted to
Senior Demonstrator of Bacteriology there and spent a good portion of
his successful career overseas. Rosamund, in contrast, was left destitute
when Sharp's chronic alcoholism destroyed his career.

Edith invited Ada Breakell and Olive Hill to accompany her to her
new home. She even made provision in her will for their right to live there
for the remainder of their lives. Ada decided to stay in London but Olive
moved with her and supported her tirelessly to the end of her life.

A last glimpse of Edith at Well Hall was left by Donald Finch, son of
an antique dealer from Blackheath. One bitterly cold day in spring 1922,
father and son arrived at Well Hall to value items Edith wished to sell. It

was Tommy who ushered them in and served them tea. Donald took him for a servant. They waited for Edith in a 'dimly lit but cosy room lined with books':

> After about ten minutes we heard someone coming and like a ship in full sail E. Nesbit appeared in the doorway. To me, at first, she seemed a rather awesome person – in black in the fashion of a previous generation – almost Victorian. She was wearing gold spectacles which helped to give her that severe look.

She put young Donald at ease by chatting about his family and she invited him to select a book from her shelves. He chose *The Railway Children*, which she inscribed with a personal message on the flyleaf in her 'firm rounded hand'. She also inscribed books for his brother and his two sisters. Donald's father negotiated a price for her Georgian silver candelabras, which had decorated the long dining table in the stone-flagged hall on so many glittering occasions. They remained in the Finch family for decades.[2]

Tommy and Edith found the perfect home on Romney Marsh on the south-east coast of England. Romney Marsh had a reputation for witchcraft and lawlessness. Visitors avoided it in ancient times, fearing its unwholesome air might carry plague. Ford Madox Ford, who lived on its fringes, called it 'an infectious and holding neighbourhood'. He wrote in *Return to Yesterday*: 'In the Middle Ages they used to say "These be the four quarters of the World: Europe, Asia, Africa and the Romney Marsh."' He knew how captivating it could be and warned: 'Once you go there you are apt there to stay.'[3]

The hamlet of Jesson, likely named after Jesson Farm and renamed St Mary's Bay in 1935, was situated in the borderland between Kent and East Sussex, close to St Mary in the Marsh, but even closer to the sea. At the end of a cul-de-sac behind Jesson Farm stood two decommissioned brick-built huts that had been used by the British Air Force as a photographic laboratory and a storehouse for medical materials. The whole structure required a great deal of renovation in order to make it habitable and Tommy and Edith completed much of this themselves. They christened the huts 'The Longboat' and 'The Jollyboat'. From their windows they could gaze out across the marshes towards the sea wall. The huts were connected by a passage they named 'The Suez Canal'. Edith brightened the walls with lithographs by Gerald Spencer Pryse and H.R.

Miller's brilliant depiction of the Queen of Babylon from *The Story of the Amulet*. Her writing room became 'the magic room'. It was there that she dedicated her final novel, *The Lark*:

> To T.T. Tucker,
> With Love
> Jesson St Mary's,
> Romney, Kent

In 1923 she completed *To the Adventurous*, a collection of short stories with a supernatural twist, but enthusiasm for her work had waned. *The Spectator* described them as 'readable little tales' and suggested: 'They might while away time in a doctor's waiting-room.'[4] When novelist and playwright Winifred Ashton, who wrote as Clemence Dane, expressed admiration for Edith's children's books at this time and begged her to write another, Edith admitted that publishers 'tell me that children don't want my sort of book any more'.[5] Her last book for children *Five of Us and Madeline*, was considered one of her weakest.

She still had literary admirers. When Gladys Bronwyn Stern had visited Well Hall with Eva Courlander, she was taken aback to find such a celebrated author baking dozens of cakes and pies. Now she came to Romney Marsh with her husband and writing partner, outspoken New Zealander Geoffrey Holdsworth. When he chastised Edith for simply disposing of her characters at the end of *Dormant*, she confessed that she had simply grown too tired of them to deal with them as she wished. Gladys and Geoffrey were both in poor health so they were grateful for Edith's 'almost divine kindness and understanding'. In a letter of thanks, Gladys assured her: 'You are quite the nicest and most comforting person I have ever met.'[6]

Another welcome visitor was the 'wildly dramatic' Agnes Thorndike. Edith knew her from Dymchurch where she owned adjoining coastguard's cottages on Marine Terrace. She brought her adult children, Sybil and Russell, both actors, although Sybil was the more famous and Russell had a larger reputation as author of the Christopher Syn mysteries, which he wrote while sitting on the sea wall at Dymchurch. It was Russell who identified the sandpit in *Five Children and It*, a gravel pit 'like a giant's wash-hand basin', as the one in St Margaret's in Rochester where Sybil and he had played as children.[7]

Sybil enjoyed Edith's company and was intrigued by her 'contempt for conventionally "good" children whose main virtues were keeping quiet and keeping clean'. She noted her preference for children who were 'curious, creative and considerate'. During the summer of 1922 Sybil visited with her son John and he described the welcome they received from the 'tiny stocky man with a beard' who was 'almost a caricature of an old sailor':

> 'Avast there me hearties!' he would shout as Anxious Annie [their car] drove up to the bungalow. 'Come aboard. Tea's ready in the Long Boat but Madam's titivating herself in the Jolly Boat.'[8]

In 1921 Edith's friend Athene Seyler, who was an actress, lent her holiday house in Dymchurch to a young writer friend named Noël Coward. He was bicycling around the district looking for a home for his mother that he could use as a writing retreat at weekends. He took a cottage in Romney Marsh, which he described in *Present Indicative* as 'nestling up against a public house [the Star Inn] in the village of St Mary in the Marsh'. It had four rooms and outside sanitation but he loved the 'superb view from the upper windows of unlimited sheep'.[9]

Coward was a huge fan of Edith's stories and was thrilled to discover she lived nearby 'with her husband, and a gentle friend, in a series of spacious huts'. He wrote in *Present Indicative*:

> There was a second-hand book-shop on the way where I could buy 'back numbers' of *The Strand Magazine* for a penny each, and I hoarded my pocket money until I could buy a whole year's worth in order to read the E. Nesbit story right through without having to wait for the next instalment. I read 'The Phoenix and the Carpet,' and 'Five Children and It,' also 'The Magic City,' but there were a few numbers missing from that year, so I stole a coral necklace from a visiting friend of Mother's, pawned it for five shillings, and bought the complete book at the Army and Navy Stores. It cost four-and-six, so that including the fare (penny half-return, Battersea Park to Victoria) I was fivepence to the good. In later years I told E. Nesbit of this little incident and I regret to say that she was delighted.[10]

Coward called on Edith and was relieved to find her 'as firm, as nice, and as humorous as her books had led me to expect'.[11] She was, he noted in a letter to his friend, children's author Noel Streatfeild, 'absolutely charming with greyish-white hair and a rather sharp sense of humour'.[12] He left a description of Tommy too: 'The skipper, her husband, was a grand old man, who loved her and guarded her devotedly through her last, rather sad years.'[13]

Edith grew fond of this talented young man and was content to discuss his plays for hours at a time. She seemed less keen on his mother and appears to have taken little trouble to hide this, since Violet Coward decided she was 'stuck-up'.[14] Yet it was Violet who suggested that Noël hire Iris Bland as costume designer for *London Calling*, his first publicly produced musical. He is said to have replied: 'I'm sure no daughter of Nesbit could make anything in the least "chic" and one can't jeopardise one's chances of success by promiscuous charity.'[15]

Edith could be sharp and much of this sharpness was the result of worry and pain. As 1922 came to a close and the weather turned colder, she was laid low with bronchial complaints. Something was dreadfully amiss, since she struggled to eat and lost a great deal of weight. She rarely got out. When she engaged the postman's daughter to help her with letters and papers, she admitted that this girl was 'the only new person I have seen lately'.[16] It was then that she renewed her friendship with Berta Ruck. They had been estranged since 1909 and it was Berta who took the blame for the breach and initiated the reconciliation. She was aware that Edith had remarried and had 'heard legends of breezy unconventionality and Old Saltiness'. At a fancy-dress dance she attended, a 'large young man in the dress of a Hawaiian native' had called her by name and asked if she remembered his sitting on her lap. She 'thought he had drink taken', but apologised when he introduced himself as Dr John Bland.[17] When she bumped into Iris and Pandora she remarked on the little girl's strong resemblance to her grandmother. Later Edith remarked to her: 'When I see Pandora in her Eighteen Seventy-Two frock, I see my own ghost: only I had less nose, and not quite such big eyes.'[18]

In 1923, when Berta learned from Iris that Edith was gravely ill, she sent a brief note with a copy of her latest book. Edith invited her to visit but warned her that she was very ill. 'I suppose I shall not get well again,' she wrote matter-of-factly. 'But like Charles II, I take an unconscionable time over the business.' She had not lost her self-deprecating humour. 'You would not know me, I am so thin,' she wrote. 'Once a Rubens Venus in figure, I am now more like a pre-Raphaelite St Simeon Stylites.'[19] That summer Berta made her way to the huts on Romney Marsh and was greeted by a 'short, hatless, collarless, unmistakably sea-faring figure, bearded like Captain Kettle'. She found Edith lying 'in the pose of someone who is too tired: too tired for more', and she described how altered her friend appeared:

> Her hair, that I knew brown as garden-earth, was grey as frost. There was no colour in her cheeks. Her hands – that was what shook me; her hands that used to be sun-burned brown as a sandal from her rowing and her garden-work were now so strangely white. Not a trace of tan, but the freckles... a challenge! They stood out, those freckles on the pale skin like a challenge from another century's arduous and ardent summers. She looked up at me and with that old imperiousness said: 'You're very late, girl?' I swallowed the lump in my throat and admitted: 'Fifteen years.' She gave a little approving nod, as at a piece of 'theatre' she liked.[20]

Berta noted with relief that, despite her obvious frailty, Edith's nature was characteristically warm:

> She talked late: the old fire was still there, the old loving curiosity for Life, and, in spite of her frail health, more than the old enjoyment of the moment. She told me – She, who had known of Love and Friendship as much as any woman in this world ever had, – 'For the first time in my life I know what it is to have *a man's whole heart.*'[21]

Since she had moved to Romney Marsh Edith had written 'occasional joyful letters' to her young friend Mavis Carter, describing how the Long Boat was taking shape, though it was 'full of shavings and carpenters'.[22] Now she reassured her:

> I have everything to make me happy except health, kindest and most loving nursing and care... a four-post bed like a golden shrine and a view of about eight miles of marsh bounded by the little lovely hills of Kent.[23]

Finding herself in Folkestone, Mavis decided to take the bus to visit Edith. The 'grave-faced little friend' who answered her knock warned her that Edith was desperately ill. Although she noted that her 'face was like ivory, the dark eyes full of pain', she detected traces of the old, exacting Edith:

Young, awkward, gawky and broken-hearted, I sat on a stiff chair and twisted my legs in desperation around its rungs, while I sought vainly for the right words. Suddenly in the old characteristic manner she scolded me violently, telling me to sit up and take Queen Mary for my model who 'always crosses her right foot over her left'. Crestfallen, I pulled myself into a more becoming posture, when with her old sweet smile she said 'Forgive me, my dear, I'm cross and fretful because I really am so very ill.'[24]

Edith talked 'with her old brilliance'. When Mavis stood to leave, she insisted that Tommy help her to the gate so she could see her off. Mavis looked back and observed 'a frail and indomitable figure, blowing me kisses, waving me "farewell"'.[25]

Edith suffered a crisis in December 1923. She told Berta she had almost died and, in response, her friend arrived with arms filled with flowers so Edith could enjoy them in life rather than have them adorn her grave. All this time, Olive and Tommy nursed her with unfailing devotion, writing her letters for her and reading her favourite books aloud: *Jane Eyre*, and *Kipps* by her old friend H.G. Wells. Her grown-up children would visit at weekends and she was as welcoming and sociable as ever. When young Angus MacPhail, who would later work as a screenwriter for Alfred Hitchcock, wrote to ask if there would be more Bastable stories, she replied: 'Alas, my dear Angus, your poor E. Nesbit lies dying and it is a long business and very tiresome. I fear the last of the Oswald saga has been sung.' She invited him to visit her in her 'government hut in the middle of Romney Marsh'.[26]

Edith was in great pain but she seemed tranquil, buoyant even, towards the end. 'What things there are still to see and to do, and to think and to be and to grow into and to grow out of!' she told Berta Ruck in March 1924.[27] Agnes Thorndike presented her with a contraption that allowed her to sit up and admire 'the marsh and the hills behind those superb sunsets that all us marsh people love so', as Sybil put it.[28] Edith wrote a poem of thanks:

On bed of state long since a Queen
Would wake to morning's starry beams
Silvering the arras blue and green
That hung her walls with cloth-of dreams;
And, where the fluted valance drooped

Above the curtains' broidered posies,
The pretty caravan cupids trooped
Festooning all her bed with roses.
Mother of Stars! Enthroned I lie
On the high bed your kindness sent,
And see between the marsh and sky
The little lovely hills of Kent;
And, 'mid the memories old and new
That bless me as the curtain closes,
Come troops of pretty thoughts of you…
And mine, too, is a bed of roses.[29]

Death held little fear for her, and she shared a lovely image with Berta:

When you were at Well Hall I used often on summer evenings to skip away from the table and go and look through the window at the rest of you finishing your desserts and your flirtations and your arguments amongst the flowers and fruits and bright glasses and think 'This is how I shall see it all some day when I am not alive any more.' Well it won't be Well Hall I shall go back to now when the time comes for it died before I died and it is quite dead whereas I am only half.[30]

'Good-bye, my dear,' she wrote. 'I really think the door will open soon now, and I may be able to scurry through at last, but I shall remember you wherever I wake.' Generous to the end, she assured Berta: 'Whenever you think of me do not forget to think how much happiness your loving kindness has given me, and how you have helped my last, long months.' She signed herself 'Your loving Duchess'.[31]

On 4 May 1924 Edith Nesbit died of 'bronchiectasis and cardiac dilatation'[32] at the age of sixty-five. The nature of her illness suggests she may have had lung cancer too. Tommy, Olive, Iris and Paul kept vigil by her bedside and she died in Iris's arms. In accordance with her wishes, she was buried in a plain oak coffin in the peaceful, country churchyard of St Mary in the Marsh, under the protective shade of a majestic elm that stood close to the road. At Tommy's request, a short funeral service concluded with a reading of the final section from *Dormant*:

'It seems such waste, such stupid senseless waste,' said Bats. 'His great thoughts, his fine body that loved life, all the friendship, the aspiration, the love… all thrown away, gone, wasted for ever.' 'Who says that it is wasted?' said the Jew. 'It is his body that has served its turn and is cast away. The great thoughts, the friendship, the aspiration, the love; can we say that these die? Nay, rather, these shall not die. These shall live in the Courts of the Lord, forever.'[33]

The *Nottingham Evening Post* reported: 'E. Nesbit (Mrs Hubert Bland), the famous writer of children's and other stories, directed that a wooden tablet bearing her name should be the only memorial over her grave.' Tommy carved the simple wooden monument that marks her grave.

Resting, E. Nesbit, Mrs Bland-Tucker,
Poet and Author died 4th May 1924 Aged 65

In Dymchurch a committee was formed to organise the establishment of a reading room and village club to her memory.[34] There was talk of an 'E. Nesbit Institute' and the muddy track leading to her home for the final two years of her life, the only home she ever owned, was renamed Nesbit Road. A correspondent to the *Derby Daily Telegraph* who had never met her wrote: 'I felt that one of my oldest and dearest friends had passed away… in her death I can but mourn one who was to me, although I never met her, a guide, philosopher, and friend in my childhood, ever ready and willing to transport me to ethereal realms.'[35]

Save for a few small bequests, the less than seven hundred pounds that Edith left went to Tommy. She instructed him to sell the copyright in her works and he used some of the proceeds to purchase an annuity of sixty pounds for Olive Hill. Mavis Carter gave him a scrapbook of Edith's uncollected stories, articles and poems that she had compiled for him as a birthday present at Edith's request. In 1931 Tommy helped Doris Langley Moore with her biography, but he complained that there was too much of him in it and not enough of Hubert. When Rosamund's marriage failed in 1932, she moved in with Tommy. She was holding his hand when he passed away peacefully, after suffering a stroke, on 17 May 1935. He was seventy-nine.

No memorial was erected in the churchyard where he is buried. Under the terms of his will, he left the Jolly Boat to Iris and the Long Boat to

Paul. What money he had went to his nephews. Sadly, Edith's children did not fare well. On 9 October 1940, after years of depression, Paul, aged sixty, ingested poison and died. Iris reached her hundredth birthday, but her life was blighted by tragedy when her daughter Pandora died in a road accident in France in 1950. A professional dancer, she had danced in Madame Pavolva's company. Iris raised her adopted children, Max and Fern. John became a brilliant bacteriologist and his research into trachoma and blindness improved many lives. They were not blood relatives, but he, like Edith, was prone to chest complaints. He died at the age of forty-six, and was praised for his 'kindness and gentleness'.[36] His birth mother, Alice Hoatson, ended her life in poverty and always spoke of her 'niece and nephew' Rosamund and John.[37]

Edward Jepson summarised Edith's literary legacy:

Mrs Bland presented and still presents to hundreds of thousands of impressionable children a sane and courageous, cheerful and kindly approach to life, which has probably been more valuable to the English than all the speeches of their politicians of the seventy odd years since she was born.[38]

In 1956 Noël Coward wrote from Jamaica:

I am reading again through all the dear E. Nesbits and they seem to me to be more charming and evocative than ever. It is strange that after half a century I still get so much pleasure from them. Her writing is so light and unforced, her humour is so sure and her narrative quality so strong that the stories, which I know backwards, rivet me as much now as they did when I was a little boy. Even more so in one way, because I can now enjoy her actual talent and her extraordinary power of describing hot summer days in England in the beginning years of the century. All the pleasant memories of my own childhood jump at me from the pages.[39]

A copy of *The Enchanted Castle* was found beside his bed when he died on 26 March 1973.

Many writers took inspiration from Edith's books. In 1947 American writer Edward Eager was delighted to discover a second-hand copy of *Wet Magic* while searching for books to read to his son. 'I have not got over the effects of that discovery yet, nor, I hope, will I ever,' he recalled, adding:

Probably the sincerest compliment I could pay her is already paid in the fact that my own books for children could not even have existed if it were not for her influence. And I am always careful to acknowledge this indebtedness in each of my stories; so that any child who likes my books and doesn't know hers may be led back to the master of us all.

He recognised the source of her talent: 'It was when the child in her spoke out directly to other children that she achieved greatness,' he wrote, and he elaborated:

But there are lucky people who never lose the gift of seeing the world as a child sees it, a magic place where anything can happen next minute and delightful and unexpected things constantly do. Of such, among those of us who try to write for children, is the kingdom of Heaven. And in that kingdom E. Nesbit stands with the archangels.[40]

C.S. Lewis borrowed Edith's wardrobe from her story 'The Aunt and Amabel', written in 1912, in which a little girl enters a magic world through a wardrobe. Of *The Story of the Amulet*, he wrote: 'It first opened my eyes to antiquity, the "dark backward and abysm of time". I can still re-read it with delight.'[41] In 1925 he presented several of her books to J.R.R. Tolkien's sons, John, Michael and Christopher. By coincidence, Tolkien had been a pupil of Richard Reynolds' at King Edward's School in Birmingham and it was Reynolds who drove him to Oxford University when he was due to start his first term in 1911.

Although Tolkien never admitted to reading Edith's books, in childhood, aged seven, he wrote a story about a 'green great dragon' at the same time as her *Book of Beasts* was being serialised in *The Strand Magazine*. In a letter to his publisher, written two years after *The Hobbit* was published, he described her as 'an author I delight in'.[42] He was invited to deliver the Andrew Lang Lecture in 1939, and early versions of his speech praise the 'triumphant formula that E. Nesbit found in the Amulet and the Phoenix and the Carpet'.[43] He removed this from later versions. Elements of Tolkien's stories appear to draw on Edith's work, and a story he told his children features a cantankerous sand-sorcerer he called a Psammead.

Fantasy writer Donald Douglas had as his bookplate:

Mr Douglas is an abject admirer of E. Nesbit, and once introduced a reference to the Ugly-Wuglies (those bloodcurdling creations in 'The Enchanted Castle') into his first novel 'The Grand Inquisitor'.[44]

Lady Antonia Fraser described *The Enchanted Castle* as 'surely the best horror story ever written'. She explained: 'The moment when the Ugly-Wuglies begin to clap stays with me and still chills as it did then. I like all Nesbit but this is the best.'[45] Her admiration was shared by the late Queen Mother, who wrote to thank Noël Coward for his gift of four of Edith's books and told him:

> I am quite sure that I shall once again be terrified of the Uglie Wugglies – oh the horror of the kid gloves clapping! Do you know, that I often take off my gloves to clap at theatres or ballet or opera, and I know that this is purely because the sound of the dull thudding of languid hands in gloves brings back vividly the dreadful Uglie-Wuglies![46]

When she delivered a lecture, 'In Celebration of Edith Nesbit,' at the Inaugural General Meeting of the Edith Nesbit Society on 29 October 1996, celebrated children's author Joan Aiken took the opportunity to acknowledge her own debt:

> She has had a powerful influence on my own writing, as can readily be seen. Her strongest point is her marvellous capacity for combining magical and fantastic ingredients with comic realistic situations.[47]

Screenwriter and novelist Frank Cottrell Boyce described her importance to him in an interview with the *Irish Times*: 'I came to her late, but it unlocked something in my head. It's way beyond an influence,' he says. 'She's massively underrated. I love comic writing – I love Damon Runyon and PG Wodehouse and David Sedaris. But none of them are in the same planet as E Nesbit.'[48] Michael Moorcock has Oswald Bastable narrate his trilogy *A Nomad of the Time Streams* (1971-81). Helen Cresswell adapted *Five Children and It* and *The Phoenix and the Carpet* for television, and wrote *The Return of the Psammead* in 1992. Booker Prize-winning novelist A.S. Byatt drew on Edith's life when writing her magnificent *The Children's Book*. Jacqueline Wilson brought the first instalment of Edith's Psammead series up to date with *Four Children and It* (2012). Kate Saunders wrote

Five Children on the Western Front as a sequal to *Five Children and It*. Emma Donoghue, acclaimed author of *Room*, was influenced by Edith's Bastable children when writing *The Lotterys Plus One*. The extraordinarily popular and prolific English writer Neil Gaiman, who loves all her books, particularly the Psammead series, included her story 'The Cockatoucan; or, Great-Aunt Willoughby', from *Nine Unlikely Tales*, in *Unnatural Creatures*, a collection of short stories about fantastical things that he edited in 2013.

When asked to name her favourite books, J.K. Rowling, hailed as the queen of modern-day writing for children, replied:

> The first of my chosen books is the famous story of the six Bastable children, who set out to restore the 'fallen fortunes' of their house: *The Story of the Treasure Seekers* by E. Nesbit. I think I identify with E. Nesbit more than any other writer. She said that, by some lucky chance, she remembered exactly how she felt and thought as a child, and I think you could make a good case, with this book as Exhibit A, for prohibition of all children's literature by anyone who can not remember exactly how it felt to be a child. Nesbit churned out slight, conventional children's stories for 20 years to support her family before producing *The Treasure Seekers* at the age of 40.
>
> It is the voice of Oswald, the narrator, that makes the novel such a tour de force. I love his valiant attempts at humility while bursting with pride at his own ingenuity and integrity, his mixture of pomposity and naivete, his earnestness and his advice on writing a book. According to Oswald, a good way to finish a chapter is to say: 'But that is another story.' He says he stole the trick from a writer called Kipling.[49]

Rowling identifies Edith's ability to empathise with children as the key to her popularity. Edith described herself as one of those people who 'feel to the end that they are children in a grown-up world'. In *Wings and the Child* she explained:

> You cannot hope to understand children by common-sense, by reason, by logic, nor by any science whatsoever. You cannot understand them by imagination – not even by love itself. There is only one way: to remember what you thought and felt and liked and hated when you yourself were a child. Not what you know now – or think you know – you ought to have thought and liked, but what you did then, in stark fact, like and think. There is no other way.[50]

She described these adult children:

They just mingle with the other people, looking as grown-up as any one – but in their hearts they are only pretending to be grown-up: it is like acting in a charade. Time with his make-up box of lines and wrinkles, his skilful brush that paints out the tints and the contours of youth, his supply of grey wigs and rounded shoulders and pillows for the waist, disguises the actors well enough, and they go through life altogether unsuspected. The tired eyes close on a world which to them has always been the child's world, the tired hands loose the earthly possessions which have, to them, been ever the toys of the child. And deep in their hearts is the faith and the hope that in the life to come it may not be necessary to pretend to be grown-up.

Such people as these are never pessimists, though they may be sinners; and they will be trusting, to the verge of what a real grown-up would call imbecility. To them the world will be, from first to last, a beautiful place, and every unbeautiful thing will be a surprise, hurting them like a sudden blow. They will never learn prudence, or parsimony, nor know, with the unerring instinct of the really grown-up, the things that are or are not done by the best people. All their lives they will love, and expect love – and be sad, wondering helplessly when they do not get it. They will expect beautiful quixotic impulsive generosities and splendours from a grown-up world which has forgotten what impulse was: and to the very end they will not leave off expecting. They will be easily pleased and easily hurt, and the grown-ups in grain will contemplate their pains and their pleasures with an uncomprehending irritation.

If these children, disguised by grown-up bodies, are ever recognised for what they are, it is when they happen to have the use of their pens – when they write for and about children. Then grown-up people will call them intelligent and observant, and children will write to them and ask the heart-warm, heart-warming question, 'How did you know?' For if they can become articulate they will speak the language that children under-stand, and children will love, not them, for their identity is cloaked with grey grown-up-ness, but what they say. There are some of these in whom the fire of genius burns up and licks away the trappings under which Time seeks to disguise them – Andersen, Stevenson, Juliana Ewing were such as these – and the world knows them for what they were, and adores in them what in the uninspired it would decry and despise.[51]

She should have added her own name to that roll.

ACKNOWLEDGEMENTS

I could never have written this biography without the tireless work of the late Doris Langley Moore OBE (1902-1989) who went to such extraordinary lengths to solicit first-hand testimony from so many of Edith Nesbit's friends and relations while they were still alive in order to produce her biography *E. Nesbit* in 1933. She cooperated with the late Professor Julia Briggs (1943-2007) in the production of her almost exhaustive biography, *A Woman of Passion*, in 1987. So well did these extraordinary women document Edith Nesbit's life that I was faced with quite a challenge when attempting to add to the body of knowledge, although I hope I have managed to do so.

The main depository for materials relating to the life of Edith Nesbit is the Edith Nesbit Archive in the McFarlin Library in the University of Tulsa, Oklahoma. My special thanks go to Tara C. Aveilhe who accessed this archive on my behalf and made me feel as if I had crossed the Atlantic. Also to I. Marc Carlson, Librarian of Special Collections and University Archives, for his prompt and generous granting of permission for me to quote from the archive.

Sarah Baxter of The Society of Authors was prompt and consistently helpful in granting me permission to quote from the letters, diaries and works of G.B. Shaw. Thanks also to The Shaw Society who welcomed me as a speaker when I was only beginning to discover the sheer genius of one of my more colourful compatriots.

The Edith Nesbit Society, of which I am a proud member, is tireless in its quest to keep the legacy of our most important writer for children alive. Special thanks go to Marion Kennett for welcoming me into the society and encouraging me in my task.

I am also grateful to the irrepressible Gaynor Wingham, Chair of Eltham Arts, who was kind enough to show me around beautiful Well Hall Pleasaunce, and who demonstrates such tireless enthusiasm for her vibrant courner of London.

Those I consulted for help in the compiling of this biography include Leonore Sell from Universität Leipzig who is undertaking important academic work on E. Nesbit's life and legacy. Also Nuria Reina, who read my early drafts and made such insightful comments. Special thanks go to Lucy Hillier at the University of Exeter who has an expert knowledge of membership of the Golden Dawn and who helped me establish that there is little evidence E. Nesbit was a member.

My thanks are due to my wonderful agent Andrew Lownie who is unfailingly encouraging and supportive. Also to Matt Casbourne, Publishing Manager at Duckworth Publishers and to my Copy Editor, Deborah Blake. I would like to express my regret at never getting the chance to meet publisher Peter Mayer who was a legend in the industry and who sadly passed away earlier this year. He was unfailingly charming, supportive and encouraging in all our correspondence and I am immensely proud to have been published by him.

Finally, with love, to Derek, Alex and Ewan for supporting me in everything I do.

IMAGE CREDITS

Edith Nesbit as a child, 1862.
Image credits: Edith Nesbit Archive, University of Tulsa, McFarlin Library, Department of Special Collections.

The Vault of Mummies, or Skeletons from St Michael's Tower, Bordeaux, 1885, by Leon Augustin Lhermitte (1844-1925). Charcoal on paper.
Image credit: Private Collection / Bridgeman Images

An illustration from *The Story of the Treasure Seekers; being the adventures of the Bastable children in search of a fortune* by E. Nesbit. Illustration by Gordon Browne.
Image Credit: Bridgeman Images / Alamy Stock Photo

Fabian Essays - Cover for a collection of essays on Socialism by the Fabian Society's members.
Image Credit: Lebrecht Music & Arts / Alamy Stock Photo

Fabian Bland, undated (shortly before his death in 1900).
Image Credit: Edith Nesbit Archive, University of Tulsa, McFarlin Library, Department of Special Collections.

Hubert Bland, photographed by Frederick H. Evans, c. 1895-1900.
Image credit: Courtesy of the J. Paul Getty Trust

The house at Well Hall where E. Nesbit lived for two decades.
Image credit: Mary Evans Picture Library

ENDNOTES

INTRODUCTION
1   E. Nesbit, *Wings and the Child* (New York and London: Hodder and Stoughton, 1913), p. 92.
2   E. Nesbit to Joan Palmer who won second prize for her review of *Five Children and It* in *The Clarion*. Edith told her that it was the best review she had ever had. Quoted in Leo Lerman 'Real Magic', *New York Times Book Review*, vol. 2 (New York: Arno Press, 1960), p. 69.
3   F.J.H. Dabton 'Nesbit, Edith', *Dictionary of National Biography 1922-1930*, edited by J.R.H. Weaver (Oxford University Press, 1937) p. 84.
4   'Mrs Hubert Bland ("E. Nesbit")', *The Strand Magazine*, no. VIII, September 1905, p. 287.
5   "A London Literary Letter" M.A.B. Mainly About Books, Vols. 15-16 (London: T. Fisher Unwin, 1922), p. 5.
6   Doris Langley Moore. E. Nesbit: A Biography (London: Ernest Benn Ltd., 1933), p. 151.
7   *Dundee Evening Telegraph*, Tuesday 3 December 1912, p. 5.
8   Marcus Crouch, *Treasure Seekers and Borrowers* (London: Library Association, 1962), p. 16.
9   Humphrey Carpenter, *Secret Gardens: A Study of the Golden Age of Children's Literature* (London: Faber and Faber, 2009), p. 126.

CHAPTER 1
1   E. Nesbit, *My School Days* (London: Dodo Press, 2017), p. 18.
2   Ibid.
3   Ibid.
4   'Mummies at Bordeaux', *Otago Daily Times*, 3 February 1875, p. 6.
5   Gustave Flaubert, *Œuvres de jeunesse inédites* (Paris: Louis Conard, 1910), p. 564.
6   Reported in John Chambers, *Victor Hugo's Conversations with the Spirit World: A Literary Genius's Hidden Life* (Rochester, Vermont: Destiny Books, 2008), p. 22.
7   *Otago Daily Times*, loc. cit.
8   Ibid. The macabre exhibition closed in 1979. The mummies were buried in a mass grave in Bordeaux's Chartreuse Cemetery and replaced by an audio-visual presentation.
9   Jean Nicolas Gannal and Richard Harlan, *History of Embalming, and of Preparations in Anatomy, Pathology, and Natural History; including an account of a new process for embalming* (Philadelphia: Judah Dobson, 1840), p. 38.

10 Gannal and Harlan, *History of Embalming*, p. 39.

11 E. Nesbit, *My School Days*, p. 19.

12 Ibid., p. 20.

13 Ibid.

14 Ibid., p. 22.

15 Ibid.

16 Fragment of a story, written on headed paper from the College of Chemistry and Agriculture, held in the Edith Nesbit Archive, University of Tulsa, McFarlin Library, Department of Special Collections & University Archives.

17 E. Nesbit, *The Wouldbegoods* (New York and London: Harper & Brothers, 1901), p. 75.

18 Ibid., p. 269.

19 E. Nesbit, *The Enchanted Castle* (London: T. Fisher Unwin, 1907), p. 199.

20 "A London Literary Letter" M.A.B. Mainly About Books, Vols. 15-16 (London: T. Fisher Unwin, 1922), p. 5.

21 The term 'intimate friend' was used by John Nesbit's nephew, Paris Nesbit, in an interview with the *Adelaide Observer*, Saturday 22 May 1926, p. 48.

22 *Illustrated London News*, Saturday 5 April 1862, p. 31; the *Salisbury and Winchester Journal* described it as a 'long and trying illness', 5 April 1862, p. 3.

23 E. Nesbit, *My School Days*, p. 13.

24 E. Nesbit, *The Wouldbegoods*, pp. 16–17.

25 Mr Paris Nesbit, K.C., 'Memories and reflections recorded by himself', *Adelaide Observer*, Saturday 22 May 1926, p. 48.

26 R.B. Prosser, 'Nesbit, Anthony (1778–1859)' in *The Dictionary of National Biography*, ed. Sidney Lee (New York: Macmillan and Co., 1894), vol XL, p. 223.

27 'Mrs. Hubert Bland ("E. Nesbit")', *The Strand Magazine*, no VIII, September 1905, p. 287.

28 New Monthly Magazine. Volume 7, January–June 1817, "Yorkshire", p. 179

29 *Sherbourne Mercury*, Tuesday 23 December 1851, p. 3; J.C. Nesbit, *On Peruvian Guano: Its History, Composition, & Fertilizing Qualities; with the best mode of its application to the soil* (London: Rogerson and Tuxford, 1856).

30 A. Nesbit & Sons, *An Essay on Education* (London: Longman & Co., 1841) p. 4.

31 Ibid., p. 5.

32 Prosser, 'Nesbit, Anthony (1778-1859)' in *Dictionary of National Biography*, vol XL, p. 223.

33 A. Nesbit, *An Introduction to English Parsing: Adapted to Murray's Grammar and Exercises, and Intended for the Use of Schools, and Private Learners* (York: Thomas Wilson and Sons, 1823), p. 175.

34 Death certificate for John Collis Nesbit, DYE 162779, General Register Office.

35 This anecdote was told to Nesbit's biographer Doris Langley Moore by Nesbit's second husband, Tommy Tucker, and is included in her interview notes held in the Edith Nesbit Archive.

36 J.C. Nesbit, *On Agricultural Chemistry, and the Nature and Properties of Peruvian Guano* (London: Longman & Company, 1858), Preface.

37 E. Nesbit, *Wings and the Child; or the Building of Magic Cities* (New York and London: Hodder and Stoughton, 1913), p. 144.

38 Ibid.

39 E. Nesbit, *My School Days*, p. 15.

40 Ibid., p. 16.

41 Sarah Nesbit to Edith Nesbit, undated, held in the Edith Nesbit Archive.

42 E. Nesbit, *Wings and the Child*, p. 40.

43 *Illustrated London News*, Saturday 5 April 1862, p. 31.

44 In the census of 1861, a Mary Ann Moore, aged twenty-eight and living with the Nesbit family, entered her profession as 'nurse'. A smiling, dark-haired woman photographed with little Edith three years later and described as her nurse, certainly looks about the right age.

45 E. Nesbit, *My School Days*, p. 14.

46 Ibid.

47 E. Nesbit, *The Wouldbegoods*, p. 8.

48 E. Nesbit, *Wings and the Child*, pp. 49–50.

49 Ibid.

50 Ibid., pp. 48-49.

51 E. Nesbit, *The Enchanted Castle*, p. 233.

52 Ibid., p. 114.

CHAPTER 2

1   E. Nesbit, *Wings and the Child*, p. 59.

2   Ibid.

3   Ibid.

4   Ibid., p. 145.

5   E. Nesbit, *Five Children and It* (London: T. Fisher Unwin, 1902), p. 14.

6   E. Nesbit, *My School Days*, p. 3.

7   Ibid., pp. 2–3.

8   Ibid., p. 3.

9   Ibid.

10 Ibid., p. 4.

11 Ibid., pp. 5–9.

12 Ibid., p. 1.

13 E. Nesbit to Berta Ruck, included in a letter from Doris Langley Moore to Berta Ruck, 20 September 1935, Edith Nesbit Archive.

14 E. Nesbit, *The Railway Children* (London: Macmillan and Company, 1905), p. 38.

15 'Mrs. Hubert Bland ("E. Nesbit")', *The Strand Magazine*, no. VIII, p. 287.

16 E. Nesbit, *My School Days*, p. 10.

17 Ibid., p. 12.

18 Ibid.

19 E. Nesbit, *Wings and the Child*, p. 39.

20 Mary Nesbit to Edward Nesbit, 26 January 1868, Edith Nesbit Archive.

21 E. Nesbit, *My School Days*, p. 24.

22 Mary Nesbit to Edward Nesbit, 26 January 1868, Edith Nesbit Archive.

23 E. Nesbit, *My School Days*, p. 30.

24 E. Nesbit, *The Wouldbegoods*, p. 244.

25 Reported in Margaret Taylor, *E. Nesbit in Eltham* (London: The Eltham Society, 1974), p. 3.

26 E. Nesbit, *My School Days*, p. 32.

27 Ibid., p. 37.

28 Ibid., pp. 43–4.

29 Ibid., p. 46.

30 E. Nesbit, *Wings and the Child*, pp. 145–6.

31 'I see children that you have seen the spinning lady.' This incident is described by Nesbit's adopted son John Bland in an interview with Doris Langley Moore, in Notebook 1, Edith Nesbit Archive.

32 E. Nesbit, *The Wouldbegoods*, p. 148.

33 E. Nesbit, *My School Days*, p. 53.

34 E. Nesbit to her mother, undated, Edith Nesbit Archive.

35 E. Nesbit, *Daphne in Fitzroy Street* (New York: Doubleday, 1909), p. 4.

36 E. Nesbit to her mother, undated, Edith Nesbit Archive.

37 E. Nesbit to her mother, 1869, Edith Nesbit Archive.

38 Mère Marie Madeline to Saretta Green, 3 November 1869, Edith Nesbit Archive.

39 E. Nesbit to her mother, 1869, Edith Nesbit Archive.

40 E. Nesbit, 'On Running Away', *Daily Chronicle*, 25 June 1910, p. 7.

41 E. Nesbit, *My School Days*, pp. 14–15.

42 Ibid., p. 15.

43 Ibid., p. 55.

44 E. Nesbit, *Wings and the Child*, p. 90.

45 Ibid., pp. 90-1.

46 E. Nesbit, *My School Days*, p. 56.

47 E. Nesbit, *The Story of the Treasure Seekers*, p. 210.

48 E. Nesbit, *My School Days*, p. 57.

49 E. Nesbit, *Wings and the Child*, p. 39.

50 E. Nesbit, *Daphne in Fitzroy Street*, p. 239; he may also have inspired an ornamental cat that comes alive in her story 'The White Cat; a wonder tale', included in *Short Stories* magazine in 1907.

CHAPTER 3

1 'Dr Marston in the Old Days', *Dundee Evening Telegraph*, Thursday 9 January 1890, p. 2.

2 T. Earle Welby, *The Victorian Romantics, 1850-70; The Early Works of Dante Gabriel Rossetti, William Morris, Burne-Jones, Swinburne, Simeon Solomon and their Associates* (London: G. Howe Ltd., 1929), p. 88.

3 William Sharp, *Dante Gabriel Rossetti: A Record and a Study* (London: Macmillan and Co., 1882), p. 35.

4 William Sharp, 'Memoir of Philip Bourke Marston' in *For a Song's Sake and Other Stories* by Philip Bourke Marston (London: W. Scott, 1887), p. xi.

5 Ibid.

6 Helen C. Black, *Notable Women Authors of the Day* (London: Maclaren & Company, 1906), pp. 199–200.

7 Thomas Purnell, "Philip Bourke Marston" in *Bookseller: the organ of the book trade*, March 4, 1887, included in collected volume *Bookseller: the organ of the book trade*, 1887 (London: J. Whitaker, 1887), 239.

8 'Philip Bourke Marston by A Woman Who Knew Him' *Pall Mall Gazette*, Wednesday 23 February 1887, p. 4.

9 Richard Garnett, 'Philip Bourke Marston 1850–1887', *Dictionary of National Biography 1885–1930*, vol. 36 (London: Smith, Elder & Co., 1893), p. 260.

10 Quoted in 'When I was a Girl' by E. Nesbit in *John O'London's Weekly*, 15 November 1919.

11 Louise Chandler Moulton, 'Biographical Sketch' in *The Collected Poems of Philip Bourke Marston* (Boston: Roberts Brothers, 1892), p. xxvi.

12 Elizabeth A. Sharp, *William Sharp (Fiona McCloud): A Memoir Compiled by his Wife* (London: William Heinemann, 1910), p. 29.

13 Louise Chandler Moulton, 'Biographical Sketch' in *The Collected Poems of Philip Bourke Marston*, Sketch p. xxiii

14 Sharp, 'Memoir of Philip Bourke Marston', p. xiv.

15 Angeli-Denis Collection, University of British Colombia Library, Letter no. 472.

16 William E. Fredeman (ed.), *The Correspondence of Dante Gabriel Rossetti 5, 1871–1872* (Cambridge: D.S. Brewer, 2012), p. 201.

17 Swinburne to his mother, 12 April 1874, quoted in 'Swinburne and the "unutterable sadness" of Philip Bourke Marston', *Literary Imagination*, vol. 15, issue 2, 1 July 2013, pp. 165–80.

18 I am indebted to Colin Fenn, vice-chair of the Friends of West Norwood Cemetery for this information. www.fownc.org.

19 E. Nesbit, 'A Strange Experience', *Longman's Magazine*, no. XVII, March 1884, p. 506.

20 Thomas Purnell, 'Philip Bourke Marston', p. 239.

21 Garnett, 'Philip Bourke Marston 1850–1887', p. 260.

22 Sharp, 'Memoir of Philip Bourke Marston' p. ix.

23 E. Nesbit to her mother, sent from the Rose and Crown, undated, Edith Nesbit Archive.

24 Information sourced from www.manfamily.org, website of the family who founded the Man Group, funders of the Man Booker Prize.

25 E. Nesbit, 'The Portent of the Shadow' in *Black and White* magazine, 23 December 1905.

26 E. Nesbit, *My School Days*, p. 58.

27 Information sourced from www.manfamily.org.

28 E. Nesbit, *My School Days*, p. 60.

29 Ibid., p. 62.

30 Ibid.

31 Reference: E. Nesbit, The Wouldbegoods, p. 187

32 E. Nesbit, 'The Brute' in *The Literary Sense* (London: Macmillan and Co., 1903), pp. 147–8.

33 E. Nesbit, *My School Days*, p. 60.

34 E. Nesbit, *The Wouldbegoods*, p. 92.

35 E. Nesbit, *My School Days*, pp. 58–9. Mrs Ewing was Juliana Horatia Ewing, English author of children's stories and notable for her insight into the life and emotions of a child.

36 E. Nesbit to Berta Ruck, 17 March 1924, Edith Nesbit Archive.

37 In *The Railway Children*, Nesbit appears to draw on an amalgam of railways and stations from around England. When she lived in Halstead the closest station was Chelsfield, located three miles along the track, but she moved her fictional station closer to home. She had left the village by the time 'Halstead for Knockholt' station opened in 1876. For further information see *Which Railway?*, Papers presented by members of the Edith Nesbit Society, September 1999.

38 E. Nesbit, *The Railway Children*, p. 30.

39 Alexander Hay Japp, *The Poets and Poetry of the Century*, vol. 8, ed. Alfred H. Miles (London: Hutchinson & Co, 1891), p. 579.

40 E. Nesbit, 'When I was a Girl' in *John O'London's Weekly*, 15 November 1919.
41 Ibid.
42 Ada Breakell to Doris Langley Moore, Edith Nesbit Archive.
43 E. Nesbit, 'The White Cat: A Wonder Tale', *Short Stories*, vol. 68, October–December 1907, p. 367.
44 E. Nesbit, *My School Days*, p. 62.

CHAPTER 4

1 Ada Breakell to Doris Langley Moore, 23 October 1931, Edith Nesbit Archive. The 'oldest and dearest friend' quote is from the dedication at the beginning of Nesbit's collection of stories *Man and Maid* (London: T. Fisher Unwin, 1906).
2 Ada Breakell to Doris Langley Moore, 23 October 1931, Edith Nesbit Archive.
3 E. Nesbit to Ada Breakell, undated, Edith Nesbit Archive.
4 'Death of Mr. Henry Bland', *Kentish Independent*, Saturday 8 September 1866, p. 4.
5 In 1861 the Blands were living at 29 Francis Street, Woolwich. Helen was seventeen and Hubert just six. The Bland Children were:
    William Henry (b. 28 December 1840, died in childhood)
    Henry Kinton (b. 7 August 1841)
    Percy Owen (b. 9 November 1842)
    Helen (b. 2 April 1844)
    Hubert (b. 3 January 1855, died 14 April 1914)
6 Hubert Bland, *Essays by Hubert Bland; chosen by E. Nesbit Bland, 'Hubert' of the Sunday Chronicle; with an introduction by Cecil Chesterton* (London: M. Goschen, 1914), p. viii.
7 George Bernard Shaw to Archibald Henderson, 3 January 1905, quoted in Archibald Henderson, *George Bernard Shaw: His Life and Works* (Cincinnati: Stewart and Kidd Company, 1911), p. 129.
8 Henderson, *George Bernard Shaw, His Life and Works*, p. 128.
9 Hubert Bland, *Essays by Hubert Bland*, p. 206.
10 Cecil Chesterton in his Introduction to *Essays by Hubert Bland*, p. xi.
11 Hubert Bland, *Essays by Hubert Bland*, p. 203.
12 Maggie was baptised on 20 January 1856. Her address in Woolwich was noted in the census of 1871.
13 The information that Maggie had a son comes from an account provided by Edith and Hubert's daughter, Iris Bland, to Doris Langley Moore. A transcript is held in the Edith Nesbit Archive.
14 E. Nesbit to Ada Breakell, undated, Edith Nesbit Archive.
15 W.C. DeVane and K.L. Knickerbocker (eds), *New Letters of Robert Browning* (London: John Murray, 1951), p. 280.
16 E. Nesbit, *The Literary Sense*, p. 117.
17 Ibid., p. 119.
18 Ibid., p. 121.
19 E. Nesbit to Ada Breakell, undated, Edith Nesbit Archive.
20 This is the very first poem she wrote into a cheap notebook, with 'Daisy Bland, Aug. 27, 1879' written inside the front cover. Quoted in Julia Briggs, *A Woman of Passion: The Life of E. Nesbit 1858-1924* (London: Penguin Books, 1987), p. 46.
21 Quoted in Briggs, *A Woman of Passion*, p. 46.
22 E. Nesbit to Francis Galton, Galton Papers, University College Library, London. https://www.ucl.ac.uk/news/news-articles/0714/100714-galton-archive-online

and http://discovery.nationalarchives.gov.uk/details/rd/N13821380 (accessed 5 November 2017).

23 Fabian Bland, *The Prophet's Mantle* (London: Belford, Clarke & Company, 1889), pp. 126–7.

24 *Lichfield Mercury*, Friday 12 October 1906, p. 6.

25 Hubert Bland, *With the Eyes of a Man* (London: T. Werner Laurie, 1905), p. 5.

26 Ibid., p. 51.

27 Ibid., p. 29.

28 E. Nesbit, *The Incredible Honeymoon* (New York and London: Harper & Brothers Publishers, 1916), p. 147.

29 Ibid., p. 56.

30 Ibid., pp. 115–16.

31 Hubert Bland, *Essays by Hubert Bland*, p. 83.

32 Ibid., p. 79.

33 Ibid., p. 152.

34 Hubert Bland, *With the Eyes of a Man*, p. 207.

35 E. Nesbit, *The Incredible Honeymoon*, p. 3.

36 Hubert Bland, *With the Eyes of a Man*, p. 53.

37 Hubert Bland, *Essays by Hubert Bland*, p. 155.

38 Hubert Bland, *With the Eyes of a Man*, p. 133.

39 According to Isabella Sutherland, a housekeeper at 17 Devonshire Square, in testimony she gave at a fraud trial on March 1, 1880. Details of her testimony is available at www.oldbaileyonline.org, case reference number t18800301-284.

40 Ada Breakell to Doris Langley Moore, Edith Nesbit Archive.

41 E. Nesbit, *The Incredible Honeymoon*, p. 160.

42 Ibid., p. 161.

43 E. Nesbit, *The Red House* (New York and London: Harper & Brothers Publishers, 1902), p. 188.

44 E. Nesbit, *The Red House*, p. 256.

45 *The London Gazette*, 6 August 1880, p. 4331: https://www.thegazette.co.uk/London/issue/24871/page/4331/data.pdf (accessed 6 November 2017), and in *Lloyds List* of Saturday 7 August 1880.

CHAPTER 5

1 G.B. Shaw, *An Unfinished Novel*, ed. Stanley Weintraub (London: Constable, 1958), p. 42.

2 *Ainslee's Magazine*, vol. 12, 1903–4, p. 75.

3 Hubert Bland, 'Who is Timothy Knapp?', *Sporting Times*, Saturday 14 March 1881, p. 2.

4 Minnie Williams, 'Timothy Knapp', *Sporting Times*, Saturday 28 May 1881, p. 7.

5 Emmeline de Vere, 'Timothy Knapp', *Sporting Times*, Saturday 11 June 1881, p. 7.

6 *Emmetsburg (Iowa) Democrat*, 1895 Christmas Souvenir Edition quoted in www.findagrave.com (accessed 6 November 2017).

7 Alice Hoatson to Doris Langley Moore, 4 July 1932, Edith Nesbit Archive.

8 E. Nesbit, *The Story of The Treasure Seekers*, p. 6.

9 E. Nesbit, *The New Treasure Seekers* (London: T, Fisher Unwin, 1904), p. 37.

10 E. Nesbit, *The Story of The Treasure Seekers*, p. 145.

11 Ibid., p. 7.

12 E. Nesbit to Ada Breakell, undated, Edith Nesbit Archive.

13 This story appeared first in *Home Chimes*, December 1887, and also in E. Nesbit, *Grim Tales* (London: A.D. Innes, 1893).

14 *Current Literature*, vol. VII, May-August 1891 (New York: The Current Literature Publishing Company, 1891) pp. 475–6.

15 E. Nesbit, *Daphne in Fitzroy Street*, p. 140.

16 Ibid., p. 141.

17 Ibid., p. 142.

18 E. Nesbit, *The Red House*, p. 63.

19 E. Nesbit, *The Railway Children*, p. 53.

20 Information on the history of Raphael Tuck & Sons sourced from https://tuckdb.org/history (accessed 6 November 2017).

21 From the account given to Doris Langley Moore by Gustave Tuck, transcript held in the Edith Nesbit Archive.

22 Interview between John Bland and Doris Langley Moore, transcript held in the Edith Nesbit Archive.

23 Ada Breakell to Doris Langley Moore, 8 May 1931, Edith Nesbit Archive.

24 E. Nesbit, 'After Many Days', *Longman's Magazine*, vol. 23, November 1893.

25 Ada Breakell to Doris Langley Moore, 8 May 1931, Edith Nesbit Archive.

26 Hubert Bland, *The Happy Moralist* (London: T. Werner Laurie, 1907), p. 169.

27 Ibid.

28 Ibid., p. 170.

29 http://leicestersecularsociety.org.uk/PHP_History/history_gimson2.php (accessed 7 November 2017).

30 E. Nesbit, *The Red House*, p. 15.

31 Edith Nesbit to Ada Breakell, 11 April 1884, Edith Nesbit Archive.

32 Edith Nesbit to Ada Breakell, 13 April 1884, Edith Nesbit Archive.

33 Edith Nesbit to Ada Breakell, 11 April 1884, Edith Nesbit Archive.

34 Edith Nesbit to Ada Breakell, undated, Edith Nesbit Archive.

35 Hubert Bland, *Essays by Hubert Bland*, p. 216.

36 Edith Nesbit to Ada Breakell, 30 March 1884, Edith Nesbit Archive.

37 E. Nesbit, *The Red House*, p. 79.

38 Alice Hoatson remembered the date as press day, 22 January 1881. However, since she also recalled Edith saying that she had a six-week-old baby and Iris was born on 2 December 1881, it must have been 1882.

39 Alice Hoatson to Doris Langley Moore, 4 July 1932, Edith Nesbit Archive.

CHAPTER 6

1 E. Nesbit to Ada Breakell, 30 March 1884, Edith Nesbit Archive.

2 Hubert Bland, 'The Faith I Hold', paper read before the Fabian Society in December 1907. Reprinted in *The New Age*, 25 January 1908.

3 William Morris and Norman Kelvin (eds), *The Collected Letters of William Morris*, vol. II, part B: *1885–1888* (Princeton: Princeton University Press, 1987), p. 670.

4 H.M. Hyndman *The Record of an Adventurous Life* (New York: The Macmillan Company, 1991), p. 323.

5 Hubert Bland, 'The Faith I Hold'.

6 E. Nesbit to Ada Breakell, undated, Edith Nesbit Archive.

7   Hubert Bland, *Essays by Hubert Bland*, p. 214.
8   Hubert Bland, 'The Faith I Hold'.
9   Hyndman, *The Record of an Adventurous Life*, p. 271.
10   Ibid., p. 307.
11   Edward Reynolds Pease, unpublished manuscript: Recollections for my sons –
     March 1930, Notes on my life (Dec. 1950), Reminiscences of E.R.P. Oct 1953 –
     held by family.
12   Ibid.
13   E. Nesbit, 'Porro Unum Est Necessarium', *Living Age*, vol. 277, 1913, p. 567.
14   Warren Sylvester Smith, *The London Heretics 1870–1914* (New York: Dodd, Mead &
     Company, 1968), p. 133.
15   Norman and Jean Mackenzie, *The Fabians* (New York: Simon and Schuster, 1977),
     p. 15.
16   E. Belfort Bax, 'The Rise and Decline of Fabianism', *Reynolds Newspaper*, Sunday 1
     July 1894, p. 3.
17   Hubert Bland, 'The Faith I Hold'.
18   Belfort Bax, 'The Rise and Decline of Fabianism', p. 3.
19   First Fabian Minute Book, held at https://digital.library.lse.ac.uk (accessed 10
     November 2017).
20   Belfort Bax, 'The Rise and Decline of Fabianism', p. 3.
21   Edward Reynolds Pease, *The History of the Fabian Society* (London: E.P. Dutton,
     1916), p. 37.
22   E. Nesbit to Ada Breakell, undated, Edith Nesbit Archive.
23   Norman and Jean Mackenzie, *The Fabians*, p. 28.
24   Pease, *The History of the Fabian Society*, p. 40.
25   G. Bernard Shaw, Fabian Tract No. 41 – *The Fabian Society: Its Early History*
     (London: The Fabian Society, 1892), p. 24.
26   Pease, *The History of the Fabian Society*, p. 64.
27   Ian Britain, *Fabianism and Culture: A Study in British Socialism and the Arts c. 1884–1918*
     (Cambridge: Cambridge University Press, 1982), p. 21.
28   Pease, *The History of the Fabian Society*, pp. 56–7.
29   *Morning Star*, 26 March 1886.
30   Ibid.
31   E. Nesbit to Ada Breakell, 6 April 1884, Edith Nesbit Archive.
32   'Political Action by Socialists' *Morning Post*, Saturday 18 September 1886, p. 2.
33   Fabian Society Executive Committee minute book, 23 Dec. 1885 – 21 Jan. 1887
     held at https://digital.library.lse.ac.uk (accessed 10 November 2017).
34   'John O'London's Weekly, 12 July 1919, 'Annie Besant – The Woman' in *John
     O'London's Weekly* Volume I, p. 413 .
35   Letter from E. Nesbit to Ada Breakell, undated, Edith Nesbit Archive.
36   Annie Besant, *An Autobiography* (London: T. Fisher Unwin, 1910), p. 188.
37   36 should read "John O'London's Weekly, 'Annie Besant - The Woman', p. 413.
38   Annie Besant, *Our Corner*, vol. 7 (London: Freethought, 1883), p. 250.
39   Annie Besant, *An Autobiography*, pp. 310–11.
40   Stanley Weintraub (ed.), *Shaw: An Autobiography 1856–1898* (London: Max
     Reinhardt, 1969), p. 393.
41   E. Nesbit, *The House of Arden* (London: T. Fisher Unwin, 1923), p. 113.
42   E. Nesbit to Ada Breakell, undated, Edith Nesbit Archive.

43   Charlotte Wilson to G. Bernard Shaw, 15 July 1889, AM 50512, fo. 161, George Bernard Shaw Papers, British Library, London.

44   E. Nesbit to Ada Breakell, undated, Edith Nesbit Archive.

45   Mrs Ashton Dilke, 'Select Socialists', *Current Opinion*, vol. 3, p. 390.

46   E. Nesbit to Ada Breakell, undated, Edith Nesbit Archive.

47   Dilke, 'Select Socialists', p. 390.

48   Pease, *The History of the Fabian Society*, p. 65.

49   E. Nesbit to Ada Breakell, undated, Edith Nesbit Archive.

50   Edgar Jepson, *Memories of an Edwardian and Neo-Georgian* (London: Richards, 1937), p. 23, Jepson confirmed 'she was one of the earliest of the chain-smokers, rolling her own cigarettes'.

51   E. Nesbit, 'The Pavilion,' *The Strand Magazine*, November 1915, included in George Newnes, ed., Volume L, July to December 1915, (London: George Newnes Ltd., 1915), 562–72.

52   Doris Langley Moore, *E. Nesbit: A Biography* (London: Ernest Benn Ltd., 1933), p. 104.

53   Havelock Ellis to Doris Langley Moore, quoted in Moore, *E. Nesbit*, p. 104.

54   'The Socialist Congress: Lively Scenes', *Weekly Irish Times*, Saturday 1 August 1896, p. 5.

55   E. Nesbit to Ada Breakell, March 1884, Edith Nesbit Archive.

56   E. Nesbit to Ada Breakell, undated, Edith Nesbit Archive.

57   Fabian Society Executive Committee minute book, 23 Dec. 1885 – 21 Jan. 1887 held at https://digital.library.lse.ac.uk (accessed 10 November 2017).

58   Ibid.

59   Moore, *E. Nesbit*, pp. 132–3; Shaw was in the habit of accusing women of feigning their swoons. On 16 March 1885 he accused actress Madge Kendal of pretending to faint during a performance of *As You Like It* in the St James's Theatre.

60   Norman and Jean Mackenzie, *The Fabians*, p. 30.

CHAPTER 7

1   Wilfrid Scawen Blunt, *My Diaries: Being a Personal Narrative of Events* (New York: Alfred A. Knopf, 1922), entry for 21 February 1920, p. 559.

2   Frank Harris, *Bernard Shaw: An Unauthorised Biography Based on Firsthand Information with a Postscript by Mr Shaw* (London: Victor Gollancz Ltd., 1931), p. 30.

3   Hesketh Pearson, *Bernard Shaw: His Life and Personality* (London: Collins, 1942), p. 41.

4   Archibald Henderson, 'The Real Bernard Shaw', *Munsey's Magazine*, January 1908, p. 453.

5   Harris, *Bernard Shaw*, p. 114.

6   GBS to Pakenham Beatty, 27 May 1887, in Dan H. Laurence (ed.), *Collected Letters 1874–1897*, p. 168; Shaw, *Sixteen Self Sketches*, (London: Dodd, Mead, 1949), p. 68

7   *Evening Dispatch*, Saturday 18 April 1914, p. 4.

8   Harris, *Bernard Shaw*, p. 31.

9   Blunt, *My Diaries*, p. 559.

10   'A Fabian', 'Individualism in Masquerade' in *Seed Time*, a magazine produced by the Fellowship of the New Life, October 1890.

11   G.B. Shaw, 'The Chesterbelloc: A Lampoon', *New Age*, 15 February 1908.

12 G. B. Shaw (1949) *Sixteen Self Sketches*, p. 94

13 G.B. Shaw to Ellen Terry, 11 June 1897 in Christopher St John (ed.), *Ellen Terry and Bernard Shaw: A Correspondence* (London: Max Reinhardt, 1922), p. 196.

14 Shaw, *Sixteen Self Sketches*, p. 14.

15 George Slyvester Viereck, *Glimpses of the Great* (London: Duckworth, 1930), p. 37.

16 Harris, *Bernard Shaw*, p. 13.

17 Shaw, *Sixteen Self Sketches*, p. 88.

18 Ibid., p. 97.

19 Fabian Society Executive Committee minute book, 23 Dec. 1885 – 21 Jan. 1887 held digitally at https://digital.library.lse.ac.uk/collections/fabiansociety/minutebooks.

20 A MANIFESTO – Fabian Tract No. 2

THE FABIANS are associated for spreading the following opinions held by them and discussing their practical consequences.

That under existing circumstances wealth cannot be enjoyed without dishonour or foregone without misery.

That it is the duty of each member of the State to provide for his or her wants by his or her own Labour.

That a life interest in the Land and Capital of the nation is the birthright of every individual born within its confines and that access to this birthright should not depend upon the will of any private person other than the person seeking it.

That the most striking result of our present system of farming out the national Land and Capital to private persons has been the division of Society into hostile classes, with large appetites and no dinners at one extreme and large dinners and no appetites at the other.

That the practice of entrusting the Land of the nation to private persons in the hope that they will make the best of it has been discredited by the consistency with which they have made the worst of it; and that Nationalisation of the Land in some form is a public duty.

That the pretensions of Capitalism to encourage Invention and to distribute its benefits in the fairest way attainable, have been discredited by the experience of the nineteenth century.

That, under the existing system of leaving the National Industry to organise itself Competition has the effect of rendering adulteration, dishonest dealing and inhumanity compulsory.

That since Competition amongst producers admittedly secures to the public the most satisfactory products, the State should compete with all its might in every department of production.

That such restraints upon Free Competition as the penalties for infringing the Postal monopoly, and the withdrawal of workhouse and prison labour from the markets, should be abolished.

That no branch of Industry should be carried on at a profit by the central administration.

That the Public Revenue should be levied by a direct Tax; and that the central administration should have no legal power to hold back for the replenishment of the Public Treasury any portion of the proceeds of Industries administered by them.

That the State should compete with private individuals – especially with parents – in providing happy homes for children, so that every child may have a refuge from the tyranny or neglect of its natural custodians.

That Men no longer need special political privileges to protect them against Women, and that the sexes should henceforth enjoy equal political rights.

That no individual should enjoy any Privilege in consideration of services rendered to the State by his or her parents or other relations.

That the State should secure a liberal education and an equal share in the National Industry to each of its units.

That the established Government has no more right to call itself the State than the smoke of London has to call itself the weather.

That we had rather face a Civil War than such another century of suffering as the present one has been.

21 Mrs Cecil Chesterton (Ada Elizabeth Jones Chesterton), *The Chestertons* (London: George G. Harrap & Company, 1931), p. 14.
22 Letter from E. Nesbit to Ada Breakell, undated, Edith Nesbit Archive.
23 E. Nesbit, *Daphne in Fitzroy Street*, p. 190.
24 Pearson, *Bernard Shaw: His Life and Personality*, p. 98.
25 *John O'London's Weekly*, 26 April 1919, p. 67.
26 G.B. Shaw and Dan H. Lawrence (ed.), *Collected Letters 1874–1897* (London: Max Reinhardt, 1965), p. 262.
27 Harris, *Bernard Shaw*, p. 237.
28 Pearson, *Bernard Shaw: His Life and Personality*, p. 139.
29 G.B. Shaw, *Love Among the Artists* (New York: Brentanos, 1910), p. 78.
30 Beatrice Webb's Diary, https://digital.library.lse.ac.uk/collections/webb.
31 Hubert Bland, 'Mr Shaw's Man and Superman' in *With the Eyes of a Man*, p. 79.
32 Shaw told Hesketh Person 'the ideal love affair is one conducted by post'. His relationship with the actress Ellen Terry was certainly epistolary in nature.
33 A.M. Gibbs, *A Bernard Shaw Chronology* (New York: Palgrave, 2001), p. 65.
34 Stanley Weintraub (ed.), *Bernard Shaw: The Diaries 1885–1897*, vol. I (University Park and London: Pennsylvania State University Press, 1986), p. 99.
35 Ibid., p. 55.
36 Ibid., p. 97.
37 Pearson, *Bernard Shaw: His Life and Personality*, p. 109.
38 Ibid.
39 Shaw, *Sixteen Self Sketches*, p. 113.
40 Weintraub, *Bernard Shaw: The Diaries 1885–1897*, vol. I, p. 34.
41 Pearson, *Bernard Shaw: His Life and Personality*, p. 112.
42 Ibid., p. 79.
43 Ibid., p. 81.
44 Ibid., pp. 80–1.
45 Rachel Holmes, *Eleanor Marx: A Life* (London: Bloomsbury, 2014), p. 211. Aveling's eventual departure and subsequent marriage provoked Marx's suicide.
46 Interview between G.B. Shaw and Doris Langley Moore, transcript held in the Edith Nesbit Archive.
47 Michael Holroyd, *Bernard Shaw: The New Biography* (London: Head of Zeus, 2015), p. 156.
48 G.B. Shaw, *Heartbreak House* (London: Constable, 1919).

49 Weintraub, *Bernard Shaw: The Diaries 1885–1897*, vol. I, p. 67.
50 Harris, *Bernard Shaw*, pp. 94, 226.
51 Weintraub, *Bernard Shaw: The Diaries 1885–1897*, vol. I, p. 108.
52 Ibid., p. 179.
53 E. Nesbit to G.B. Shaw, 29 June 1886, in Shaw Papers, British Library Add. MSS 50511, quoted in Briggs, *A Woman of Passion*, p. 89.
54 E. Nesbit, *Daphne in Fitzroy Street*, pp. 144–5.
55 *New Yorker*, vol. 43, part 1, 1925, p. 34.
56 Briggs, *A Woman of Passion*, p. 92.
57 Weintraub, *Bernard Shaw: The Diaries 1885–1897*, vol. I, p. 199.
58 Ibid., p. 209.
59 Ibid., p. 34.
60 Pearson, *Bernard Shaw: His Life and Personality*, p. 115.
61 Quoted in *The Collected Works of Bernard Shaw*, vol. 6 (New York: W.H. Wise, 1930), p. 98.
62 Holroyd, *Bernard Shaw: The New Biography*, p. 88.
63 G.B. Shaw to Charles Charrington dated 28 January 1890 in Dan H. Laurence (ed.), *Collected Letters 1874–1897*, p. 240.
64 E. Nesbit, *Daphne in Fitzroy Street*, p. 185.
65 Dan H. Laurence (ed.), *Bernard Shaw: Collected Letters 1911–1925*, vol. III (London: Max Reinhardt, 1985), p. 904. Letter from G.B. Shaw to Molly Tompkins 22 February 1925. Edith Nesbit died on 4 May 1924.
66 *John O'London's Weekly*, 15 November 1919.
67 Held in the Butler Library of Columbia University, New York, and quoted in full in Briggs, *A Woman of Passion*, p. 95.
68 G.B. Shaw and Dan H. Laurence (ed.), 'Found at Last – A New Poet' in *Unpublished Shaw* (University Park, PA: Pennsylvania State University Press, 1996), pp. 108–9.
69 Pearson, *Bernard Shaw: His Life and Personality*, p. 114.
70 Weintraub, *Bernard Shaw: The Diaries 1885–1897*, vol. I, p. 268.
71 Ibid., pp. 228, 302.
72 E. Nesbit, *Daphne in Fitzroy Street*, p. 404.
73 Interview between G.B. Shaw and Doris Langley Moore, transcript held in the Edith Nesbit Archive.
74 Shaw, *Sixteen Self Sketches*, p. 6.
75 Weintraub, *Bernard Shaw: The Diaries 1885–1897*, vol. I, p. 229.
76 Shaw, *An Unfinished Novel*, p. 35.
77 Ibid., p. 42.
78 Ibid., p. 88.
79 Ibid., pp. 91–2.
80 Ibid., p. 77.
81 Ibid., p. 78.
82 Shaw, *Sixteen Self Sketches*, p. 113.
83 Ibid., pp. 113, 115.
84 Wilfrid Scawen Blunt, *My Diaries 1900–1914 The Coalition Against Germany* (London: A.A. Knopf, 1923), p. 136.
85 Holroyd, *Bernard Shaw: The New Biography*, p. 432.
86 Shaw, *Sixteen Self Sketches*, p. 115.

CHAPTER 8

1   E. Nesbit to Ada Breakell, undated, Edith Nesbit Archive.
2   E. Nesbit to Ada Breakell, undated, Edith Nesbit Archive.
3   Podmore married Eleanor Oliver Bramwell on 11 June 1891. Alan Gauld, his
    biographer, writes: 'In 1907 Podmore was compelled to resign without pension from
    the Post Office because of alleged homosexual involvements. He separated from his
    wife, and went to live with his brother Claude, rector of Broughton, near Kettering.'
    (*Oxford Dictionary of National Biography*, Oxford: Oxford University Press, 2004).
4   Alice Hoatson to Doris Langley Moore, 4 July 1932, Edith Nesbit Archive.
5   E. Nesbit, 'The Moat House' in *Lays and Legends* (London: Longmans, Green,
    1887), p. 21.
6   E. Nesbit, *The Story of the Treasure Seekers*, p. 258.
7   E. Nesbit, *The Wouldbegoods*, p. 146.
8   E. Nesbit, *The Red House*, p. 14.
9   Alice Hoatson to Doris Langley Moore, 4 July 1932, Edith Nesbit Archive.
10 This series included 'Morning Songs and Sketches', 'Noon Songs and Sketches',
    'Eventide Songs and Sketches', 'Night Songs and Sketches', 'Spring Songs and
    Sketches', 'Summer Songs and Sketches', 'Autumn Songs and Sketches' and
    'Winter Songs and Sketches'.
11 E. Nesbit, *The Red House*, p. 18.
12 Alice Hoatson to Doris Langley Moore, 4 July 1932, Edith Nesbit Archive.
13 Alice Hoatson to Doris Langley Moore, 4 July 1932, Edith Nesbit Archive.
14 Eric Bellingham-Smith to Vera Bellingham Smith (Hugh's wife), 3 August 1966,
    owned by Mrs Shirley Colqhoun and quoted in Briggs, *A Woman of Passion*, pp.
    132–3.
15 E. Nesbit, *The Red House*, p. 87.
16 'Mrs Hubert Bland ("E. Nesbit")' in *The Strand Magazine*, no. VIII, p. 287.
17 Andrew Lang to Thomas Longman, 18 July 1886, quoted in Moore, *E. Nesbit*, p. 120.
18 'Lays and Legends by E. Nesbit' *Vanity Fair* and reproduced in *The Globe*,
    Wednesday 15 December 1886, p. 8.
19 'Recent Poetry & Verse' in *The Graphic*, Saturday 8 January 1887, p. 22.
20 E. Nesbit to Berta Ruck, 17 March 1924, written in Olive Hill's handwriting with
    a PS from E. Nesbit, Edith Nesbit Archive.
21 *The Bookseller, Newsdealer and Stationer*, vol. 23, 1905, p. 511.
22 Oscar Wilde to E. Nesbit, in M. Holland and R. Hart-Davis (eds), *The Complete
    Letters of Oscar Wilde* (London: Fourth Estate, 2000), p. 287.
23 Oscar Wilde's review of *Women's Voices*, an anthology of poetry edited by Elizabeth
    Sharp, in 'Literary and Other Notes' in *The Women's World*, November 1887.
24 Oscar Wilde (writing anonymously) 'The Poets' Corner', *Pall Mall Gazette*, Friday
    16 November 1888, p. 2.
25 Oscar Wilde, 'English Poetesses', originally published in *Queen*, 8 December 1888,
    reproduced in Oscar Wilde and E. V. Lucas, ed., *A Critic in Pall Mall*; reviews and
    miscellanies (New York: G.P. Putnam & Sons, 1920), 130; J.M. Barrie, 'A Publisher
    of Minor Poets: A Chat with Mr. John Lane,' *The Sketch*, 4 December 1895, 6.
26 Coulson Kernahan, *Swinburne As I Knew Him, with some unpublished letters from the poet
    to his cousin, the Hon. Lady Henniker Heaton* (London: John Lane, 1919), pp. 68–70.
27 Ibid., p. 65; Jerome K. Jerome, 'Gossips' Corner' in *Home Chimes* new series 3, no.
    2, March 1887, pp. 155–60.

28 Philip Bourke Marston to Thomas Purnell, quoted in *The Bookseller*, 4 March 1887, p. 239.
29 Elizabeth A. Sharp, *William Sharp (Fiona McLeod): A Memoir Compiled by his wife Elizabeth A. Sharp* (New York: Duffield & Company, 1910), p. 74.
30 Louise Chandler Moulton in her introduction to *Lyrics and Sonnets from the Book of Love* by Philip Bourke Marston (London: Elkin Matthews, 1891), pp. 11–12.
31 E. Nesbit to George Bernard Shaw, 18 February 1887, Shaw Papers, British Library, MSS 50511.
32 May Bowley to Doris Langley Moore, 11 November 1931, Edith Nesbit Archive.
33 Weintraub (ed.), *Bernard Shaw: The Diaries 1885–1897*, vol. I, p. 429.
34 Rosamund Bland to Doris Langley Moore, 12 December 1931, Edith Nesbit Archive.
35 E. Nesbit, 'The Prince, Two Mice and Some Kitchen-maids', *Nine Unlikely Tales* (London: Ernest Benn Ltd., 1901)
36 Nesbit. The Literary Sense (London: Macmillan Company, 1903), p. 8.
37 Briggs, A Woman of Substance, p.120
38 Helen Macklin to Doris Langley Moore, 9 June 1933, Edith Nesbit Archive.
39 Edgar Jepson, *Memories of an Edwardian and Neo-Georgian* (London: Richards, 1937), pp. 19–20.
40 Hubert Bland, *Letters to a Daughter* (London: T. Warner Laurie, 1907), p. 118.
41 Ibid., p. 190.
42 Review of *Lays and Legends* in *The Graphic*, Saturday 16 July 1892.
43 'Bland, Edith 1858-1924' in *Dictionary of National Biography 1922–1930*, p. 84.
44 *The Primitive Methodist Magazine*, vol. 71, Conference Offices, 1890, p. 756.

CHAPTER 9
1 Jepson, *Memories of an Edwardian and Neo-Georgian*, p. 24.
2 Cecil Chesterton, Introduction to *Essays by Hubert Bland*, p. vii.
3 Hubert Bland, *With The Eyes of a Man*, p. 94.
4 H.G. Wells, *H.G. Wells in Love* (London: Faber and Faber, 2011), p. 68.
5 Richard Le Gallienne to John Lane, 25 May 1888, held among the John Lane Papers; Richard Le Gallienne, *The Romantic '90s* (New York: Doubleday, Page & Company, 1925), p. 15.
6 James Lewis May, *John Lane and the Nineties* (London: John Lane, 1936), p. 128.
7 May, *John Lane and the Nineties*, p. 96.
8 May, *John Lane and the Nineties*, p. 33.
9 Richard Le Gallienne to Doris Langley Moore, 26 August 1931, Edith Nesbit Archive. It is likely they had met earlier through Lane.
10 Le Gallienne, *The Romantic '90s*, p. 165.
11 Frederick Rogers, *Labour, Life and Literature: Some Memories of Sixty Years* (London: Smith, Elder & Co., 1913), p. 173.
12 Lewis May, *John Lane and the Nineties*, pp. 127, 154.
13 Le Gallienne 'Women as a Supernatural Being' in *Vanishing Roads and Other Essays* (London: Putnam, 1915), p. 17.
14 E. Nesbit to R. Le Gallienne, undated, Harry Ransome Research Centre, University of Texas at Austin.
15 Information included on a card written by Doris Langley Moore, Edith Nesbit Archive.

16 Rogers, *Labour, Life and Literature*, p. 173.
17 This is the opinion of Richard Whittington Egan and Geoffry Smerdon in *The Quest for the Golden Boy* (London: Unicorn Press, 1960), p. 255.
18 Brian Tyson (ed.), *Bernard Shaw's Book Reviews: 1884–1950* (Pennsylvania State University Press, 1991), p. 154.
19 Richard Le Gallienne, 'Women Poets of the Day', *English Illustrated Magazine*, vol. II, no. 127–32, 1894, pp. 652–3.
20 Le Gallienne, *Vanishing Roads and Other Essays*, pp. 74–5.
21 E. Nesbit, 'The Bibliophile's Reverie', *The Library Chronicle*, vol. IV, 1887, p. 96.
22 Jepson, *Memories of an Edwardian and Neo-Georgian*, p. 24.
23 Ibid., p. 21.
24 Interview between Iris Bland and Doris Langley Moore, transcript held in the Edith Nesbit Archive.
25 'Gossip – mainly about people', reproduced in the *Dundee Evening Telegraph*, Monday 7 May 1888, p. 2.
26 Fabian Bland, 'Only a Joke', *Longman's Magazine*, vol. 14, 1889, p. 390.
27 Hubert Bland 'The Outlook' in *Fabian Essays in Socialism* (London: Walter Scott, 1889), p. 205.
28 Daily Chronicle, quoted in Hubert Bland, The Happy Moralist, piii
29 *Manchester Evening News*, Wednesday 15 April 1914, p. 4.
30 'A Bookman's Gossip', *The Bystander*, 12 April 1905, p. 88.
31 Ada Chesterton, *The Chestertons*, p. 56.
32 Cecil Chesterton, Introduction to *Essays by Hubert Bland*, p. ix.
33 Ada Chesterton, *The Chestertons*, pp. 56–7.
34 Tyson (ed.), *Bernard Shaw's Book Reviews: 1884–1950*, p. 60.
35 *Overland Monthly*, series 2, vol. 15, 1890, p. 103.
36 William Archer, 'Miss E. Nesbit: (Mrs. Bland)' in *Poets of the Younger Generation* (London: John Lane, 1902), pp. 272–83.
37 Olive Schreiner to Havelock Ellis, 22 October 1888, NLSA Cape Town, Special Collections. Available at www.oliveschreiner.org.
38 Olive Schreiner to Edward Carpenter, 20 July 1888. Sheffield Libraries, Archives & Information, Olive Schreiner Letters Project transcription. Available at www. oliveschreiner.org.
39 E. Nesbit to Olive Schreiner, quoted in Moore, *E. Nesbit*, pp. 136–7.
40 Olive Schreiner to Havelock Ellis, 22 October 1888, NLSA Cape Town, Special Collections. Available at www.oliveschreiner.org.
41 Hubert Bland, *Essays by Hubert Bland*, p. 35.

CHAPTER 10

1 '"E. Nesbit" the Poetess', *Glasgow Evening Citizen*, Tuesday 17 September 1889, p. 2.
2 'General Gossip of Authors and Writers', *Current Opinion*, September 1889, vol. 3, July–December 1889, p. 196.
3 Margaret Dilke, 'Select Socialists – Mrs Ashton Dilke – Syndicated Letter' in the November 1889 issue of *Current Literature*, vol. III, June to December 1889 (New York: Current Literature Pub. Co.), p. 390.
4 Ada Moore to Doris Langley Moore, 6 June 1931, Edith Nesbit Archive.
5 Jepson, *Memories of an Edwardian and Neo-Georgian*, p. 24.
6 E. Nesbit, *The Railway Children*, p. 2.

7   May Bowley to Doris Langley Moore, 11 November 1931, Edith Nesbit Archive.

8   Jepson, *Memories of an Edwardian and Neo-Georgian*, p. 24.

9   Alice Hoatson to Doris Langley Moore, 4 July 1932, Edith Nesbit Archive.

10   C.K.S., 'A Literary Letter: Reminiscences of the Fabian Society', T*he Sphere*, 25 September 1915, p. 334.

11   'Jock and Saccharissa', *English Illustrated Magazine*, vol. 20, 1898/9 (New York: Macmillan and Co.), pp. 285–90; Jepson, *Memories of an Edwardian and Neo-Georgian*, pp. 19–20.

12   Jepson, *Memories of an Edwardian and Neo-Georgian*, p. 26.

13   Ibid., p. 25.

14   E. Nesbit to John Lane, undated, held among the Lane Papers, Austin, Texas.

15   From an account given to Doris Langley Moore by Bower Marsh.

16   Adeline Sergeant to E. Nesbit, 1897, quoted in Moore, *E. Nesbit*, p. 173.

17   'Old Fashioned Novels', *Literary World*, vol. 31, 1900, p. 71.

18   'The Secret of Kyriels by E. Nesbit', review in *Book News*, vol. 18, p. 241.

19   'Current Literature', *Current Opinion*, vol. 9, January–April 1892, p. 639.

20   E. Nesbit, *The Red House*, p. 178.

21   Alice Hoatson to Doris Langley Moore, 4 July 1932, Edith Nesbit Archive.

22   E. Nesbit, *Dormant* (London: Methuen & Co. Ltd., 1911), p. 117.

23   May Bowley to Doris Langley Moore, 11 November 1931, Edith Nesbit Archive.

24   Ibid.

25   E. Nesbit, 'Picnics', *Daily Chronicle*, 11 June 1910, p. 7.

26   Hubert Bland, 'In the South', *Essays by Hubert Bland*, p. 234.

27   May Bowley to Doris Langley Moore, 11 November 1931, Edith Nesbit Archive.

28   Hubert Bland, 'In the South', *Essays by Hubert Bland*, p. 237.

29   Ibid., p. 238.

30   Ibid., p. 235.

31   May Bowley to Doris Langley Moore, 11 November 1931, Edith Nesbit Archive.

32   Hubert Bland, 'In the South', *Essays by Hubert Bland*, p. 242.

33   May Bowley to Doris Langley Moore, 11 November 1931, Edith Nesbit Archive.

34   Ibid.

35   *The Spectator*, 18 August 1906, p. 21.

36   E. Nesbit, 'The Treasure Seekers' in *Father Christmas*, 1897, p. 30.

37   E. Nesbit to Sarah Nesbit, undated, quoted in Briggs, p.196.

38   E. Nesbit to Sarah Nesbit, undated, quoted in Briggs, p.196.

39   'Christmas Books' in *The Athenaeum*, no. 3759, 11 November 1899, p. 653.

CHAPTER 11

1   Jepson, *Memories of an Edwardian and Neo-Georgian*, p. 19.

2   E. Nesbit, 'After Many Days', *Longman's Magazine*, no. CXXXILL, November 1893, p. 52.

3   'Mrs Hubert Bland ("E. Nesbit")', *The Strand Magazine*, no. VIII, p. 287.

4   Ada Moore to Doris Langley Moore, 6 June 1931, Edith Nesbit Archive.

5   'Humanitarian Work in Deptford', *Kentish Mercury*, Friday 25 January 1895, p. 2.

6   Ibid.

7   'Free Tea to Schoolchildren', *Blackheath Gazette*, 15 January 1892.

8   E. Nesbit, *Harding's Luck* (London: Hodder & Stoughton, 1909), p. 1.

9   E. Nesbit, *Wings and the Child* (London: Hodder & Stoughton, 1913), p. 179.

10 Ibid., p. 178.
11 Ibid., pp. 98–9.
12 Ibid., p. 15.
13 Ibid., p. 29.
14 Ibid., p. 179.
15 'Entertainments at Hughes' Fields Board Schools, Deptford', *Kentish Mercury*, Friday 17 January 1896, p. 5.
16 Ada Moore to Doris Langley Moore, 6 June 1931, Edith Nesbit Archive.
17 Alice Hoatson to Doris Langley Moore, 4 July 1932, Edith Nesbit Archive.
18 *Yorkshire Evening Post*, Monday 23 December 1912, p. 4.
19 E. Nesbit, 'The Town in the Library in the Library in the Town', *Nine Unlikely Tales*, pp. 245–66.
20 E. Nesbit (1909) 'The Criminal', *These Little Ones* (London: George Allen & Sons, 1909), p. 107. Originally published in *The Neolith*, no. 1, November 1907.
21 E. Nesbit, 'The Criminal', *These Little Ones*, p. 107.
22 Laurence Housman, *The Unexpected Years* (London: Jonathan Cape, 1937), pp. 127–8.
23 Laurence Housman to Doris Langley Moore, 12 July 1931, Edith Nesbit Archive.
24 Lewis May, *John Lane and the Nineties*, pp. 207–8.
25 Briggs, *A Woman of Passion*, p. 150.
26 E. Nesbit, 'The Ballad of the White Lady', *English Illustrated Magazine*, vol. II, 1893–94, pp. 308–9.
27 Briggs, A Woman of Passion, p. 150.
28 Laurence Housman to E. Nesbit, undated, reproduced in full in Moore, *E. Nesbit*, p. 142.
29 'Lewisham Liberal Club', *Blackheath Gazette*, Friday 15 October 1897, p. 5.
30 *London Daily News*, Wednesday 11 December 1889, p. 6.
31 Note from E. Nesbit to John Lane quoted in Briggs, *A Woman of Passion*, p. 153.
32 Marshall Steele, 'E. Nesbit: An Appreciation', *Harper's Bazaar*, January 1903, reprinted in *The Writer*, vols 16–18, 1903–06, p. 8. Scrapbook albums compiled by the Steele daughters, Olivia (1894–1902) and Mildred (1896–1953), contain verses written by Edith and drawings done by Iris, a talented artist who later attended the Slade School of Art.
33 Laura M. Zaidman, *British Children's Writers, 1880–1914* (Detroit: Gale, 1994), p. 208.
34 *Kentish Mercury*, Friday 16 February 1894.
35 'Dramatic Performance at New Cross Hall', *Blackheath Gazette*, Friday 23 February 1894, p. 5.
36 'Dramatic Entertainment at New-Cross', *London Daily News*, Thursday 22 February 1894, p. 3.
37 'Entertainments at Hughes Fields Schools Deptford', *Blackheath Gazette*, Friday 24 January 1886, p. 5.
38 'Humanitarian Work in Deptford', *Kentish Mercury*, Friday 25 January 1895, p. 2.
39 Fabian Tract Number 120, *After Bread Education: A Plan for the State Feeding of School Children*. p. 2.
40 Alice Hoatson to Doris Langley Moore, 4 July 1932, Edith Nesbit Archive.

CHAPTER 12

1   'Literary Folk and their Ways', *Saturday Evening Post*, 10 February 1906, vol. 178, January–June 1906, p. 31.
2   *The Bookman*, vol. 23, March–August 1906, p. 480.
3   'Rational Exercise and Women's Dress', *Cheshire Observer*, Saturday 16 June 1894, p. 2.
4   Berta Ruck, *A Story-Teller Tells the Truth* (London: Hutchinson & Co., 1935), p. 143.
5   Moore, *E. Nesbit*, p. 239.
6   Colin N. Manlove, *The Impulse of Fantasy Literature* (London: Macmillan, 1983), p. 62.
7   Moore, *E. Nesbit*, p. 196.
8   Interview between Noel Griffith and Doris Langley Moore, Edith Nesbit Archive.
9   Interview between Noel Griffith and Doris Langley Moore, Edith Nesbit Archive.
10 E. Nesbit, *Salome and the Head: A Modern Melodrama* (London: Alston Rivers Ltd., 1909), pp. 73–4.
11 E. Nesbit, *The Incredible Honeymoon*, pp. 118–19.
12 William Archer, 'Miss E. Nesbit: (Mrs. Bland)', *Poets of the Younger Generation*, pp. 272–83.
13 E. Nesbit, *The Wouldbegoods*, p. 95.
14 E. Nesbit, *Salome and the Head*, pp. 62–3.
15 Walter James Turner, *The Englishman's Country* (London: Collins, 1945), p. 15.
16 'The "Anchor Inn," Yalding', *The Courier*, 12 March 1909.
17 E. Nesbit, *Salome and the Head*, p. 60.
18 E. Nesbit, *The Incredible Honeymoon*, p. 111.
19 Ibid., p. 112.
20 E. Nesbit, *Salome and the Head*, p. 58.
21 Note from E. Nesbit to H.G. Wells, among the H.G. Wells Papers.
22 E. Nesbit to her mother from the Rose and Crown, undated, Edith Nesbit Archive.
23 E. Nesbit, 'Coals of Fire', *In Homespun* (London: John Lane, 1896), p. 174.
24 E. Nesbit, *The Railway Children*, p. 175.
25 E. Nesbit, The Incredible Honeymoon, p. 145.
26 Ibid., pp. 117–18.
27 Ibid., pp. 116–17.
28 Ibid., p. 117.
29 Ibid., pp. 115–16.
30 Ibid., p. 116.
31 Ibid., p. 34.
32 John Sloan, *John Davidson, First of the Moderns: A Literary Biography* (Oxford: Clarendon Press; New York: Oxford University Press, 1995), p. 100.
33 E. Nesbit to Ada Breakell, 1884, Edith Nesbit Archive.
34 Fanny Woodcock in an interview with Doris Langley Moore, p. 126.
35 Jepson, *Memories of an Edwardian and Neo-Georgian*, p. 100.

CHAPTER 13

1   E. Nesbit, *The Incredible Honeymoon*, p. 292.
2   E. Nesbit, *The New Treasure Seekers*, p. 238.
3   Ibid., p. 214.
4   A.D. Innes. 'Something Wrong. By E. Nesbit', *The Spectator*, 18 November 1893, p. 37.
5   E. Nesbit, *The House of Arden* (Harmondsworth: Puffin, 1986), p. 76.
6   E. Nesbit, *Oswald Bastable and Others* (London: Weels Gardner, Darton & Co. Ltd., 1905), p. 35.

7   E. Nesbit, 'The Millionairess', *Man and Maid* (London: T. Fisher Unwin, 1906), pp. 103–33.
8   E. Nesbit, 'Rack and Thumbscrew' in *Man and Maid*, p. 87.
9   Jepson, *Memories of an Edwardian and Neo-Georgian*, p. 142.
10   H.G. Wells, *Kipps: The Story of a Simple Soul* (New York: Charles Scribner's Sons, 1922), p. 16.
11   G. Law, *Serializing Fiction in the Victorian Press* (Basingstoke and New York: Palgrave, 2000), p. 111.
12   E. Nesbit, *My School Days*, p. 62.
13   E. Nesbit, *The Red House*, p. 15.
14   Sidney Webb to Beatrice Webb, 9 April 1900, quoted in Norman MacKenzie (ed.), *The Letters of Sidney and Beatrice* Webb, vol. 2: *Partnership 1892–1912* (Cambridge: Cambridge University Press, 2008), p. 128.
15   *Book News*, vol. 21, September 1902–August 1903, p. 381.
16   W.L. Alden, 'Mr Alden's Views', *New York Times*, Saturday 7 March 1903, p. 154.
17   *Horn Book Magazine* (Boston: Horn Books, 1945).
18   Jepson, *Memories of an Edwardian and Neo-Georgian*, p. 26.
19   Andrew Lang to E. Nesbit, February 1903, quoted in Moore, *E. Nesbit*, p. 199.
20   Charlotte Perkins Gilman, *The Living of Charlotte Perkins Gilman: An Autobiography* (New York: D. Appleton-Century, 1935), p. 211.
21   Ibid., p. 268. Yet Hubert wrote an exceptionally harsh review of her book *Women and Economics* for the *Manchester Chronicle* under the heading 'A Sane World in a Mad Controversy'.
22   E. Nesbit, 'Fortunatus Rex and Co.', *Nine Unlikely Tales*, p. 208.
23   E. Nesbit, *Five Children and It*, p. 1.
24   S.P. Bedson, 'Obituary: John Oliver Wentworth Bland (Born 6th October 1899. Died 10th May 1946)', *Journal of Pathology*, vol. 59, issue 4, October 1947, pp. 716–21.
25   Margaret Taylor, *E. Nesbit in Eltham* (London: The Eltham Society, 1974), p. 6.
26   Interview between Laurence Housman and Doris Langley Moore, transcript held in the Edith Nesbit Archive.

Chapter 14

1   This information is included in the letter from Alice Hoatson to Doris Langley Moore, 4 July 1932, Edith Nesbit Archive.
2   Hubert Bland, *Letters to a Daughter*, p. 4.
3   E. Nesbit, 'The Criminal', *The Neolith*, issue 1, 1907.
4   E. Nesbit, 'Absalom, or In the Queen's Garden', The Neolith, issue 1, 1907.
5   E. Nesbit, *The Wouldbegoods*, p. 62.
6   E. Nesbit, *Harding's Luck* (New York: Frederick A. Stokes Company, 1910), pp. 196–7.
7   E. Nesbit, *The Wouldbegoods*, p. 185 and p. 1.
8   Berta Ruck, *A Story-Teller Tells the Truth* (London: Hutchinson, 1935), p. 147.
9   Berta Ruck, *A Smile For The Past* (London: Hutchinson, 1959), p. 118.
10   E. Nesbit, *The Railway Children*, pp. 204–5.
11   Berta Ruck, *A Story-Teller Tells the Truth*, p. 146.
12   'Short Stories', *The Athenaeum*, 4 January 1902.
13   E. Nesbit, *Five Children and It*, p.299.
14   E. Nesbit, *Five Children and It*, p. 6.

15   Reproduced in the *Totnes Weekly Times*, Saturday 14 October 1899, p. 5.

16   'Safety Cheques', *Belfast Newsletter*, Thursday 24 March 1881, p. 8.

17   *Journal of Science*, Volume IV, (Third Series), June 1882, pp. 35–52.

18   'Painting the Lily', *The Globe*, Wednesday 5 July 1882, p. 1.

19   'Chemicals and Flowers', *The Globe*, Thursday 4 September 1913, p. 6.

20   E. Nesbit, *The Lark* (London: Hutchinson, 1922), p. 98 and p. 11.

21   E. Nesbit, *The Incredible Honeymoon*, p. 192.

22   E. Nesbit to the Reverend C.H. Grinling, 22 May 1896, Edith Nesbit Archive. Grinling was also a Labour activist and Editor of *The Pioneer*.

23   Jepson, *Memories of an Edwardian and Neo-Georgian*, p. 24.

24   Quoted in Norman and Jeanne MacKenzie, *The Life of H.G. Wells: The Time Traveller* (London: Hogarth Press, 1987), p. 175.

25   Ruck, *A Story-Teller Tells the Truth*, p. 206.

26   Ibid.

27   Ada Chesterton, *The Chestertons*, p. 58.

28   Ibid.

29   Ruck, *A Story-Teller Tells the Truth*, p. 147.

30   Ruck, *A Smile for The Past*, p. 115.

31   Berta Ruck to Doris Langley Moore, 23 January 1932, Edith Nesbit Archive.

32   Account given to Doris Langley Moore by Nina Griffith, Edith Nesbit Archive.

33   Ruck, *A Smile for the Past*, p. 115.

34   Ruck, *A Story-Teller Tells the Truth*, p. 146.

35   Taylor, *E. Nesbit in Eltham*, p. 9.

36   Arthur Ransome and Rupert Hart-Davis, *The Autobiography of Arthur Ransome* (London: Jonathan Cape, 1976), p. 100.

37   'Personal', *Hackney and Kingsland Gazette*, Wednesday 31 October, 1888, p. 3.

38   Cecil Chesterton, Introduction to *Essays by Hubert Bland*, p. xi.

39   Sean O'Casey, *Drums Under the Window* (New York: Macmillan, 1960), p. 8.

40   May, *John Lane and the Nineties*, p. 82.

41   A.J.A. Symons, *The Quest for Corvo: An Experiment in Biography* (New York: Macmillan, 1934), p. 108.

42   Clarence A. Andrews, 'A Baron Corvo Exhibit', *Books at Iowa* 1, 1964, pp. 18–27.

43   Symons, *The Quest for Corvo*, p. 255.

44   Account given to Doris Langley Moore by Nina Griffith, Edith Nesbit Archive.

45   Doran, M. and Co., Dyers, etc. are listed as operating from 31 High Street, Beckenham in the Beckenham Directory for 1898, printed and published by T.W. Thornton. In 1901 Maggie, 'dyer and cleaner', was registered at that address as head of household. She lived with her brother Tom, a photographer who would later become a dyer and cleaner (probably taking over from Maggie), his wife Jane, their children Hubert (15) and Samuel (13), and her sister's child Edith (8), daughter of Edith Doran. Information on Tom Doran can be found at http://www.photohistory-sussex.co.uk/BTNDoranF.htm (accessed 10 September 2017).

46   Jepson, *Memories of an Edwardian and Neo-Georgian*, p. 125.

47   Ruck, *A Story-Teller Tells the Truth*, p. 147.

48   Rudyard Kipling, *Puck of Pook's Hill* (Leipzig: B. Tauchnitz, 1906), p. 253.

49   Reproduced in Benjamin F. Fisher, 'The Critical Reception of A Shropshire Lad' in Alan W. Holden and J. Roy Birch (eds), *A.E. Housman: A Reassessment*

(Basingstoke: Macmillan, 1999), p. 22; Edith reviewed A.E. Housman's poetry in the *National Observer*: 'the dominant characteristic of Mr Housman's work is dignified simplicity... of expression... Here is no struggle for effect; only achievement without apparent effort. And that the effort was, there is only the excellence of the result to prove.'

50   Nesbit, E., *The Story of the Treasure Seekers*, pp. 57–61.
51   Ibid., p. 262.
52   Reprinted in the *Kipling Journal*, vol. XV, no. 86, July 1948, p. 13.
53   Ibid.
54   Hubert Bland, 'The Decadance of Rudyard Kipling', *Essays by Hubert Bland*, pp. 33–53.
55   E. Nesbit, *The Enchanted Castle*, pp. 176–7.
56   E. Nesbit, *The New Treasure Seekers*, p. 85.
57   Kathleen Waters to Doris Langley Moore, undated, Edith Nesbit Archive.

CHAPTER 15

1   Ada Chesterton, *The Chestertons*, p. 58.
2   Jepson, *Memories of an Edwardian and Neo-Georgian*, p. 48.
3   Douglas Kennedy to Doris Langley Moore, 13 February 1933, Edith Nesbit Archive.
4   'Authoress of Our Next Serial', *London Daily News*, Friday 8 March 1907, p. 11 – this magazine claims that *Old and Young* had published a fairy tale by her.
5   *Lippincott's Monthly Magazine*, May 1914, vol. XCIII, no. 557, January–June 1914, p. 513.
6   *Gloucester Journal*, Saturday 15 August 1908, p. 8.
7   Sandra Kemp, Charlotte Mitchell and David Trotter, 'Dorothea Deakin', *Oxford Companion to Edwardian Fiction* (Oxford: Oxford University Press, 1997), p. 92.
8   *Hampstead and Highgate Express*, Saturday 1 December 1906, p. 5. The exhibition was held in the premises of Messrs Cox and Co., 4 High Street.
9   'Writers of the Day', *The Writer* (Boston), vol. 20, 1908, p. 57.
10   The catalogue is online at https://archive.org/stream/parissalon1904ie00unse#page/157/mode/2up/search/Rosamund (accessed 1 December 2017).
11   Ruck, *A Story-Teller Tells the Truth*, p. 75.
12   Ibid., p. 142.
13   Ibid.
14   Ibid., p. 143.
15   'The Joy of Laughter', *Thanet Advertiser*, Tuesday 16 May 1933, p. 4.
16   Ruck, *A Story-Teller Tells the Truth*, p. 147.
17   Ibid., p. 145.
18   Ibid., p. 144.
19   Ibid., pp. 144–5.
20   Justus Miles Forman, *Tommy Carteret, a novel* (New York: Doubleday, 1905), p. 307.
21   Ruck, *A Story-Teller Tells the Truth*, p. 144.
22   E. Nesbit, *The Incomplete Amorist, a novel* (London: Archibald Constable & Co., 1906), pp. 285–6.
23   E. Nesbit, *The Railway Children*, p. 138.

24 E. Nesbit to Berta Ruck, 20 June 1923, Edith Nesbit Archive.
25 Reproduced in the *Belfast Newsletter*, Saturday 6 September 1913, p. 10.
26 *Kindergarten Review*, vol. 17, 1906–7, p. 237.
27 'Some Holiday Books', *Kindergarten Magazine and Pedagogical Digest*, vol. 19, 1906–7, p. 295.
28 E. Nesbit, *Daphne in Fitzroy Street*, pp. 167–8.
29 Ibid., p. 171.
30 'Great Britain and Russia', *Manchester Courier and Lancashire General Advertiser*, Thursday 27 June 1907.
31 *St James's Gazette*, Saturday 24 April 1897, p. 8.
32 'E. Nesbit and the Yorkshire Post', *The Author*, vol. XVII, no. 9, p. 252.
33 *Pall Mall Gazette*, Thursday 20 December 1906, p. 9.
34 *Morning Post*, Friday 25 January 1907.
35 E. Nesbit. The Story of the Amulet (London: T. Fisher Unwin, 1906), p. 249.
36 E. Nesbit. The Enchanted Castle (London: T. Fisher Unwin, 1907), p. 58.
37 E. Nesbit to Berta Ruck, 21 April 1924, Edith Nesbit Archive.

CHAPTER 16

1   H.G. Wells, *Experiment in Autobiography: Discoveries and Conclusions of a Very Ordinary Brain* (Philidelphia and New York: J.B. Lippencott Company, 1967), p. 513.
2   Ibid.
3   E. Nesbit to H.G. Wells, 1905, reproduced in Moore, *E. Nesbit*, p. 202.
4   H.G. Wells to E. Nesbit, 17 December 1904, reproduced in Moore, *E. Nesbit*, p. 212.
5   Note from E. Nesbit to H.G. Wells, reproduced in Moore, *E. Nesbit*, p. 228.
6   *McClure's Magazine*, vol. 32, November 1908–April 1909, p. 613.
7   E. Nesbit to H.G. Wells, 11 February 1905, Wells Papers, University of Illinois.
8   Ruck, *A Smile for the Past*, p. 147.
9   Berta Ruck to Doris Langley Moore, 23 January 1932, Edith Nesbit Archive.
10 H.G. Wells to E. Nesbit, 13 August 1905, reproduced in Moore, *E. Nesbit*, pp. 228–9.
11 Ada Chesterton, *The Chestertons*, pp. 58–9.
12 Ruck, *A Story-Teller Tells the Truth*, p. 207.
13 E. Nesbit to H.G. Wells, August 1905, Wells Papers, University of Illinois.
14 'Writers of the Day', *The Writer* (Boston), vol. 20, 1908, p. 57.
15 Iris Bland to Jane Wells, 23 March 1906, Wells Papers, University of Illinois.
16 Wells, *Experiment in Autobiography*, p. 519.
17 Ibid., p. 516.
18 Ibid., p. 517.
19 Wells, *H.G. Wells in Love*, p. 69.
20 Hubert Bland, *Letters to a Daughter*, pp. 1–2.
21 Ibid., p. 2.
22 Ibid., p. 129.
23 Norman and Jeanne Mackenzie, *H.G. Wells: A Biography* (New York: Simon and Schuster, 1973), p. 225.
24 Wells, *H.G. Wells in Love*, pp. 68–9.
25 Ibid., pp. 68–9.
26 Wells, *Experiment in Autobiography*, p. 513.

27 Ibid., p. 514.
28 Ibid., p. 515.
29 Ibid., p. 515–16.
30 Ibid., p. 518.
31 H.G. Wells to G.B. Shaw, undated, among the Shaw Papers.
32 Weintraub, *Shaw: An Autobiography 1898–1950*, pp. 176–7.
33 Ford Madox Ford, *Mightier than the Sword* (London: Allen & Unwin, 1938), pp. 160–1.
34 Pease, *History of the Fabian Society*, p. 165.
35 G.B. Shaw, 'H.G. Wells: the man I knew' available at http://www.newstatesman.com/archive/2013/12/h-g-wells-man-i-knew (accessed 3 December 2017).
36 Ada Chesterton, *The Chestertons*, pp. 57–9.
37 Ruth Fry, *Maud and Amber: A New Zealand Mother and Daughter and the Women's Cause, 1865–1981* (Christchurch, NZ: Canterbury University Press, 1992), p. 52.
38 Beatrice Webb's typescript diary, 2 January 1901 to 10 February 1911, August 1909, available at https://digital.library.lse.ac.uk/objects/lse:won715bor/read/single#page/550/mode/2up (accessed 3 December 2017).
39 Shaw, 'H. G. Wells: the man I knew' available at http://www.newstatesman.com/archive/2013/12/h-g-wells-man-i-knew (accessed 3 December 2017).
40 Norman and Jeanne Mackenzie, *H.G. Wells*, p. 270.
41 H.G. Wells, *The New Machiavelli* (London: John Lane, 1911), p. 317.
42 Ibid., pp. 461–2.
43 Ibid., pp. 462–3.
44 Leonard Woolf, *Beginning Again: An Autobiography of the Years 1911–18* (London: Mariner Books, 1964), pp. 129–30.
45 Rosamund Sharp to H.G. Wells, 26 January 1930, Wells Papers, University of Illinois.
46 Rosamund Sharp to H.G. Wells, 3 September [1930], Wells Papers, University of Illinois, ALS 127.
47 Ibid.
48 Rosamund Bland, *The Man in Stone House* (London: John Miles Ltd., 1936), p. 33.
49 Ibid.
50 Ibid., p. 206.

CHAPTER 17

1 E. Nesbit to J.B. Pinker, April 1905, held in the Berg Collection, New York Library.
2 E. Nesbit, *Dormant*, p. 28.
3 'The Lounger', *Putnam's Monthly*, vol. 3, October 1907–March 1908, p. 511.
4 E. Nesbit to Evelyn Sharp, June 13, 1910, held in the Bodleian Library, MSS Eng Lett d. 277.
5 Interview between Graily Hewitt and Doris Langley Moore, February 1933, transcript held in the Edith Nesbit Archive.
6 Gerald Gould, 'E. Nesbit', *Week-End Review*, 28 January 1933.
7 H.L. Mencken, George Jean Nathan and Willard Huntington Wright, *Europe after 8:15* (New York: John Lane Company, 1914), pp. 180–1.
8 *Morning Post*, Saturday 21 December 1907, p. 10.
9 'Miscellaneous', *Burlington Magazine*, February 1908, 59, vol. 12, p. 320.
10 E. Nesbit to Lord Dunsany, 9 October 1907, quoted in Moore, *E. Nesbit*, p. 243.

11   E. Nesbit, *Dormant*, p. 29.

12   E. Nesbit to Lord Dunsany, quoted in Moore, *E. Nesbit*, p. 243.

13   Henry Savage, *Richard Middleton: The Man and his Work* (London: Cecil Palmer, 1922), p. 47.

14   Richard Middleton to E. Nesbit, 1908, quoted in Moore, *E. Nesbit*, p. 244.

15   A.E. Housman to Laurence Housman, 30 April 1907, quoted in Alfred Edward Housman and Archie Burnett (eds), *The Letters of A. E. Housman* (Oxford: Clarendon, 2007), p. 206.

16   Jepson, *Memories of an Edwardian and Neo-Georgian*, pp. 100–1.

17   Interview Kathleen Waters with Doris Langley Moore, transcript held in the Edith Nesbit Archive.

18   E. Nesbit to Lady Dunsany, January 1910, quoted in Moore, *E. Nesbit*, p. 265.

19   Margaret Bondfield (later a Labour politician, trade unionist and women's rights activist) to Doris Langley Moore, 24 August 1931, Edith Nesbit Archive.

20   H.G. Wells, *Little Wars and Floor Games: The Foundations of Wargaming* (London: Courier Dover Publications, 2015), p. 165.

21   E. Nesbit, *Wings and the Child*, p. 96.

22   Albert Coumber to Doris Langley Moore, 15 July 1931, Edith Nesbit Archive.

23   Stanley Kunitz, Howard Haycraft and Wilbur Crane Hadden, *Authors Today and Yesterday*, a companion volume to *Living Authors* (New York: H.W. Wilson Company, 1934), p. 490.

CHAPTER 18

1   Berta Ruck to Doris Langley Moore, 23 January 1932, Edith Nesbit Archive.

2   Laurence Housman to Doris Langley Moore, 12 July 1931, Edith Nesbit Archive.

3   E. Nesbit to Evelyn Sharp, 13 June 1910, Bodleian Library (Eng. Lett. D.277).

4   Gerald Gould, in *Week-End Review*, 28 January 1933, vol. 7, issues 148–72, p. 89.

5   E. Nesbit, 'Property, Taxes, Votes', *Sheffield Daily Telegraph*, Monday 22 January 1912, p. 8.

6   *Fabian Women's Group – Three Years' Work 1908–1911*, p. 1.

7   Ibid.

8   Ibid. A huge emphasis was placed on the compiling of statistics and the group documented the difficulties faced by working-class women and their families in Lambeth, publishing their findings in 'Round About a Pound a Week'.

9   *Fabian Women's Group – Three Years' Work 1908–1911*, p. 2.

10   Kay Daniels, 'Emma Brooke: Fabian, Feminist and Writer', *Women's History Review* 12:2, 2003, 153–68.

11   *Fabian Women's Group – Three Years' Work 1908–1911*, p. 10.

12   'England's Strenuous Suffragettes', *Wilshire's Magazine*, January 1909, p. 7.

13   E 111/4 Summary of Seven Papers and Discussions upon the Disabilities of Women as Workers, issued for private circulation only by the Fabian Women's Group, 1909.

14   *Fabian Women's Group – Three Years' Work 1908–1911*, p. 10.

15   Minutes of the Fabian Women's Group held at the Nuffield Library, Oxford.

16   *Fabian Women's Group – Three Years' Work 1908–1911*, p. 10.

17   Amanda Farrell Hollander, *The Fabian Child: English and American Literature and Socialist Reform 1884-1915*, PhD thesis, UCLA, 2015, p. 6. Original in Fabian Society Papers, Box E, Folder 111.

18   Hubert Bland, *Letters to a Daughter*, p. 108.

19   Hubert Bland, *Essays by Hubert Bland*, p. 209.
20   Hubert Bland, 'On Being Delightful', *Letters to a Daughter*, p. 29.
21   Hubert Bland, *Letters to a Daughter*, p. 31.
22   Hubert Bland, *Essays by Hubert Bland*, p. 67.
23   Ibid., p. 68.
24   E. Nesbit to Ada Breakell, April 1884, Edith Nesbit Archive.
25   Ruck, *A Story-Teller Tells the Truth*, p. 145.
26   E. Nesbit, 'The Goodwife's Occupation Gone' reprinted in the *Burnley Express*, Saturday 30 May 1914, p. 13.
27   E. Nesbit, 'Miss Lorrimore's Career', *Sylvia's Journal*, February 1894, pp. 27–31.
28   E. Nesbit, 'The Slaves of the Spider', *Living Age*, 26 February 1916, vol. 288, no. 3738, p. 571.
29   Ibid.
30   Ibid., p. 572
31   E. Nesbit. The Railway Children, p. 78.
32   Hubert Bland, *Essays by Hubert Bland*, p. 69.
33   E. Nesbit. The Wonderful Garden (London: Macmillan & Co., 1911), p. 240.
34   E. Nesbit. The Magic City (London: Macmillan & Co., 1910), p. 161.
35   Ibid.
36   E. Nesbit. The New Treasure Seekers, p. 209.

CHAPTER 19
1   E. Nesbit, *The Enchanted Castle*, p. 170.
2   Ernest Wallis Budge to Doris Langley Moore, 14 May 1931, Edith Nesbit Archive.
3   E.A. Wallis Budge, *Egyptian Magic* (London: Kegan Paul, Trench, Trübner & Co, 1899), 43.
4   Ibid., p. x.
5   E. Nesbit. The Story Of The Amulet. (London: T. Fisher Unwin , 1906), p. 166.
6   Ibid.
7   E. Nesbit. The Story Of The Amulet, p. 74.
8   E. Nesbit. The Story Of The Amulet, p. 126.
9   Ernest Wallis Budge to Doris Langley Moore, 14 May 1931, Edith Nesbit Archive.
10   E. Nesbit, 'The Kiss', *American Magazine*, April 1907.
11   Ernest Wallis Budge to Doris Langley Moore, 14 May 1931, Edith Nesbit Archive.
12   Roger Luckhurst, *The Mummy's Curse: The True History of a Dark Fantasy* (Oxford: Oxford University Press, 2014), p. 140. The friend was Victoria Markham.
13   'Torch-bearers', *Lucifer, a Theosophic Magazine* (edited by Madame Blavatsky and Annie Besant), vol. 6, 1890, p. 29.
14   Jepson, *Memories of an Edwardian and Neo-Georgian*, pp. 23–4.
15   E. Nesbit. The Story Of The Amulet, p. 191.
16   Maud Gonne, *A Servant of the Queen: Her Own Story* (Dublin: Golden Eagle Books, 1950), p. 248.
17   For example Alex Owen in *The Place of Enchantment: British Occultism and the Culture of the Modern* (Chicago: University of Chicago Press, 2004).
18   E. Nesbit, 'Accidental Magic; or don't tell all you know', *The Magic World* (London: Macmillan & Co., 1912), p. 59.
19   E. Nesbit, Introduction to *The Children's Shakespeare* (London: Raphael Tuck & Sons Ltd., 1897).

20   Ruck, *A Smile for the Past*, p. 115.
21   Professor Andrade to Doris Langley Moore, 9 June 1932, Edith Nesbit Archive.
22   Professor Andrade to Doris Langley Moore, 9 June 1932, Edith Nesbit Archive.
23   Ibid.
24   Ibid.
25   E. Nesbit to Harry Nesbit, 1912. Quoted in Briggs, *A Woman of Passion*, p. 347.
26   E. Nesbit to Harry Nesbit, undated. Quoted in Briggs, *A Woman of Passion*, p. 350.
27   Joan Evans de Alonso, 'E. Nesbit's Well Hall, 1915–1921: A Memoir', *Children's Literature*, vol. 3, 1974, pp. 147–52.
28   George Seaver, 'Memories of E. Nesbit' held at the Grenwich Local History Library.
29   Dan H. Laurence (ed.), *GBS Collected Letters: 1898–1910*, Volume 2 p. 927.
30   Professor Andrade to Doris Langley Moore, 9 June 1932, Edith Nesbit Archive.
31   E. Nesbit, The Wonderful Garden, p. 27.
32   E. Nesbit to A.P. Watt, 1912, held in the Berg Collection, NY Public Library.
33   E. Nesbit, *The Incredible Honeymoon*, p. 199.
34   E. Nesbit, *The Incredible Honeymoon*, pp. 199–200.
35   E. Nesbit, *The Incredible Honeymoon*, p. 202.
36   Hubert Bland, *The Happy Moralist*, pp. 40–1.
37   E. Nesbit, 'Shakespeare', letter in the *Sheffield Daily Telegraph*, 22 January 1912, p. 11.
38   E. Nesbit, 'An Iconoclast in Stratford', *New Witness*, April 29, p. 674.

CHAPTER 20

1   Taylor, *E. Nesbit in Eltham*, p. 9.
2   E. Nesbit to Harry Nesbit, 1911. Quoted in Briggs, *A Woman of Passion*, p. 336.
3   E. Nesbit, *The Incredible Honeymoon*, pp. 73–4.
4   E. Nesbit to Lady Dunsany written towards the end of 1913. Quoted in Moore, *E. Nesbit*, p. 279.
5   Mavis Strange, 'E. Nesbit, As I Knew Her', *Horn Book* 34, October 1958, p. 359.
6   Strange, 'E. Nesbit As I Knew Her', p. 360.
7   E. Nesbit to Harry Nesbit, 1912. Quoted in Moore, *E. Nesbit*, p. 274.
8   E. Nesbit, *Wings and the Child*, pp. 127–8.
9   Lesley Gordon, *Peepshow into Paradise* (New York: J. de Graff, 1953), pp. 158–9.
10   Letters in the Macmillan Archive quoted in J. Bavidge, 'Exhibiting Childhood: E. Nesbit and the Children's Welfare Exhibitions', in A.E. Gavin and A.F. Humphries (eds), *Childhood in Edwardian Fiction* (London: Palgrave Macmillan, 2009).
11   E. Nesbit to Harry Nesbit, 1 December 1913. Quoted in Briggs, *A Woman of Passion*, p. 354.
12   E. Nesbit to Lady Dunsany, late 1913. Quoted in Moore, *E. Nesbit*, p. 279.
13   A.E.L., 'Pioneers at Well Hall', *The Pioneer*, Friday 1 June 1917.
14   E. Nesbit, *The Lark*, p. 114.
15   Ruck, A Smile For The Past, p. 134.
16   *Sunday Chronicle* (Manchester), 19 April 1914.
17   Alice Hoatson to Doris Langley Moore, 4 July 1932, Edith Nesbit Archive.
18   E. Nesbit, Essays by "Hubert" of the Sunday Chronicle, p. 284.
19   E. Nesbit, *Essays by Hubert Bland*, p. 284.
20   Taylor, *E. Nesbit in Eltham*, p. 10.
21   E. Nesbit to Mavis Carter, 8 June 1915. Quoted in Moore, *E. Nesbit*, p. 288.

22 Ruck, *A Story-Teller Tells the Truth*, p. 146.
23 May Bowley to Doris Langley Moore, 11 November 1931, Edith Nesbit Archive.
24 Jepson, *Memories of an Edwardian and Neo-Georgian*, p. 20.
25 *Liverpool Echo*, Saturday 13 June 1914.
26 *Yorkshire Post and Leeds Intelligencer*, Saturday 13 June 1914, p. 9.
27 *Hull Daily Mail*, 22 September 1914.
28 Hamilton Fyfe, *My Seven Selves* (London: G. Allen & Unwin Ltd., 1935).
29 E. Nesbit to Edward Andrade, 28 March 1915. Quoted in Briggs, *A Woman of Passion*, p. 367.
30 E. Nesbit to Mavis Carter, 8 June 1915. Quoted in Moore, *E. Nesbit*, p. 288. Although *The Incredible Honeymoon* was published in America in 1916, it did not appear in the United Kingdom until 1921.
31 E. Nesbit to Harry Nesbit, late 1915. Quoted in Moore, *E. Nesbit*, p. 288.
32 *Daily Gazette for Middlesborough*, Monday 21 June 1915, p. 2.
33 Elsa Courlander quoted in Moore, *E. Nesbit*, p. 290.
34 G.K. Chesterton to E. Nesbit, 1914. Quoted in Moore, *E. Nesbit*, p. 289.
35 Berta Ruck to Doris Langley Moore, 23 January 1932, Edith Nesbit Archive.
36 E. Nesbit to Edward Andrade, 28 March 1915. Quoted in Briggs, *A Woman of Passion*, p. 367.
37 Ruck, *A Story-Teller Tells the Truth*, p. 142.

CHAPTER 21
1   A.E.L., 'Pioneers at Well Hall', *The Pioneer*, Friday 1 June 1917, p. 22.
2   E. Nesbit, 'The Voyage of the Hut', *The Graphic*, 21 February 1920, p. 276.
3   E. Nesbit to Edward Andrade. Quoted in the Edith Nesbit Society Newsletter, June 2016.
4   A.E.L., 'Pioneers at Well Hall', p. 22.
5   E. Nesbit, 'The Voyage of the Hut', p. 276.
6   *Leeds Mercury*, Friday 11 May 1917, p. 8.
7   'Poetess and Poultry Culture', *Sevenoaks Chronicle and Kentish Advertiser*, Friday 15 September 1916.
8   Joan Evans de Alonso, 'E. Nesbit's Well Hall, 1915–1921: A Memoir', *Children's Literature*, vol. 3, 1974, pp. 147–52.
9   Ibid., p. 149.
10 Ibid., p. 151.
11 Ibid., p. 147.
12 Ibid., p. 148.
13 Mavis Strange, 'E. Nesbit As I Knew Her', *The Horn Book Magazine*, vol. XXXIV, no. 5, October 1958, pp. 361–2.
14 E. Nesbit to Edward Andrade, 12 July 1916, Edith Nesbit Archive.
15 E. Nesbit, *The Lark*, p. 179.
16 E. Nesbit, *The Lark*, p. 200.
17 Peter Blundell to Doris Langley Moore, 7 November 1931, Edith Nesbit Archive.
18 Peter Blundell to Doris Langley Moore, 6 February 1933, Edith Nesbit Archive.
19 A.E.L., 'Pioneers at Well Hall' in *The Pioneer and Labour Journal*, Friday June 1 1917, reproduced in Laura Probert, *The Well Hall Garden Parties* (London: The Edith Nesbit Society, 2007), p. 23.

20 E. Nesbit, 'The Voyage of the Hut', p. 276.

21 A.E.L., 'Pioneers at Well Hall' in *The Pioneer and Labour Journal*, Friday June 1 1917, reproduced in Laura Probert, *The Well Hall Garden Parties*, p. 24.

22 E. Nesbit, 'The Voyage of the Hut', p. 276.

23 E. Nesbit to Paul Bland, June 1916. Quoted in Briggs, *A Woman of Passion*, p. 373.

24 A.E.L., 'Pioneers at Well Hall' in *The Pioneer and Labour Journal*, Friday June 1 1917, reproduced in Laura Probert, *The Well Hall Garden Parties*, p. 24.

25 'What the Women are Doing', *The Pioneer*, Friday 28 May 1915, reproduced in Laura Probert, *The Well Hall Garden Parties*, p. 4.

26 *The Pioneer*, Friday 18 June, reproduced in Laura Probert, *The Well Hall Garden Parties*, (London: Edith Nesbit Society, 2005), p.4.

27 *The Pioneer* Saturday 26 June, reproduced in Laura Probert, *The Well Hall Garden Parties*, p. 8.

28 Probert, The Well Hall Garden Parties, p. 4.

29 *North West Kent Family History*, vol. 4, no.1, March 1986, p. 16 and the *Pioneer* report.

30 E. Nesbit to Harry Nesbit, February 1917. Quoted in Briggs, *A Woman of Passion*, pp. 373–4.

31 Iris gave this account to Doris Langley Moore.

32 E. Nesbit to Edward Andrade, 7 February 1917. Quoted in Briggs, *A Woman of Passion*, p. 374.

33 E. Nesbit to Harry Nesbit, February 1917. Quoted in Briggs, *A Woman of Passion*, pp. 373–4.

34 Russell Green to Doris Langley Moore, Edith Nesbit Archive.

35 E. Nesbit to Berta Ruck. Quoted in Moore, *E. Nesbit*, p. 220.

36 Briggs, *A Woman of Passion*, p. 379.

37 E. Nesbit to Gertrude Nebel, 11 November 1918, Edith Nesbit Archive.

38 E. Nesbit to Edward Andrade, 7 February 1917. Quoted in Briggs, *A Woman of Passion*, p. 374.

39 E. Nesbit, *Wings and the Child*, p. 53.

CHAPTER 22

1 Will of Edith Bland-Tucker, Probate, London 12 June 1924, London Probate Department.

2 Account included in Taylor, *E. Nesbit in Eltham*.

3 Ford Madox Ford, *Return to Yesterday* (New York: Liveright, 1932), p. 27.

4 'Light Fiction', *Spectator*, 28 April 1923, p. 25.

5 E. Nesbit to Clemence Dane, dated March 1921, Edith Nesbit Archive.

6 G.B. Stern interview with Doris Langley Moore, transcript held in the Edith Nesbit Archive.

7 William Rose Benet, 'The Phoenix Nest', *Saturday Review*, 17 November 1934, p. 302.

8 John Cason, *Lewis & Sybil: A Memoir* (London: Collins, 1972), p. 98.

9 Noël Coward, *Present Indicative* (Methuen Drama, 2008), p. 141.

10 Ibid., p. 12.

11 Ibid., p. 141.

12 Noël Coward to Noel Streatfield, in Barry Day (ed.), *The Letters of Noël Coward* (London: Bloomsbury Publishing, 2014), p. 74.

13 Coward, *Present Indicative*, p. 141.

14 Cole Lesley, *Remembered Laughter: The Life of Noël Coward* (New York: Knopf, 1976), p. 68.

15 Philip Hoare, *Noël Coward: A Biography* (New York: Simon and Schuster, 2013), p. 111 n. 3.

16 E. Nesbit to Berta Ruck, 17 March 1924, in Olive Hill's handwriting with a PS from E. Nesbit, Edith Nesbit Archive.

17 Ruck, *A Story-Teller Tells the Truth*, p. 148.

18 E. Nesbit to Berta Ruck, 23 June 1923, Edith Nesbit Archive.

19 E. Nesbit to Berta Ruck, 20 June 1923, Edith Nesbit Archive.

20 Ruck, *A Story-Teller Tells the Truth*, p. 150.

21 Ibid., p. 150.

22 Mavis Strange, 'E. Nesbit as I knew her', *Horn Book Magazine*, vol. 34, p. 363.

23 Moore, *E. Nesbit*, p. 317.

24 Mavis Strange, 'E. Nesbit as I knew her', p. 363.

25 Ibid., p. 363.

26 Moore, *E. Nesbit*, p. 316.

27 E. Nesbit to Berta Ruck, 17 March 1924, in Olive Hill's handwriting with a P.S. from E. Nesbit, Edith Nesbit Archive.

28 'The New Books', *Saturday Review of Literature*, vol. 11 (New York: Saturday Review Associates, 1934), p. 302.

29 Moore, *E. Nesbit*, pp. 321–2.

30 Ruck, *A Story-Teller Tells the Truth*, p. 215.

31 E. Nesbit to Berta Ruck, 21 April 1924, Edith Nesbit Archive.

32 Death Certificate for Edith Nesbit.

33 E. Nesbit, *Dormant*, p. 312.

34 *Nottingham Evening Post*, Tuesday 23 September 1924, p. 4.

35 *Derby Daily Telegraph*, Tuesday 6 May 1924, p. 2.

36 L.J.W., 'Obituary for J.O.W. Bland M.D.', *British Medical Journal*, 1 June 1946, p. 853 https://www.ncbi.nlm.nih.gov/pmc/articles/PMC2059002/pdf/brmedj03835-0030b.pdf.

37 Taylor, *E. Nesbit in Eltham*, p. 6.

38 Jepson, *Memories of an Edwardian and a Neo-Georgian*, p. 21.

39 Cole Lesley, *Remembered Laughter*, pp. 370–1.

40 Edward Eager, 'Daily Magic', *The Horn Book*, 1 October 1958, pp. 347–9.

41 C.S. Lewis, *Surprised by Joy: The Shape of My Early Life* (New York: Harcourt Brace & Co., 1955), p. 14.

42 Christina Scull and Wayne G. Hammond, *The J.R.R. Tolkien Companion & Guide* (Boston: Houghton Mifflin, 2006), p. 639.

43 The connection between E. Nesbit and J.R.R. Tolkien is explored at http://nansen-tolkien.co.uk/enesbit.html (accessed 13 December 2017).

44 'E. Nesbit', *Saturday Review of Literature*, vol. 1, Saturday Review Associates, 1934, p. 59.

45 *Illustrated London News*, Friday 2 November 1984, p. 12.

46 Barry Day (ed.), *The Letters of Noël Coward* (London: Methuen/Drama, 2007), p. 60.

47 Joan Aiken (1996) *In Celebration of Edith Nesbit* (London: The Edith Nesbit Society).

48 Anna Carey, 'Flying High on Page and Screen', *Irish Times*, Tuesday 1 November 2011. https://www.irishtimes.com/culture/books/flying-high-on-page-and-screen-1.5928 (accessed 24 April 2018).

49 J.K. Rowling, 'From Mr Darcy to Harry Potter by way of Lolita', *Sunday Herald*, 21

May 2000 (this appears to be the transcript of her contribution to a BBC Radio 4 show about famous people and their favourite books.) http://www.accio-quote.org/articles/2000/0500-heraldsun-rowling.html (accessed 13 January 2017).

50 E. Nesbit, *Wings and the Child*, p. 20.

51 Ibid., pp. 6–8.

INDEX